# SEVENTEENTH CENTURY COLONIAL ANCESTORS

# Seventeenth Century Colonial Ancestors

*of Members of the*

## NATIONAL SOCIETY COLONIAL DAMES XVII CENTURY
### 1915-1975

*Compiled by*

**Mary Louise Marshall Hutton**

GENEALOGICAL PUBLISHING CO., INC.
*Baltimore 1984*

## Introduction

The National Society Colonial Dames 17th
Century was organized in 1915, during the
meeting of the International Genealogical
Congress at the Pan-Pacific International Ex-
position, under the leadership of Miss Mary
Florence Taney as founder. The objectives of
the Society are (1) to aid in the preserva-
tion of the records and of the historic sites
of our country; (2) to foster interest in
historical colonial research; (3) to aid in
the education of the youth of our country;
(4) to commemorate the noble and historic
deeds of our ancestors, the founders of our
great republic; (5) to maintain zealously
those high principles of virtue, courage and
patriotism which led to the independence of
the colonies and the foundation and establishment of the United States of America; (6)
to aid in the establishment of a library of
heraldry, working with various genealogical
societies; and (7) to develop a library
specializing in seventeenth century colonial
data.

Since its organization, Chapters have been
formed in 37 states, with a current membership of over 8,000. A prime requirement for
membership in this Society has always been a
proven line of descent from a colonial settler. From 1915 to 1942 this colonial ancestor could have come or have been in one of
the thirteen original colonies at any time in
the colonial period, namely, to 1775. In
1942, this ruling was changed and since that
time, this early settler must have been here
before 1701. Thus the Society's records include the names of some 600 colonists who came

later than 1700, and descent from whom no longer fulfills the requirement for eligibility to membership. Status of members who joined under the former ruling remained unchanged, but no new members were admitted who showed descent from colonists who came later than 1700. In this Roster, therefore, it has been thought best to list those colonists of later date separately. Names in the list appearing on p.1-291 are definitely of the seventeenth century. A second alphabetizing, p.291-96, contains names on which information was received in the first months of 1976, too late to include in the main list. Following p.296 is a list of eighteenth century colonial ancestors who were here before the American Revolution, but are no longer acceptable in lines of descent for membership in the Society under the present ruling.

Since 1915, our members have proven over 13,000 blood lines from colonial ancestors. It is thought that a listing of these early settlers, giving vital dates, name of wife and service, as shown in the Society's records will prove of value to those interested in colonial history. Lineages are not included, but are preserved in the Society's Headquarters at 1300 New Hampshire Avenue, Washington, D.C. 20036. Included in this volume are only the names of colonists from whom members have proven descent. The compiler is not responsible for the research on which the data here given is based. In these early documents one often finds that dates vary and thus much use is made of the symbol "c" (circa) indicating that records disagree, or are approxmate.

It has been found that the spelling of
many family names differs, even in the same
lineage. One form has been chosen in such
cases, with reference from other forms of the
name. Such names as Clark (Clarke) and
Brown (Browne) appear in one alphabet, without regard to the spelling, since both forms
are often found in the same lineage.

When there are several entries under the
same name, with different dates, as in the
case of grandfather, father and son of the
same name, same colony, arrangement has been
made chronologically; also "M", "Mac" and
"Mc" are arranged in one alphabetic sequence
because these forms may vary within a single
lineage and the searcher does not know which
form has been used.

In the note as to service, it has been
necessary to reduce information to several
words because of lack of space. Individual
military titles are not included. Many in-
teresting occupations are noted - as Snow-
shoemaker, Tax Collector, High Sheriff, Blacksmith, Master Mariner, Ferryman, Surveyor,
Shipbuilder, etc. The Society's bylaws include a list of services for the ancestor,
establishing his "eligibility" - as Historic
Founder, Officer, Military or Civil Officer,
Attorney, Minister, Physician, Patriot, Landowner, etc., many of which are noted in these
entries.

In the course of this compilation, The
Society has become indebted to many who have
contributed in time and effort to this project
- especially to Mrs. Harry A. Emrick, Miss
Vera Walker Morel and Mrs. M. Miles Snider

Valuable advice and counsel have been given
by the members of our Committee on Special
Publications - Mrs. Donald Boaz, Mrs. George
L. Bott, and Mrs. Esmond Grosz. Particular
thanks go to the members of the successive
Executive Boards, 1965-76, for their continued interest and support. And finally,
the compilation could never have been com-
pleted without the help of the Registrars of
Chapters all over the country who have given
their whole-hearted cooperation in making
this Roster possible.

Mary Louise M. Hutton

Abbe, John (c1613-89/90) Mass.; m. Mary Boring.
Constable; Freeman.
Abbe, Thomas (1656-1728) Conn.; m. Sarah Fairfield.
Military service; Landowner.
Abbott, Daniel (1589-1647) R.I.; m. Margaret ---.
Landowner.
Abbott, George (1615-81) Mass.; m. Hannah Chandler.
Landowner.
Abbott, George (1631-88/89) Mass.; m. Sarah Farnum.
Constable.
Abbott, George (1658/59-1724) Mass.-Conn.; m. Eliza-
beth Ballard. Landowner.
Abbott, James (1665- ) N.Y.; m. Martha ---.Military
service.
Abeel, Johannes (1667-1711) N.Y.; m. Catherine Schuy-
ler. Mayor; Assemblyman.
Abell, Joshua (1632- ) Va.; m. Experience Smith.
Military service; Landowner.
Abell, Robert ( -1663) Mass.; m. Joanna ---.
Freeman; Proprietor.
Abernathy, Robert (1624-90) Va.; m. Christian Gillman.
Landowner; Juryman.
Abney, Dannett (c1669-1732) Va.; m. Mary ---. Land-
owner.
Abney, George (1613-61) Va.; m. Bathsheba ---. Land-
owner.
Abney, George (c1652/53-96) Va.; m. Mary Lee. Land-
owner.
Abney, Sir James (1675-1733) Va.; m. Damatis Andrews.
Justice; Surveyor.
Abney, Paul (1652-c96) Va.; m. Mary Lee. Landowner.
Ackerman, David (1614-62) N.J.; m. Elizabeth de Vil-
liers. Justice.

Adair, James R. (    -1705) S.C.; m. Ann McCarty.
Physician.
Adams, Abraham (1639-1714) Mass.; m. Mary Pettingill.
Military service.
Adams, Charles (    -1694) N.H.; m. Temperance ---.
Juryman.
Adams, George (c1647-96) Mass.; m. Frances ---.
Military service.
Adams, Henry (1583-1646) Mass.;m. Edith Squire; Mary
Alexander. Military service; Founder.
Adams, Henry (c1604-1676) Mass.; m. Elizabeth Paine.
Military service; Assemblyman.
Adams, Jeremy (1604-83) Conn.; m. Rebecca Greenhill.
Proprietor; Military service.
Adams, John (    -1633) Mass.; m. Ellen Newton. Land-
owner.
Adams, Joseph (1664-1701) Mass.; m. Margaret Eames.
Landowner.
Adams, Philip (--- ---) Mass.; m. ---. Freeman;
Juryman.
Adams, Robert (1602-82) Mass.; m. Eleanor Wilmot.
Landowner.
Adams, Robert (1628-    ) Va.; m. ---. Burgess.
Adams, Robert (1690-1740) Va.; m. Mourning Lewis.
Proprietor.
Adams, Samuel (1616/17-88/89) Mass.; m. Rebecca
Graves (1); Esther Sparhawk (2). Freeman; Town-
clerk.
Adams, Thomas (1612-88) Mass.; m. Mary Blackmore.
Ancient and Honorable Artillery.
Adams, William (    -1685) Mass.; m. Mary Manning;
Alice Bradford. Minister.
Addison, John (1667-1706) Md.; m. Rebecca(Wilkinson)
Dent. Military service; Landowner.
Adgate, Thomas (c1620-1707) Conn.; m. Mary (Marvin)
Bushnell. Deacon; Landowner.

Adkins, John (--- ---) Va.; m. Isabelle Brach.
Landowner.
Adkins, Josiah ( -1690) Conn.; m. --- Andrews.
Landowner.
Agee, Matthew (1670-1735/40) Va.; m. Ann Godwin.
Landowner.
Aiken, John (1663-1746) Mass.; m. Hanna Briggs.
Selectman; Military service.
Ainsworth, Edward (c1652-c1740/4 ) Mass.; m. Joanna
Hemingway. Founder.
Akers, William (--- ---) N.J.-Va.; m. ---. Landowner.
Founder.
Albritton, Francis (1609-67) Va.; m. ---. Landowner;
Juror.
Albro, John (1619-1712) N.Y.-R.I.; m. Dorothy Potter.
Councilman.
Alden, John (1599-1687) Mass.; m. Priscilla Mullins.
Mayflower Passenger.
Alden, Joseph (1624-97) Mass.; m. Mary Simmons.
Freeman; Proprietor.
Alderman, Thomas (1683-1775) Conn.; m. Mary Seagraves.
Landowner.
Alderman, William (1640-97) Conn.; m. Mary Case.
Landowner.
Alderson, Richard (c1640-97/98) Va.; m. Margaret ---.
Landowner.
Alderson, Richard (c1680-1753) Va.; m. Sarah ---.
Landowner.
Aldrich, Clement (c1601-c1668) Va.; m. Susan Boswell.
Landowner.
Aldrich, Peter (c1631-c1694) Del.; m. Mary (Sigfridus)
Wessels. Landowner.
Alexander, Andrew (1648-c1700) Md.; m. Abigail McKnitt.
Landowner.
Alexander, Anthony (c1665-1741) N.C.; m. Ann ---.
Proprietor.

Alexander, James (1652-1740) Md.; m. Mary ---.
Landowner.

Alexander, John (1603-77) Va.; m. Agnes Graham;
Elizabeth ---. Landowner, Sheriff.

Alexander, Joseph (c1669-1730) Md.; m. Abigail Mc-
Knitt. Landowner.

Alexander, Phillip (1657-1705) Va.; m. Sarah Ashton.
Sheriff.

Alexander, William ( -1707) Va.; m. Agnes Ann Reid.
Military Service.

Alexander, William (1666-1735) Md.; m. Catherine ---.
Minister.

Alford, William (1620-1674/75) Va.; m. Dorothy ---.
Juryman; Landowner.

Alger, Andrew (1610-75) Me.; m. Agnes ---. Constable.

Allen, Ananias (c1670-1717) N.J.;m. Mary ---. Military service.

Allen, Arnold ( -c1645) Me.; m. Mary Reynolds.
Juror; Appraiser.

Allen, George (1568-1648) Mass.; m. Catherine ---.
Deputy to Court.

Allen, George (1619-93) Mass.; m. Hannah ---. Landowner.

Allen, George (1672-1714) Mass.; m. Elizabeth Hulitt.
Landowner.

Allen, Jedediah (1600-58) Mass.; m. Esther Swift.
Assemblyman.

Allen, Jedediah (1646-1712) Mass.-N.J.; m. Elizabeth
Howland. Justice; Assemblyman.

Allen, Joseph (1642-1704) Mass.; m. Sarah Hull.
Town Treasurer.

Allen, Ralph (c1600-91) Mass.; m. Susannah ---.
Attorney; Landowner.

Allen, Ralph (1615-c1663) Mass.; m. Esther Swift.
Founder; Landowner.

Allen, Richard (1613-c1670) Conn.; m. ---. Landowner.

Allen, Richard (1648/50-1724/25) Va.; m. Elizabeth Holt. Landowner.

Allen, Richard (1687-1715) Va.; m. Ann ---. Military service.

Allen Samuel (1588-1648) Conn.Me.; m. Ann ---. Landowner; Juryman.

Allen, Samuel (1596-1659) Mass.; m. Ann ---. Freeman; Minister.

Allen, Samuel (1632-1703) Mass.; m. Sarah Partridge. Town clerk; Legislator.

Allen Valentine ( -1676) Va.; m. Mary Page. Landowner.

Allen, William (1602-78) N.Y.; m. Elizabeth Bradley. Juryman; Selectman.

Allen, William (1602-86) Mass.; m. Ann Goodale. Landowner.

Allen, William (1613/16-78) Mass.; m. Mary --. Freeman; Surveyor.

Allen, William (1677-1740) Va.; m. Margaret Waggoner. Landowner.

Allen, William (c1692-1752) Va.; m. Mary (Hunt) Minge. Justice; Landowner.

Allen SEE ALSO Allyn.

Allerton, Isaac (1583-1653) Mass.; m. Mary Norris; Fear Brewster. Mayflower passenger.

Allerton, Isaac (1630-1702) Va.; m. Elizabeth Willoughby. Burgess; Councilman.

Allibone, Joseph (c1660-1733) Pa.; m. ---. Landowner.

Alling, Roger I. (1612-74) Conn.; m. Mary Nash. Provincial treasurer.

Allis; William (1613-78) Mass.; Mary ---. Mary (Brownson) Graves. Freeman; Selectman.

Allison, Robert (c1620-1666) Va.-Md.; m. Hannah
  Gerard.  Sheriff.
Allison, Thomas (1637/38-1677) Md.; Mary Roberts.
  Landowner.
Allyn, John (1642-1709) Conn.; m. Elizabeth Gager.
  Landowner.
Allyn, Matthew (1604-71) Conn-Mass.; m. Margaret Wyatt.
  Freeman; Colonial Commissioner.
Allyn, Robert (c1608-73) Mass.-Conn.; m. Sarah ---.
  Selectman; Constable.
Allyn, Thomas ( - )Mass.; m. Winifred ( ) Woolcot.
  Assemblyman; Justice.
Allyn    SEE ALSO    Allen
Almy, Christopher (1632-84) R.I.; m. Mary Unthank.
  Assistant Governor.
Allricks,Peter (c1631-94) Del.; m. Marie Wessels.
  Judge; Assemblyman
Alston, John (1673-1756) N.C.; m. Mary Clark; Ann
  Clark.  Sheriff; Tax collector.
Alston, Peter (c 1660- ) N.H.; m. Sarah Miller.
  Grand Juryman.  Constable.
Alvord, Alexander (c 1627-87) Conn.; m.  Mary Vore.
  Freeman.
Alvord, Benedict (   -1683) Conn.; m. Jane Newton.
  Military service.
Alward, Henry (1664-1718) N.J.; m. Judith Hendrick-
  son.  Founder; Military service.
Amadowne, Roger (   -1673) Mass.; m. Jeanne Harwood.
  Founder; Freeman.
Ames, John (1647-1726) Mass.; Sarah Willis.   Mili-
  tary service.
Ames, Joseph (c 1672-1709) Va.; m. Ester Gray.
  Landowner.
Amis, Louis (1670-1750) Va.; m.------.  Founder.
Amis, Thomas ( - ) Va.; m. ---.  Landgrave;
  Huguenot.

Ammonette, Jacob ( - ) Va.; m. ---. Military
Service; Huguenot.
Anderson, Charles (1670-1718) Va., m. Frances ---.
Minister.
Anderson, David (c1634-1721) Va., m. Frances ---.
Landowner.
Anderson, George ( -c1707) Va.; m. Mary Matthews.
Sheriff.
Anderson, James (1695-1783) Va.; m. Margaret ---.
Landowner.
Anderson, John (c1664-c1735) Va.; m. Sarah Waddy.
Landowner.
Anderson, Richard (1618- ) Va.; m. ---. Minister.
Anderson, Robert (1640-1712) Va.; m. Cecilia Massie.
Landowner.
Anderson, Robert (1663-1716) Va.; m. Mary Overton.
Military service.
Andrews, Francis ( -1662/63) Conn.; m. Anna Smith.
Founder; Landowner.
Andrews, Henry (1611-52) Mass.; m. Mary ---. Repre-
sentative.
Andrews, James ( -1684) Va., m. Elizabeth Starkey.
Proprietor.
Andrews, John ( -1681) Conn.; m. Mary ---. Free-
man; Landowner.
Andrews, John ( -1683) Mass.; m. Jane Jordan.
Selectman.
Andrews, Joseph (1651-1706) Mass.; m. Rebecca ---.
Constable; Representative.
Andrews, Thomas ( -1770) Va.; m. ---.- Landowner.
Andriessen (Alias Staleup), John (1617-86) Del.; m.
Christina Carrols. Landowner; Military service.
Andriessen, Luykes (1625/28-1700) N.Y.; m. Aefje
Laurens. Landowner.
Angell, Thomas (1618-1694/95) R.I.; m. Alice Ashton.
Freeman; Commissioner.

Annable, Anthony (    -1674) Mass.; m. Jane ---; Ann
  Clark; Ann Barker.  Founder; Representative.
Anthony, Allard (    -1685) N.Y.; m. Henrica Wessells.
  Burgomaster; Delegate.
Anthony, John (1607-75) R.I.; m. Susanna Potter.
  Freeman; Landowner.
Apperson, John (c1678-1736) R.I.; m. ---.  Landowner.
Appleton, Samuel (1586-1670) Mass.; m. Judith Everard;
  Martha ---.  Grand Jury; Freeman.
Appleton, Samuel (c1624-96) Conn.; m. Hannah Paine;
  Mary Oliver.  Military service.
Applewaite  SEE ALSO  Applewhite.
Applewhite, Henry (    -1704) Va.; m. ---.  Justice;
  Burgess.
Applewhite, John (    -1704) Va.; m. Mary ---.  Justice.
  Military service.
Archer, George (    -    ) Va.;m. Elizabeth Harris.
  Landowner.
Armistead, Anthony (1645-c1710) Va.; m. Hannah Ellyson.
  Burgess; Sheriff.
Armistead, John (1635-98) Va.; m. Judith Robinson.
  Burgess; Councilman.
Armistead, William (c1610-61) Va.; m. Ann ---.
  Landowner.
Armistead, William (c1640-1715) Va.; m. Rebecca Miss;
  Hannah Hind.  Burgess; Sheriff.
Armstrong, Joseph (    -1761) Pa.; m. ---.  Assembly-
  man; Justice.
Arne, William (1654-1731) Mass.; m. Joanna Hawks.
  Military service.
Arnold, Benjamin (c1660-c1723) Va.; m. Anne ---.
  Landowner; Sub-sheriff.
Arnold, Eleazer (1651-1722) R.I.; m. Eleanor Smith.
  Civil officer; Landowner.
Arnold, Isaac (1684-1758) Va.; m. Margaret Coffe.
  Landowner; Vestryman.

Arnold, Richard (1640-1710) R.I.; m. Mary Angell.
Councilman.
Arnold William (1587-1675) R.I.-Mass.; m. Christina
Peake. Commissioner; Deputy to Court.
Arrington, William (   -1725) Va.; m. Elizabeth Peden.
Landowner.
Asball, George (cl598-1672) Va.; m. Anne Marks. Land-
owner.
Asbury, Henry (1650/55-1707) Va.; m. Mary Durant.
Military service.
Ashbrook, John (1657-cl727) N.J.; m. Mary Howell.
Assemblyman.
Ashby, Thomas (1660-1752) Va.; m. Rose ---. Land-
owner.
Ashe, John (   -1704) S.C.; m. ---. Landowner.
Ashfordby, William (1639-92) N.Y.; m. Martha Burton.
Assemblyman; Sheriff.
Ashmead, John (1648-88) Pa.; m. Mary Courier. Land-
owner.
Ashton, John (1623-77) Va.; m. Grace ---. Justice.
Ashton, Peter (cl634-1669) Va.; m. Grace Meese.
Burgess; Landowner.
Aspinwall, Peter (cl619-1687/92) Mass.; m. --- Merrill;
Alice Sharp; Remember Palfrey. Surveyor; Constable.
Aston, George (   -1728) Pa.; m. Elizabeth Hunter.
Justice.
Aston, Walter (1607-56) Va.; m. --- Warbowe; Hannah
Jordan. Burgess; Military service.
Aten, Adrian Henricks (1630-1708) N.Y.; m. Elizabeth
Thomas. Landowner.
Athearn, Simon (1643-1714) Mass.; m. Mary Butler.
Representative.
Atherton, Humphrey (1609-1661) Mass.; m. Mary Wales.
Freeman; Ancient and Honorable Artillery.

Atkinson, James (    -1723) Va.; m. Mary Holliman.
Landowner.
Atkinson, John (    -1713) Mass.; m. Eliza ---.
Minister.
Atkinson, Thomas ( 1645-1726) Va.; m. Mary ---.
Landowner.
Atwood, John (    -1675) Conn.-Mass.; m. Sarah Masterson.
Founder; Colonial treasurer.
Aubrey, Henry (    -c1711) Va.; m. ---Sheriff.
Augustine    SEE    Gustin
Ault, John (1601-77/78) N.H.; m. Remembrance Tibbetts.
Constable; Juryman.
Austin, Anthony (1634-1708) Conn.; m. Esther Huggins.
Freeman; Civil officer.
Austin, John (1700-c1760) Va.; m. Hannah Love.
Constable.
Avent, Thomas (1671-1757) Va.; m. Margaret Elizabeth
Gooch. Justice; Landowner.
Avery, Alexander (c1690-  ) Va.; m. Olive ---.
Military service.
Avery, Christopher (1590-70) Conn.; m. Margery
Stephens. Selectman.
Avery, Christopher (1679-1753) Mass.-Conn.; m.
Prudence (Payson) Wheeler. Landowner.
Avery, James (1620-98) Conn.-Mass.; m. Joanna Green-
slade. Selectman; Train Band.
Avery, James (1648-1728) Conn.; m. Deborah Stallion.
Military service.
Avery, James (1673-1784) Mass.-Conn.; m. Margery
Griswold. Founder.
Avery, William (1622-87) Mass.; m. Margaret Albright.
Freeman; Physician.
Axtell, Thomas (1619-46) Mass.; m. Mary Rice.
Landowner.
Ayer, John (1587-1657) Mass.; m. Hannah Webb.
Military service.

Ayer, John N. (1690-1757) Mass.; m. ---. Proprietor.
Aylesworth, Arthur (1653-1725) R.I.; m. Mary Brown.
Assessor; Supervisor of highways.

-B-

Babb, Philip ( -c1671) N.H.-Me.; m. Mary ---.
Commissioner; Magistrate.
Babb, Thomas (c1666-c1751) N.H.-Me.; m. Bethsheba
Hussey; Elizabeth (Conway) Booth. Landowner.
Babcock, George ( -1671) Mass.; m. Mary ---.
Viewer of highways.
Babcock, John (1644-73) R.I.; m. Susannah Clark.
Freeman; Assessor.
Babcock     SEE ALSO Badcock.
Baber, John (c1670-1736) Va.; m. Mary Walton. Clerk
of court.
Baber, Robert (c1650-1718) Va.; m. Sarah ---. Land-
owner.
Bachelder  SEE        Batchelder.
Bachiler   SEE        Batchelder.
Bachilor   SEE        Batchelder.
Backus, William (1614-64) Conn.; m. Sarah Charles
Legislator; Landowner.
Bacon, Edmund (1641-1705) Va.; m. Anne Lyddall.
Sheriff; Military service.
Bacon, Geoege (1592-1642) Mass.; m. Margaret ---.
Landowner.
Bacon, Michael (1608-88) Mass.; m. Mary ---; Mary
Noyes. Military service.
Bacon, Nathaniel (1630/35-1705/06) Conn.; m. Ann
Miller. Founder; Military service.
Bacon, Nathaniel (1642-76) Va.; m. Elizabeth Duke.
Military service; Assemblyman.
Bacot; Pierre (1638-1702) S.C.; m. Jacquine Menecier.
Landowner.

Bacot, Pierre (1684-1735) S.C.;m. Marie Personneau. Landowner.

Badcock, James (1612-79) R.I.; m. Sarah ---. Elizabeth ---. Commissioner; Military service.

Badcock, Robert (c1620-94) Mass.; m. Joanna ---. Military service.

Badcock SEE ALSO Babcock.

Badger, Giles (1595-1647) Mass.; m. Elizabeth Greenleaf. Proprietor.

Badgley, Anthony (c1670-1712/20) N.Y.; m. Elizabeth ---. Landowner.

Bailey, Daniel (1601-74) Pa.; m. Mary ---. Founder.

Bailey, Joel (1659-1732) Pa.; m. Ann Short. Proprietor; Constable.

Bailey, Samuel (1691- ) Va.; m. Sarah Lewis. Justice.

Bailey SEE ALSO Bayley; Baily

Baily, SEE ALSO Bailey

Bainbridge, John (1605-87) N.J.; m. Alice ---. Justice; Sheriff.

Baird, John (1665-1755) N.J.; m. Mary ---. Landowner.

Baker, Alexander (1606-85) Mass.; m. Elizabeth Farrar. Proprietor.

Baker, Francis (1612-96) Mass.; m. Isabel Twining. Surveyor; Freeman.

Baker, Henry ( 1610-1700) Va.; m. Sarah ---. Landowner.

Baker, Henry (1630/42-1712) Va.; m. Mary Bennett. Justice; Burgess.

Baker, Henry (1645-1700) Pa.; m. Margaret Hardman. Councilman.

Baker, Joseph (1655-1716) Pa.; m. Mary ---. Constable; Councilman.

Baker, Martin (c1605- ) Va.; m. ---. Landowner; Sheriff.

Baker, Richard (c1625-1698) S.C.; m. Elizabeth Wilson.
Landowner.
Baker, Thomas (1618-1700) N.Y.-Conn.; m. Alia Dayton.
Magistrate; Constable.
Balch, Benjamin (1628/29-1706) Mass.; m. Sarah Gardner.
Military service.
Balch, Freeborn (1660-1729) Mass.; m. Elizabeth Fair-
field. Landowner.
Balch, Hezekiah (c1684/86-  ) Md.; m. Martha Bloomer.
Landowner.
Balch, John (c1579-c1648) Mass.-Pa.; m. Margery Lovell.
Selectman.
Baldridge, James (  -  ) Va.; m. Jane ( ) Baynham.
Councilman.
Baldwin, Benjamin (1681 -  ) Conn.; m. Sarah Sanford.
Proprietor.
Baldwin, George (1624-80/81) N.Y.; m. Abigail Sweet.
Landowner.
Baldwin, John (c1600-82) Va.- Md.; m. Elizabeth Wilkens.
Tax collector; Proprietor.
Baldwin,John (c1612-1681) Conn.; m. Hannah Burchard;
Mary Bruen. Proprietor.
Baldwin, John (1614-87) Mass.; m. Mary Richardson.
Landowner.
Baldwin, John (1630-1714) Va.-Md.; m. Hester ---.
Landowner.
Baldwin, John (1648-81) Conn.; m. ---. Landowner.
Baldwin, Joseph (c1639-84) Va.; m. Hannah Whitlock.
Freeman; Landowner.
Baldwin, Nathaniel (  -1648) Conn.; m. Joanna ( )
Westcoat; Abigail Camp. Landowner.
Baldwin, Richard (c1622-65) Conn.; m. Elizabeth Alsop.
Founder; Military service.

Baldwin, Thomas (1657-1731) Pa.; m. Mary ---. Landowner; Supervisor.

Ball, Allen (c1610-1700) Conn.; m. Dorothy Tuttle.
Military service.

Ball, Edward (1642-   ) Conn.-N.J.; m. Abigail Blatchley. Sheriff; Committeeman.

Ball, Edward (c1675-1726) Va.; m. Keziah Williamson.
Sexton; Landowner.

Ball, Joseph (1649-1711) Va.; m. Mary Johnson;
Elizabeth Romney. Military service.

Ball, William (c1615-80) Va.; m. Hannah Atherold.
Burgess; Commissioner.

Ballagh, William (1660-1739) S.C.; m. Mary ---.
Landowner.

Ballard, Charles (   -1676/77) Md.; m. Sarah ( ) Elzey.
Justice; Landowner.

Ballard, Thomas (1630-89) Va.; m. Ann Thomas; Frances
---. Burgess; Councilman.

Ballard, Thomas (c1655-1711) Va.; m. Katherine
Hubbard. Burgess; Justice.

Ballard, William (1603-89) Mass.; m. Elizabeth ---.
Ancient and Honorable Artillery; Military service.

Ballinger, Henry (1660-1733) N.J.; m. Mary Harding.
Assemblyman.

Ballou, Maturin (1610/25-1661/63) R.I.; m. Hannah
Pike. Proprietor.

Bancroft, Thomas (1649-1718) Mass.; m. Sarah Poole.
Military service.

Bangs, Edward (1592-1678) Mass.; m. Lydia Hicks;
Rebecca (Hobart) Tracy. Deputy to court.

Banks, Adam (   -   ) Va.; m. ---. Landowner.

Bankston, Andrew (1640-1706) Pa.; m. Gertrude Rambo.
Landowner.

Banta, Jacob Epke (1620-70) N.Y.; m. Sitske ---.
Landowner.

Barber, Charles (1676-1726) Va.; m. Mary Tarpley.
Burgess; Clerk of court.

Barber, Luke (c1625-74) Md.; m. Elizabeth Younger.
Physician.

Barber, Thomas (1614-62) Conn.; m. Jane Coggin.
Juror; Military service.

Barber  SEE ALSO  Barbour

Barbour, William (1640-97) Va.; m. Elizabeth ---;
Mary (Gray) Tarplay. - Military service.

Barbour, William (1675-1733) Va.; m. Ann Archer.
Burgess.

Barbour  SEE ALSO  Barber

Barding, Nathaniel ( -1674) Conn.; m. ---. Selectman.

Barecock, Thomas (c1653-1721) N.C.; m. --- Jennings.
Landowner.

Barham, Charles (c1626/27-53) Va.; m. Elizabeth Ridley.
Sheriff; Military Service.

Barker, James ( -1678) Mass.; m. Grace ---. Proprietor; Freeman.

Barker, John (1680- ) Va.; m. Letitia ---. Landowner.

Barker, Luke (c1625-73) Md.; m. Elizabeth Youngs.
Physician; Councilor.

Barker, Nathanial (1644-1722) Mass.; m. Mary ---.
Freeman.

Barker, Richard (c1643-1692 ) Mass.; m. Joanna ---.
Selectman.

Barker, Samuel (1643-1720) Del.; m. ---. Landowner.

Barksdale, William (1629-94) Va.; m. ---. Proprietor.

Barlow, George ( - ) Mass.; m. Jane ( ) Bessey.
Constable.

Barlow, John ( -1674) Conn.; m. Ann Ward. Freeman;
Landowner.

Barlow, Sir Thomas ( -c1725)Va.; m. ---. Landowner.

Barnard, Francis (1617-98) Mass-Conn.; m. Hannah
Marvis. Freeman; Military service.
Barnard, Joseph (1641-95) Mass.; m. Sarah Strong.
Town officer.
Barnard, Robert (    -1682) Mass.; m. Joanna Harvey.
Military service; Founder.
Barnes, Henry (    -1676) Md.; m. Sarah Coffer.
Military service.
Barnes, Jonathan (1684-    ) Mass.; m. Sarah Bradford.
Landowner.
Barnes, Thomas (    -c1671) Conn.; m. Mary Andrews.
Landowner; Military service.
Barnes, Thomas (1623-93) Conn.-Mass.; m. Elizabeth
---. Signed Colony Constitution.
Barnes, Sir Thomas William (1568-1619) Va.; m. Anne
Sandys. Member London Co.
Barney, Jacob (1600-73) Mass.; m. Elizabeth ---.
Freeman; Representative.
Barnum, Thomas (1625-95) Conn.; m. Sarah Hurd.
Proprietor.
Barrett, Arthur (c1682-    ) Va.; m. Lydia Chambers.
Landowner.
Barrett, Benjamin (    -1690) Mass.; m. Sarah Graves;
Mary Alexander. Military service.
Barrett, Humphrey (1598-1662) Mass.; m. Mary ---.
Freeman; Ensign.
Barron, Ellis (    -1676) Mass.; m. Grace ---. Free-
man; Selectman.
Barrow, John (c1700-76) Va.; m. ---. Landowner.
Barrows, John (1609-92) Mass.; m. Anne ---. Land-
owner; Fence surveyor.
Barstow, William (1612-68) Mass.; m. Anne ---.
Freeman; Bridge builder.
Bartholomew, Andrew (1670-1752/55) Conn.; m. Hannah
Frisbie. Landowner.

Bartholomew, **Henry** (1607-92) Mass.; m. Elizabeth
Scudder. Proprietor.
Bartholomew, William (1602/03-1680) Mass.; m. Anna
Lord. Freeman; Representative.
Bartlett, Richard (1575-1647) Mass.; m. ---..
Landowner; Minister.
Bartlett, Robert (1603-1676) Mass.; m. Ann ---;
Mary Warren. Founder; Constable.
Bartlett, Stephen (1691-1773) Mass.; m. Hannah
Webster. Cordwainer.
Barton, Benjamin (1645-1720) R.I.; m. Susanna
Gorton. Freeman.
Barton, Edward ( -1674) Mass.; m. Sarah Stone;
Elizabeth ---. Oath of Fidelity; Freeman.
Barton, John (c1670-1711) Md.; m. ---. Landowner.
Barton, Rufus ( -1648)Mass.-R.I.; m. Marguerite ---.
Magistrate; Commissioner.
Barton, Samuel (1663-1732) Mass.; m. Hannah Bridges.
Landowner.
Barton, **Thomas** (1680-1732) Va.; m. Mary Wells.
Churchman.
Barton, William (1605-c1675) Md.; m. ---. Burgess;
Commissioner.
Barton, William ( -1717) Md.; m. **Eliza Smoote.**
Landowner.
Barwick, John (c1640/44-1717)Md.;m. ---. Landowner.
Bass, Nathaniel (1589-1654) Va.; m. Mary Jorden.
**Burgess; Landowner.**
Bass, Samuel (1600-94) Mass.; m. Anna ---. Deputy
to court.
Bassett, Samuel (1692-1764) Conn.; m. Deborah Bennett.
Selectman; Military service.
Bassett, William (c1600-67) Mass.; Elizabeth Tilden;
Bridget Cary. Military service.
Bassett, William (1624-1701) Mass.; m. Mary or
Sarah Burt. Selectman; Deputy to court.

Bassett, William (1628-84) Conn.; m. --- (Hannan)
Ives. Military service.
Bassett, William (1671-1723) **Va.; m. Joanna Burwell.**
Burgess; Military service.
Batchelder, David (1673-1766) **Mass.;** m. Susanna Whipple.
Military service.
Batchelder, John (1638-98) Mass.; m. Sarah Goodale.
Freeman.
Batchelder, Joseph (   -1647) Mass.; m. Elizabeth ---.
Landowner; Freeman.
Batchelder, Stephen (1561-1660) N.H.; m. Helen (Mer-
cer) Mason; Ann Bate; Mary Beedle; Deborah ---.
Minister.
Batchelder, William (1630-1710) N.H.; Constable;
Selectman.
Batcheller   SEE Batchelder
Bateman, William (   -1658) Mass.-Conn.; m. ---.
Freeman; Landowner.
Bates, Clement (1595-1671) Mass.; m. Ann Dalrumple.
Freeman.
Bates, Henry (   -1721) Va.; m. Mary ---. Burgess.
Bates, John (c1598/99-1666) Va.; m. Elizabeth Winston.
Landowner.
Bates, William (1640-84) Va.; m. Martha Willard.
Landowner.
Bathurst, Lancelot (1646-1704/05 ) Va.; m. Susanna ---;
Susan Rich. **Sheriff.** Attorney.
Batson, Thomas (c1650-1725) Va.-N.C.; m. Susannah ---.
Landowner.
Batte, Henry (   -1721) **Va.;** m. Mary Lound. Burgess;
Justice.
Batte, John (c1595-1652) Va.; m. Martha Mallory.
Military service.
Batte, Robert (   -   ) **Va.;** m. Mary Parry. Landowner.
**Batte, Thomas** (1630-   ) Va.; m. Mary Randolph.
Burgess; Military service.

Batte, Thomas (1656-1736) Va.; m. Any Kent. Land-
owner.
Battel SEE Battle
Battle, John (1633-90) Va.; m. Elisabeth ---. Land-
owner.
Battle, John (1660- ) Va.-N.C.; m. Margaret Sowsby.
Landowner.
Battle, Mathew ( -1681) Va.; m. Ann ---. Landowner.
Battle, William (1682-1749) Va.; m. Sarah Hunter.
Landowner.
Baudouin, Pierre ( -1647) Mass.; m. Elizabeth ---.
Physician.
Baudouin SEE ALSO Bowdoin
Baugh, William (1610-87) Va.; m. Jane ---. Justice.
Baulstone, William (1600-78) Mass.-R.I.) m. Elizabeth
---. Military service.
Baxter, George ( - ) Va.; m. Mary Love. Landowner.
Bayard, Balthazar Lazare ( -1643) N.Y.; m. Judithde
Vos Beyens. Minister.
Bayard, Nicholas (1644-1707) N.Y.; m. Blanchina Conde.
Minister; Councilman.
Bayard, Petrus (1644-99) N.Y.; m. Blandina Kierstadt.
Minister; Landowner.
Bayes, Thomas (1615-80) Mass.; m. Anne Baker. Select-
man; Proprietor.
Bayldon, Richard (1591-1665) Conn.; m. ---. Propri-
etor.
Bayles, John (1617-82) N.Y.; m. Rebecca ---. Townsman;
Constable; Magistrate.
Bayles, Samuel (1667-c1732) N.Y.; m. Hannah Goulder.
Proprietor.
Bayles SEE ALSO Bayless
Bayless, Humphrey (c1695- ) Va.; m. Ann ---. Land-
owner.
Bayless, John (1617-82) Conn.; m. Rebecca Stillwell.
Justice; Town clerk.

**Bayless** SEE ALSO Bayles
Bayley, John (1613-91) Mass.; m. Eleanor Emery.
Proprietor.
Bayley SEE ALSO Bailey
Baylor, John (1650-1721) Va.; m. Lucy (Todd) O'Brien)
Burgess.
Baytop, Thomas ( -c1635) Va.; m. Alexander. Land-
owner.
Beach, Benjamin (1673/74- ) Conn.-N.J.; m. Mary
Hitchcock. Landowner.
Beach, George ( -- ) Va.; m. ---. Landowner.
Beach, John (1623-77) Conn.; m. Mary Staples. Free-
man; Landowner.
Beach, John (1690-1773) Conn.; m. Mary Royce.
Founder; Deacon.
Beadon, George ( -1705) S.C.; m. Elizabeth ---.
Landowner.
Beal; Beale SEE Beall
Beall, Alexander (1649-1744) Md.; m. Elizabeth Dick.
Magistrate.
Beall, James (1698-1793) Md.; m. Margaret Edmonston.
Landowner.
Beall, John (1588-1688) Mass.; m. Nazareth ---; Mary
( ) Jacob. Deputy to court.
Beall, John (1649-1748) Md.; m. Verlinda Magruder.
Burgess.
Beall, John (1657-1726) Pa.; m. Mary Clayton. Land-
owner; Governor, Quaker meeting.
Beall, John (1685-1747) Pa.; m. Sarah Bowater.
Landowner.
Beall, John (1700-67) Md.; m. Elizabeth Cameron.
Military service.
Beall, Ninian (1625-1717) Md.; m. Ruth Moore; Eliza-
beth Gordon. Sheriff; Military service.

Beall, Robert (1670-1748) Md.; m. Mary Berry. Landowner.

Beall, Thomas (1621-1700) Va.; m. Alice ---. Councillor; Military service.

Beall, Thomas (1638-1732) Md.; m. Elizabeth Lee; Landowner.

Beaman, Simon ( -1676) Conn.; m. Alice Young. Landowner.

Bean, Lewis (1671-1721) Mass.; m. Mary (Austin) Sayre. Governor; Military-service.

Beard, Richard (1620-75) Va.-Md.; m. Rachel Robbins. Assemblyman.

Beardslee SEE Beardsley

Beardsley, William (1605-61) Conn.; m. Mary Harvey. Military service; Deputy to court.

Beatty, John (1675-1721) N.Y.; m. Susanna Ashfordby. Founder; Sheriff.

Beauchamp, Edmund (1625-91) Md.; m. Sarah Dixon. Military service.

Beauford SEE Buford.

Beaufort SEE Buford.

Bebout, John ( -1697) N.J.; m. Mary Miller. Landowner.

Bechinoe, Edward (1628-1679) Va.; m. Mary ---. Collector.

Becker, Jan Janrisenszen ( -1697) N.Y.; m. Maria Adriaens. Commander; Alderman.

Beckman, William (1650-1720) Va.; m. --- Randolph. Landowner.

Beckley, Richard (c 1615-90) Conn.; m. ---. Landowner.

Beckwith, Joseph (1679-1741) Conn.; m. Susannah Tallman. Military service.

Beckwith, Matthew (1610-81) Conn.; m. Elizabeth ---. Landowner.

Beech SEE Beach

Beekman, Gerardus (1653-1723) N.Y.; m. Magadelene
Abeel. Physician; Military service.

Beekman, Hendrick (    -1703) N.Y.;m. ---. Assemblyman; Military service.

Beekman, Wilhelmus (1623-1707) N.Y.; m. Cataline de
Boogh. Military service.

Beeson, Edward (1652-1714) Pa.; m. Rachel Pennington.
Landowner.

Behethland, Robert (    -    ) Va.; m. Mary Nicholson.
Landowner.

Belangee, Ive (c1670-c1720) N.J.; m. Crejanne de la
Plaine. Landowner.

Belcher, Gregory (    -1659) Mass.; m. Catherine ---.
Freeman.

Belcher, William (    -1705) Va.; m. Ann ---. Landowner.

Belknap, Abraham (1589/90-1643) Mass.; m. Mary ---.
Landowner.

Bell, Robert (    -1634) Va.; m. Alice Colston.
Justice; Commissioner.

Bell, Thomas (1600-44) Va.; m. ---. Landowner.

Bellagh, William (    -1717) S.C.; m. ---. Landowner.

Bellinger, Edmund (1657-1707) S.C.; m. Elizabeth
Cartwright. Surveyor; Landgrave.

Bellinger, Henry (1660-    ) Mass.; m. Mary Harding.
Landowner.

Belt, Humphrey (1615-63) Md.; m. Anne ---. Landowner.

Belt, John (1645-98) Md.; m. Elizabeth Tidings.
Landowner.

Belt, Joseph (1680-1761) Md.; m. Esther Beall.
Burgess; Justice.

Benedict, Thomas (1617-90) Mass.-Conn.; m. Mary Brid-
gnow. Magistrate; Landowner.

Benmore, Philip (    -1676) N.H.; m. Rebecca(Tibbett)
Nocke. Landowner.

Bennet    SEE    Bennett

Bennett, David (1615-1715/19) Mass.; m. Mary ---;
Rebecca Spencer. Physician.

Bennett, Edward (1577-64) Va.; m. Mary Bourne.
Burgess.

Bennett, Henry (c1648-1726) Conn.; m. Sarah Champion.
Military service.

Bennett, James (1620-86) N.C.; m. Ann Wilks. Burgess;
Governor's Committee.

Bennett, John (1656-1709) Pa.; m. Ann Brinton. Landowner; Assemblyman.

Bennett, Richard (1606-76) Va.; m. Mary Ann Utie.
Governor.

Bennett, Samuel (1582-1638/39) Va.; m. ---. Landowner.

Bennett, Thomas (1590-1632/35) Va.; m. Alice ( )
Pierce. Burgess.

Bennett, William (c1700-1765) Va.-N.C.; m. Grace ---.
Landowner.

Bennett, William Adrianse (c1615-1643) N.Y.; Mary
Braskhoenger; Marritje (Thomas) Badie. Military
service; Landowner.

Benson, John ( - ) Vt.; m. Mary ---. Military
service.

Benson, Robert (1682-1757) Va.; m. Frances Prou.
Landowner.

Bent, John (1596-1672) Mass.; m. Martha ---. Freeman;
Landowner.

Bentley, William (1645-1720) Mass.; m. Sarah Eldred.
Landowner.

Benton, Andrew (1620-83) Conn.; m. Hannah Stocking;
Ann ---. Freeman.

Bergen, Hans Hansen ( -1659) N.Y.; m. Sarah Rapelje.
Shipowner.

Bernard, William (1603-1665) Va.; m. Lucy (Higginson)
Burwell. Councillor; Military service.

Berrien, John (1669-1711) N.Y.; m. Ruth Edsall.
Landowner.

Berry, James (c1610-1685) Va.-Md.; m. Elizabeth ---.
Founder.

Berry, Joseph (1691-1749) Va.; m. Catherine ---.
Military service.

Berry, Samuel ( -c1753) Md.; m. ---. Physician.

Berry, William ( -1677) Va.; m. Ann ---. Landowner.

Berryman, Benjamin (c1665-1729) Va.; m. Elizabeth
Newton. Landowner.

Berryman, John ( -1680) Va.; m. Jane Tucker. Landowner; Minister.

Bertrand, John ( -1701) Va.; m. Charlotte de Jolme.
Minister.

Besselieu, Mark Anthony (c1670-c1739) S.C.; m. ---.
Landowner.

Bethea, John (c1635-c1735) S.C.-N.C.; m. ---. Landowner.

Betts, John ( - ) Conn.; m. Abigail Elderkin.
Landowner.

Betts, Richard (1613-1688) N.Y.; m. Joanna ---.
Councillor; Freeman.

Betts, Thomas (1618-88) Conn.; m. Mary ---. Freeman;
Founder.

Beverley, Harry ( -1730) Va.; m. Elizabeth Smith.
Magistrate; Justice.

Beverley, Peter (c1668-94) Va.; m. Elizabeth Peyton.
Burgess; Surveyor general.

Beverly, Robert (1636-86) Va.; m. Elizabeth Armistead;
Mary Keeble. Burgess; Military service.

Beverly SEE Beverley

Bevier, Louis (1646-1720) N.Y.; m. Marie LeBlanc.
Founder; Military service.

Bevill, Essex (c1644-1682/83) Va.; m. Amy Butler.
Justice; Landowner.

Bevin, Arthur (1652-1697) Conn.; m. Mary ---. Land-
owner.
Bevin, Richard (c1620-  ) Va.; m. ---. Landowner.
Bibb, Benjamin (1640-1702) Va.; m. Mary ---. Pro-
prietor.
Biddle, William (1650-1712) N.J.; m. Sarah ( ) Kempe.
Justice; Proprietor.
Bidlack, Christopher (1661-1740) Mass.; m. Sarah
Fuller. Landowner.
Bidwell, John (c1620-87) Conn.; m. Sarah Wilcox.
Landowner; Freeman.
Bigelow, John (1617-1703) Mass.; m. Mary Warren;
Sarah Bemis. Selectman; Military service.
Bigelow, Joshua (1655-1745) Mass.; m. Elizabeth
Flagg. Landowner; Military service.
Bigger, James (1684-1770) Va.; m. ---. Landowner.
Biglo SEE Bigelow
Bilbo, Jean Jacques (  -c1739) Va.; m. ---. Founder.
Biles, William (1650-1710) Pa.; m. Jane Atkinson.
Councillor; Pennsylvania Great Charter.
Biles, William (1672-1747) Pa.; m. Sarah Langhorne.
Proprietor; Assemblyman.
Bill, Phillip (1665-1729) Mass.; m. Mercy Houghlow.
Military service.
Billingsley, Francis (1620-84) Md.; m. Ann ---.
Assemblyman.
Billingsley, John (1647-93) Md.-Va.; m. Sarah ---.
Maritime trader; Landowner.
Billingsley, William (1628-57) Va.; m. Sarah Bowman.
Maritime trader; Landowner.
Billingsley, William (1670-1716) Md.; m. Clearanna
Bowles. Landowner; Tax assessor.
Billington, Luke (  -  ) Va.; m. Elisia Russell.
Landowner.
Bingham, James (c1668-1714) Pa.; m. Ann ---. Vestry-
man; Landowner.
Bingham, Thomas (1642-1710) Conn.; m. Mary Rudd.
Founder.
Binns, Henry (c1622-69) Va.; m. Martha ---; Elizabeth
Alston. Justice; Commissioner.

Binns, Thomas (1638-78) Va.; m. Elizabeth Aston.
Justice; Landowner.
Bird, Abraham (c1660-98) Md.; m. ---.  Landowner.
Bird, Robert (    -1686) Va.; m. Frances Williamson.
Landowner.
Bird, Thomas (c1700-26) Conn.-Del.; m. Sarah Empson.
Landowner.
Bird,    SEE ALSO    BYRD
Bishop, Edward (    -1716 ) Mass.; m. Hannah Raymond.
Military service.
Bishop, James (1625-91) Conn.; m. Mary (Lewen) Curtis;
Elizabeth Tompkins.  Deputy Governor; Landowner.
Bishop, John (1589-1660) Conn.-N.J.; m. Anne ---.
Founder; Justice.
Bishop, John (c1640-58) Va.; m. Elizabeth ---.  Burgess.
Bishop, John (    -c1716) Va.; m. Sarah Lawrence.
Landowner.
Bissell, John (1591-1677) Conn.; m. Mary Drake.  Mili-
tary service; Freeman.
Bixby, Joseph (1621-1704) Mass.; m. Sarah Gould;
Sarah Heard.  Military service.
Black, Samuel (    -1770) Va.; m. Catherine Shaw.
Minister.
Blackburn, Benjamin (c1698-1790/91) Va.; m. Mary ---.
Military service.
Blackburn, William (1679-1739) Va.; m. Elizabeth ---.
Landowner.
Blackledge, William (    -1713/18) Pa.; m. Mary Duf-
field.  Landowner.
Blackman, Adam (1598-1665) Conn.; m.  Jane Wheeler.
Minister.
Blackman, William (    -1698) Va.; m. Dorothy ---.
Landowner; Sheriff.
Blackshaw, Robert (1632-  ) Del.; m. Ellinor ---.
Landowner.
Blackshaw, Robert (1677-  ) N.J.-Del.; m. ---.  Land-
owner.
Blackshaw, Thomas (1631-84) N.J.-N.Y.; m. Ellinor ---.
Landowner.
Blackwell, Robert (1650-1717 ) N.Y.; m. Mary Manning-
ham.  Landowner.

Blackwell, Samuel (1680-1732) Va.; m. Margery D.
Hudnall. Justice; Vestryman.

Blair, Archibald (1663-1736) Va.; m. Mary Harrison;
Sarah(Archer) Fowler; Mary (Wilson) Cary. Burgess;
Physician.

Blair, John (1687-1771) Va.; m. Mary Monro. Governor;
Treasurer.

Blake, John ( -1744) Va.; m. Jane ---. Landowner.

Blake, Thomas (1626-92) Md.; m. Patience Pope. Constable; Freeman.

Blake, Thomas (c1640-1702) Va.; m. Alice --; Jane
Isaac. Landowner.

Blake, William (c1594-1663) Mass.; m. Agnes Bond.
Recorder; Ancient and Honorable Artillery.

Blakeman, Adam (1598-1665) Conn.; m. Jane Wheeler.
Minister.

Blanchan, Matthys ( - ) N.Y.; m. Madeline Jorisen.
Landowner.

Blanchard, Benjamin (1657-1719) Va.; m. Catherine ---.
Judge; Landowner.

Blanchard, Jean ( - ) N.Y.; m. ---. Justice;
Committeeman.

Blanchard, John (c1630-1693) Mass.; m. Hannah Brackett.
Landowner.

Blanchard, Thomas (c1600-54) Mass.; m. ---. Landowner.

Bland, James ( -1708) Va.; m. Margaret ---. Landowner.

Bland, Theodore (1629-71) Va.; m. Anne Bennett.
Justice; Burgess.

Blasdell, Ralph (1618-49) Mass.; m. Elizabeth ---.
Constable; Deputy to court.

Blatchley, Thomas (1615-74) Md.; m. Susanna Hall.
Landowner; Military service.

Blatt, Robert ( -c1659) Mass.; m. Susanna ---.
Freeman.

Bledsoe, George (c1652-c1704) Va.; m. Ann Ball.
Surveyor.

Bledsoe, William ( - ) Va.; m. ---. Sheriff; Military service.

Blish, Abraham ( -1683) Mass.; m. Anne ---. Surveyor; Landowner.

Bliss, John (  -  ) Mass.; m. Patience Burt. Land-
owner.
Bliss, Thomas (1580/85-1639) Mass.-Conn.; m. Margaret
Lawrence. Founder; Military service.
Blodgett, Samuel (1633-1720) Mass.; m. Susannah ---.
Selectman; Deputy to court.
Blodgett, Thomas (1661-1740) Mass.; m. Rebecca Tidd.
Freeman; Landowner.
Blood, James (1588-c1641) Mass.; m. ---. Freeman.
Blood, Richard (1617-83) Mass.; m. Isabel ---. Town
Officer; Military service.
Bloomfield, Thomas (1638-  ) N.J.; m. ---. Founder;
Landowner.
Blossom, Thomas (  -1633) Mass.; m. Ann Heilson.
Landowner.
Blount, James (c1620-95/96) N.C.; m. Ann Willis;
Claire ---. Assemblyman; Councillor.
Blount, James (1635-86) Va.; m. ---. Burgess; Land-
owner.
Blumston, John (1644-1723) Pa.; m. Eleanor Branton.
Assemblyman; Speaker of House.
Blush  SEE  Blish
Boardman, Samuel (c1615-73) Conn.; m. Mary Betts.
Deputy to Court; Governor's Assistant.
Boardman, Thomas (  -1670) Mass.; m. Margaret ---.
Tax Collector; Landowner.
Boardman, William (1627-1709) Md.; m. Sarah Sinley.
Judge; Burgess.
Boarman  SEE ALSO  Boardman
Boddie, John (1675-1730) Va.; m. Elizabeth Thomas.
Founder.
Boddie, William (1630/33-1717) Va.; m. Elizabeth Thom;
Ann ---; Mary ( ) Griffin. Landowner.
Bodie  SEE  Boddie
Bogardus, Anneke Jans (1600-63) N.Y.; m. Rev. Everar-
dus Bogardus. Landowner.
Bogardus,Everardus (1607-47) N.Y.; Annetse Jans (Webb-
er) Roeloff. Minister.
Bogardus, Pieter (1645-1703) N.Y.; Wyntje C. Van West-
brock. Magistrate; Sheriff.

Bogardus, Willem (1638/39-1711 (N.Y.; m. Wyntje
   Sybrairt. Military service.
Bohun, Edmund (1644/45-99) S.C.; m. Mary Brampton.
   Justice; Commissioner.
Boice    SEE   Boys
Bollen, James (1600-82) N.J.; m. Martha Ann ---.
   Provincial Secretary; Landowner.
Bolles, Joseph (   -1678) Me.; m. Mary Howell. Com-
   missioner; Town clerk.
Bolling, John (1676-1729) Va.; m. Mary Kannon.
   Burgess; Military service.
Bolling, Penelope (   -1754) Va.; m. Christopher Clark.
   Landowner.
Bolling, Robert (1646-1709) Va.; m. Jane Rolfe; Ann
   Stith. Burgess; Justice.
Bolling, Thomas (1584-   ) Va.; m. Mary ---. Landowner.
Boltwood, Robert (   -1684) Mass.; m. ---. Freeman;
   Founder.
Bond, Peter (c1640-1706) Md.; m. Alice ---. Military
   service.
Bond, William (1625-95) Mass.; m. Sarah Briscoe.
   Founder.
Bondurant, Jean Pierre (   -1734) Va.; m. Elizabeth
   Ann Chastaine. Physician.
Bonham, George (1604-1704) Mass.; m. ---. Landowner.
Bonneau   SEE   Bonnell
Bonnell, Antoine (1658-1743) S.C.; m. Catherine Du-
   bliss. Military service.
Bonnell, Daniel (c1664-c1740) S.C.; m. Marie Izambent.
   Proprietor; Landowner.
Bonnell, Nathaniel (c1644-c1696) N.J.; m. Susannah
   Whitehead. Proprietor.
Bonner, John (1699-   ) Va.; m. Jane Cook. Landowner.
Bonner, Thomas (1690-1765) N.C.; m. Abigail. Sheriff;
   Assemblyman.
Bonum, Samuel (   -1726) Va.; m. Margaret Phillpot.
   Landowner.
Booker, Edward (1590-1648) Va.; m. --- Glover. Mil-
   itary service; Landowner.
Booker, Richard (1652-1704) Va.; m. Rebecca Leak.
   Military service.

Boon, Thomas (c1648-1723) Va.; m. Elizabeth ---.
Landowner.
Boone, George (1666-1749) Pa.; m. Mary Maugridge.
Landowner; Trustee.
Boone, John (c1648-c1711) S.C.; m. Elizabeth Paty.
Landowner; Councillor.
Boone, Squire (1690-1765) Pa.; m. Sarah Morgan.
Landowner.
Boosey, James (    -1649) Conn.; m. Alice ---. Town
Clerk.
Booth, Humphrey (    -  ) Va.; m. Margaret Underwood.
Commissioner.
Booth, John (1653-  ) Conn.; m. Dorothy Hawley.
Military service.
Booth, Richard (1606/09-c1688) Conn.; m. Elizabeth
Hawley. Landowner.
Booth, Robert (c1610/16-57) Va.; m. Frances ---.
Burgess; Justice.
Borde, Richard (1563-1620) R.I.; m. Joan ---. Govern-
or's Assistant.
Borden, Benjamin (1649-1728) Va.; m. Abigail Grover.
Landowner.
Borden, Benjamin (1692-1743) Va.; m. Zuriah Winter.
Landowner.
Borden, Richard (1595-1671) R.I.-N.J.; m. Joan Fowle.
Commissioner; Treasurer.
Bordner, Balthasar (1698-1747) Pa.; m. Mercelessa ---
Landowner.
Boreman  SEE  Boardman
Borland, Archibald (c1700-c1774)N.C.; m. Jane ---.
Landowner.
Borsboom, Pieter Jacob (    -1686) N.Y.; m. Maretje
Dirke. Proprietor.
Borton, John (c1638-1687) N.J.; m. Anne Kinton.
Assemblyman; Constable.
Bosley, Walter (1677-1715) Md.; m. ---. Attorney;
Landowner.
Bosmen; Bossman  SEE  Bozman
Bostick, William (    -  ) Va.; m. ---. Landowner.
Boston, Henry (c1620-76) Md.; m. Ann Walker.
Landowner.

Bostwick, Arthur (1603-80) Conn.; m. Jane Whittle;
Ellen ---. Founder; Landowner.
Bostwick, John (1638-88/89) Conn.; m. Mary Brins-
mead. Landowner.
Bostwick, Nathaniel (1699-1756) Conn.; m. Abigail
Walker; Jane Whittel. Deputy to court; Justice.
Boswell, John (c1700-41) Va.; m. Ann Ransom.
Landowner.
Bosworth, Jonathan (1613-87/88) Mass.; m. Elizabeth
---. Surveyor; Constable.
Boteler    SSS    Butler
Botsford, Henry (    -1683/85) Conn.; m. Elizabeth
---. Military service.
Bouchelle, Legide (    -c1700) Md.- N.Y.; m. Eliza-
beth ---. Huguenot.
Boudinot, Elias (1674-1719) N.Y.; m. Marie Catherine
Carreje. Landowner; Military service.
Boudouin    SEE    Bowdoin
Bouldin, William (1650-1717) Va.; m. Elizabeth ---.
Landowner.
Boulding, Thomas (1580-1655) Va.; m. ---. Landowner.
Bourne, Richard (    -1685) Mass.; m. Bathsheba Hal-
let. Freeman; Deputy to court.
Bourne; Thomas (1581-1664) Mass.; m. Elizabeth ---;
Martha ---. Deputy to court.
Bouton, John (c1636-1707) Conn.; m. Abigail Marvin.
Landowner.
Bovee, Jacob (1698-    ) N.J.; m. Donna Switzer. Land-
owner.
Boveington, Richard (1654-1747/48) N.J.-Pa.; m.
Anne ---. Landowner; Constable.
Bowdle, Thomas (    -    ) Md.; m. Joanna ---. Justice.
Bowdoin, Pierre (    -1706) Mass.; m. Elizabeth ---.
Merchant; Landowner.
Bowan    SEE    Bowen
Bowen, Griffith(    -1767) Mass.; m. Margaret Fleming.
Surveyor.
Bowen, John (    -1688) Va.; m. Rebecca ---. Land-
owner.
Bowen, Moses (1698-    ) Pa.; m. Rebecca Reese. Land-
owner; Merchant.

Bowen, Obadiah (1627-1710) Mass.; m. Mary Clifton.
Surveyor; Juryman.
Bowen, Richard (1600-74/75) Mass.; m. Ann ---; Eliza-
beth ( ) Marsh. Proprietor; Freeman.
Bowles, Thomas ( -1679/86) Va.; m. Tabitha Edloe.
Justice; Councillor.
Bowling    SEE    Bolling
Bowman, Nathaniel (1610-82) Mass.; m. Ann ---. Free-
man; Landowner.
Bowne, James (1636-95) Mass.-N.J.; m. Mary Stout.
Justice; Assemblyman.
Bowne, John (1626-95) Mass.; m. Hannah Feake. Land-
owner.
Bowne, William ( -1677) N.J.; m. Anne ---. Magis-
trate; Landowner; Huguenot.
Boyce, Cheney (1599-1649) Va.; m. Sara ---. Burgess;
Landowner.
Boyce    SEE ALSO    Boys
Boykin, Edward (1650-1725) Va.; m. Ann(Marshall)
Williams. Burgess; Proprietor.
Boynton, Joseph (1644-1730) Mass.; m. Sarah Swan;
Elizabeth Wood. Town clerk; Military service.
Boynton, Joshua (1646-1736) Mass.; m. Hannah Barnet.
Military service.
Boynton, William (1606-86) Mass.; m. Elizabeth Jack-
son. Landowner.
Boys, Jan Cornelius (c1624/29- ) N.Y.; m. Femmetje
Jans. Landowner.
Bozman, William (1649-65) Md.-Va.; m. Bridget ---.
Landowner.
Bracewell, Robert (1612- ) Va.; m. ---. Minister;
Burgess.
Bradbury, Thomas (1574- ) Mass.; m. Elizabeth Whit-
gift. Commissioner; Judge.
Bradbury, Thomas (1610/11-95) Mass.; m. Mary Perkins.
Freeman; Judge.
Bradford, John (1651-1736) Mass.; m. Mercy Warren.
Military service.
Bradford, Joseph (c1589-1657) Mass.; m. Alice Carpen-
ter. Landowner.

Bradford, Joseph (1630-1715) Mass.; m. Jael Robert.
Landowner.
Bradford, Nathaniel (    -1690) Va.; m. Joan ---.
Landowner.
Bradford, William (1590-1657) Mass.; m. Alice (Car-
penter) Southworth. Governor.
Bradford, William (1623/24-1708) Mass.; m. Alice
Richards; Mary Wiswall; Mary Holmes. Landowner.
Bradford, William (1655-87) Mass.; m. Rebecca Bart-
lett. Landowner.
Bradford, William (1663-1752) Mass.; m. Elizabeth
Soule. Landowner.
Bradley, Henry (    -1650)Va.; m. Frances ---. Land-
owner.
Bradstreet, Ann (Dudley) (1603-72) Mass.; m. Simon
Bradstreet. Author of extant diary.
Bradstreet, Humphrey (c1594-c1657) Mass.; Bridget---.
Freeman.
Bradstreet, Simon (1603-97) Mass.; m. Ann Dudley;
Ann (Downing) Gardner. Colonial Secretary; Deputy
Governor.
Bradt, Arent Andriess (    -    ) N.Y.; m. Catalyntje
Dirks. Founder.
Bragdon, Arthur (1597-1678) Me.; m. Mary ---. Con-
stable; Alderman.
Bragg, Edward (    -1708) Mass.; Elizabeth ---.
Proprietor; Town clerk.
Bragg, Hugh (c1678-1736) Va.; m. Elizabeth ---.
Landowner.
Brainerd, Daniel (c1641-1715) Conn.; m. Hannah Spencer.
Deputy to court; Justice.
Braithwaite, William (c1600-1679) Md.; m. Heleanor
Stephenson. Acting Governor; Assemblyman.
Bramble, John (1689-1735) Md.; m. Elizabeth ---.
Landowner.
Brammer, Thomas (1605-c70) Va.; m. Margarette ---.
Burgess, Assemblyman.
Branch, Benjamin (c1627-68) Va.; m. ---. Landowner.
Branch, Sir Christopher (1595-1681) Va.; m. Addie
Hoey. Burgess; Justice.

Brandon, John (1691-1756) Pa.-N.C.; m. Elizabeth
Locke. Justice; Assemblyman.
Brandt, Randolph (    -1698) Md.; m. Mary ---. Founder.
Branton, William (1633-74) R.I.; m. Martha Burton.
Colonial President; Governor.
Brashall, Henry (c1620/25-1661/62) S.C.; m. ---.
Landowner.
Brashear, Benjamin (c1620-62) Md.; m. Mary Richford.
Justice; Landowner.
Brashear, Robert (1615-65) Va.-Md.; m. Florence ---.
Burgess; Assemblyman.
Brashear, Robert (1630/40-63) Md.; m. Mary ---. Land-
owner.
Brashear, Samuel (1673-1740) Md.; m. Ann Jones.
Landowner.
Brashier    SEE    Brashear
Brasseur    SEE    Brashear
Brassy, Thomas (    -1690) Pa.; m. ---. Juryman.
Braswell, Richard (1652-1730) Va.; m. Sarah ---.
Landowner.
Braswell, Robert (1613-68) Va.; m. Elizabeth ---.
Minister; Burgess.
Bratt    SEE    Bradt
Braun, Philip (1693-1767) Pa.; m. Elizabeth Magdalene.
Landowner.
Bray, John (    -1716) N.J.; m. Anne(Seabrook) Bowne
Minister.
Bray, William (    -    ) N.C.; m. Abigail Forbes.
Deputy marshal; Landowner.
Brayton, Francis (1611/12-92) R.I.; m. Mary ---.
Freeman.
Brearly, John (1645-1720) N.J.; m. Sarah ---. Land-
owner.
Breckinridge, Alexander (c1667/68-1743) Va.; m. Jane
Preston. Military service.
Breed, Allen (1630-    ) Mass.; m. Mary ---. Landowner.
Brent, George (    -    ) Va.; m. Elizabeth Green. Mil-
itary service.
Brent, Giles (c1600-71) Va.-Md.; m. Mary K---. Mili-
tary service; Governor.

Brent, Hugh (c1620-71) Va.; m. ---. Constable;
Landowner.
Brenton, William (1633-74) R.I.; m. Martha Burton.
Landowner.
Bretton, William (       -c1671) Md.; m. Mary Nabbs.
Proprietor; Justice.
Brevard, Jean (       -1730) Md.-N.C.; m. Mary McKnitt.
Huguenot.
Breward, James (       -1709) Md.; m. Anne ---. Land-
owner; Vestryman.
Brewer, John (1565-1635) Va.-Md.; m. Mary Butler.
Landowner.
Brewster, Mary (Wentworth) (1565/68-1637/38) Mass.;
m. William Brewster. Mayflower passenger.
Brewster, William (1567-1644) Mass.; m. Mary Went-
worth. Landowner; Acting Minister.
Brice, William (       -1710) N.C.; m. ---. Landowner.
Brick, John (       -1753 ) N.J.; m. Hannah Davis. Con-
stable; Military service.
Bridell, Francis (1631/32-1712) Va.; m. Mary ( )
Williams. Landowner.
Bridge, John (c1577-1665) Mass.; m. ---. Landowner;
Selectman.
Bridger, Joseph (1584-1650) Va.; m. Mary ---. Mili-
tary service.
Bridger, Joseph (1628-86) Va.; m. Hester Pitt.
Burgess; Landowner.
Bridgman, James (c1640-76) Mass.; m. Sarah ---.
Surgeon; Constable.
Briggs, John (       -1697) R.I.; m. Frances ---. Land-
owner.
Brigham, Samuel (1652-1708) Mass.; m. Elizabeth
(Ward) Howe. Military service.
Brigham, Thomas (1603-53) Mass.; m. Mercy Hurd. Con-
stable; Freeman.
Brinson, Adam (1689-1769) N.C.; m. Sara ( ) Sterling.
Military service; Juror.
Brinton, William (1636--1700) Pa.; m. Ann Bagley.
Landowner; Grand Juror.
Briscoe, John (c1540-c1634) Md.; m. Elizabeth Dubois.
Ark and Dove Expedition; Physician.

Briscoe, Philip (1648-1724) Md.; m. Susannah Swan.
Military service; Justice.

Bristol, Henry (1625-95) Conn.; m. Lydia Brown.
Landowner.

Brittain, James (c1699-c1779) N.C.; m. Mary Witty.
Landowner.

Brittingham, William (c1642-1709) Mass.; m. Elizabeth
Williams; Mary (Roach) Martin. Landowner.

Britton, Nathaniel (c1613-84) N.Y.; m. Ann Stillwell.
Commissioner.

Broaddus, Edward (1672-1749) Va.; m. ---. Landowner.

Broadnax   SEE   Brodnax

Brock, Henry (   -1652) Mass.; m. Elizabeth Barger.
Proprietor.

Brockett, John (1609/11-90) Conn.; m. ---.   Commissioner; Deputy to court.

Brockett, Richard (1612-95) Mass.; m. Alice ---.
Military service.

Brocklebank, Samuel (c1628-76) Mass.; m. Jane ---.
Deacon; Military service.

Brockman, Henry (1647-   ) Va.; m. Rebecca Salmon.
Landowner.

Brodhead, Daniel (1604-67) N.Y.; m. Ann Tye.  Military service.

Brodhead, Richard (1666-1758/59) N.Y.; Wynte Pawling.
Landowner; Trustee.

Brodnax, John (1608-1657) Va.; m. Dorothy ---.  Landowner; Military service.

Brodnax, William (1675-1727) Va.; m. Rebecca (Champion) Travis. Burgess.

Brokaw, Abraham (1684-   ) N.Y.-Pa.; m. Marylie David.
Military service.

Bronson, Abraham (1647-74) Conn.; m. Anne Griswold.
Landowner.

Brooke, Michael (1616-63) Md.; m. Frances ---. Burgess.

Brooke, Robert (1602-55) Md.; m. Mary Baker; Mary
Mainwaring. Governor; Minister.

Brooke, Robert (1654-1712) Va.-Md.; m. Catherine
Booth; Eleanor Matton. Justice; Coroner.

Brooke, Roger (1637-1700 ) Md.; m. Deborah Griswold;
Dorothy Neal. Justice; Sheriff.

Brooke, Roger (1673-1718) Md.; m. Elizabeth Hutchins.
Burgess.
Brooke, Thomas (1590-1612) Md.; m. Susan Forster.
Assemblyman; Sheriff.
Brooke, Thomas (1632-78) Md.; m. Eleanor Hatton.
Burgess; Acting Governor.
Brooke, Thomas (c1640-95) Pa.-Va.; m. Joanne ---.
Landowner.
Brooke  SEE ALSO  Brooks
Brooks, John (1680-1766) N.C.; m. Susan ---. Land-
owner.
Brooks, Thomas (1613/17-67) Mass.; m. Grace Wheeler.
Freeman; Landowner.
Brooks, Thomas (1679-1732) Conn.; m. Hannah Blakeslee.
Military service.
Brooks  SEE ALSO  Brooke
Brossius, John George (1698-  ) Pa.; m. ---. Burgess.
Broucard, Bourgon (1645-1720) N.Y.; m. Catherine Le
Febre. Landowner.
Brower, Adam (1696-1768) N.Y.; m. Deborah Allen.
Landowner.
Brown, Abell (   -1702) Md.; m. --- Harwood. Sheriff.
Browne, Abraham (1590-1650) Mass.; m. Lydia ---.
Freeman; Selectman.
Browne, Chad (   -1662) Conn.-R.I.; m. Elizabeth
Sharperowe. Juryman; Surveyor.
Brown, Francis (c1607-85) Conn.; m. Martha Chapman.
Assemblyman; Constable.
Brown, George (c1600/10-  ) Pa.; m. Mercy Wright.
Landowner.
Browne, Henry (c1600-c1662) Va.; m. Ann ---. Land-
owner.
Browne, John (c1632-  ) Mass.; m. Esther Makepeace.
Landowner.
Browne, John (   -1673) Md.; m. ---. Ship's officer;
Landowner.
Brown, John (1671-1731) R.I.; m. Elizabeth Cranston.
Landowner.
Brown, Nicholas (   -1694) R.I.; m. ---. Freeman.
Browne, Originale (   -   ) Va.-Md.; m. Jane (Brookes)
Wickliffe. Landowner; Military service.

Browne, Peter (1633-   ) Mass.-Conn.; m. Mary ---.
Mayflower passenger.
Brown, Richard (1616-86/87) Mass.; m. Hannah King.
Military service.
Browne, Samuel (1694-1769) Pa.; m. Ann Clark.  Land-
owner.
Brown, Thomas (c1612-88) Mass.; m. Bridget ---.  Pro-
prietor.
Brown, William (   -   ) N.C.; m. ---.  Committee of
Safety.
Browne, William (   -   ) N.J.; m. Anne ---.  Magis-
trate; Landowner.
Browne, William (1620-1703) Va.; m. Mary Brown.
Burgess.
Browne, William (1639-1716) Mass.; m. Hannah Curwin.
Judge; Councillor.
Brown, William (1669-c1780) Va.; m. Sarah Long.
Committee of Safety; Provincial Congressman.
Browne SEE   Brown
Brownell, Thomas (1618-65) R.I.; m. Ann Bourne.
Freeman; Commissioner.
Browning, John ( 1588-1646 ) Va.; m. ---.  Burgess;
Military service.
Browning, William (c1615-c79) Va.; m. ---.  Landowner.
Brownsen  SEE   Brownson
Brownson, John (1600-   ) Conn.; m. Elizabeth ---.
Deputy to court;  Military service.
Brownson, Richard (1617-87) Conn.; m. Abigail Wilbourn.
Proprietor; Landowner.
Bruce, William (   -1683) Va.; m. ---.  Landowner.
Bruen, Obadiah (1606-84) N.J.-Conn.; m. Sarah ---.
Selectman; Freeman.
Brundige, John (c1585-c1639) N.Y.; m. Rachel ---.
Town clerk.
Brunson  SEE   Brownson
Bryan, Alexander (c1602-79) Conn.-Mass.; m. Ann Bald-
win.  Military service; Judge.
Bryan, Edward (1663-1737) Va.; m. Christina Council.
Landowner.
Bryan, Edward (1690-1746) Va.; m. Ann ( ) Hands.
Landowner; Justice.

Bryan, John (c1680-1741) N.C.; m. Ann Norwood.  Military service; Commissioner.
Bryan, Jonathan (1690-1782) S.C.; m. Janet Cochran. Councillor.
Bryan, Joseph (     -1732) S.C.; m. Janet Cochrane. Landowner.
Bryan, Morgan (1671-1763) Pa.; m. Martha Strode. Landowner.
Bryan, Needham (1690-67) N.C.; m. Anne Rambeau; Sarah Woodward. Justice; Assemblyman.
Bryan, Richard (     -     ) Conn.; m. Mary Pantry. Landowner.
Bryan, William (1655-1742) Va.; m. Alice Needham. Assemblyman; Justice.
Bryant, Cornelis Aertszen (1607-     ) N.J.; m. Belitje Hendricks. Landowner.
Bryant, James (c1650-1731/32) Va.; m. Sarah ---. Landowner; Military service.
Bryant, Thomas (1635-99) Va.; m. --- Wright.  Landowner.
Brydell, Francis (1625/30-1712) Va.; m. Mary ---. Landowner.
Buchanan, John (1599-1687) Va.; m. Margaret Patton. Landowner.
Buchanan, John (1615-     ) Va.; m. Jean ---.  Military service; Landowner.
Buck, Richard (1623/24-     ) Va.; m. ---.  Minister.
Buck, Thomas (1618-59) Va.; m. ---.Landowner.
Buckingham, Thomas (1605/06-57) Mass.-Conn.; m. Hannah ---.  Founder; Deputy to court.
Buckman, William (1690-1755) Pa.; m. Sarah ---; Esther Penquite. Landowner.
Buckner, John (1631-95) Va.; m. Deborah Ferrers. Burgess; County clerk.
Budd, John (     -1670) Mass.-Conn.-N.Y.; m. Katherine Brown. Landowner.
Budd, William (1615-73) N.J.; m. Joanna Knight. Juror; Landowner.
Budd, William (1649-1732) N.J.; m. Anne Claypoole. Justice; Assemblyman.

Buell, Samuel (1641-1720) Conn.; m. Deborah Griswold.
Assemblyman; Military service.

Buell, William (1610-81) Conn.; m. Mary Post. Landowner.

Buffington, Richard (1653-1748) Pa.; m. Frances Grubb.
Constable.

Buford, John (1642-1722) Va.; m. Elizabeth Parrott.
Proprietor; Military service.

Buford, Richard (1617-  ) Va.; m. Margaret ---.
Landowner.

Bugbee, Edward (1594-1669) Mass.; m. Rebecca ---.
Constable; Landowner.

Bugby    SEE    Bugbee

Bugg, Samuel (1640-1716) Va.; m. Deborah Sherwood.
Landowner.

Bulkley, Gershon (1636-1713) Conn.; m. Sarah Chauncey.
Physician; Justice.

Bulkley, Peter (1582-1658/59) Mass.; m. Grace Chet-
wood. Minister.

Bulkley, Peter (1643-88) Mass.; m. Jane Allen; Rebecca
Wheeler. Military service; Justice.

Bulkley, Peter (1664-1701) Conn. m. Rachel Talcott.
Military service.

Bull, Sarah(Wells) (1694-1796) N.Y.; m. William Bull.
Landowner.

Bull, Stephen (c1635-1706) S.C.; m. ---. Assemblyman.

Bull, Thomas (1610-  ) Conn.; m. Susannah ---. Military service.

Bullard, Benjamin (c1634-89) Mass.; m. Martha Pidge;
Elizabeth ---. Military service.

Bullen, James (   -   ) N.J.; m. ---. Provincial
Secretary.

Bullock, Edward (c1665/70-1753) Va.; m. Sarah ---.
Landowner.

Bullock, Hugh (c1600-  ) Va.; m. Mary ---. Burgess;
Landowner.

Bullock, John (1650-1705) Md.; m. Elizabeth ---.
Landowner; Freeman.

Bullock, Richard (1622-67) Mass.; m. Elizabeth Ingra-
ham. Founder; Freeman.

Bullock, Richard (1640-1703) Va.; m. Mary Hawkins.
Landowner.

Bullock, William (1610-90) Va.; m. Mary (Lewis) Taylor.
Councillor.

Bumpas, Edward (c1605-93) N.C.; m. Hannah ---. Landowner.

Bunce, Thomas (1612-82) Mass.-Conn.; m. Sarah ---.
Proprietor; Constable.

Bunker, George (  -1664) Mass.; m. Judith ---.
Freeman; Constable.

Bunn, Edward (1612-73) Mass.; m. ---. Proprietor.

Bunting, Samuel (1678-1724) N.J.; m. Mary Faulke.
Minister; Juror.

Burbank, John (c1600-82/83) Mass.; m. Jemima ---.
Freeman; Proprietor.

Burdette, William (1580-1633) Va.-Md.; m. Frances ( )
Saunders; Alicia Travelley. Burgess; Vestryman.

Burdick, Robert (  -1692) R.I.; m. Ruth Hubbard.
Deputy to court; Military service.

Burgess, Thomas (1603-85) Mass.; m. Dorothy ---.
Deputy to court; Military service.

Burgess, William (1622-86) Md.; m. Elizabeth Robins.
Councillor; Deputy Governor.

Burke, Richard (1640-93) Mass.; m. Mary Parmenter.
Proprietor.

Burnap, John (1627-95) Mass.; m. Ann ---. Landowner;
Military service.

Burnap, Robert (c1595-1688/89) Mass.; m. Ann ---.
Selectman.

Burnham, John (1618/26-1694) Mass.; m. Mary ---.
Deacon; Military service.

Burnham, Thomas (1617-88) Conn.; m. Ann ---; Martha
Gayer. Landowner.

Burnham, Thomas (1623-94) Mass.; m. Mary Tuttle.
Deputy to court; Military service.

Burnley, John ( 1673-c1762) Va.; m. Phoebe Davis.
Landowner.

Burr, Benjamin (c1630-81) Conn.; m. Anne ---. Freeman;
Proprietor.

Burr, Daniel (c1660-1722) Conn.; m. Elizabeth Pinckney. Landowner.

Burr, Jehue (1600-70) Mass.; m. ---.  Landowner;
Deputy to court.

Burrell, Benjamin (1605-78) Conn.; m. Anne Wilmot.
Oath of Allegiance.

Burrell, Philip Duday (1662-1740) Me.; m. --- Purring-
ton.  Military service.

Burrett    SEE    Burritt

Burrill, John (1631-1703) Mass.; m. Lois Ivory.  Selectman.

Burritt, Stephen (c1635-97) Conn.; m. Sarah Nicols.
Landowner; Military service.

Burritt, William (    -1651) Conn.; m. Elizabeth ---.
Landowner; Blacksmith.

Burroughs, John (c1616/17-1678) Conn.; m. Elizabeth
Reed. Landowner; Founder.

Bursley, John (1599-1660) Mass.; m. Joanna Hull.
Founder; Freeman.

Burt, Henry (c1609-1662 ) Mass.; m. Eulalia Marche.
Town clerk; Military service.

Burton, Francis (c1555-   ) Va.; m. ---.  Landowner.

Burton, John (c1634-1685) Va.-N.J.; m. Susanna Allen;
Rachel Hutchings.  Landowner.

Burton, John (1666-1734) Va.; m. Elizabeth Fowler.
Landowner.

Burton, Richard (    -   ) Va.; m. Katherine Christian.
Landowner.

Burton, Robert (c1647-1725) Pa.; m. Catherine Cotton.
Assemblyman; Juror.

Burton, Robert (1665-1748) Va.; m. Priscilla ---.
Landowner.

Burton, Thomas (1634-86) Va.; m.  Susannah Allen.
Landowner.

Burwell, Dorothy (Bedell) (    -1648) Va.; m. Edward
Burwell.  Landowner.

Burwell, Lewis (1621-1653) Va.; m. Lucy Higginson.
Burgess; President of Council.

Burwell, Lewis (1649-1710) Va.; m. Abigail Smith.
Councillor; Landowner.

Burwell. Nathaniel (1680-1721) Va.; m.    ---.
Burgess; Justice.

Bush, Isaac (1647-95) Mass.; m. ---. Representative;
Military service.

Bush, John (   -1624) Va.; m. Elizabeth ---. Landowner.

Bush, Richard (c1655-1700) Va.; m. Elizabeth Bibby.
Landowner.

Bush, William (c1661-1716) N.C.; m. Martha ---. Tax
collector; Landowner.

Bushnall    SEE    Bushnell

Bushnell, Francis (c1580-1646) Conn.; m. Rebecca ---;
Ferris Quenell. Guilford Compact.

Bushnell, Richard (1620-58) Conn.;   m. Mary Marvyn.
Military service.

Bushnell, Richard (1652-1727 ) Conn.; m. Elizabeth
Adgate. Judge; Commissioner.

Bussey, George (1622-93) Md.; m. Ann Keene or Ann
Williams. Landowner.

Bustin, John (   -1688) Va.; m. Margaret ---. Landowner.

Butcher, John (   -1707) Pa.; m. Hannah ---. Landowner.

Bute, James (1582-1635) Mass.; m. Alice Glover.
Founder.

Bute, James (1625-1718) Mass.; m. Anne Withington.
Founder.

Butler, Benjamin (1672-1755) Va.; m. Thankful Sage.
Landowner.

Butler, John (1677-1759) Mass.; m. Elizabeth Wilson.
Founder.

Butler, Nicholas (1595-1671) Mass.; m. Joyce Baker.
Freeman; Landowner.

Butler, Richard (c1610-84) Mass.-Conn.; m. Elizabeth
Bigelow. Founder; Juror.

Butler, Shem (c1672-1718) S.C.; m. Esther ---. Landowner.

Butler, Thomas (1603-46) Va.; m. Joan Christopher.
Landowner.

Butt, Thomas (   -1722) Va.; m. Elizabeth ---.
Landowner.

Butter, William (1630-92) Mass.; m. Mary --. Landowner.

Butts, Samuel (1673-1747) Mass.; m. Sarah Maxfield.
Deputy to court.

Bye, Thomas (c1640-1726) Pa.; m. Margaret Davis.
Landowner.

Byram, James (1649-   ) Va.; m. Jane Wright.  Landowner.

Byram, Nicholas (   -1688) Mass.; m. Susanna Shaw.
Military service; Councillor.

Byrd, Abraham (1639-99) Md.; m. Margaret Huling.
Landowner.

Byrd, John (1668-1716) N.C.; m. Rebecca Bayard.
Justice; Landowner.

Byrd, William (c1610-c72) Va.; m. Hannah (Grandin)
Jennings.  Landowner.

Byrd, William (1652-1704) Va.; m. Mary Horsmanden.
Burgess.

-C-

Cabaniss, Henri (   -1725) Va.; m. Marie ---.; Magdalene ---.  Landowner.

Cabell, William (1695-1774) Va.; m. Elizabeth Burks.
Burgess.

Cade, Robert (1626-c1685 ) Va.; m. ---.  Landowner.

Cadwallader, John (1676-1742) Pa.; m. Mary Cassell.
Minister.

Caldwell, John (1624-92) Mass.; m. Sarah Dillingham.
Surveyor.

Calkins, Hugh (c1600-1690) Mass.-Conn.; m. Ann (Robert)
Eaton.  Freeman; Selectman.

Callaway, Francis (1675-1774) Va.; m. ---.  Landowner.

Callaway, Joseph (c1700-c1730) Va.; m. Elizabeth
Tilley.  Landowner.

Callaway, Thomas (c1648-   ) Va.; m. ---.  Landowner.

Calthorne, Christopher (   -1667) Va.; m. Anne ---.
Commissioner; Burgess.

Calthrope, James (   -1689) Va.; m. Elizabeth ---;
Mary ---.  Justice.

Calvert, Cecilius (1605-75) Md.; m. Anne Arundel.
Ark and Dove.

Calvert, Charles (1637-1715) Md.; m. Mary (Thorpe)
Banks.  Lord Proprietor.

Calvert, George (1580/82-1632) Md.; m. Joane ---;
Anne Wynne. Member of a Virginia Company.
Calvert, John (1649-1742) Pa.; m. Judith Stamper.
Landowner.
Calvert, Lenard (c1610-47) Md.; m. Anne Brent.
Governor.
Calvert, William (1642/43-82) Md.; m. Elizabeth Stone.
Secretary of colony; Burgess.
Camac SEE Cammack
Cammack, Warwick (1636-c85) Va.; m. Margaret Williams.
Executor; Landowner.
Camp, Edward (1650-1721) Conn.; m. Mehitable Smith.
Proprietor; Landowner.
Camp, Thomas (1691- ) Va.; m. --- Marshall. Land-
owner.
Campbell, Duncan (c1643- ) Pa.-Va.; m. Mary McCay.
Landowner.
Campbell, James (1682-1753) Va.; m. ---. Landowner.
Campbell, John (1674-1747) Pa.; m. Grissell (Grace)
Hoy. Councillor.
Canby, Phebe (1699-1774) Pa.; m. Robert Smith.
Quaker minister.
Canfield, Matthew (1604-73) N.J.; m. Sarah Treat.
Delegate to court.
Canfield, Thomas (c1634- ) Conn.; m. Phoebe Crane.
Delegate to court; Military service.
Cannon, Thomas (c1633-98) Md.; m. ---. Landowner.
Canterbury, John (1665-1716 ) Va.; m. Ruth Williams.
Landowner.
Cantey, George (c1650-c1714) S.C.; m. Martha ---.
First fleet 1670.
Cantey, Teige (1619-c79) S.C.; m. Elizabeth ---.
Landowner.
Cantey, William (c1672-1729) S.C.; m. Arabella Oldye.
Landowner.
Cantrill, Richard(1689-1753) Pa.; m. Dorothy Jones.
Military service; Proprietor.
Capen, John (1613-92) Mass.; m. Mary Bass. Military
service.
Capers, Richard (1657-94) S.C.; m. Mary Barnett.
Landowner.

Capers, William (    -1718) Va.; m. Mary ---.  Vestry-man.

Cappell, Robert (1654-c1744 ) Md.; m. Susannah Holland. Landowner.

Capps, William (1575-1639) Va.; m. Catherine Jernigan. Burgess.

Card, Richard (    -1674) R.I.; m. Rebecca ---.  Free-man; Landowner.

Carey, John (1610-81) Conn.; m. Elizabeth Godfrey. Town clerk; Constable.

Carlile, John (    -1725) N.J.; m. Mary Goodwin. Quaker; Landowner.

Carlock, David (1679-1763) Va.; m. ---.  Road Com-missioner; Surveyor.

Carlton, Edward (1605/7-91) Mass.; m. Eleanor Denton. Founder; Freeman.

Carlton, John (1630-68) Mass.; m. Hannah Jewett. Town clerk; Selectman.

Carman, John (1606-58) N.Y.; m. Florence Fordham. Landowner.

Carpenter, Daniel (1669-1721) Mass.; m. Bethia Bliss. Military service.

Carpenter, Henry (--- -  ) Pa.; m. Anne Morget. Physician; Landowner.

Carpenter, Henry (1673-1747/49) Pa.; m. Salome (Rufen-er) Blumenstein.  Landowner; Physician.

Carpenter, William (1605-59) Mass.; m. Abigail ---. Delegate to court; Commissioner.

Carpenter, William (1608-85) Conn.-R.I.; m. Elizabeth Arnold.  Military service.

Carr, Caleb (1592-1635) R.I.; m. Martha Hardington. Commissioner; Treasurer.

Carr, Caleb (1624-95) R.I.; m. Mary (or Mercy) Vaughan; Sarah Clarke.  Freeman; Governor.

Carr, Sir Robert (1614-81) R.I.; m. Elizabeth ---. Landowner.

Carr, Thomas (1678-1737) Va.; m. Mary Dabney.  Justice; Burgess.

Carraway, John (c1619-69) Va.; m. Anne ---.  Landowner.

Carroll, Charles (1635-90) Md.; m. Mary Darnell.
  Attorney General.
Carroll, Charles (1660-1720) Md.; m. Elizabeth Brook.
  Landowner.
Carter, George (1635-c1665) Va.; m. Mary ---. Land-
  owner.
Carter, George (1692-1750) Va.; m. Elizabeth ---.
  Landowner.
Carter, Giles (c1634-1701/02) Va.; m. Hannah Crews.
  Surveyor of highways.
Carter, John (     -1669) Va.; m. Sarah Ludlow; Eliza-
  beth Landon; Anne ---; Jane Glynn. Burgess; Mili-
  tary service.
Carter, Robert (1663-1732) Va.; m. Mary Walker; Judith
  Armistead. Burgess; Governor.
Carter, Theodore (1676-1737) Va.; m. Elizabeth ---.
  Landowner; Constable.
Carter, Thomas (1610-84) Mass.; m. Mary Dalton.
  Minister.
Carter, Thomas (1630/36-1700) Va.; m. Mary Parkhurst;
  Katherine Dale. Military service; Burgess.
Carter, Thomas (1672-1733) Va.; m. Arabella Williamson.
  Attorney; Landowner.
Carter, William ( 1600-54) Va.; m. Alice Croxon.
  Landowner.
Carter, William (c1660-1709/11) Va.; m. Mary Goodloe.
  Landowner.
Carterett, Hugh (     -1693) S.C.; m. Anne ---. Mili-
  tary service; Assemblyman.
Cartledge, Edmund (1639-1703) Pa.; m. Mary Need.
  Landowner.
Cartwright, John (1602-   ) Md.; m. Jannecke Lawrence.
  Landowner.
Cartwright, Matthew (1634-c1688) Md.; m. Sarah ---.
  Census taker.
Cartwright, Thomas (1670-1705) Va.; m. Alice ---.
  Landowner.
Carver, John (     -1621) Mass.; m. Katherine White.
  Mayflower passenger.
Carver, John (c1637-   ) Mass.; m. Millicent Ford.
  Freeman.

Carver, Robert (1594-1680) Mass.; m. Christian ---.
Landowner; Sawyer.

Cary, John (  -  ) Va.; m. Elizabeth Hereford.
Military service.

Cary, John (1645-1701) Va.; m. Jane Flood.  Landowner.

Cary, Miles (1622/24-1667) Va.; m. Anne Taylor.
Burgess; Councillor.

Cary, Miles (1655-1708) Va.; m. Mary (Wilson) Roscow.
Burgess; Surveyor General.

Cary, Miles (1671-1724) Va.; m. Elizabeth Cocke.
Landowner.

Cary, Thomas (1647-1708) Va.; m. Anne Milner.  Military service.

Case, Henry (c1637-1665) N.Y.; m. Martha Corwin.
Landowner.

Case, John (1616-1704) Conn.; m. Sarah Spencer.
Assemblyman; Representative.

Cassell, Johannes (c1639-92) Pa.; m. Mary ---.  Councillor.

Cassell, Mary (1639-c91) Pa.; m. Johannes Cassell.
Landowner.

Castle, Henry (1613-98) Conn.; m. Abigail (Dickerson)
Finch.  Landowner.

Castleberry, Henry (  -  ) Pa.; m. Katherine ---.
Landowner.

Catcher, Thomas (   -c1637) Md.; m. ---.  Minister.

Catchings, Henry(c1610-  ) Va.-Md.; m. ---.  Landowner.

Cater, Thomas (1655-1731) S.C.; m. ---.  Landowner.

Catlett, John (1658-1721) Va.; m. Elizabeth (Gaines)
Underwood.  Burgess; Military service.

Catlin, John (c1647-87) Conn.; m. Mary ---.  Landowner.

Catlin, Robert (1650-  ) Md.; m. Ann ---.  Landowner.

Caulkins  SEE  Calkins

Cawthorn, Richard (1644-87) Va.; m. Anne Cox.  Landowner.

Caytlan  SEE  Catelin; Catlin

Cecil, John (c1658-1698) Md.; m. Mary ---.  Landowner.

Cecil, John (1690-1757/58) Md.; m. Elizabeth Selles.
Landowner.

Cecil, William (1665-1749) Md.; m. ---. Landowner.
Cessna  SEE  Decessna
Chadbourne, William (1584-  ) Md.; m. Helen Tawnley.
Carpenter.
Chaffee, Thomas (   -1680) Mass.; m. ---. Landowner.
Chaires, John  (c1625-  ) Md.; m. Elizabeth Ader.
Landowner.
Chaires, John (1668-1718) Md.; m. Catherine Collins.
Justice; Vestryman.
Chalker, Alexander (   -c1675) Conn.; m. Katherine
Past. Founder.
Challis, Philip (1617-81) Mass.; m. Margaret Sargent.
Deputy to court; Military service.
Chamberlain, Henry (1596-1674 ) Mass.; m. Jane ---.
Freeman.
Chamberlain, Henry (1659-88/89) Mass.; m. Ann West.
Landowner.
Chamberlain, John (c1633-c1667) R.I.; m. Ann Brown.
Landowner.
Chamberlain, John (c1688-1739) N.J.; m. Rebecca Morris.
Landowner.
Chamberlain  SEE ALSO Chamberlin
Chamberlin, Peter (1660-1727) Pa.; m. Lucy ---.
Landowner.
Champion, Edward (   -c1668) Va.; m. Elizabeth ---.
Landowner.
Champion, Henry (1616/17-1708/09) Conn.; m. Sarah
Bennet. Freeman.
Champlin, William (1678-1718) R.I.; m. Mary Babcock.
Military service.
Champney, Richard (c1609-69) Mass.; m. Jane ---.
Elder; Landowner.
Chandler, ( ) Jane (c1645-c1669) Pa.; m. George
Chandler. Landowner.
Chandler, Robert (c1627-69) Va.; m. Elizabeth Davis.
Juror; Landowner.
Chandler, Robert (1695-  ) Va.; m. Elizabeth ---.
Landowner.
Chandler, Roger (1637-1716/17) Mass.; m. Mary Simonds.
Mechanic.

Chandler, William (1595-1641) Mass.; m. Annie Bayford;
   Annie Alcock. Proprietor.
Chandler, William (1695-  ) Va.; m. Elizabeth ---.
   Landowner.
Chapin, Josiah (1634-1726) Mass.; m. Mary King.
   Selectman; Freeman.
Chapin, Samuel (1598-1675) Mass.; m. Cecily Penny;
   Phillipa Euston. Freeman; Founder.
Chapin, Seth (1668-1746) Mass.; m. Bettie Thurston.
   Surveyor; Selectman.
Chaplaine  SEE   Chaplin
Chapline   SEE   Chaplin
Chaplin, Francis (   -1707) Md.; m. Martha ---.
   Landowner; Vestryman.
Chaplin, Isaac (1584-c1628) Va.-Md.; m. Mary Calvert.
   Burgess; Commissioner.
Chapman,  Abraham (1684-1752) Pa.; m. Susanna Olden.
   Justice.
Chapman, Edward (   -1688) Mass.; m. Mary Symonds.
   Landowner.
Chapman, Ralph (1615-72) Mass.; m. Lydia Wells.
   Founder.
Chapman, Robert (1616-87) Conn.; m. Ann Bliss.
   Military service.
Chapman,  William (1627-79) Conn.; m. ---.  Landowner.
Chappell, George (1615-1709) Mass.; m. Margery ---.
   Landowner.
Chappell, James (1694-1769) Va.; m. Elizabeth Briggs.
   Landowner.
Chappell, John ( 1588-1612) Va.; m. Mary (Barker)
   Cravesend. Ship's captain.
Chappell, Thomas (1612-58) Va.; m. Mary Banister.
   Member of London  Company; Landowner.
Chappell, Thomas (1650-1700) Va.; m. Elizabeth Jones.
   Member London Company; Landowner.
Chappell, Zachariah (   -  ) Va.; m. ---.  Shipmaster.
Chappelle  SEE   Chappell
Charles, John (1595-1650) Mass.-Conn.; m. Sarah (Moss)
   Geare. Minister; Proprietor.
Charles, John (1641-90) Conn.; m. Abigail Welles.
   Landowner.

Charles, John (1686-   )  Mass.; m. Elizabeth Swetman.
Landowner.
Chase, Aquilla (1618-70) Mass.- N.H.; m. Ann Wheeler.
Landowner.
Chase, Jonathan (   -1676) Mass.; m. ---. Military
service.
Chase, William (1595/1600-1659) Mass.; m. Mary ---.
Freeman; Constable.
Chauncey, Charles (1592-1673) Mass.; m.  Catherine
Ayre.  Minister.
Cheatham, Thomas (1645-1726) Va.; m. Margaret ---.
Landowner.
Cheche, Philipe (c1675-1749) S.C.; m. Martha Jeanne.
Landowner.
Chedsey  SEE   Chidsey
Cheever, Ezekiel (1614-1708) Mass.; m. Ellen Lothrop.
Teacher.
Chenault, Stephen (1675-   ) Va.; m. ---. Landowner;
Military service.
Cheney, Richard (  ⌐c1688) Md.; m. Charity ---.  Land-
owner.
Cheney, Thomas (c1637-1694) N.Y.-Mass.; m. Jane
Atkinson; Military service.
Cheney, William (1603-67) Mass.; m. Margaret Mason.
Member of Militia.
Cherry, John (1610-70) Va.; m. ---. Landowner.
Cherry, John (1635-99) Va.; m. Frances Turberville.
Freeman.
Cherry, Lemuel (c1700-54) N.C.; m. ---. Committee
of Safety; Military service.
Cheseborough, William (1594-1667) Conn.; m. Anne
Stevenson.  Founder.
Chesley, Philip (--- --) N.H.; m. Elizabeth Thomas;
Sarah ---.  Joanna ---.  Landowner.
Chesnut, Alexander (   -1749 ) Va.; m. Mary ---.
Landowner.
Chester, Leonard (c1609-46) Mass.; m. Mary ---. Juror.
Chester, Thomas (   -1759) Va.; m. Sarah (Cartmell)
---.  Justice; Military service.
Chew, Benjamin (1670/71-1699) Md.; Elizabeth Benson.
Landowner.

Chew, John (1590-1652) Va.; m. Sarah Walker.  Burgess;
Justice.
Chew, Larkin (c1650-1728) Va.; m. Hannah Roy. Burgess.
Chew, Samuel (1625-76) Va.-Md.; m. Anne Ayres.
Physician; Military service.
Chew; Samuel (1660-1718) Va.-Md.; m. Anne---; Eliza
( ) Coale.  Landowner.
Chewning, Robert (1659-98) Va.; m. Ann Poole.  Land-
owner; Military service.
Cheyney  SEE  Cheney
Chidsey, John (1621-88) Conn.; m. Elizabeth ---.
Deacon.
Child, Benjamin (1630-78) Mass.; m. Mary Bowen.
Founder of School.
Child, John (1638-76) Mass.; m. Mary Warren.  Repre-
sentative.
Childers, Abraham (1655-93/98) Va.; m. Ann Pew.
Landowner.
Chiles, Walter (1600-c53) Va.; m. Elizabeth Maury.
Burgess, Councillor.
Chiles, Walter (1622-71) Va.; m. Mary Page; Susannah
---.  Military service.
Chilton, James (c1580-1620) Mass.; m. Mary ---;
Frances ---.  Mayflower passenger.
Chilton, John (1646-1700) Va.; m. Jane ---.  Land-
owner.
Chilton, John (1654-1726) Va.; m. --- Ball.  Mili-
tary service.
Chilton, Thomas (1699-1765/75) Va.; m. Jemima Cook.
Sheriff.
Chinn, John (c1692- ) Va.; m. Alice ---.  Constable.
Chinn, Raleigh (1684-1741/42) Va.; m. Easter Ball.
Landowner.
Chipman, John (1614-1708) Mass.; m. Hope Howland.
Elder; Magistrate
Chittenden, Isaac (1621-76) Mass.; m. Mary Vinal.
Military Service.
Choate  SEE  Chute
Christian, Thomas (1627-1712) Va.; m. ---.  Landowner.
Christian, Thomas (1636-1703) Va.; m. ---.  Landowner.

Christopher, Richard (1662-  ) Conn.; m. Lucretia
Bradley. Commissioner; Assemblyman.
Church, Caleb (1642-1722) Mass.; m. Johanna Sprague.
Freeman; Selectman.
Church, Edward (1628-1704) Mass.; m. Mary Hopkins.
Freeman; Selectman.
Church, Garrett (1611-c1662) Mass.; m.  Sarah ---.
Proprietor; Freeman.
Church, Richard  (1610-68) Mass.; m. Ann Marsh;
Elizabeth Warren. Founder;Proprietor.
Church, Richard (  -1705/06) Va.; m. Mary  Savage.
Burgess.
Church, Samuel (1636-84) Conn.; m. Mary Churchill.
Selectman.
Churchill, John ( -1662/63 ) Mass.; m. Hannah Porter.
Freeman; Landowner.
Churchill, Josiah (  -c1686 ) Conn.; m. Elizabeth
Foote. Military service.
Churchill, William (1649--1710) Va.; m. Elizabeth
(Armistead) Wormsley; Mary ---.  Burgess, Coun-
cillor.
Chute, Lionel (1580-1645) Mass.; m. Rose (Barker)---.
Teacher.
Clack, James (1660-1723) Va.; m. Jane Bolling.
Minister.
Claflin, Daniel (1674-1775) Mass.; m.  Sarah Edwards.
Treasurer.
Claflin, Joanna (Warner)(c1640-c1670) Mass.; m. Robert
Macklothlan. Landowner.
Claflin, Macklothlan (1630-c1690) Mass.; m. Jeanne
Warner. Landowner.
Claflin, Sarah Edwards (c1680-1743) Mass.; m. Daniel
Claflin. Landowner.
Clagget, Thomas (1635-1675) Md.; m. Sarah Patterson;
Mary (Nutley) Hooper. Landowner.
Claiborne, Thomas (1647-83) Va.; m. Sarah Fenn.
Military service.
Claiborne, William (1587-1676 ) Va.; m. Elizabeth
Butler; Jane Butler. Surveyor; Councillor.
Clapp, Roger (1684-1762) Mass.; m. Elizabeth Bartlett.
Ancient and Honorable Artillery.

Clap    SEE Clapp
Clapp, Nicholas (1612-79) Mass.; m. Sarah ---.
Deacon; Juror.
Clapp, Roger (1609-91) Mass.; m. Johannah Ford.
Ancient and Honorable Artillery; Military service.
Clapp, Thomas (1639-91) Mass.;m. Mary Fisher.
Landowner.
Clare, Timothy (   -1726) N.C.; m. Mary Bundy.
Burgess; Justice.
Clark,  Christopher (1668-1754) Va.; m. Penelope
(Bolling) Johnston.  Sheriff; Justice.
Clark, Daniel (1622-1710) Conn.; m. Mary Newberry.
Magistrate; Military service.
Clark, Edward (1604/06-   ) Va.; m. ---.  Landowner.
Clark, Edward (    -1736) Va.; m. Ann  Christopher.
Military service.
Clark, George (1610-73) Conn.; m. Sarah Northrup.
Deputy to court.
Clarke, Jeremiah (1605-1651) R.I.; m. Frances (Lath-
om) Dungan.  Governor; Provincial Treasurer.
Clark, John (1614-74) Conn.; Mary Colen.  Freeman.
Clark, John (c1630-1709/10) Conn.; m. ---.  Surveyor.
Clarke, John (1636-89) Va.-N.C.; m. Mary Bird; Mary
Palin.  Landowner; Military service.
Clark, John (   -1690) Mass.; m. ---.  Physician.
Clarke, Joseph (1597-c1720) Mass.; m. Alice Pepper.
Landowner.
Clarke, Joseph (1618-94) R.I.-Mass.; m. Margaret ---;
Alice Potter.  Freeman; Selectman.
Clark, Richard (   -   ) Va.; m. ---.  Landowner.
Clark, Richard (1632/40-1697) N.J.; m. Elizabeth Moore.
Landowner.
Clarke, Thomas (   -1678) Mass.; m. Elizabeth ---.
Ancient and Honorable Artillery.
Clarke, Thurston (1590-   ) Mass.; m. Faithe ---.
Landowner.
Clark, William (c1615-81) Conn.; m. ---.  Proprietor;
Landowner.
Clarke    SEE ALSO    Clerke
Clay, Charles (1638-86) Va.; m. Hannah Wilson; Ann---.
Military service.

Clay, Henry (1672-1760) Va.; m. Mary Mitchell.
Landowner.
Clay, John (1587-1656) Va.; m. Elizabeth ---;  Ann
England.  Landowner.
Clay, William (    -1663) Va.; m. Emlin ---.  Land-
owner.
Claypoole, Norotn (1640-88) Del.-Va.; m. Rachel ---.
Judge.
Clayton, John (c1700-1759) Va.; m. Elizabeth ---.
Burgess; Assemblyman.
Clayton, William (1635-89) Pa.; m. Prudence Mikel.
Councillor; Proprietor.
Cleeve, George (c1574-1666/67) Me.; m. Joan ---.
Freeman; Deputy President.
Clement, Augustine (    -1674 ) Mass.; m. Elizabeth
---.  Freeman; Landowner.
Clement, James (    -   ) Conn.; m. Jane ---.  Land-
owner.
Clement, Robert (1595-1658) Mass.; m. Lydia ---;
Judith ---.  Deputy to court; Founder.
Clement, William (1680-1760) Va.; m. Anne ---.
Landowner.
Clerke, James (c1600-   ) Conn.; m. Sarah Harvey.
Landowner.
Clerke   SEE ALSO   Clarke
Clesson, Matthew (    -1709) Mass.; m. Mary Phelps.
Freeman.
Cleveland, Alexander (1659-1770) Va.; m. Milly Press-
ley.  Landowner.
Cleveland, John (1695-1779) Va.; m. Martha Coffee.
Landowner.
Cleveland, Moses (1624-1701/02) Mass.; m. Ann Wynn.
Landowner; Freeman.
Clifford, George (1590-   ) N.H.; m. Elizabeth ---.
Founder; Ancient and Honorable Artillery.
Clift, Joseph (    -c1753) Md.; Mary Noble.  Landowner.
Clopton, William (c1585-c1632) Va.; m. Margaret ---.
Landowner; Justice.
Clopton, William (1655-1733) Va.; m. Ann (Booth)
Dennett.  Justice; Constable.

Cloud, William (1620-1700) Del.-Pa.; m. Susan James.
  Landowner; Quaker.
Cloud,    SEE ALSO    Cloyd
Clough, Jonathan (1648-1718) Mass.; m. Mercy Page.
  Ancient and Honorable Artillery.
Cloyd, James (1680-   ) Pa.; m. ---. Landowner.
Cloyd    SEE ALSO Cloud
Clute, Frederic (1656-   ) N.Y.; m. Francyntje Dumond.
  Freeman.
Coate, Samuel (1675-1723) N.J.-Pa.; m. Mary  Sanders.
  Proprietor.
Coate, William (1684-1749) N.J.; m. Rebecca Sharp.
  Landowner.
Cobb,  Edward (c1649-1742) Va.; m.  Dorothy ---.
  Landowner.
Cobb, Joseph (1593-c1653/54) Va.; m.  Elizabeth Flin-
  ton.  Tobacco Viewer.
Cobb, Nicholas (c1620-   ) Va.; m. Susan ---.  Land-
  owner.
Cobbs, Ambrose (1590-   ) Va.; m. Anne ---.  Landowner.
Coburn, Edward (1618-1700) Ve.; m. Hannah ---.
  Landowner.
Cocke, James (c1666-1721) Va.; m. Elizabeth Pleasants.
  Clerk of court.
Cocke, Nicholas (   -1687) Va.; m.  Elizabeth Holt;
  Jane ( ) Curtis.  Landowner; Vestryman.
Cocke,  Richard (1600-65) Va.; m. Mary Aston; Temper-
  ance Bayley; --- ( ) Bronson.  Burgess; Sheriff.
Cocke, Richard  (1639-1706) Va.; m.  Elizabeth ---.
  County Surveyor; Justice.
Cocke, Thomas (1638-96) Va.; m. Margaret (Wood) Jones.
  Sheriff; Coroner.
Cocke, William (   -   ) Va.; m. ---.  Landowner;
  Justice.
Cockerham,  William (   -1699 ) Va.; m.  Ann Spencer;
  Hannah ---; Mary ---.  Military service; Landowner.
Codd,  St. Leger (1635-1707) Va.; m.  Anne (Bennett)
  Bland.  Landowner.
Coddington,  William (1601-78) R.I.; m. Anne Wase.
  Governor; Magistrate.
Codman, Robert (   -c1678) Mass.; m. ---.  Freeman;
  Landowner.

Cody, Philip (1668-1743) Mass.; m. Martha LeBrocq.
Landowner.
Coe, Benjamin (1628-1710) Mass.; m. Abigail Carman.
Landowner.
Coe, Robert (1596-1672) Conn.; m. Maria ---. Deputy
to court; Founder.
Coe, Robert (1626-59) Mass.; m. Hannah Mitchell.
Landowner; Sheriff.
Coffin, James (1640-1720) Mass.; m. Mary Severance.
Founder; Landowner.
Coffin    SEE ALSO    Coffyn
Coffyn, Tristram (1605-c81) Mass.; m. Dionis Stephens.
Founder; Magistrate.
Coffyn, Tristram (1632-1704) R.I.; m. Judith Green-
leaf.  Proprietor.
Coffyn    SEE ALSO    Coffin
Coggeshall, John (1591/1601-1647) R.I.; m. Mary ---.
Assemblyman; Provincial President.
Coggeshall, John (1618-1708) Mass.; m. Elizabeth
Bankston.  Landowner.
Coggeshall, John (1659-1727) R.I.; Mary  Stanton.
Landowner.
Cogswell, John Francis (1592-1669) Mass.; m. Elizabeth
Thompson.  Treasurer; Freeman.
Coit, John (    -1659) Conn.; m. Mary Jenners.  Select-
man; Landowner.
Coker, John (    -1711) Va.; m. Margaret ---.  Land-
owner.
Colburn, Edward (1618-1712 ) Mass.; Hannah ---.
Landowner.
Colburn, Joseph (1662-1728) Mass.; m. Mary Holbrook.
Constable; Surveyor.
Colburn, Nathaniel (    -1691) Mass.; m. Priscilla
Clarke.  Proprietor; Selectman.
Colburn, William (    -1682) Mass.; m. Margery ---.
Freeman; Deacon.
Colby, Anthony (c1590-1660/61 ) Mass.; m. Susanna
(Sargent) Haddon.  Freeman; Landowner.
Colcough, Benjamin (c1669-1722) Va.; m. Rachel ---.
Landowner.

Cole, Daniel (1614-94) Mass.; m. Ruth Chester. Selectman; Deputy to Court.

Cole, Henry ( -1676) Conn.; m. Sarah Rusco. Landowner.

Cole, James (1600-30) Mass.; m. Mary Lobel. Surveyor; Constable.

Cole, James (c1625- ) Mass.; m. Mary Tilson. Surveyor; Deputy to court.

Cole, Rice ( -1646) Mass.; m. --- Arrold. Freeman.

Cole, Stephen (c1660-c1700) Pa.; m. Elizabeth ---. Landowner.

Cole, Thomas ( -1678) Mass.; m. Ann ---. Landowner.

Cole, William (1597/98-1664) Va.; m. Frances ---. Landowner; Burgess.

Cole, William (1637/38-1693/94) Va.; m. Susannah ---; Anne Digges; Mary Lear. Councillor; Provincial Secretary.

Cole, William (1692-1729) Va.; m. Mary Roscow. Sheriff; Burgess.

Coleman, Daniel (1672-1722) Va.; m. Patience ---. Military service.

Coleman, Robert (c1622-1680) Va.; m. Elizabeth Grizzell. Landowner.

Coleman, Thomas (1636- ) Conn.; m. ---. Court Procurer.

Coleman, William (1619-80) Mass.; m. ---. Landowner.

Coleman, William ( -1747) Va.; m. Jane ---. Landowner.

Coles, James ( -1714) Va.; m. Mary ( ) Peterson. Carpenter; Landowner.

Collier, Dowty ( -1775) Md.; m. Priscilla Nicholson. Military service.

Collier, Isaac ( 1668) Va.; m. Mary Lecky. Military service; Landowner.

Collier, John (1685-1735) Va.; m. Nancy Ann Eppes. Landowner.

Collier, William (c1585-1670) Mass.; m. Jane ---. Assistant Governor; Landowner.

Collins, Benjamin ( -c1692) Mass.; m. Elizabeth ( ) Putnam. Freeman.

Collins, Edward (c1603-89) Mass.; m. Martha ---.
Deacon; Freeman.
Collins, Elizur (1622-83) R.I.; m. Sarah Wright.
Attorney; Landowner.
Collins, Francis (1635-1720) N.J.; m. Mary (Budd)
Gosling. Judge; Proprietor.
Collins, Henry (1606-87) Mass.; m. Ann ---. Land-
owner.
Collins, John (1680-1735) Va.; m. Ann Eppes. Vestry-
man.
Collins, Joseph (c1677-1748/57) Va.; Catherine
Robertson; Susannah Lewis. Landowner; Military
service.
Collins, Nathaniel (1642-84) Mass.-Conn.; m. Mary
Whiting. Minister.
Collins, William (1610-70) Va.; m. Ann Wilds. Land-
owner.
Colton, George (1644-99) Conn.-Mass.; m. Deborah
Gardner. Military service; Freeman.
Comegys, Cornelius (1628-1708) Md.; m. Willementje
Gysart; Rebecca ---. Committee of Safety.
Compton, William (1622-79) N.Y.; m. ---. Landowner;
Constable.
Comstock, Daniel (1630-83) Conn.; m. Paltiah Elderkin.
Military service; Landowner.
Comstock, David (1671-1746) Conn.; m. Elizabeth
Prentice. Landowner.
Comstock, John (1624-80) Conn.-Mass.-N.Y.; m. Abigail
Chappell. Proprietor.
Comstock, William (1595-1683) Conn.; m. Elizabeth
Daniel. Military service; Landowner.
Conant, John (1652-1724) Mass.; m. Bethiah Mansfield.
Military service.
Conant, Roger (1592-1679) Mass.; m. Sarah Horton.
Governor of colony; Deputy to court.
Concklane   SEE   Conklin
Concklin   SEE ALSO Conklin
Condit, John ( -1713) N.J.; m. ---. Landowner.
Condit, Samuel (1696-1777) N.J.; m. Mary Dodd.
Landowner.
Cone, Daniel (1626-1706) Conn; m. Mahitable Spencer;
Mary Gates. Freeman; Selectman.

Cone, Daniel (1666-1725) Conn.; m. Mary Gates. Justice.

Cone, James (1698-1774) Mass.-Conn.; m. Grace Spencer. Military service.

Cone, Oliver ( -1697) Pa.; m. Rebecca ---. Land-owner.

Coney, John (1628-90) Mass.; m. Elizabeth Nash. Free-man; Ancient and Honorable Artillery.

Conger, John (1642-1712) N.J.; m. Mary Kelly; Sarah ---. Town clerk; Justice.

Conklin, Ananias (c1605-57) Conn.; m. Mary Launders. Selectman; Landowner.

Conklin, Benjamin (c1600-57) N.Y.; m. Mary Lavender. Constable; Assessor.

Conklin, John (c1600-84) Mass.; m. Elizabeth Also-brooke. Founder.

Conklin, Nicholas (1661-1751) N.Y.; m. Sarah Hunt. Landowner.

Conklin, Timothy (c1640-1720) Conn.-Mass.; m. Sarah Scudder. Landowner.

Conklin, Timothy (1670-1734) N.Y.; m. Abigail Scudder. Military service.

Conner, Jeremiah (1672-1747) N.H.; m. Ann Gove. Pro-prietor.

Conner   SEE ALSO   Connor

Connor, Philip (1613-c1634) Md.; m. Mary ---. Land-owner.

Connor, Thomas (1678-1768) S.C.; m. Margaret ---. Landowner.

Connor   SEE ALSO   Conner

Convers, Edward (1590-1663) Mass.; m. Sarah ---; Jane Clark. Selectman; Deputy to court.

Convers, James (1645-1706) Mass.; m. Hannah Carter. Selectman; Councillor; Speaker of House.

Convers, Samuel (1637-1669) Mass.-Conn.; m. Judith Carter. Military service.

Conway, Dennis (c1641-1709) Va.; m. ---. Landowner.

Conway, Edwin (1610-75) Va.; ---; Martha ( ) Eltonhead. Clerk of court.

Conway, Edwin (1680-1763) Va.; m. Ann Ball. Burgess.

Conway, Thomas (c1640-1689/95) Pa.; m. Mary Hollings-worth; Elizabeth ---. Landowner.

Cory, John (c1614-1685/86) N.Y.-N.J.; m. Anne ---.
Founder; Proprietor.

Cory, John (c1639-85/86) N.Y.; m. Mary Cornish.
Landowner.

Coryell, Emanuel (c1663-   ) N.J.; m. ---.  Huguenot;
Landowner.

Cosby, Charles (c1585-1656) Va.; m. Mary Loftus.
Landowner.

Cosby, John (1623- 96) Va.; m. Sarah Higanisar.
Surveyor.

Cossart, Jacques (1639-85) N.Y.; m. Lydia Willems.
Oath of allegiance.

Cottle, Edward (1628-1710) Mass.; m. Dorothy ---.
Founder; Fence Viewer.

Cotton, George (   -1699) Mass.; m. Deborah Gardner.
Freeman.

Cotton, John (1585-1652) Mass.; m. Sarah (Hawkridge)
Story. Minister; Teacher.

Cotton, John (1625-91) N.C.; m. Ann Hucheson. Justice;
Landowner.

Cotton, John (1658-1729) N.C.; m. Martha (Godwin)
Jones. Landowner.

Cotton, William (c1610-36) Va.; m. Anne Graves.
Minister.

Cotton, William (1615-78) N.H.; m. ---.  Selectman;
Justice.

Couch, Simon (c1633-88 ) Conn; m. Mary Andrews.
Freeman.

Council, Hodges (1643-1699) Va.; m. Lucy Hardy.
Landowner.

Coursey, William (1620-1717) Md.; m. Julianna ---.
Burgess; Landowner.

Courten   SEE   Van Voorhees

Courts, Sir John (1620-c97) Md.; m. Margaret Calvert.
Burgess.

Courts, John (1655-c1702) Md.; m. Charity Henley.
Speaker of the House; Councillor.

Cousins, Jacob (c1656-  ) N.J.; m. ---.  Landowner.

Coutant, Jean (1658-c1717) N.Y.; m. Susanna Gouin.
Oath of allegiance.

Couwenhoven    SEE    Van Couwenhoven
Covey, James (1687-   ) R.I.; m. Mary Lamphere.  Military service.
Covington,  William (1670-1721) Va.; m. Rosamond ---.
   Landowner.
Coward, James (    -1717) Va.; m. Mary  Collidge.
   Landowner; Deputy  Sheriff.
Cowdery, William (1602-87) Mass.; m. Joanna ---.
   Deacon; Selectman.
Cowles, John (1598-1675) Conn.; m. Hannah ---.
   Landowner.
Cowles, Samuel (1639-91) Conn; m. Abigail Stanley.
   Landowner.
Cowles, Thomas (1650-1704) Va.; m. ---.  Burgess.
Cowper, William (1660-93) Va.; m. Ann Hurtley.
   Landowner.
Cowper   SEE ALSO   Cooper
Cox, James (    -c1758) Va.; m. Elizabeth ---.  Landowner.
Cox, Joshua (c1690-1747) Pa.; m. Mary Rankin.  Landowner.
Cox, Thomas (    -1743) N.C.; m.  Anne ---.  Landowner.
Cox   SEE ALSO   Coxe
Coxe, Thomas (    -1681) N.J.; m. Elizabeth Blackford.
   Town agent; Proprietor.
Coxe, William (1598-c1656) Va.; m. Elizabeth Hutchins.
   Landowner.
Coye, Richard (1625-75) Mass.; m. Martha Hayfield.
   Military service.
Crafford, Carter (1652-1744) Va.; m. Sarah Swann.
   Landowner.
Crafford, Robert (1620-1714/15) Va.; m. Elizabeth
   Carter.  Landowner; Military service.
Crafford   SEE ALSO   Crawford
Craft   SEE   Croft
Cragin, John  (c1634-1708) Mass.; m. Sarah Dawes.
   Landowner.
Craig,  Andrew (1662-1739) N.J.; m. Susannah ---.
   Alderman; Landowner.
Cram, John (1596/97-1682) N.H.; m. Hester ---.
   Townsman; Lot Layer.

Crandall, John (1600-c1676) R.I.; m. Sarah ---;
   Hannah Gaylord; Mary Opps. Elder; Freeman.
Crane, Azariah (1648-1730) N.J.; m. Mary Treat.
   Founder.
Crane, Benjamin (c1630-91) Conn.; m. Mary Backus.
   Proprietor.
Crane, Henry (1635-1711) Conn.; m. Concurrence Meigs.
   Governor's Assistant; Teacher.
Crane, Jasper (1605-81) Conn.-N.J.; m. Hannah ---;
   Alice ---. Magistrate; Freeman.
Crane, Jonathan (1638-1735) Conn.; m. Deborah Griswold.
   Military service.
Crane, Stephen (1640-c1700) N.J.; m. ---. Founder.
Cranston, John (1629-80) R.I.; m. Mary Clarke.
   Attorney General; Deputy Governor.
Cranston, Samuel (1659-1727) R.I.; m. Mary Hart.
   Governor.
Crary, Peter (    -1708) Conn.; m. Christobel Gallup.
   Landowner.
Craven, Peter (1672-1754) N.J.; m. ---. Landowner.
Cravens, Mary (Harrison) (1696-1781) N.Y.; m. Robert
   Cravens. Furnished supplies to Army.
Crawford, Daniel (c1662-c1762) Va.; m. Elizabeth Smith.
   Landowner.
Crawford, David (1623-1710) Va.; m. ---. Landowner;
   Military service.
Crawford, John (1600-76) Va.; m. ---. Landowner;
   Military service.
Crawford, Sarah (1670-1766) Va.; m. Thomas Poindexter.
   Landowner.
Crawford, William (1692-1732) Va.; m. Honoria Valen-
   tine; Land agent.
Crawford  SEE ALSO  Crafford
Crehore, Teague (c1640-1695) Mass.; m. Mary Spurr.
   Landowner.
Cresap, Thomas (1671-   ) Md.; m. Hannah Johnson.
   Governor; Committee of Safety.
Cresson, Pierre (    -1681) N.Y.; m. Rachel Cloos.
   Military service.
Crisp, Benjamin (c1611-1631/32) Mass.; m. Bridget ---.
   Freeman; Proprietor.

Crisp, Nicholas (c1665-   )  N.C.; m. ---Wilkins.
Commissioner; Vestryman.
Crispin, Silas (1653-1711) N.J.; m. Mary (Stockton)
Shinn; Hester Holme.  Surveyor; Landowner.
Crocker, Anthony (   -1693) Va.; m. Ann Francis.
Appraiser; Landowner.
Crocker, William (c1612-1692/93) Mass.; m. Alice Hoyt
or Foster.  Deacon; Selectman.
Crockett, Richard (1640-1727) Md.; m. Alice ---.
Founder.
Croft, Griffin (1600-59) Mass.; m. Alice----.  Deputy
to court; Landowner.
Crom   SEE   Crum
Cromwell, William (   -1684/85) Md.; m. Elizabeth
Traherna.  Military service.
Croom, David (c1663-1716) Va.; m. Elizabeth ---.
Landowner; Vestryman.
Croom, Joel (1635-1703) Va.; m. Susanna ---.  Land-
owner.
Crosby, George (1681-1745) Va.; m. Sarah Glasscock.
Landowner.
Crosby, John (1672-1750) Pa.; m. Susanna Dunbabin.
Justice.
Crosby, Simon (1608-59) Mass.; m. Ann Brigham.  Free-
man; Selectman.
Crosby, Thomas (c1608-37) Mass.; m. Anne Brigham.
First printer.
Croshaw, Joseph (1610/12-67) Md.; m. ---( ) Finch;
Ann ( ) Hodges; Margaret ( ) Tucker; Mary ( ) Brom-
field.  Burgess; Justice.
Croshaw, Raleigh (   -1624) Va.; m. ---.  Landowner.
Croshaw, Richard (1622-67) Va.; m. Elizabeth ---.
Landowner.
Cross, John (1584-1681) Mass.; m. Ann ---.  Surveyor;
Deputy to court.
Cross; Peter (   -1681) N.Y.; m. Rachel Closs.  Mil-
itary service.
Crossdale, Thomas (c1644-92) Pa.; m. Agnes Hatherwaite.
Landowner.
Crosson   SEE   Cross

Crow, John (1606-86) Mass.-Conn.; m. Elizabeth Good-
win. Landowner; Founder.
Crow, William (c1670-c1740) Md.; m. ---. Church
warden.
Crowson, Robert ( -c1702) Va.; m. Comfort Littleton.
Landowner.
Cruger, John ( -1744) N.Y.; m. Maria Cuyler. Alder-
man; Merchant.
Crum, Floris Williamse (c1644-1706) N.Y.; m. Cata-
lyndje Ariens. Sheriff; Assemblyman.
Crump, Thomas (1600-c53) Va.; Elizabeth Buck. Burgess;
Juror.
Crymes, William (c1650-c1725) Va.; m. ---. Physician.
Cubberley, James (c1680-1753) N.J.; m. Mary ---.
Landowner.
Cudworth, James (1590/91-1672) Mass.; m. Mary Drake.
Military Service.
Cullen, Thomas ( -1689) Va.; m. ---. Judge;
Councillor.
Culver, Edward (1610-85) Mass.-Conn.-R.I.; m. Anna
Ellis. Landowner; Founder.
Culver, John (1700-66) Md.; m. Mary ---. Landowner.
Cummings, Isaac (1601-77) Mass.; m. ---. Freeman;
Juror.
Cummings, Isaac (1630-1700) Mass.; m. Alice (French)
Howlett. Landowner.
Cunningham, William (c1590- ) Va.; m. Elizabeth ---.
Landowner.
Cureton, Richard (1650- ) Pa.; m. Margaret ---.
Landowner.
Curle, Thomas (1640-1700) Va.; m. Anne ---. Justice.
Curling, Joseph (c1655-1719) Va.; m. Rebecca ---.
Landowner.
Curtis, Bartholomew (1629-59) Va.; m. Jane ---.
Landowner.
Curtis, John (1614-1707) Conn.-N.J.; m. Elizabeth Ann
Wells. Landowner; Justice.
Curtiss, William (1577- ) Conn.; m. Elizabeth Hutch-
ins. Military service; Deputy to court.
Cushman, Elkanah (1651-1727) Mass.; m. Martha Cooke.
Landowner.

Cushman, Robert (1577-1625) Mass.; m. Sarah Reder.
Agent, London Company.
Cushman, Thomas (1608-91) Mass.; m. Mary Allerton.
Elder.
Custis, Henry (c1657-c1708/09) Va.; m. Rachell Revell.
Military service.
Custis, John (1630-96) Va.; m. Joan ---; Elizabeth
Robinson. Councillor; Military service.
Custis, John (    -1732) Va.; m. Anne Upshur. Mili-
tary service.
Custis, William (1650-c1726) Va.; m. Frances( )Stockley.
Justice; Military service.
Cutler, James (1606-94) Mass.; m. Ann ---. Military
service.
Cutler, James (1635-85) Conn; Lydia (Moore) Wright.
Military service.
Cutler, Robert (    -1665) Mass.; m. Rebecca ---.
Freeman; Military service.
Cutler, Thomas (1606-94) Mass.; m. ---. Landowner.
Cutler, Thomas (1648-1722) Mass.; m. Abigail Reed.
Landowner; Assessor.
Cutler, Thomas (1678-1718) Mass.; m. Tabitha Rice.
Landowner.
Cutt, Robert (   -1674) N.H.-Me;m. Mary Hall. Shipowner.
Cutter, Richard (c1621-93) Mass.; m. Elizabeth ---.
Military service.
Cutting, Richard (1622-95) Mass.; m. Sarah ---.
Landowner.

-D-

Dabney,Cornelius (1640-1701) Va.; m. Suzanne or Sarah
Swann; Estelle ( ) Jennings Interpreter; Landowner.
Dabney, John Pettus (c1672-   ) Va.; m. Anne Overton.
Burgess.
Dafnell, William (c1625-86) Va.; m. Mary Jones. Juror;
Constable.
Daggett, John (    -1673 ) Mass.; m. Hepzibah ---.
Freeman; Military service.
Daggett, John (1662-1724) Mass.; m. Sarah ---.
Landowner.

Daggett, Thomas (c1650-91) Mass.; m. ---. Clerk of court.

Dakin, Thomas (c1624-1708) Mass.; m. Susanna Stratton. Tithingman; Constable.

Dale, Edward (c1655-95) Va.; m. Diana Skipwith. Burgess; Military service.

Dale, John (1686-1778) Md.; m. Elizabeth McKnight. Landowner.

Dalton, William (1650-1733) Va.; m. Mary Brockenborough. Landowner.

Dam, John (c1600-89/90) N.H.; m. Elizabeth Pomfret. Proprietor; Landowner.

Dameron, Lawrence (c1620-89) Va.; m. Dorothy ---. Landowner.

Damme  SEE  Dam

Damon, John (1628-77) Mass.; m. Katherine Merritt. Representative; Military service.

Dana, Richard ( -1690) Mass.; m. Ann Bullard. Landowner.

Danforth, Jonathan (1627/28-1712) Mass.; m. Elizabeth Poulter. Surveyor.

Danforth, Nicholas (1589-1638) Mass.; m. Elizabeth Symes. Landowner; Deputy to court.

Danforth, Thomas (1623-99) Mass.; m. Mary Withington. Deputy Governor.

Daniel, James (1664-1740) Va.; m. ---. Landowner.

Daniel, John (--- ) Mass.; m. Mary Chappell. Landowner.

Daniel, Roger ( --- )Va.; m. Kinshaw (Miles) Carey. Landowner.

Daniel, William (1625/30-98) Va.; m. Dorothy Forth; Jochebed ---. Military service; Deputy to court.

Daniell, Robert ( -1636) Mass.; m. Elizabeth Morse. Freeman

Daniell, Robert (1648-1718) S.C.-Va.; m. Martha Walwright; Dorothy Chamberlain. Landowner; Attorney General.

Darby, Samuel (1640/44- ) Md.; m. ---. Landowner.

Darby  SEE ALSO  Derby

Darden, Stephen (1611-79) Va.; m. ---. Military service; Landowner.

Darnell, Edward (1671-1754)Md.; m. Sarah Roby. Landowner.
Darnell, Henry (c1651-1711) Md.; m. Eleanor (Hatton)
Brooke; Elizabeth Diggs. Sheriff; Councillor.
Dart, Richard(1664-1724)Conn.; m. Bethia --. Landowner.
Dashiel, George (1634-97) Md.; m. Ann Cannon. Land-
owner.
Dashiell, James (1634-97) Md.; m. Anne ---. Burgess;
Justice.
D'Aubighy   SEE   Dabney
D'Auge, Jacques (1660-1719) Va.; m. Mary Bonney.
Landowner.
Davenport, Charles (1652-1720) Mass.; m. Waitstill
Smith. Military service.
Davenport, John (1597-1670) Mass.; m. Elizabeth Wolby.
Minister.
Davenport, Martin (1675-1735) Va.; m. Sarah Partloe.
Landowner.
Davenport, Thomas (--- --) Mass.; m. Mary ---.
Landowner.
Davenport, William (1693-1771) Va.; m. Elizabeth
Heale. Landowner.
David, Morgan (1622/23-94/95) Pa.-N.C.; m. Catherine
---. Landowner.
David, Peter (   -1730) Va.; m. Ann ---. Landowner.
Davies, David (1680-1759) Del.; m. Martha Thomas.
Landowner.
Davies, Moses (c1645-c1700) Va.; m. ---. Military
service.
Davies   SEE ALSO   Davis
Davis, Dolor (1593-1673) Mass.; m. Margery Willard.
Military service; Ancient and Honorable Artillery
Company.
Davis, Evan (1685-1748) Pa.-Del.; m. Jane Rees.
Landowner.
Davis, Faulk (1615-c1692) N.Y.; m. ---. Landowner.
Davis, Francis (c1620-1709) Mass.; m. Gertrude Emerson.
Proprietor; Military service.
Davis, Hopkin (   -1793) N.H.; m. Ruth Roberts.
Landowner.
Davis, James (   -c1625) Va.; m. Rachell ---. Mili-
tary service.

Davis, James (1662-1749) N.H.; m. Elizabeth Chesley.
Military service; Judge.
Davis, John (c1625-85) N.H.; m. Jane Peasley.  Freeman.
Davis, John (    -1687) Va.; m. Mary ( ) Burton.  Land-
owner.
Davis, Nathaniel (    -c1704) Va.; m. Wickette (Indian).
Shipmaster; Trader.
Davis, Robert (    -1693) Mass.; m. Anne ---.  Mili-
tary service.
Davis, Samuel (    -1725) Md.-Del.; m. Mary Simpson.
Minister.
Davis, Thomas (1603-83) Mass.; m. Christian ---.
Selectman; Landowner.
Davis, Tobias (    -1690) Mass.; m. Sarah Mirrill.
Ancient and Honorable Artillery.
Davis, William (1617-83) Mass.; m. Elizabeth ---.
Military service.
Davisson, Daniel (1630-93) Mass.; m. Margaret Low.
Proprietor; Military service.
Davisson, Daniel (1662-1703) Conn.-Mass.; m. Sarah
Dodge.  Landowner.
Davol, Jonathan (    -1709) Mass.; m. Hannah Audley.
Landowner.
Davol, Joseph (    -1726) Mass.; m. Mary  Soule.
Landowner.
Davol, William (1622-83) Mass.; m. ---.  Freeman;
Landowner.
Daw, Nicholas (1670-1743) N.C.; m. Abigail Wallis.
Representative.
Dawson, John (    -1762) N.C.; m. Mary Thomas.
Landowner.
Dawson, William (1600-c1625) Va.; m. Joan ---.
Landowner.
Day, James (c1650-1701) Va.; m. Mary Thompson.
Burgess; Military service.
Day, Nicholas (1658-1704) Md.; m. Sarah ---.  Land-
owner.
Day, Robert (1604-48) Va.; m. Editha Stebbins.
Landowner.
Day, Robert (    -1648) Conn.; m. ---.  Proprietor.

Dayton, Ralph (1598-1658) Mass.; m. Alice Wilton.
Landowner.
Deane, John (1648-1712) Va.; m. Elizabeth Thacher.
Surveyor; Constable.
Dean, Samuel (    -c1784) Pa.; m. ---. Military
service.
Deane, Stephen (    -1634) Mass.; m. Elizabeth Ring.
Freeman.
Deane, Walter (  -  ) Mass.; m. Eleanor Cogan.
Founder; Military service.
Dearborn, Godfrey (    -1686) N.H.; m. ---. Landowner.
Deatherage, George (1674-1764) Va.-N.C.; m. Sarah Gar-
ner. Landowner.
Deaver, Richard (1627-1701) Md.; m. Grace Fitzmorris.
Landowner; Indian fighter.
DeBoog, Frederick (    -1686) N.Y.; m. Elizabeth
Solomons. Ship captain.
DeBoog, Frederick (1686-1776) N.J.-N.Y.; m. Hannah
Van Hook. Military service.
deBordeaux, Jacques (    -1699) S.C.; m. Madeleine
Garilion. Landowner.
Decamp, Laurent (c1645-  ) N.Y.; m. Eloise Mandeville.
Minister.
DeCessna, John (    -1751) Pa.; m. Priscilla Foulke.
Huguenot.
DeCou, Isaac (    -1686) Pa.; m. Susanna Asher.
Huguenot; Landowner.
Dedman, Henry (    -1655) Va.; m. Katherine ---.
Landowner.
DeForest, Henricus (1657-1715) N.Y.; m. Femmetje
Fliesbeeck. Justice; Glazier.
DeForest, Isaac (    -1672) N.Y.; m. ---. Landowner.
DeGarmo, Pierre (c1660-1741) N.Y.; m. Catina Van der
Heyden. Landowner.
DeGerno    SEE    DeGarmo
DeGrosse, Roger (c1617-75) Md.; m. Anne ---. Justice;
Commissioner.
DeHaven, Evert (  -  ) Pa.; m. Elizabeth Schipbower.
Founder of church.
DeJarnet, Jean (1680-1765) Va.; m. Mary Mumford.
Landowner.

DeKay, Jacob Teunis (c1635-91) N.Y.; m. Helgonda
Teunisse Quick. Landowner.
De la Mare, Francis ( -1713) N.C.; m. Susanna ( )
Travis. Justice.
De la Mater, Claude (1620-83) N.Y.; m. Hester DuBois.
Magistrate; Landowner.
De la Montagne, Johannes (1595-c1670) N.Y.; m. Rachel
DeForest. Physician; Councillor.
Delaney SEE ALSO Dulaney
Delano, Jonathan (1647-1720) Mass.; m. Mercy Warren.
Military service.
Delanoye, Phillippe, (1602-81) Mass.; m. Hester
Dewsbury. Freeman; Surveyor.
Delano SEE ALSO Delaney; Delanoye
DelaPlaine, Nicholas (1592-1697) N.Y.; m. Susanna
Cresson. Lawyer; Burgher.
Dell, Thomas (1665/66-1750) Pa.; m. Mary (Elder)
Shaw. Proprietor.
DeLoach, Michael (c1600-c1678) Va.; m. Jane Griffith.
Landowner.
DeMeyer, Nicholas ( -1729) N.Y.; m. Lydia Van Dyke.
Landowner.
DeMille, Anthony (1625-89) N.Y.; m. Elizabeth Van der
Liphor. Magistrate.
Deming, John (1610/15-1705) Conn.; m. Honor Treat.
Freeman; Deputy to court.
Deming, John (1694-1763) Conn.; m. Elizabeth Perkins.
Landowner.
Deming, Jonathan (c1617-1705) Conn.; m. ---. Freeman;
Selectman.
Deming, Samuel (1646-1709) Conn.; m. Sarah Kirby.
Landowner.
Denise, Teunis Nyssen ( -1661) N.J.; m. Femmetje
Seale Jans. Magistrate.
Denison, George (1618-94) N.J.-Conn.; m. Ann Borodell;
Bridget Thompson. Landowner.
Denison, George (1671-1720) Conn.; m. Mary (Witherell)
Harris; --- Avery; --- Starr. Landowner.
Denison, William (c1571-1653/54) Mass.; m. Margaret
Chandler. Deputy to Court; Freeman.

Dennison   SEE   Denison

Denny, Frederick (1662-1728) N.J.-Pa.; m. Eleanor ---.
Landowner.

Denslow, Nicholas (1576-1666) Conn.; m. ---.  Freeman; Landowner.

Denson, William (c1620-1675/76) Va.; m. Frances ---.
Burgess.

Dent, George (1690-1754) Md.; m. Ann Herbert.
Sheriff; Military service.

Dent, John (1635-1712) Md.; m. Mary (Shercliff) Hatch.
Justice; Military service.

Dent, Thomas (1630-76) Md.; m. Rebecca Wilkinson.
Justice; Sheriff.

Dent, William (1660-1705) Md.; m. Elizabeth Fowke.
Solicitor.

Denton, Richard (c1586-1663) N.Y.; m. Helen Windibank.
Founder of church.

DePew, Moses (1657-   ) N.Y.; m. Maria Wyncoop. Landowner.

DeProuitt, Roger (c1660/80-   ) Va.; m. Mary Byrd.
Founder.

DeProuitt   SEE ALSO   Prewitt

Derby, Edward (   -   ) Mass.; m. Susannah Hooke.
Landowner; Founder.

DeRichbourg, C. Phillippe (1650-1718) S.C.-Va.; m.
Anne Chastaine. Landowner; Minister.

Dernall   SEE   Darnall

Derrickson, Andreas (c1670-   ) Md.; m. Mary Andrews.
Landowner.

DeSaye, Abraham (c1665-c1694) Va.; m. --- Wilson.
Landowner.

DeSaye, Richard (   -   ) Del.; m. ---.  Surveyor.

DeSille, Nicasius (1610-74) N.Y.; m. Cornelia
Neulmanys. Councillor; Proprietor.

D'Esley   SEE   Easley

Des Marets, David (1620-95) N.J.; m. Marie Sohier;
Elizabeth Herbuq. Constable; Delegate to Court.

DeTeurneur   SEE   Turner

DeVeaux, Andre (1682-1716) S.C.; Hannah Palmer;
Sarah Eberson; Ann LaSade. Landowner.

DeVeaux, Andries (1700-98) N.Y.; m. Susanna Bradt.
Magistrate; Deputy Director.
Devotion, Edward (1621-85) Mass.; m. Mary ---.
Landowner.
Dew    SEE    Dewe
Dewe, John (c1630-78) Va.; m. Elizabeth Shearer.
Burgess.
Dewe, Thomas (1600-77) Va.; m. Elizabeth Bennett.
Burgess; Councillor.
Dewees, Garrett Hendrick (c1688-c1701) Pa.; m. Zynthia
---. Landowner.
Dewey, Jedediah (1676-1728) Mass.; m. Rebecca
Williams. Landowner.
Dewey, Josiah (    -c1649) Conn.; m. Frances ( ) Clark.
Landowner.
Dewey, Josiah (1641-1732) Conn.; m. Hepsibah Lyman.
Military service.
Dewey, Thomas (    -c1648) Mass.-Conn.; m. Frances
Clark. Landowner.
Dewitt, Tjerck Claessen (1620-1700) N.Y.; m. Barbara
Andriessen. Signer of treaty; Magistrate.
Dewolf, Edward (1646/47-1712) Conn.; m. Rebecca ---.
Military service; Landowner.
Dexter, Richard (1606-80) Mass.; m. Bridget ---.
Landowner.
Dey, Dirck Jansen (    -c1687) N.Y.; m. Jannetje
Theunis. Military service.
Dey, James (1680-    ) N.Y.-N.J.; m. Mary ---. Dedham
Covenant.
Diaz, Juan (1599-    ) Fla.; m. Maria de Arsian. Land-
owner.
Dibble, Robert (    -c1640) Conn.; m. ---. Freeman;
Landowner.
Dibble, Thomas (1612-1700) Conn.; Mary Grant. Mili-
tary service; Landowner.
Dibert, Charles Frederick (1660-1707) Va.; m. Magda-
lene Margaret ---. Military service.
Dickerman, Isaac (1677-1758) Conn.; m. Mary Atwater.
Deputy to court.
Dickerson, Philemon (1598-1672) Mass.; m. Mary Pains.
Freeman; Landowner.

Dickinson, Henry (    -  ) Va.; m. Agnes Jennings.
Military service; County clerk.
Dickinson, John (1693-  ) Md.; m. Rebecca (Powell)
Wynne. Civil officer.
Dickinson, Nathaniel (c1600-76) Mass.; m. Anna (  )
Gull. Deputy to court; Military service.
Dickinson, Walter (1620/21-81) Pa.; m. Jane Yarrett.
Commissioner; Landowner.
Dicks, Peter (c1656-1704) Pa.; m. Esther Maddock.
Landowner.
Dicks, Peter (c1694-1760) Pa.; m. Sarah (Hays) Powell.
Minister.
Diefendorf, John Jacob (1677-1784) N.Y.; m. Rebecca
(Ash) Crosner. Military service.
Digges, Cole (1692-1744) Va.; m. Elizabeth Powers.
Burgess; Commander in Chief.
Digges, Sir Dudley (1665-1710) Va.; m. Susannah Cole.
Member of Parliament.
Digges, Edward (1620/21-75) Va.; m. Elizabeth ---.
Councillor; Military service.
Dike, Anthony (   -1638) Mass.; m. ---.  Founder
Ship's captain.
Dillard, George (c1624-1704) Va.; m. Mary Daniel.
Landowner.
Dimacon; Demacon   SEE   Macon
Dimick   SEE   Dimmock
Dimmock, Shubael (c1644-1732) Mass.; m. Joanna Bursley.
Selectman; Deputy to  Court.
Dimmock, Thomas (1604-1658/59) Mass.; m. Anne Hammond.
Founder; Selectman.
Dimon, Moses (1672-1748) Conn.; m. Jane Pinkney.
Military service.
Disbrow, Peter (1631-88) N.Y.; m. Sarah (Everton)
Knapp. Founder.
Dixon, Ambrose (1609-87) Md.; m. Mary Peddington.
Constable; Assemblyman.
Dixon, Thomas (    -1670) Va.; m. Maris Boddie.
Landowner.
Dixon   SEE ALSO   Dixson
Dixson, Henry (    -c1690) Del.; m. ---.  Quaker.

Doane, Daniel (c1636-1712) Mass.; m. ---. Selectman;
Deacon.
Doane, Israel (1672-1735) Mass.; m. Ruth Freeman.
Surveyor.
Doane, John (1590-1629) m. ---. Freeman; Governor's
Council.
Doane, John (1685-1708) Mass.; m. Hannah Bangs;
Rebecca Pettee. Selectman.
Doane, Walter (1612-91) Me.; m.---. Deputy to court.
Dobbins SEE Dobyns
Dobyns, Daniel (c1650-1712/13) Va.; m. Elizabeth ( )
Hodgkins. Magistrate.
Dockery, Mathias (c1665-1740) Md.; m. Mary ---.
Landowner.
Dodd, Daniel (1615-1665/66) Conn.; m. Mary Wheeler.
Landowner.
Dodge, John (1631-1711) Mass.; m. Sarah ---. Select-
man; Deputy to court.
Dodge, Richard (1602-71) Mass.; m. Edith ---.
Landowner.
Dodge, Tristam (1625-  ) R.I.; m. ---. Freeman;
Landowner.
Dodge, William (1604-1686/92) Mass.; m. Elizabeth ---.
Landowner.
Dodson, Charles (1645/49-1703) Va.; m. Anne ---.
Landowner.
Dodson, Thomas (1649-1702) Va.; m. ---. Registrar.
Doggett, Benjamin (1636-82) Va.; m. Jane ( ) Garrard.
Minister.
Donaldson SEE ALSO Donelson
Donelson, John (   -1736) Va.; m. Catherine Davis.
Minister.
Doniphan, Alexander (1650-1716) Va.; m. Margaret Mott.
Military service.
Doniphan, Mott (c1692-c1776) Va.; m. Rosannah Ander-
son. Vestryman.
Donovan SEE ALSO Doniphan
Doodes, Meinert (1610-77) Va.; m. Mary Geret. Mili-
tary service.
Doolittle, Abraham (1620-90) Conn.; m. Joan Allen;
Abigail Moss. Sheriff.

Dorlandt, Lambert Janse  (1639-1720) N.Y.-Pa.; m.
Hermione (Janse) Peters.  Magistrate.
Dorman, John (c1610-56) Va.; m. Sarah ---.  Landowner.
Dornell  SEE  Darnell
Dorr, Edward (1648-1733) Mass.; m. Elizabeth Hawley.
Selectman.
Dorsey, Edward (1616-59) Md.-Va.; m.  Ann ---.  Land-
owner.
Dorsey, Edward (1640/45-1705) Md.; m. Sarah Wyatt;
Margaret Larkin.  Judge; Burgess.
Dorsey, John (1663-1714 ) Md.; m. Pleasance (Ely)
Ludwell.  Assemblyman; Military service.
Doty, Edward (1590-1655) Mass.; m. Faith Clark.
Military service.
Doty, James (1686-  ) N.J.; m. Phebe Slater.  Assembly-
man.
Doty, Joseph (1651-1732/35) Mass.; m. Deborah Hatch.
Landowner;  Surveyor.
Doty, Samuel (1643-1715) Mass.-N.J.; m. Jeane Harman.
Military service.
Doude, Henry (   -1668) Conn.; m. Elizabeth ---.
Landowner.
Doughty, Elias (1632-c90) N.Y.; m. ---.  Military
service.
Douglas, John (1636-78) Md.; m. Sarah Bonner.  Land-
owner.
Douglas, John (1697-1761) Va.; m. Martha Heron.
Bounder.
Douglas, William (1610-85) Va.; m. Ann Mattle.    Free-
man; Moderator.
Douglas, William (1645-1725) Conn; m. Abiah Hough.
Military service.
Dow, Henry (1605-59) Mass.; m. Joan Nudd.  Selectman;
Deputy to court.
Dowling, Robert (c1700-c1756) Va.; m. ---.  Landowner.
Downer, Joseph (1615-  ) Mass.; m. Mary Knight.  Mil-
itary service.
Downing, Edmond (   -  ) Mass.; m. Lucy Northrop.
Founder.
Downing, Emanuel (1589-1656/60) Mass.-Conn.; m. Lucy
Winthrop.

Downing, John (1645-   ) Va.; m. ---. Burgess; Justice.
Downing, William (c1651-c83) Va.; m. ---. Justice.
Downman, William (c1600-c1655) Va.; m. Dorothy
Nicholls. Landowner.
Downs, John (   -   ) Conn.; m. ---. Landowner.
Doze, Andrew (   -1680/1707) Pa.; m. Ann ---. Vine-
yard keeper.
Dozier, Leonard ( c1643-1692/93) Va.; m. Elizabeth
---. Proprietor.
Dragou, Pierre (1669-1712) N.Y.; m. Elizabeth Tavaud.
Landowner.
Drake, Francis (1615-87) N.J.; m. Mary Walker.
Founder, Surveyor.
Drake, John (1592-1659) Mass.-Conn.; m. Elizabeth
Rodgers. Freeman; Proprietor.
Drake, John (1612-89) Conn.; m. Hannah Moore. Land-
owner.
Dresser, John (1640-1724) Mass.; m. Martha Thorla;
Rebecca ( ) Dickinson. Landowner; Military service.
Drew, Anthony (1660-1720) Md.; m. Mary Ann Utie.
Burgess; Justice.
Drew, George (c1695-1734) Md.; m. Johannah Lushy.
Landowner.
Driver, Robert (c1590-1680) Mass.; m. Phebe ---.
Landowner.
Drummond, William (1620-99) Va.-N.C.; m. Sarah (Swann)
Prescott. Governor.
Drury, Hugh (   -1689) Mass.; m. Lydia ---. Military
service; Landowner.
Dryden, William (c1640-c85) Md.; m. Agnes ---. Land-
owner.
D'Schomp SEE Schomp
Dubois, Louis (1627-96) N.Y.; m. Catherine Blanchon.
Landowner; Military service.
Dubois, Mattheus (1679-1748) R.I.; m. Sarah Mathysen.
Trustee; Justice.
Dubose, Isaac (1661-1726) S.C.; m. Suzanne Couillan-
deau (or Coutelandeau). Huguenot; Landowner.
Duday-Durrell SEE Durrell
Dudley, Edward (c1605-c1655) Va.; m. Elizabeth (Hester)
Prichard. Landowner.

Dudley, Richard (c1623-c1687) Va.; m. Mary Sewell (Seawell). Sheriff; Military service.

Dudley, Richard (   -1716/17) Va.; m. Elizabeth Stevens. Military service.

Dudley, Samuel (c1608-83) Md.; m. Elizabeth ---; Mary Winthrop. Minister; Founder.

Dudley, Thomas (1576-1653) Mass.; m. Dorothy Yorke; Catherine Deighton. Governor; Commander-in-Chief.

Dudley, William (1639-c1700) Conn.; Mary Roe. Deacon; Commissioner.

Duffield, Benjamin (1661-1741) Pa.; m. Elizabeth Watts. Landowner.

Duke, Henry(  -  ) Va.; m. Elizabeth Cluverius. Councillor.

Duke, Henry (1653-1714) Va.; m. Lydia Hansford. Sheriff; Burgess.

Duke, William (c1679-c1726) N.C.-S.C.; m. Mary ---. Landowner.

Dulaney, Daniel (1685-1755) Md.; m. Rebecca Smith. Speaker of the House.

Dulaney, Joseph (1682-1769) Va.; m. Mary Lewis. Military service.

Dumas, Jerome (  -1734) Va.; m. Unity Lucy. Physician; Landowner.

Dumbleton, John (c1620-1702) Mass.; m. Mercy ---. Selectman.

Dumont, Walran (Wallerand) (1657-1713) N.Y.; m. Margaret ( ) Hendricks. Military service.

Dunbar, Robert (c1634-93) Mass.; m. ---. Freeman.

Dungan, Thomas (c1634-97) Pa.; m. Elizabeth Weaver. Minister.

Dunham, Benjamin (1640-80) Mass.; m. Elizabeth Tilson. Court officer.

Dunham, John (1588-1669) Mass.; m. Abigail(Wood) Baillou. Military service; Deputy to court.

Dunham, Lewis Ford (1659-1731) N.J.; m. Jane Tutwill. Surgeon.

Dunn, Hugh (1640-94) N.J.; m. Elizabeth Drake. Landowner.

Dunning, Theophilus (c1625-c1649) Mass.; m. ---. Landowner.

Dunster, Henry (1610/1657/59) Mass.; m. Elizabeth
Glover. Ancient and Honorable Artillery.
Du Pré, Josias (1640-1712) S.C.; m. Martha ---.
Landowner.
Du Pré, Josias (c1686-1747) S.C.; m. Sarah Garnier.
Tax collector; Huguenot Minister.
Dupree, Joseph (c1654- ) Va.; m. ---. Landowner.
Dupree SEE ALSO Dupré
Dupuy, Bartholomew (1658-1743) Va.; m. Contessa Susan-
nah Lavilliau. Proprietor.
Dupuy, Nicholas (1625-91) N.Y.; m. Caterina (Reynard)
De Vos. Landowner; Military service.
Durant, George (1632-94) N.C.; m. Anne Marwood;
Sarah Tooker. Burgess; Attorney.
Durant, John ( - ) Mass. m. Susan Dutton. Land-
owner.
Durborow, Hugh (c1660-1740) Pa.; m. Elizabeth Taylor.
Minister.
Durden, Jacob (1677-1759) Va.; m. Mary ---. Land-
owner.
Durden, Stephen (1611-81) Va.; m. Mary ---. Landowner.
Durfee, Thomas (1643-1712) R.I.; m. Deliverance(Hall)
Tripp. Freeman; Constable.
Durfee, Thomas (1669/70-1729) R.I.; m. Anne Freeborne.
Assemblyman.
Durrell, Philip (1662-c1740) Me.-N.H.; m. --- Puring-
ton. Military service.
De Sauchoy, Marcus (1626-c1700) N.Y.; m. Elizabeth
Rossignol. Huguenot; Landowner.
Dustin SEE Duston
Duston, Hannah (Webster) Emerson (1657-1736) Mass.;
m. Thomas Duston. Landowner.
Duston, Thomas (1606-c1662) Mass.; m. Hannah Emerson.
Military service; Founder.
Dutearque, Lewis ( -1748) S.C.; m. Christian Maris.
Landowner.
Dutrieux, Philip (c1586-1649/53) N.Y.; m. Jacquemine
Noirett. Landowner.
Duval, Daniel ( - ) Va.; m. ---. Burgess.
Duval SEE ALSO Duvall

Duvall, Mareen (1629-94) Md.; Elizabeth ---; Susannah Brasseur; Mary Stanton. Commissioner.

Duvall, Mareen (1661-75) Md.; m. Frances Stockett. Military service.

Duvall, Mareen (1680-1741) Md.; m. Elizabeth Jacob. Landowner.

Duvall, Samuel (1665-1741) Md.; m. Elizabeth (Ijams) Clark. Military service.

Du Vos, Andries ( - ) N.Y.; m. Margitje ---. Landowner.

Duytsch, Jan Laurenszen (c1644- ) N.Y.; Janetje Jurious ---. Surveyor.

Duytszen, Laurens (1639-68) N.J.; m. Ytie ---. Landowner.

Dwight, John (c1600-60) Mass.; m. Hannah Eloyes. Deputy to court.

Dwinnell, Michael ( -1718) Mass.; m. Mary ---. Surveyor.

Dyckman, Cornelius (1647-c1732) N.Y.; m. Jannet Claesson. Landowner.

Dye, Arthur (1670-c1706) Va.; m. Katherine Hopkins. Landowner.

Dye, Avery (c1698-1757) Va.; m. Katherine Mackmelion. Landowner.

-E-

Eames, Anthony (1595-1686) Mass.; m. Marjorie Prisse. Military service; Deputy to court.

Earle, John (1614-60) Va.; m. Mary Symons. Landowner.

Earle, Ralph (1605-78) R.I.; m. Joan Savage; Mary Brown. Treasurer.

Earle, Samuel (1638-96) Va.; m. Bridgett Hale. Landowner.

Earle, Samuel (1692-1771) Va.; m. Anna Sorrell; Elizabeth Holbrook. Burgess; Military service.

Early, John (c1640-1693) Va.; m. Margaret Loyall. Landowner.

Easley, Robert (c1655-1711/12) Va.; m. Ann Parker. Landowner.

Easter, William ( -1732) Va.; m. Mary ---.
Landowner.

Eastham, Robert ( - ) Va.; m. Anne Lawson. Sheriff;
Military service.

Eastman, Joseph (1659-92) Mass.; m. Mary Tilton.
Military service.

Eastman, Joseph (1697-1760) N.H.; m. Patience Smith.
Landowner.

Eastman, Roger (1610/11-94) Mass.; m. Hannah Kimball.
Carpenter.

Eastman, Samuel (1657-1725/26) Mass.- N.H.; m. Elizabeth Severance. Landowner.

Easton, Nicholas (1593-1675) R.I.; m. Patience Strachey. Governor.

Eaton, Francis (c1595-1633) Mass.; m. Christian Penn.
Mayflower passenger.

Eaton, John (1686-1717/19) Va.; m. Ann ---. Military
service.

Eaton, Theophilus (1590-1657) Conn.; m. Anna (Lloyd)
Yale. Founder; Governor.

Eaton, Thomas (c1631-1715) Mass.; m. Eunice Singleton.
Selectman.

Eaton, William (1690-1759) Va.; m. Mary Reeves;
Rebecca Cocke. Assemblyman; Military service.

Echols, John (1650-1712) Va.; m. Mary Cave. Landowner.

Eddy, Samuel (1608-87) Mass.; m. Elizabeth ---. Freeman; Landowner.

Eddy, Zachariah (1639-1718) Mass.; m. Alice Paddock;
Abigail ( ) Smith. Landowner.

Edelen, Richard (1635-95) Md.; m. Elizabeth Banton.
Military service.

Edgar, George (c1689-c1765) Va.; m. Elizabeth ---.
Landowner.

Edge, John (c1646-1711) Pa.; m. Jane ---. Quaker;
Landowner.

Edgerly, Thomas (c1634-1715/17) N.H.; m. Rebecca
(Ault) Hallowell. Judge; Landowner.

Edmiston, Thomas ( - ) Md.; m. Martha Campbell.
Landowner.

Edmond, Andrew (1639-95) R.I.; m. Mary Hendern.
Military service.

Edmondson, Thomas (1667-1715) Va.; m. Mary ---.
Landowner.
Edmondson   SEE ALSO   Edmondston
Edmondston, Archibald (c1670-1734) Md.; m. Jane Beall.
Landowner.
Edmondston   SEE ALSO   Esmondston
Edmunds, Howell (c1675-1729) Va.; m. Elizabeth Blunt.
Military service.
Edson, Samuel (1612-92) Mass.; m. ---.  Councillor;
Military service.
Edward, Edward (1616-97) Va.; m. Dorothy ---.  Burgess.
Edward   SEE ALSO   Edwards
Edwards, Alexander (    -1690) Mass.; m. Sarah (Bald-
win) Searle.  Landowner.
Edwards, John (c1600-64) Conn.; m. Dorothy ( ) Finch.
Founder.
Edwards, Nathaniel (    -1771) Va.; m. ---.  Justice;
Military service.
Edwards, Richard (    -   ) Va.; m. Mary ---.  Physi-
cian.
Edwards, William (1616-97) Va.; m. Dorothy ---.
Founder.
Edwards, William (1648-98) Va.; m. Ann Mansfield.
Burgess; Landowner.
Edwards, William (1687-   ) N.Y.; m. Mary Nicholson.
Landowner.
Egbert, Tunis (1662-1721) Md.; m. Susannah Tilje.
Supervisor; Road Commissioner.
Eggleston, Bigod (1587-1674) Conn.; m. Mary Talcott;
Sarah Talcott.  Freeman; Selectman.
Eggleston, James (1620-80) Conn.; m. Hester Williams.
Founder; Military service.
Eggleston, Joseph (1678-1730) Va.; m. Anne Pettus.
Burgess.
Egmont, Cornelis (    -   ) N.Y.; m. Brechie Jacobs.
Landowner.
Elam, Gilbert (    -1693) Va.; m. ---.  Landowner.
Elam, Martin (c1635-91/92) Va.; m. ---.  Landowner;
Military service.
Elam Robert (    -c1625) Va.; m. ---.  Landowner.

Eldred, Samuel (1620-   ) R.I.-Mass.; m. Elizabeth.
Military service.
Eldridge, Samuel (c1666-c1708) Va.; m. ---. Landowner.
Eliot, Jared (1685-1763) Conn.; m. Elizabeth Smithson.
Minister.
Eliot, John (1664-90) Mass.; m. Ann (Mountford)
Moore. Minister; Established Roxbury Latin School.
Eliot, Joseph (1638-94) Mass.; m. Mary Wyllys.
Minister.
Eliot, Philip (1602-57) Mass.; m. Elizabeth ---.
Delegate to court.
Elkington, George (1650-1713) N.J.; m. Mary Humphrey.
Landowner; Secretary of State.
Elliott, Daniel (c1662-   ) Mass.; m. Hannah Cloyes.
Proprietor; Landowner.
Elliott, Edward (1639/40-c1713) Md.; m. Elizabeth
( ) Frith. Landowner.
Elliott, Thomas (c1670-c1731/32) S.C.; m. Hebzibah
---. Landowner; House of Commons.
Ellis, Elizabeth (Freeman) (c1624-1714) Mass.; m.
John Ellis. Landowner.
Ellis, Ellis (   -1705) Pa.; m. Lydia Humphrey.
Supervisor of roads.
Ellis, Jeremiah (   -1727) Va.; m. ---. Military
service.
Ellis, John (c1661-1728) Va.; m. Suzannah Ware.
Grantee of Charter.
Ellis, Lydia (Humphrey) (   -1742) Pa.; m. Ellis
Ellis. Landowner.
Ellis, Robert (   -1697) Pa.; m. Eline (Ellen) ---.
Landowner.
Ellis, Rowland (1650-1731) Pa.; m. Margaret Roberts;
Minister.
Ellis, Thomas (1635-1688) Pa.; m. Ellen Rees.
Minister; Registrar-General.
Ellsworth, Jeremiah (c1649-1724) Mass.; m. Sarah
Jewett. Constable; Military service.
Ellsworth, John (   -   ) Conn.; m. Anne Edwards.
Military service.
Ellyson, Robert (   -c1662) Va.; m. Hannah Gerard;
Elizabeth Ann Mayhill. Physician; Burgess.

Ellyson, Robert (1695-1722) Va.; m. Mary Lide. Landowner.

Elmer, Edward (1609-76) Conn.-Mass.; m. Mary ---.
Landowner.

Elsen, Abraham ( -1648) Conn.; m. Rebecca ---.
Landowner.

Elsworth, Josiah (1629-89) Conn.; m. Elizabeth Holcomb. Founder.

Eltinge, Jan Roelofse (1632-92) N.Y.; m. Jacomynte
Steckt. Landowner.

Elwell, Robert ( -1683) Mass.; m. Joane ---.
Selectman.

Ely, George (1682-1750) N.J.; m. Jane Pettit. Landowner.

Ely, Joshua (1647-1702) N.J.; m. Mary Senior. Councillor; Military service.

Ely, Nathaniel (1605-75) Mass.; m. Martha ---.
Landowner.

Ely, Richard (1610-84) Conn.-Mass.; m. Joan Phipps;
Lady Boteler. Assemblyman.

Ely, William (1647-1717) Conn.; m. Elizabeth Smith.
Councillor.

Emerson, Ellis (c1590-1626) Va.; m. Ann ---. Landowner.

Emerson, Michael (c1625-1715) Mass.; m. Hannah Webster.
Landowner; Constable.

Emery, Anthony (c1660-c1680) R.I.; m. Frances ---.
Selectman.

Emery, Daniel (1667-1722) Me.; m. Margaret Gowen.
Surveyor.

Embry, Henry (1690-1763) Va.; m. Martha ---. Justice;
Burgess.

Emery, James (1630-c1714) R.I.; m. Elizabeth ---.
Juror; Selectman.

Emery, John (1598-1694) Mass.; m. Alice Grantham.
Freeman; Selectman.

Emery, John (1628- ) Va.; m. Mary (Shatewell) Webster.
Landowner.

Emlen, George ( -1712) Pa.; m. Hannah Garrett.
Vineyard keeper; Landowner.

Emperour, Francis (c1621-c1659 ) Va.; m. Mary Tully.
   Commissioner; Sheriff.
Empson, Cornelius (1660-1712) Del.; m. Mary Sanderson;
   Ann ---. Assemblyman; Justice.
Empson, Richard (c1635-75) Del.; m. Ann ---. Land-
   owner.
Endicott, John (1588-1663) Mass.; m. Elizabeth Gibson;
   Ann Gower. Governor.
England, Francis (1609-77) Va.; m. Sarah ---. Land-
   owner.
England, William (   -  ) R.I.; m. Elizabeth ---.
   Landowner.
English, Clement  (1646-83) Mass.; m. Mary Waters.
   Civil officer.
English, John (   -1675) Va.; m. ---. Military service.
Ensign, James (   -1670) Conn.; m. Sarah Elson. Magi-
   strate; Constable.
Enyard, John (   -1763) N.J.; m. Mary ---. Military
   service.
Epperson   SEE   Apperson
Eppes, Daniel (   -1692) Mass.; m. Elizabeth ---.
   Landowner.
Eppes, Francis (1597-1655) Va.; m.  Marie Bawlett.
   Military service; Justice.
Eppes, Francis (1628-78) Va.; m. Elizabeth (  )
   Worsham. Burgess; Councillor.
Eppes, Francis (1659-1718/19) Va.; m. Ann Isham.
   Burgess; Sheriff.
Erskine, James (1659-1725) Pa.; m. ---. Landowner.
Erskine, John (1632-72) Va.-Del.; m. Jane ---.
   Landowner.
Eskridge, George (1650-1735) Va.; m. Rebecca Bonum.
   Burgess.
Esmonton, Thomas (1648-90) Md.; m. ---. Landowner.
Estes, Abraham (1669-1720) Va.; m. Barbara ---.
   Landowner.
Estes, Elisha (c1701-90/91) Va.; m. Frances ---.
   Landowner.
Estes, Richard (1647-1740) Mass.; m. Elizabeth Beck.
   Weaver; Landowner.

Estey, Isaac (c1630-1712) N.Y.-Mass.; m. Mary Towne.
Landowner.
Estey, Jeffry   (1587-1657) Mass.- Conn.; m. Margaret
Pate. Proprietor.
Estill, John (c1670-c1702) N.J.; m. ---. Landowner.
Estill, Thomas (1623-88) N.J.-Pa.; m. Lucia Wallace.
Minister.
Estill, William (1698-1792) Va.; m. Mary Ann Campbell.
Landowner.
Etheridge, Henry (1700/04-65) Va.; m. Elizabeth ---.
Landowner.
Etheridge, Thomas (c1620-71) Va.; m. Christian Yates.
Landowner.
Evans, David (   -1709/10) Pa.; m. Mary Jones.
Land Commissioner.
Evans, John (1647-1693/94) Va.; m. Mary Rieves.
Indian trader.
(AP) Evans, Owen (1659-1723) Pa.; m. Elizabeth ---.
Landowner.
(AP) Evans, Thomas (1651-1738) Pa.; m. Ann ---.
Landowner.
Evans, Walter (   -1721) Md.; m. Mary Powell. Land-
owner.
Evelyn, George (c1608- )Md.-Va.; m. Jane Crane.
Landowner; Military service.
Everett, John (1646-1715 ) Mass.; m. Elizabeth Pepper.
Landowner.
Everett, John (1676-1751) Mass.; m. Mary Brown. Land-
owner.
Everett, Nathan (c1680-1749) N.C.; m. ---. Landowner.
Everett, Richard (c1600-82) Mass.; m. Mary ---.
Proprietor.
Eves, Thomas (   -1726/27) N.J.; m. Anne (Hannah) ---.
Proprietor.
Evetts, James (   -   ) N.J.; m. ---. Landowner.
Evevett   SEE   Averett
Ewell, Charles (1680-1722) Va.; m. Mary Ann Bertrand.
Landowner.
Ewen, Richard  (c1649-c1675) Md.; m. Sophia Ewell.
Sheriff; Justice.

Ewen, William Nicholas (   -   ) Va.; m. ---. Land-
owner.
Ewer, John (1676-1712) N.J.; m. Ann Allen. Landowner.
Ewer, Thomas (1595-1638) Mass.; m. Sarah Learned.
Town officer.
Ewing, Alexander (1656-1738) Md.; m. Jane Porter.
Landowner.
Exum, Jeremiah (c1650-1720) Va.; m. Ann Lawrence.
Judge.
Exum, William (   -c1700) Va.; m. Jane ---. Land-
owner.
Eyams  SEE  Ijams
Ezell, George (c1648-92/93) Va.; m. Elizabeth Clarke.
Military service.

- F -

Fairbanks, Jabez (1670-1758) Mass.; m.  Mary Wilder.
Military service.
Fairbanks, Jonathan (c1595-1668) Mass.; m. Mary ---.
Signed Dedham Covenant.
Fairbanks, Jonathan (1633-88) Mass.; m. Grace Smith.
Landowner.
Fairchild, Thomas (1610-70) Conn.; m. Emma Seabrook.
Magistrate; Delegate to court.
Fairchild, Zachariah (1651-1703) Conn.; m. Hannah
Beach. Landowner.
Fairfield, John (c1610-1646) Mass.; m. Elizabeth Knight.
Freeman; Proprietor.
Fairfield, Thomas (1610-70) Conn.; m. ---.  Merchant;
Landowner.
Fales, James (   -1708) Mass.; m. Ann Brock.  Freeman.
Fales, John (1658-1735) Mass.; m. Abigail Hawes.
Landowner.
Fanning, Edmund (c1620/25-1683) Conn.; m. Ellen ---.
Military service; Landowner.
Farley, George (1615-93) Mass.; m. Christian Barth.
Landowner.
Farley, John (1647-  ) Va.; m. Mary ---. Landowner.
Farley, John (1670-1758) Va.; m. Elizabeth ---.
Landowner.

Farley, Thomas (c1600-    ) Va.; m. Jane Sefton.  Landowner; Military service.

Farmer, Edward (c1640-1727) Mass.; m. Mary ---.
Landowner.

Farmer, Samuel (1680-1752) Md.; m. Sarah Duvall.
Juror; Churchman.

Farmer, Thomas (c1594-1652) Va.; m. ---.  Burgess.

Farnifold, John (1625-1702) Va.; m. Mary Brooks.
Minister.

Farnsworth, Matthias (1612-89) Mass.; m. Dorothy
Robinson; Mary Farr.  Selectman; Constable.

Farnum, Ralph (1603-66) Mass.; m. Alice ---.  Proprietor.

Farr, George (1594-1662) Mass.; m. Elizabeth Stower.
Shipwright; Landowner.

Farrar, William (1594/95-1637) Va.; m. Cecely Jordan.
Attorney; Councillor.

Farrar, William (1626-77) Va.; m. Mary ---.  Burgess;
Military service.

Farrar, William (1657-1721) Va.; m. Priscilla(Baugh)
(Branch) Gower.  Burgess; Justice.

Farrington, Daniel (1664-1718) Mass.; m. Abigail
Fisher.  Proprietor.

Farrington, John (c1624-76) Mass.; m. Mary Bullard.
Proprietor.

Farrow, Abraham (c1650-1730) Va.; m. Margaret ( )
Mason.  Landowner.

Farrow, John (   -1687) Mass.; m. Frances ---.  Landowner.

Farwell, Henry (c1605-1670) Mass.; m. Olive Welby.
Freeman.

Farwell, Joseph (1640/41-1722) Mass.; m. Hannah
Learned.  Military service.

Fassett   SEE   Fawcett

Fauconnier, Pierre (1659-1746) N.J.; m. Madeleine
Pasquerlau.  Merchant.

Faulkman, John (1654-1715 ) Mass.; m. Sarah Abbott.
Military service.

Faulkner, Daniel R. (1617-c1700) Pa.; m. Mary.
Minister.

Faulkner, Edmund (    -1687) Mass.; m. Dorothy
Robinson. Landowner.
Faunce, Thomas (1647-1745) Mass.; m. Jane Nelson.
Town clerk; Elder.
Fauntleroy, Moore (1610-63) Va.; m. Mary Hill.
Burgess; Military service.
Faure, Pierre (1684-1745) Va.; m. Judith Benzile.
Church warden.
Faure (Widow ?) (    -  ) Va.; m. ---. Landowner.
Founder.
Fawcett, John (c1639-73) Va.; m. Rhoda Lamberton.
Attorney.
Fawcett, William (1662-1735) Md.; m. Mary (Fenwick)
Harrison. Military service.
Fawden, George (1606-56) Va.; m. Ann Smith. Burgess;
Justice.
Fay, John (1648-90) Mass.; m. Mary Brigham. Military
service.
Feake, Robert (c1608-62) Mass.; m. Elizabeth (Fone)
Winthrop. Delegate to court.
Fearing, John (    -1665) Mass.; m. Margaret ---.
Selectman.
Fears, William (    -  ) Va.; m. Frances Sadler.
Founder; Landowner.
Featherston, Charles (c1635-81) Va.; m. Rebecca ---.
Founder; Military service.
Feild, Abram (1630/36-74) Va.; m. Mary Ironmonger.
Landowner.
Feild    SEE ALSO    Field
Feke    SEE    Feake
Fellows, William (1608-  ) Mass.; m. --- Ayers.
Landowner.
Felt, George (1601-93) Mass.; m. Elizabeth Wilkinson.
Landowner.
Felton, Nathaniel (1615-1705) Mass.; m. Mary Skelton.
Military service.
Fenn, Benjamin F. (    -1672) Conn.; m. Sara Baldwin.
Founder; Magistrate.

Ferebee, John (c1642-1715) Va.; m. Elizabeth (Green) Ellis. Surveyor; Deputy exchequer.

Ferebee, Thomas (1682-1739) Va.; m. ---Fenford. Landowner.

Ferguson, James (1680-1725 ) Va.; m. ---. Military service.

Ferniside, John (c1611-c1683) Mass.; m. Elizabeth Starr. Proprietor.

Ferre, Charles (1637-95) Mass.; m. Sarah Harmon. Freeman.

Ferring, John (1615-63) Mass.; m. Margaret Hawks. Freeman; Landowner.

Ferris, Jeffrey (c1619-66) Conn.; m. ---. Freeman.

Ferris, John (1639-1715) N.Y.; m. Mary ---. Landowner.

Ferris, Richard (1596-1637) Va.; m. ---. Landowner.

Ferry, Charles (c1638-99) Mass.; m. Sarah Harmon. Proprietor; Landowner.

Few, Richard (c1626-88) Pa.; m. Julian ---. Grand Juror.

Fewox, James (   -1711) N.C.; m. Ann ---. Landowner.

Fidler, John (1684-1759) N.J.; m. Sarah Smith. Constable.

Field, Henry (1611-67) Va.; m. ---. Landowner.

Field, John (1579-  ) Va.; m. Elen Hutchinson. Burgess; Military service.

Field, Peter (1647-1707) Va.; m. Judith(Sloan) Randolph. Justice; Sheriff.

Field, Robert (1605-73) N.Y.-R.I.; m. Elizabeth Taylor; Ruth Fairbanks; Charity ---. Landowner.

Field, Robert (1613-75) Mass.; m. Mary Stanley. Freeman; Proprietor.

Field, Zechariah (1596-1666) Mass.; m. Mary ---. Proprietor; Military service.

Field   SEE ALSO   Feild

Fifield, William (1614/18-1700) N.H.; m. Mary ---. Juror; Constable.

Filer, Walter (   -1683) Conn.; m. ---. Deputy to court; Landowner.

Filmer, Henry (1600-73) Va.; m. Elizabeth ---. Burgess.

Filmore   SEE   Filmer
Finch, Edward (c1689-1750/60) Va.; m. Agnes ---.
  Landowner.
Finch, John (    -1657) Mass.; m. ---. Governor.
Finckley, Thomas (    -1694) Va.; m. Elizabeth ---.
  Physician; Landowner.
Finney, Andrew (1632-69) Va.; m. Jane Major. Land-
  owner; Military service.
Fish, Jonathan (    -1734) N.Y.-Conn.; m. Elizabeth
  ---. Minister.
Fish, Nathaniel (1635-  ) N.Y.; m. Mary ---. Mili-
  tary service.
Fish, Thomas (1618/19-87) R.I.; m. Mary Soule. Free-
  man; Councillor.
Fisher, Anthony (1591-1671) Mass.; m. Mary Fisher.
  Selectman; Ancient and Honorable Artillery Company.
Fisher, George (1650-1733) Pa.; m. Wilhemina ---.
  Landowner.
Fisher, Thomas (    -1638) Mass.; m. Elizabeth ---.
  Freeman.
Fiske, Nathan (c1615-76) Mass.; m. Susanna ---.
  Freeman; Selectman.
Fiske, Phineas (1600-83) Mass.; m. Sarah Francis.
  Representative; Constable
Fiske, William (c1613-54) Mass.; m. Bridgett Muskett.
  Town clerk.
Fiske, William (1642/43-1728) Mass.; m. Sarah Kilborn.
  Military service.
Fitch, James (1622-1702) Conn.; m. Priscilla Mason;
  Abigail Whitfield. Minister.
Fitch, John (1667-1743) Conn.; m. Elizabeth Waterman.
  Town clerk; Judge.
Fitch, Joseph (    -c1713) Conn.; m. Mary Stone.
  Freeman; Representative.
Fitch, Samuel (1673-1742) Mass.; m. Elizabeth Walker.
  Selectman; Clerk.
Fitch, Thomas (1612-1704) Conn.; m. Anna Stacey.
  Military service; Landowner.
Fitch, Thomas (1665-1731) Conn.; m. Sarah ---.
  Commissioner.

Fithian, William (    -1678) N.Y.; m. Margaret ---.
Landowner; Miller.

Fitzhugh, Henry (1686/87-1755) Va.; m. Susannah Cooke.
Burgess; Sheriff.

Fitzhugh, William (1650-1701) Va.; m. Sarah Tucker.
Burgess; Landowner.

Fitzrandolph, Edward (c1607-84/85) Mass.-N.J.; m.
Elizabeth Blossom. Military service; Builder.

Fitzrandolph, Nathaniel (1642-1713) Mass.; m. Mary
Holley. Provincial Secretary; Assessor.

Fitzrandolph, Nathaniel (1666-1703) Mass.-N.J.; m.
Grace Hull. Landowner.

Fladger, Hugh (c1693-    ) S.C.; m. ---. Landowner.

Flagg, Gersham (1641-90) Mass.; m. Hannah Lipping-
well. Freeman.

Flagg, Thomas (1621-1697/98) Mass.; m. Mary Underwood. Selectman; Military service.

Flake, Robert (1652-1717) Va.; m. Mary ---. Landowner.

Flanders, Steven (1646-84/89) Mass.; m. Abigail
Carter. Landowner.

Fleete, Henry (c1600-c1660) Md.-Va.; m. Sarah (Conway)
Burden. Explorer; Burgess.

Fleming, Sir Alexander (1612-68/69) Va.; m. Ursula
(  ) Brown. Landowner.

Fleming, Charles (1660-1720) Va.; m. Susana Tarleton.
Surveyor; Military service.

Fleming, John (1697-1756) Va.; m. Mary Bolling.
Military service; Landowner.

Fleming, Sir Thomas (1630/35-83) Va.; m. Judith
(Ursula) Tarlton. Landowner.

Fleming, William (1662-1725) Del.-Pa.; m. Mary Moore.
Landowner.

Fletcher, Ralph (1676-1728) Va.-N.C.; m. Jane Morgan.
Justice; Councillor.

Fletcher, Robert (1592-1677) Mass.; m. Elizabeth
Wheeler. Juror.

Fletcher, William (1622-77) Mass.; m. Lydia Bates.
Selectman; Freeman.

Fletcher, William (1650-1710) Va.; m.; Elizabeth ---.
Landowner.
Flint, Henry (c1607-68) Mass.; m. Margery Hoar.
Freeman; Minister.
Flint, Richard ( -1715) Va.; m. Martha ---. Land-
owner.
Flint, Thomas ( -1663) Mass.; m. Ann ---. Landowner.
Flint, Thomas (1645-1721) Mass.; m. Mary Sounton.
Military service.
Flood, John (1593/94-1661) Va.; m. Margaret (Finch)
Fortman Jordan. Burgess; Military service.
Flournoy, Francis (1687-1778) Va.; m. Mary Gibson.
Landowner.
Flournoy, Jacob (1663-1748) Va.; m. Martha Morel.
Military service.
Floyd, Nathaniel ( -1699) Va.; m. ---. Landowner.
Flynt   SEE   Flint
Foissin, Elias (c1672-1739) S.C.; m. Elizabeth ---.
Petitioner; Elder.
Folger, John (c1590-1660) Mass.; m. Meribah Gibbs.
Landowner.
Folger, Peter (1617-90) Mass.; m. Nancy Morrell.
Proprietor.
Follansbee, Thomas (c1640-c1726) N.H.-Mass.; m.
Sarah ---. Landowner.
Folsom, John (c1618-81) N.H.; m. Mary Gilman.
Civil Officer.
Fontaine, Nicholas (1640-1708/09) Md.; m. Grace ---.
Military service.
Fontaine   SEE ALSO   Fonteyn
Fontayn   SEE   Fontaine
Fonteyn, Charles ( -1687) N.Y.; m. Katherine de
Bailley. Landowner.
Fonville, John (1675-1741) Va.; m. Ann ---. Land-
owner.
Foote, Nathaniel (1593-1644) Conn; m. Elizabeth
Deming. Delegate to court; Representative.
Foote, Nathaniel (1652-1715) Mass.; m. Elizabeth
Herrick. Attorney.
Foote, Samuel ( -1690) Mass.; m. Hannah Currier.
Representative; Military service.

Footman, John (   -c1660/64) Va.; m. Jane ---.
Landowner.
Forbes, John (1674-   ) Mass.; m. Abigail Robinson.
Landowner.
Ford, James (1650/60-   ) S.C.; m. ---. Landowner.
Ford, Joseph (1666-1749) Mass.; m. Lois Stetson.
Founder; Landowner.
Ford, Peter (1679-1744) Va.; m. Elizabeth ---.
Landowner.
Ford, Stephen (c1680-c1731) S.C.; m. ---. Landowner.
Ford, Thomas (   -1675/76) Mass.-Conn.; m. ---Cooke;
Joan Wayne. Freeman; Representative.
Ford, William (1604-76) Mass.; m. Anna ---. Pro-
prietor.
Fordham, Robert (1605-74) Mass.-Conn.; m. Elizabeth
Benning. Founder.
Foreman, Robert (1605-71) N.Y.; m. Johanna ---.
Magistrate.
Foreman, William (1654-1730) Md.; m. Elizabeth ---.
Landowner.
Foreman    SEE ALSO    Forman
Forman, Samuel (1662-1740) N.Y.-N.J.; m. Mary Wilbur.
Sheriff.
Forman    SEE ALSO    Foreman
Forrest, Thomas (c1580-c1650) Va.; m. ---. Landowner;
Military service.
Fort, Elias (c1645-78) Va.; m. Phillis Champion.
Landowner.
Fort, Elias (1660-1719) Va.; m. Catherine ---.
Landowner.
Fortman, John (c1600-1664) Va.; m. Jane ---. Land-
owner.
Forwood, William (1692-1777) Del.; m. Mary Stedman.
Landowner.
Fosdick, Samuel (1655-1702) Conn.; m. Mercy Picket.
Landowner.
Fosdick, Stephen (1583-1664) Mass.; m. Anna Marre;
Sarah Fraser. Surveyor; Freeman.
Fosque, Simon (1604-80) Va.; m. Elizabeth ---.
Landowner.

Foster, Christopher (    -    ) Va.; m. Mary Jordan.
Landowner.
Foster, Edward (1610-44) Mass.; m. Lettice Hanford.
Military service; Town officer.
Foster, John (1626-87) Mass.; m. Marie Tompkins.
Landowner.
Foster, John (1675-1735) Va.; m. Mary Fort.  Land-
owner.
Foster, John (1680-1759) Mass.; m. Margaret Ware.
Representative.
Foster, Reginald (c1598-1681) Mass.; m. Judith ---.
Landowner; Military service.
Foster, Richard (1620-87) N.C.; m. Alice ---.
Burgess; Military service.
Foulke, Thomas (1624-1714) N.J.; m. Mary ---.
Commissioner.
Foulke, Thomas (1662-1737) N.J.; m. Elizabeth Curtis.
Sheriff.
Fowkes, Gerard (1630/36-69/71) Va.; m. Anne (Thorough-
good) Chandler. Burgess; Justice.
Fowkes, James (c1592-    ) Va.; m. Rachel ---.  Land-
owner.
Fowkes, James (1655-1722) Va.; m. Sarah (Dorrington)
Fisher.  Judge; Ship Captain.
Fowler, Ambrose (    -1704) Conn.; m. Jane Alvord.
Churchman.
Fowler, Godfrey (1670-1747) Va.; m. Susannah ---.
Landowner.
Fowler, Henry (1652/53-87) N.Y.; m. Rebecca Newell.
Landowner.
Fowler, John (c1670-1683) Va.; m. ---.  Landowner.
Fowler, Philip (1592-1670) Mass.; m. Mary Winsley.
Landowner.
Fowler, Philip (1640-1715) Mass.; m. Elizabeth
Herrick.  Attorney.
Fowler, William (1596-1661) Conn.; m. ---.    Oath
of Fidelity.
Fox, Henry (    -1714) Va.; m. Ann West.  Justice;
Burgess.
Fox, Richard (c1641-1708) Conn.; m. Beriah Smith.
Landowner.

Fox, Thomas (1608-93) Mass.; m. Ellen Green.  Freeman; Selectman.

Fox, Thomas (1690-1760) Md.; m. Rebecca Purtee. Landowner.

Foy  SEE  Fox

Frampton, William (1646-86) Pa.; m. Elizabeth Potter. Registrar-General.

Francis, John (c1610-77) Va.; m. Jane ---.  Landowner.

Francis, Robert (c1629-1711/12) Conn.; m. Joan Sibberance.  Freeman; Surveyor.

Francks, John Martin (1680-1744) N.C.; m. Sibella Fonville.  Assemblyman; County Treasurer.

Frank  SEE  Francks

Franklin, Josiah (1657-   ) Mass.; m. Abiah Folger; Ann Child.  Candlemaker.

Frary, John (1638-95) Mass.; m. Prudence ---. Founder.

Frary, Sampson (c1640-1704) Mass.; m. Mary Daniels. Landowner.

Frazer, Joseph (1640-1713/14) N.J.; m. Mary Osborne. Founder.

Frederickes, Myndert (   -1706) N.Y.; m. Petertje Tennise Van Vechten.  Armourer; Deacon.

Freeborn, William (1574-1670) R.I.; m. Mary ---. Founder.

Freeman, Bridges (c1600-31) Va.; m. ---.  Landowner.

Freeman, Edmund (1596-1682) Mass.; m. Bennet Hodsell; Elizabeth ---.  Judge; Deputy to court.

Freeman, Henry (1669/70-1763) Pa.-N.J.; m. Elizabeth Brown.  Judge; Commissioner.

Freeman, John (1626-1719) Mass.; m. Mary Prence. Founder; Notary.

Freeman, Robert (c1670-c1704) Va.; m. Ann Robins. Landowner.

Freer, Hugo (1668-1706) N.Y.; m. Marie Anne LeRoy. Landowner.

Freich, Joseph (1640-94) Mass.; m. Experience Goster. Military service.

French, John (1612-92 ) Mass.; m. Grace ---.  Freeman; Founder.

French, Thomas (1639-79) N.J.; m. Jane Atkins.
Proprietor; Commissioner of highways.
French, William (1687-1745) Mass.; m. Elizabeth Symmes.
Military service.
Frey, Heinrich (1652-1736) Pa.; m. Anna Catherine
Levering. Town Clerk.
Frink, John (1630-1717) Conn.; m. Grace Stevens.
Landowner; Military service.
Frith, Nathaniel (1627-77) Va.; m. Elizabeth ---.
Landowner.
Frohman  SEE  Froman
Frost, Charles (1631-97) Me.; m. Mary Bolles. Mili-
tary service; Town clerk.
Frost, William ( - ) Conn.; m. ---. Landowner.
Frye, John (1601-93) Mass.; m. Anne ---. Freeman.
Fucque, Gill ( - ) Va.; m. Jane Ayres. Landowner.
Fuller, Edward (1575-1620/21) Mass.; m. Ann ---;
Frances ---. Mayflower passenger.
Fuller, Ezekiel (c1653-1723) Va.; m. Deborah Spivey.
Landowner.
Fuller, Matthew (1603/05-78) Mass.; m.  Frances.
Councillor; Surgeon general.
Fuller, Robert ( -1706) Mass.; m. Sarah Bowen;
Margaret Waller. Proprietor.
Fuller, Samuel (1580-1633) Mass.; m. Jane Lathrop;
Mary Ide; Bridget Lee. Military service.
Fuller, Thomas (1618-90/95) Mass.; m. Hannah Flower;
Elizabeth Todd. Selectman; Military service.
Fuller, William ( -c1705) S.C.; m. Sarah ---.
Councillor.
Furman, John (c1600- ) Mass.; m. ---. Governor.
Furman, Josiah (1685-1775) S.C.; m. Sarah Wood.
Landowner.
Fyler, Walter (c1610-83) Conn.; m. Jane ---.
Freeman; Delegate to court.

-G-

Gage, John, 1604-72/73) Mass.; m. Amy Keyes. Freeman; Military service.

Gage, Thomas (1656-1707) Mass.; m. Sarah ---.  Military service.

Gager, John (c1630-1703) Conn.; m.  Elizabeth ---.
Proprietor; Freeman.

Gaillard, Joachim (1625-   ) S.C.; m. Esther Paporel.
Landowner.

Gaillard, Peter (c1660-c1710) S.C.; m. Elizabeth
LeClair. Huguenot.

Gaineau, Etienne (   -   ) N.Y.; m. Lydia Mestereau.
Landowner; Huguenot.

Gaines, Bernard (1623-83) Va.; m. ---.
Justice; Burgess.

Gaines, Daniel (1623-82) Va.; m. Margaret Bernard.
Military service.

Gaines, Richard (1686-1758/59) Va.; m. ---.  Landowner.

Gaines, Thomas (c1590/95-1650) Va.; m. ---.  Military service.

Gaither, John (1599-c1666) Va.; m. Grace ---; Ruth
(Moseley) Beard.  Landowner.

Galbraith, John (1690-1753) Pa.; m. Janet ---.  Grist
miller; Sheriff.

Gale, Abell (   -1642) N.Y.; m. Dinah ---.  Commissioner; Fence viewer.

Gale, Christopher (1680-1734) N.C.; m. Sarah (Laker)
Harvey.  Attorney.

Gale, Richard (1596-1678/79) N.Y.; m. Mary Castle.
Founder.

Gallup, John (1595-1650) Mass.-Conn.; m. Christobel
Crabbe; Hannah Lake.  Delegate to court; Military
service.

Gallup, Robert (c1660-1720) Mass.-Conn.; m. Elinor ---.
Grand Juror.

Gantt, Thomas (c1660-   ) Md.; m. Mary Graham.
Justice.

Garat    SEE   Garrard: Gerrard

Gardiner, David (1636-89) Conn.; m. Mary Herringham.
Proprietor.

Gardiner, George (1600-c1679) R.I.; m. Heriodius
(Long) Hicks.  Freeman; Commissioner.

Gardiner, Lion (1599-1653) Conn.; m. Marichje(Willemsen) Deurcant. Landowner.
Gardiner, Richard ( -1649) Md.; m. ---. Landowner.
Gardiner, Thomas (1633- ) N.J.; m. Elizabeth Satterthwaite. Assemblyman.
Gardiner SEE ALSO Gardner
Gardner, Richard (1626-88) Mass.; m. Sarah Shattuck. Landowner; Magistrate.
Gardner, Thomas (1592-1674) Mass.; m. Margaret Fryer. Freeman; Governor.
Gardner SEE ALSO Gardiner
Garfield, Richard (1605-72) Mass.; m. Rebecca ---. Freeman.
Garland, Edward (c1660-1719) Va.; m. Jane Hensley. Landowner.
Garlington, Christopher (c1663-c1680) Va.; m. Elizabeth Ball; Jeane ---. Vestryman; Landowner.
Garner, John (1633-1703) Va.; m. Susanna Keene. Landowner.
Garnett, John (c1649-1703) Va.; m. ---. Landowner.
Garnett, Thomas (1584/85- ) Va.; m. Elizabeth ---. Landowner.
Garnier, Daniel (c1650-c1698) S.C.; m. Elizabeth Fanton. Landowner.
Garnsey, Henry (1620/25-92) Mass.; m. Hannah Munnings. Landowner.
Garnsey, Joseph (1649-1730) Conn.; m. Hannah Cooley. Delegate to court; Leather inspector.
Garretson, Casparius (1676-1726) Del.; m. ---. Quaker minister.
Garretson, Henry ( -1721) Del.; m. Ann ---. Landowner.
Garretson, John ( -1694) Del.- Pa.; m. Ann ---. Landowner.
Garrett, William (1643-1724) Pa.; m. Ann Kirk, Assemblyman.
Garvine, Patrick ( - ) N.Y.; m. Mary ---. Landowner.
Gascoigne, Thomas (c1591-1665) Va.; m. Sarah Magdalen. Proprietor.

Gaskill, Edward (1678-c1717) Mass.; m. Sarah South-
wick. Landowner.
Gaskins, Thomas (1601-c1665) Va.; m. ---. Landowner.
Gassaway, Nicholas (c1630-91) Md.; m. Anne Beeson.
Military service.
Gates, George (1634-1724) Conn.; m. Sarah Olmstead.
Landowner.
Gates, Isaac (1673-   ) Mass.; m. Mercy Benjamin.
Landowner.
Gates, Stephen (1638-1662) Mass.; m. Ann (Veare) Hill.
Landowner; Military service.
Gatlin, John (1616-98) Va.; m. ---. Landowner.
Gavit, Philip (1641-1714) R.I.; m. Hannah Maechone.
Landowner.
Gay, Henry (c1686-1705) Va.; m. Joan Sanders. Land-
owner.
Gay, John (    -1688) Mass.; m. Joanna Baldwicke.
Freeman; Proprietor.
Gay, Nathaniel (1642-1713) Mass.; m. Lydia Starr.
Freeman; Selectman.
Gayden, Ralph (c1654-c92) Va.; m. Johanna Webster.
Sub-sheriff.
Gayer, William (1644-1710) Mass.; m. Dorcas Starbuck;
Mary Guard. Justice; Representative.
Gaylord, James (c1681-   ) Va.; m. Anne ---. Landowner.
Gaylord, William (1582-1673) Conn-Mass.; m. Sarah
Walter. Deacon; Selectman.
Gee, Charles (1660-1709) Va.; m. Hannah ---. Land-
owner.
Geer, George (1621-1726) Conn.; m. Sarah Allyn.
Military service.
Geer, Thomas (1623-1722) Conn.; m. Deborah Davis.
Landowner; Moderator.
Gelpin, Philip (    -1685) Mass.; m. Elizabeth Smith.
Juror; Founder.
Gendron, Phillippe (    -1724) S.C.; m. Madeline Chardon.
Landowner.
Gentry, Nicholas (1660-c1735) Va.; m. ---. Military
service; Landowner.
Gentry, Nicholas (1697-1779) Va.; m. Jane ---.
Landowner.

George, John (1604/06-78) Va.; m. Jane Cole. Military service.

Gerow, Daniel (1680-1757) N.Y.; m. Jeanne Dorcas. Surveyor; Landowner.

Gerrard, Thomas (c1605-c1671) Va.-Md.; m. Susanna Snow; Rose Fitzburgh. Physician; Assemblyman.

Gerrard   SEE ALSO   Garrard

Gerrish, William (1617-87) Mass.; m. Joanna ---. Military service.

Gholston, Antony (1680-1763) Va.; m. Jane ---. Landowner.

Gibbes   SEE   Gibbs

Gibbins, Ambrose (1598-1656) N.H.; m. Rebecca ---. Founder; Magistrate.

Gibbons, James (1614-   ) Me.; m. Judith Lewis. Landowner.

Gibbs, Giles (   -1641) Conn.; m. Katherine ---. Assessor; Freeman.

Gibbs, Jacob (1668-1708/09) Conn.; m. Elizabeth Andros. Landowner.

Gibbs, John (1680-1725) Va.; m. Mary Mullens. Civil Officer.

Gibbs, Robert (1644-1715) S.C.; m. Mary ---. Justice; Governor.

Gibson, John (c1601-94) Mass.; m. Rebecca Thompson. Freeman; Petitioner.

Giddings, George (1610-76) Mass.; m. Jane (Tuttle) Lawrence. Selectman.

Giddings, John (1639-91) Mass.; m. Sarah ---. Landowner.

Giddings, Thomas (1683-   ) Mass.; m. Sarah Butler. Landowner.

Gilbert, Garvis (1632-1739) Md.; m. Margaret ---. Landowner.

Gilbert, Henry (1615-1656/57) Mass.; m. Elizabeth ---. Landowner.

Gilbert, Humphrey (   -   ) Conn.; m. Elizabeth ---. Landowner.

Gilbert, Jonathan (1618-82) Conn.; m. Mary Welles. Tax collector; Military service.

Gilbert, Josiah (1628-84) Conn.; m. Elizabeth
  Belcher. Surveyor; Constable.
Gilbert, Matthew (   -1680) Conn.; m. Jane Baker.
  Deputy Governor; Magistrate.
Gilbert, Thomas (1582-1659) Conn.; m. Lydia ---.
  Landowner.
Gildersleeve, Richard (1601-81) Mass.-Conn.; m.
  ---. Landowner.
Gile, Ephraim (1661-  ) Mass.; m. Martha Bradley.
  Military service.
Giles, James (1628/29-90) N.J.; m. Elizabeth Tidd.
  Justice; Proprietor.
Gill, Benjamin (   -1655) Md.; m. ---. Founder;
  Proprietor.
Gill, Stephen (   -1646/52) Va.; m. ---. Physician;
  Landowner.
Gillam, Benjamin (c1634-85) Mass.; m. Hannah Savage.
  Military service.
Gillett, Jonathan (   -1677) Conn.; m. Mary Dolbere.
  Philanthropist.
Gillett, Nathan (1600-70) Mass.; m. Elizabeth ---.
  Freeman; Landowner.
Gilliam, John (   -1651) Va.; m. Margaret Henshaw.
  Landowner.
Gilman, Edward (c1587-1655) N.H.; m. Mary Clarke.
  Proprietor.
Gilman, John (1624-1708) N.H.;m Elizabeth ---.
  Selectman; Councillor.
Gilman, Nicholas (1672-1749) Mass.; m.  Sarah Clark.
  Landowner.
Gilmore, John (c1660-1743) Mass.; m. Agnes ---.
  Landowner.
Gilson, Andrew ( c1640-  ) Va.; m. ---. Landowner.
Gilson, James (c1648-  ) Mass.; m. Mary ---.
  Landowner.
Gilson   SEE ALSO   Jillson
Gist, Christopher (1655-90) Md.; m. Edith Cromwell.
  Grand Juror.
Gist, Richard (1683-1741) Md.; m. Zipporah Murray.
  Justice; Assemblyman.

Givens, George (1679-1740) Va.; m. Sarah Cathey;
Elizabeth Mason. Church worker.

Givens, Richard (1634-92) Va.-Md.; m. Amy Lewis.
Minister; Committee of Peace.

Givens, Samuel (1698-1740) Va.; m. Sarah Cathey.
Justice.

Glascock, Gregory (c1622-   ) Va.; m. Jane ---.
Landowner.

Glascock, Thomas (1610-c1663) Va.; m. Jane Just.
Justice; Landowner.

Glenn, Johannes Sanders (1648-1731) N.Y.; m.  Annetje
Peek. Military service.

Glover, Charles (   -1665) Mass.; m. Elizabeth ---.
Landowner.

Glover, Charles Worth (1638-1732) S.C.; m. Sarah
Sanders. Landowner.

Glover, John (1600-55) Mass.; m. Anne ---. Representative.

Glover, Jonathan (1677-   ) Mass.; m. Abigail Henderson. Landowner.

Goad, Abraham (c1660-1734) Va.; m. Katherine Williams.
Landowner.

Godfrey, George (c1620-c1688) Mass.; m. ---.
Founder.

Godfrey, John (1640-c91) S.C.; m. ---. Military
service; Attorney general.

Godfrey, John (c1646-1722) N.C.; m. Elizabeth (Donne)
Nicholson. Landowner; Military service.

Godfrey, John (1663-1690) S.C.; m. Mary ---. Acting
Governor; Councillor.

Godfrey, Richard (1595-c1652) Mass.; m. Jane Turner;
Mary ---. Proprietor.

Godwin, Thomas (   -1676/77) Va.; m. ---. Burgess;
Military service.

Godwin, Thomas (   -1713) Va.; m. Martha Bridges.
Burgess.

Godwin, Thomas (1680-   ) Va.; m. Mary ---. Landowner.

Goff, Aaron (1658-1711/12) Conn.; m. Hannah Cole.
Landowner.

Goff, Anthony (   -1727) Mass.; m. Sarah Carpenter.
Founder.
Goff, John (1700-86) N.H.; m. Hannah Griggs.  Judge;
Military service.
Goff, Philip (   -1674) Conn.; m. Rebecca ---.  Land-
owner; Town clerk.
Goforth, William (1600-77) N.J.; m. Mary ---.  Land-
owner.
Goforth, William (1632-78) Pa.; m. Ann  Shipwith.
Landowner.
Goldman, Thomas(c1684-1699)Va.; m. Dorothy ( ) Aubray.
Burgess.
Goldsborough, Robert (1660-1746) Md.; m. Elizabeth
Greenberry.  Attorney.
Goldsmith, Samuel (1600/10-70)   Md.; m. Johanna
---.  Deputy to court; Burgess.
Goldthwaite, Thomas (1610-83) Mass.; m. Elizabeth
---.  Constable.
Gooch, William (   -   ) Va.; m.  Rebecca Staunton.
Landowner.
Goodale, Richard  (c1638-66) Mass.; m. Dorothy ---.
Landowner.
Goodale, Robert (1604-82) Mass.; m.; Katherine Killam.
Proprietor; Military service.
Goodby, John (1654-1720 ) S.C.; m. Elizabeth Dalli-
son.  Landowner; Military service.
Goode, John (c1630-1709) Va.; m. Frances Mackennon;
Anne Bennett; Martha Isabel Mackarness.  Landowner;
Military service.
Goodell SEE  Goodale
Goodenow, Edmund (1611-88) Mass.; m. Hannah ---.
Military service; Deputy to court.
Goodhue, Joseph  (1639-97) Mass.; m. Sarah Whipple.
Landowner.
Goodhue, William (1612/13-99) Mass.; m. Margery
Watson.  Deacon; Selectman.
Goodloe, George (1639-1710) Va.; m. Mary Weeks.
Landowner; Juror.
Goodloe, Henry (1675-1748) Va.; m. Elizabeth Eastham.
Landowner.

Goodman, Henry (c1662-c1745) N.C.; m. ---. Justice.

Goodman, Richard (1609-76) Mass.-Conn; m. Mary Terry.
Freeman; Deacon.

Goodman, William ( - ) Va.; m. Mary ---. Minister.

Goodrich, David (1667-1755) Conn.; m. Prudence
Churchill. Military service.

Goodrich, John (1652-96) Va.; m. Anne Bechinos.
Burgess.

Goodrich, John ( -1749) Va.; m. Honour Wilson.
Landowner.

Goodrich, Richard ( -1676) Conn.; m. Dinah ---.
Landowner.

Goodrich, Thomas (1614-79) Va.; m. Ann Sherwood.
Justice; Military service.

Goodrich, William (1605-47) Mass.; m. Margaret ---.
Freeman; Landowner.

Goodrich, William ( -1676) Conn.; m. Sarah Marvin.
Military service.

Goodridge SEE Goodrich

Goodspeed, Roger ( -1685) Mass.; m. Alice Layton.
Freeman; Grand Juror.

Goodwin, James (c1620-87 ) Va.; m. Rachel Porter.
Burgess.

Goodwin, John (c1650-1701) Va.; m. Elizabeth Moore.
Justice; Church warden.

Goodwin, Ozias (c1596-1683) Conn.; m. Mary Woodward.
Landowner.

Goodwin, Thomas (c1665-c1773)Va.; m. Mary Harrison.
Landowner.

Goodwin, William ( -1673) Conn.; m. Susannah ---.
Elder; Landowner.

Goodyear, Stephen (1600-58) Conn.; m. Mary ---.
Deputy Governor.

Gooken, Daniel ( -1632/33) Mass.; m. Mary Byrd.
Landowner.

Gooken, Daniel (1612-87) Mass.; m. Mary Dolling.
Landowner.

Gookin SEE Gooken

Gorham, Jabez (1656-1724/25) Mass.; m. Hannah (Sturgis)
Gray. Landowner.

Gorham, John ( 1621-76) Mass.; m. Desire Howland.
Selectman; Military service.
Gorsage    SEE    Gorsuch
Gorsuch, Anne(Lovelace)(1610-   ) Va.; m. John Gorsuch.
Landowner.
Gorsuch, Charles (1642-1716) Md.; m. Ann Loveland.
Landowner.
Gorsuch, Charles (1687-1746/47) Md.-Va.; m. Sarah
Cole. Landowner.
Gorsuch, John (1600-c47) Va.; m. Anne Lovelace.
Minister.
Gorsuch, Richard (    -c1703) Va.; m. Sarah Shelton.
Justice.
Gorton, Samuel (c1592-1677) R.I.; m. Mary Maplet.
Provincial President; Judge.
Goud, Abraham (    -1734) Va.; m. Katherine Williams.
Landowner.
Gould, Daniel (    -   ) R.I.; m. Waite Coggeshell.
Landowner.
Gould, John (1635-1709) Mass.; m. Sarah Baker.
Minister; Selectman.
Gould, Nathan (1614-1692/94) Mass.-Conn.; m. Sarah
(Phippen) Yeo; Elizabeth ---.  Landowner; Military
service.
Gould, Nathan (1663-1723) Conn.; m. Sarah ---.  Chief
Justice; Deputy Governor.
Gould, Zaccheus (1589-1670) Mass.; m.  Phebe Deacon.
Founder; Landowner.
Goulding, Palmer (1695-1770) Mass.; m. Abigail Rice.
Military service.
Gouldman    SEE    Goldman
Gouldsmith    SEE    Goldsmith
Gove, John (1651-1737) Mass.-N.H.; m. Sarah Russell.
Selectman; Landowner.
Gowen, William (c1683-1726) Va.; m. Katherine ---.
Landowner.
Graeff, Hans (1661-   ) Pa.-Md.; m. ---.  Landowner.
Graeff, Herman Op den (1585-1642) Pa.-Del.; m. Gritjen
Plitjer.

Graeff, Herman Op den (    -1708) Del.; m. Deborah Van
   Bibber. Landowner.
Graff   See   Graeff
Graffenried, Barbara (Needham De) (1688-1744) Va.; m.
   Christopher Graffenreid. Landowner.
Graffenried, Christopher De (1691-1742) N.C.-S.C.; m.
   Lady Barbara Needham. Landowner.
Graham, Christopher (1670-1745) Va.; m. Margaret
   Florence Risk. Landowner.
Granberry, Moses (c1700-53) Va.; m. Elizabeth ---.
   Landowner.
Granberry, William (c1653-  ) Va.; m. Ann ---;
   Sarah ---. Landowner.
Grandy, Charles (c1630-87) Va.; m. Elizabeth Sawyer.
   Landowner.
Granger, Lancelot (    -1689) Mass.; m. Joanne Adams.
   Landowner.
Grant, Matthew (1601-81) Conn.; m. Priscilla Grey.
   Town clerk; Surveyor.
Grant, Peter (1632-1718) Mass.; m. Johannah Ingersoll.
   Tax collector; Surveyor of fences.
Grant, William (c1670-1762) Va.; m. Elizabeth Mott.
   Landowner.
Graves, Francis (c1630-91) Va.; m. Jane McGuffey.
   Landowner.
Graves, Francis (c1678-1774) Va.; m. Mary Reynolds.
   Landowner.
Graves, George (    -1673) Conn.; m. Sarah ---.
   Landowner; Deacon.
Graves, George (1631-92) Conn.; m. Elizabeth Ventres.
   Representative; Marshal.
Graves, Isaac (c1620-1677) Mass.; m. Mary Church.
   Freeman; Military service.
Graves, John (c1621-77) Conn.; m. Mary Smith. Free-
   man.
Graves, John (1645-  ) Mass.; m. Mary Hoar. Petition-
   er to court.
Graves, John (1670-1747) Va.; m. Susannah ---.
   Landowner.
Graves, Thomas (1580-1655/56) Va.; m. Katherine
   Cooshaw; Virginia ---. Representative; Military
   service.

Graves, Thomas (1605-53) Mass.; m. Katherine Gray.
Sea Captain; Rear-Admiral.

Gray, Edward   (1623-81) Mass.; m. ---.  Landowner.
Grand Juror.

Gray, Francis (1630-79) Va.-Md.; m. Mary ---; Alice
Moorman.  Military service.

Gray, James (1664-1719/20) Va.; m. ---.  Landowner;
Military service.

Gray, John (c1660-1733/39) Mass.; m. Elizabeth ---.
Landowner.

Gray, Thomas (1593-1659) Va.; m. Anis Rebecca Shelton.
Landowner.

Gray, Thomas (1661-1710) Va.; m. Elizabeth ---.
Landowner.

Gray,  William (1620/30-c1675) Va.; m. Maudlin (Cane-
mock) Ingram.  Landowner.

Grayson, John (1665-1745) Va.; m. Susanna White.
Military service; Landowner.

Green, Farnefold (1674-1714) N.C.; m. Abigail ---.
Landowner.

Greene, James (1655-c1728) R.I.; m. Elizabeth ---.
Founder.

Greene, Job (1656-1744) R.I.; m. Phoebe Sayles.
Deputy to court.

Green, John (1596/97-1658) Mass.-R.I.; m. Joan
Tattersall.  Surgeon; Magistrate.

Green, Thomas (1600-51) Md.; m. Ann Cox; Winifred
Seyborn.  Assemblyman; Governor.

Green,  Thomas (1600/06-67) Mass.; m. Elizabeth ---;
Frances (Wheeler) Cook.  Selectman; Grand Juror.

Green, Thomas (1630-91) Pa.; m. Margaret ---.
Landowner.

Green, Thomas (1635-  ) Va.; m. Martha Filmore.
Landowner.

Greenberry, Nicholas (1627-97) Md.; m. Ann ---.
President of Council; Acting Governor.

Greenfield, Thomas (1640-1730) Md.; m. Martha ---.
Burgess; Sheriff.

Greenleaf, Edmund (1574-1670/71) Mass.; m. Sarah Dole.
Military service.

Greenwood, John (1687-1765) Va.; m. Lydia Holmes.
Minister.

Greer, James (1655-97) Md.; m. Ann Taylor. Landowner.

Gregg, John (1685/95-1758) Va.-Pa.; m. Nancy Ann
Woods. Military service.

Gregg, William (1640/48-87) Del.; m. ---. Landowner.

Gregory, Benjamin (c1680-1738) Conn.; m. Abigail
Sturgis. Landowner.

Gregory, Henry (c1590-1655) Conn.; m. ---. Landowner.

Gregory, John ( -1670) Va.; m. Elizabeth Bishop.
Vestryman; Landowner.

Gregory, John ( -1689) Conn.; m. Sarah ---. Selectman; Proprietor.

Gregory, Judah (c1642- ) Mass.; m. Sarah Burt.
Landowner.

Gregory, Richard ( -c1699) Va.; m. ---. Justice.

Gregory, Samuel (1645-1702) Conn.; m. Rebecca
Wheeler. Landowner.

Grele, Philip (1644-1718/19) Me.; m. Sarah Haley.
Freeman; Surveyor.

Griffith, Samuel ( -1717) Md.; m. Elizabeth ---.
Landowner.

Griffith, William ( -1699) Md.; m. Sarah Maccubbin.
Founder; Landowner.

Griffith, William (c1662-1739) Mass.; m. Lydia ---.
Proprietor.

Griggs, Thomas (1585-1646) Mass.; m. Mary ---.
Founder.

Griggs. Thomas (1603-46) Mass.; m. Grace Wells.
Landowner.

Grigsby, John ( -1729) Va.; m. Sarah Rosser.
Landowner.

Grimball, Paul ( -c1696) S.C.; m. Mary Stoney.
Proprietor; Secretary.

Grimes, Charles (1612-60) Va.; m. Rose (Tucker)
Gerrard. Minister.

Grimes, Charles (c1651-1706) Va.; m. Katherine Dedman;
Frances Jennings. Minister.

Grimes, Thomas (1660-1709) Va.; m. Alice Townley;
Sarah Worner. Military service; Burgess.

Grinnalda, Richard (1659-1724) Va.; m. Mary ---.
Constable.

Griswold, Edward (1607-91) Conn.; m. Margaret ---.
Landowner; Representative.

Griswold, Francis (1629/32-71) Conn.; m. Mary Tracy.
Proprietor; Deputy to court.

Griswold, Matthew (1620/98 ) Conn.; m. Anna Wolcott.
Landowner.

Groesbeek, Claas Nicholas (1624-1713 ) N.Y.; m.
Councillor.

Groff    SEE    Graeff

Groome, Peter (    -1726) N.J.; m.  Elizabeth ---.
Landowner.

Groot, Symon Symon (    -c1698) N.Y.; m. Rebecca du
Trieux. Landowner.

Grosvenor, John (1640-91) Mass.; m. Esther Clarke.
Landowner.

Grover, Edmund (1600-82) Mass.; m. Margaret ---.
Proprietor.

Grover, James (c1646-85/86) N.Y.; m. Rebecca or Mary
---. Delegate to court; Military service.

Grubb, John (1652-1708) Pa.; m. Helen Vivian;
Frances Vane. Landowner; Assemblyman.

Grymes    SEE    Grimes

Guerram    SEE    Guerrant

Guerrant, Peter (    -1750) Va.; m. Magdalene Malm.
Landowner.

Guerri    SEE    Guerry

Guerry, Pierre (c1670-1737) S.C.; m. Jeanne Broussard.
Landowner; Vestryman.

Guild, John (1616-45) Mass.; m. Elizabeth Crooke.
Freeman; Landowner.

Guilliam, Pieter Cornellis (    -1666) N.Y.; m. ---.
Military service.

Gulick, Jochem (    -  ) N.Y.; m. Jacomynth Van Pelt.
Landowner.

Gunn, Jasper (1606-71) Conn.; m. Ann ---.  School
  master; Attorney.
Gunn, Thomas (1689-  ) Va.; m. Sarah ---.  Landowner.
Gunnell, William (1630-1700) Va.; m. ---.  Landowner.
Gunnison, Elihu ( 1650-1729) Mass.-Me.; m. Elizabeth
  ---.  Justice; Selectman.
Gurganey, Edward (   -c1619/20) Va.; m. Anne ---.
  Landowner; Assemblyman.
Gustine, John (c1647-1719) Mass.; m. Elizabeth Browne.
  Landowner.
Gutridge   SEE   Goodrich
Guyton, Nathaniel (1669-  ) S.C.; m. ---.  Civil
  office.
Gwyn, Hugh (1618-99) Va.; m. Elizabeth Fielding;
  Ann ---.  Vestryman; Burgess.
Gwyn, Owen (c1580-c1660) Va.; m. Grace Williams.
  Landowner.
Gyles   SEE   Giles

-H-

Hackley, James (1680/85-c1748) Va.; m. Elizabeth
  Shippey.  Landowner.
Hackley, John (c1638-  ) Va.; m. ---.  Landowner.
Hackley, John (c1660-1698) Va.; m. Elizabeth Bowler.
  Landowner.
Hackley, Richard (c1646-  ) Va.; m. Jane Brook.
  Landowner.
Haden,  Anthony (1694-1797) Va.; m. Margaret Douglass.
  Landowner.
Hadley, Dennis (1650-1741) Mass.-N.H.; m. ---.
  Landowner.
Hadley, Simon (1667-1725) Va.; m. Ruth ---.  Land-
  owner; Quaker.
Hadsell, Richard (1622-  ) Mass.; m. Joan Bateman.
  Landowner.
Haggard, James (1677-  ) Va.; m. ---.  Teacher;
  Landowner.
Haines, Margaret (   -1753) N.J.; m. ---.  Landowner.
  Quaker.
Haines, Richard (1665-1746) N.J.; m. Mary Carlile.
  Landowner.

Haines, Samuel (1611-c86) N.H.; m. Eleanor Neate.
Landowner.
Haines, Samuel (1641-88) N.H.; m. Mary Fifield.
Landowner.
Haines, William (1672-1754) N.J.; m. Sarah Paine.
Landowner.
Haines  SEE ALSO  Haynes
Hale, George (1632-98) Va.; m. Ellen Rogers.  Justice.
Hale, Henry (1676-1721/22) Md.; m. Mary Duvall.
Minister.
Hale, Nicholas (    -c1663) Va.; m. Mary Travers.
Burgess; Landowner.
Hale, Robert (    -1659) Mass.; m. Jane (Joanna) ---.
Deacon.
Hale, Samuel (1610-93) Conn.; m. Mary ---.  Military
service; Selectman.
Hale, Samuel (1669/70-  ) Conn.-Mass.; m. Sarah
Haselton.  Military service.
Hale, Thomas (1606-82) Mass.; m. Thomasine Dorsett.
Judge.
Hale, Thomas (1633-88) Mass.; m. Mary Hutchinson.
Military service; Judge.
Hale  SEE ALSO  Heale
Hall, Elihu (1692-1753) Md.; m. ---.  Landowner.
Hall, Jacob (    -  ) Pa.; m. Mary Charlesworth.
Judge; Landowner.
Hall, John (1584-1673) Mass.-Conn.; m. Esther ---.
Founder; Proprietor.
Hall, John (c1605-76) Mass.; m. Jane Woolen.  Select-
man; Military service.
Hall, John (1627-1701) Mass.; m. Elizabeth Green.
Landowner.
Hall, Thomas (1614-c1689) Conn.-N.Y.; m. ---.
Founder; Deputy to court.
Hallett, Samuel (1678-1756) N.Y.; m. Bridgett Black-
well.  Landowner.
Hallock, Peter (1590-  ) N.Y.; m. ---.  Landowner.
Hallowell, John (1650-  ) Pa.; m. Mary Holland.
Constable; Freeman.
Hallowell, Thomas (1621-87) Va.; m. Alice ---.
Landowner.

Hally    SEE    Hawley

Halsey, Thomas (1592-1678) Mass.-Conn.; m. Elizabeth
  Wheeler; Mary ---; Phoebe Banett.  Marshal; Representative.

Halstead, Jonas (  -  ) N.J.; m. ---.  Constable.

Halstead, Timothy (c1640-1703) Conn.; m. Abigail
  Williams.  Selectman.

Ham, William (  -c1672) N.H.; m. Honor ---.  Freeman;
  Selectman.

Hamer, John (c1660-1729) Md.; m. Ann ---.  Landowner.

Hamilton, John (1682-1730) Md.; m. Elizabeth  Burdit.
  Deputy sheriff.

Hamlin, Giles (1622-89) Mass.; m. Hester Crow.  Deputy to court.

Hamlin, Stephen (c1638-c1665) Va.; m. Agnes ---.
  Burgess; Landowner.

Hamlyn    SEE    Hamlin

Hammond, Benjamin (1621-1703) Mass.- N.H.; m. Mary
  Vincent.  Selectman.

Hammond, Charles (c1672-1713) Md.; m. Hannah Howard.
  Assemblyman; Military service.

Hammond, Elizabeth (Payne)(  -c1634/40) Mass.; m.
  William Hammond.  Landowner.

Hammond, Jabez (1679-1786) Mass.; m. Abigail Faunce.
  Landowner.

Hammond, Job (1654-1718) Va.; m. Elizabeth ---.
  Proprietor.

Hammond, John (1643-1707) Md.; m. Mary Howard.
  Justice; Burgess.

Hammond, John (1668-1762) Md.; m. Anne Greenberry.
  Justice; Burgess.

Hammond, John (1690-1779) Va.; m. Catherine Dobbyns.
  Sheriff.

Hammond, Thomas (c1600-c78) Md.; m. ---.  Quaker;
  Landowner.

Hammond, Thomas (1618-55) Mass.; m. Hannah Cross.
  Proprietor.

Hammond, Thomas (1656-1724) Mass.; m. Sarah Pickard.
  Selectman; Military service.

Hammond, Thomas (c1663-1724) Md.; m. Rebecca Larkin.
  Commissioner; Assemblyman.

Hammond, William (1575-1662) Mass.; m. Elizabeth
Payne. Freeman; Proprietor.

Hampton, John (1650-1712) Va.; m. Mary Mann. Military service.

Hampton, Thomas (1621/23-90) Va.; m. ---. Minister.

Hampton, Thomas (1658-1703) Va.; m. Elizabeth Bridell.
Landowner.

Hampton, William (1586-1652) Va.; m. Joan ---.
Landowner.

Hancock, Nathaniel ( -1648) Mass.; m. Joanna ---.
Landowner.

Hancock, Richard ( -1689 ) N.J.; m. Elizabeth Denne.
Surveyor; Justice.

Hancock, Simon ( -1652/54) Va.; m. Sarah ( ) Gayne.
Landowner.

Hancock, Thomas (c1640-97) Va.; m. ---. Landowner.

Hancock, Timothy (c1664-c1713) N.Y.; m. Susannah Ives.
Landowner.

Hancock    SEE ALSO    Handcock

Hand, John (1610-60) N.Y.-Mass.; m. Alice (Stansborough) Gransden. Magistrate; Landowner.

Handcock, William ( -1739) N.C.; m. Elinor ---.
Vestryman; Commissioner.

Handcock    SEE ALSO    Hancock

Haney, William (c1650-c1713 ) Pa.; m. ---. Landowner.

Hanford, Thomas (1624-93) Conn.; m. Mary (Miles)
Ince. Landowner.

Hanks, William (1650-1704) Va.; m. Sarah ---.
Landowner.

Hanna, John (1700-70) Pa.; m. Jane Andre. Landowner.

Hannum, John ( -1730) Pa.; m. Margery Southery.
Landowner; Constable.

Hansen, Hans ( -1704) Md.; m. Martha (Skelton)
Ward. Landowner.

Hansford, Charles ( -1702) Va.; m. Elizabeth Foliot.
Justice.

Hansford, John (1580-1661) Va.; m. Elizabeth ---.
Military service.

Hanson, Samuel (1685-1740) Md.; m. Elizabeth Story.
Commissioner; County clerk.
Hapgood, Shadrack (1642-75) Mass.; m. Elizabeth Tread-
way. Military service.
Haptonstall, Abraham (c1690-c1774 ) N.Y.; m. ---.
Landowner.
Harbour, Thomas (1692-c1778) Va.; m. ---. Landowner.
Harcom, William ( -c1650) Va.; m. Lidia ---.
Physician.
Hardaway, Thomas (c1680-1745) Va.; m. Jane Stith.
Landowner.
Hardenbergh, Gerrit Janse (1639-95) N.Y.; m. Jaepie
Schepegues. Landowner.
Hardewyn   SEE    Hardin
Hardin, Marcus (1681-1734 ) Va.; m. Mary Hogge(Hogue).
Landowner.
Hardin, Martin ( -c1681) N.Y.; m. Madeline DuSauchoy.
Landowner.
Harding, John  (1683-1752) Md.; m. Elizabeth ---.
Landowner.
Harding, Thomas (1639-74) Va.; m. Anne Moseley or
(Elizabeth ---). Landowner.
Harding, Thomas ( -1708) N.J.; m. Eleanor ---.
Physician; Landowner.
Hardwick, James ( -1696) Va.; m. ---. Landowner.
Hardwick, William (1618-68) Va.-Md.; m. Elizabeth
Sturmer. Military service.
Hardy, George (1633-93) N.C.; m. Mary Jackson.
Landowner.
Hardy, John  (1613-70/77) N.C.-Va.; m. Olive Council.
Burgess; Justice.
Hardy, John (1637-77) Va.; m. Alice (Bennett) Johnson.
Burgess, Justice.
Hardy, John ( -1719) N.C.-Va.; m. Rebecca---;
Charity O'Dyer. Landowner.
Hardy, Thomas (1605-78) Mass.; m. Lydia ---.
Landowner.
Hardyman, John ( -1711) Va.; m. Mary Epps. Justice.
Harker, Samuel ( - ) N.J.; m. ---. Military
service.

Harkness, John (1690-1747) Mass.; m. Margaret ---.
Landowner.

Harlan, George (cl650-1714) Pa.-Del.; m. Elizabeth
Duck. Governor; Quaker.

Harlow, William (cl624-91) Mass.; m. Rebecca Bartlett.
Military service.

Harmanson, Thomas (1626-1702) Va.; m. Jeane (Jane)
Andrews. Attorney.

Harmon, John (1617-61) Me.-Mass.; m. Elizabeth ---.
Constable; Supervisor.

Harper, John (   -1714) Pa.; m. ---. Landowner.

Harrell, Abraham (1698-1765) N.C.; m. ---. Juror.

Harriman, John (   -1683) Con.; m. Elizabeth---.
Landowner.

Harriman, Joseph (cl686-1758) N.J.; m. Elizabeth ---.
Landowner.

Harrington, Cornelius (cl693-   )Md.; m. Rachel Jones.
Landowner.

Harrington, Robert (cl616-1707) Mass.; m. Susanna
George. Freeman; Proprietor.

Harris, Adria (Gurganey)(1598-cl626) Va.; m. Thomas
Harris. Landowner.

Harris, Daniel (1618-1701) Mass.; m. Mary Wild.
Founder.

Harris, Edward (1670-1734) Va.; m. Mary Thorpe.
Physician.

Harris, John (1588/89-1638) Va.; m. Dorothy Calcote.
Burgess; Military service.

Harris, John (1605/06-   ) Mass.; m. ---. Freeman.

Harris, John (1651/52-1732) Mass.; m. Grace Searle.
Military service.

Harris, John (1673-1748) Pa.; m. Esther Hickman.
Trader; Landowner.

Harris, Nathaniel (1693-1775) N.J.; m. Miriam Brooks.
Military service.

Harris, Robert (1630-1712) Va.; m. Mary (Claiborne)
Rice. Landowner; Burgess.

Harris, Robert (1680-1765 ) Va.; m. Mourning Glenn.
Landowner.

Harris, Samuel (1695-1770) Mass.; m. Abigail Presbury.
Minister.

Harris, Thomas ( -c1633) Mass.; m. Elizabeth Hills. Landowner.

Harris, Thomas (1612-1697) Mass.; m. Martha Lake; Ruth James. Landowner; Military service.

Harris, Thomas (1587-1658) Va.; m. Adria Osborne; Joane Gurganey. Burgess; Military service.

Harris, Thomas ( -1686) R.I.; m. Elizabeth Leatherland. Commissioner.

Harris, William (1622-78) Va.; m. Lucy Stewart. Burgess; Military service.

Harris, William (c1640-1709) Md.; m. Mary ---. Landowner.

Harris, William (1669-1753) Va..; m. Temperance Overton; Mary ---. Landowner.

Harrison, Andrew (1650-1715) Va.; m. Eleanor Ellitt. Landowner.

Harrison, Anthony ( -1685) Va.; m. Thomasina ---. Landowner.

Harrison, Benjamin (1608-48/49) Va.; m. Mary ---. Burgess; Councillor.

Harrison, Benjamin (1645-1713) Va.; m. Hannah Churchhill. Burgess; Treasurer.

Harrison, Benjamin (1673-1710) Va.; m. Elizabeth Burwell. Landowner; Attorney General.

Harrison, Burt (1637-1706) Va.; m. Mary Smith; Sarah(Francis)Burdette. Burgess.

Harrison, Burt (Burr) (1699-1790) Va.; m. Ann Barnes. Landowner.

Harrison, Cuthbert (1607-80) Va.; m. ---. Landowner.

Harrison, Harmon (c1580/88-c1675) Va.; m. ---Hill. Member of Virginia Company.

Harrison, Isaac ( -1676) Mass.; m. Martha Montague. Landowner.

Harrison, Isaiah (1666-1738) N.Y.-N.J.; m. Elizabeth Wright; Abigail Smith. Proprietor; Landowner.

Harrison, James ( -1712) Va.; m. Elizabeth Mott. Justice; County Clerk.

Harrison, John ( -1683) Conn.; m. Elizabeth ---. Councillor; Treasurer.

Harrison, Joseph (c1686-1758) Conn.; m. ---. Commissioner; Treasurer.

Harrison, Richard (1560-1603) Va.; m. ---. Margaret Pilkington. Landowner.

Harrison, Richard (1600-53) Conn.-N.J.; m. ---. Ancient and Honorable Artillery Company.

Harrison, Richard (1630-77) Md.; m. Elizabeth (Burgess) Smith. Merchant; Landowner.

Harrison, Richard (1650-    ) Va.; m. ---. Landowner.

Harrison, Thomas (1619-82) Va.; m. Katherine Bradshaw. Chaplain

Harrison, Thomas (1665-1785) Md.; m. Jane Delahage. Military service.

Harrison, Thomas (    -1746) Va.; m. Alythea Short or Annie ---. Burgess; Justice.

Harrison, William (1682/83-1742) Va.; m. Hannah Christopher. Landowner.

Harrisperger, Jacob (c1668-1740) S.C.; m. ---. Landowner.

Hart, Edward (1610-c71) N.Y.; m. Margaret ---. Founder, Town Clerk.

Hart, Edward (1685-    ) N.J.; m. Martha ---. Military service.

Hart, Edward (    -1712/13) N.Y.-N.J.; m. Nancy ---; Mary ---. Military service.

Hart, Howard (1610-71) Mass.-Conn.; m. Margaret ---. Founder; Town Clerk.

Hart, John (1651-1714) Pa.-N.J.; m. Susannah Rush; Mary ---. Military service; Assemblyman.

Hart, Stephen (1605-88) Conn.-Mass.; m. Sarah ---. Landowner.

Hart, Stephen (1632-62) Conn.-Mass.) m. Margaret (Smith) Form. Founder; Delegate to Court.

Hart, Thomas (1643/44-1726) Conn.; m. Ruth Hawkins. Justice; Councillor.

Hart, Thomas (c1679-c1755) Va.; m. Susanna Rice. Landowner.

Hartley, Edward (1681-c1744) Pa.; m. Mary ---. Landowner.

Hartsborne, Richard (1638-1722) N.J.; m. Margaret ---. Sheriff; Councillor

Hartshorn, Thomas (1614-83) Mass.; m. Sarah ( ) Landon. Freeman.

Hartwell, William (1613-90) Mass.; m. Jazan ---.
Founder.
Harvey, Daniel (1618-92) Mass.; m. Abigail Andrews.
Selectman.
Harvey, John (1639-1702) N.C.; m. Mary ---.
Governor.
Harvey, Nicholas (c1604-47) Md.; Jane Calvert.
Landowner.
Harvey, Stephen (c1620-71) Md.; m. Sarah Williams.
Burgess; Founder.
Harvey, Thomas (c1612-  ) Va.-N.C.; m. Margaret ---.
Landowner.
Harvey, Thomas (c1665-99) Va.-N.C.; m. Sarah Laker.
Councillor; Governor.
Harvey, William (  -1658) Mass.; N.H.; m. Joan
Hucker; Martha Copp. Churchman; Landowner.
Hasbrouck, Abraham (  -1717) N.Y.; m. Marie Deye.
Assemblyman.
Haseltine, John (1620-90) Va.; m. Joan Auter. Free-
man; Founder.
Haskell, Roger (1613-  ) Mass.; m. Elizabeth Harvey.
Surveyor; Constable.
Haskell, William (1617-93) Pa.; m. Mary Tybbot.
Selectman.
Hassell, James (c1700-79) N.C.; m. Rachel ---.
President of Council.
Hastings, Thomas (1605-85) Mass.; m. Margaret Chamey;
Susanna ---. Freeman.
Hatch, Anthony (1620-1688/89) N.C.; m. Elizabeth ---.
Landowner; Justice.
Hatch, Anthony (1660-1726) N.C.; m. Elizabeth Durant.
Treasurer; Justice.
Hatch, John (  -1681) Md.; m. ---. Member of
London Company.
Hatch, Thomas (1603-63) Mass.; m. Grace ---.
Landowner.
Hatch, William (1598-1657) Mass.; m. Jane Young;
Elizabeth Holbrook. Elder; Surveyor.
Hatcher, Benjamin (1644-1727) Va.; m. Elizabeth
Greenbough. Landowner.

Hatcher, William (1613-78) Va.; m. Mary ---.  Burgess.

Hatchett, John (1680-1747) Va.; m. Elizabeth Bass.
Landowner.

Hathaway, Arthur (c1656-  ) Mass.; m. ---.  Oath of
Fidelity.

Hathaway, John (1629-1705) Mass.; m. Martha Shepherd.
Freeman; Military service.

Hathaway, William (1636-92) Va.; m. ---.  Landowner;
Civil Officer.

Haughton, William (1685-1749) N.C.; m. Mary Luten.
Shipmaster.

Haven, Richard (1620-1703) Mass.; m. Susannah Newhall.
Military service.

Havens, William (1618-83) R.I.; m. Divinia ---.
Landowner.

Hawes, Daniel (1652-1738) Mass.; m. Abiel Gay.  Military service.

Hawes, Daniel (1684-1763) Mass.; m. Beriah Mann.
Landowner.

Hawes, Edward (   -1686) Mass.; m. Elinor Lumbar.
Landowner.

Hawes, Samuel (1695-1753) Va.; m. (Elizabeth) Anne
Spencer.  Freeman.

Hawkins, Anthony (c1620-73/74) Conn.; m. Isabel Brown.
Landowner; Governor's Assistant.

Hawkins, Henry (c1630-99) Md.; m. Elizabeth Wynn.
Burgess.

Hawkins, Holland (1665-1745/46) Md.; m. Joan Greenfield.  Assemblyman.

Hawkins, Richard (1620-c1650) Va.; m. ---.  Landowner.

Hawkins, Samuel (   -   ) Va.; m. Sarah Smith.  Landowner.

Hawkins, Timothy (   -1661) Mass.; m. Hannah Hammond.
Landowner.

Hawkins, William (1609-  ) R.I.; m. Margaret Harwood.
Landowner; Freeman.

Hawks, John (   -1662) Conn.; m. Elizabeth ---.
Freeman.

Hawley, John (1690-1755/56) Md.; m. Easter Burch.
Landowner.

Hawley, Joseph (1605-90) Conn.; m. Catherine Birdsey.
Recorder.

Haworth, George (c1676-1724) Pa.; m. Sarah Scarborough. Landowner.

Hay, John (c1620-   ) Va.; m. Mary Wade. Burgess;
Landowner.

Hay, Peter (1657-1748) Mass.; m. Mary Kibbe. Civil
Officer.

Hayden, Nehemiah (1647-1718) Mass.; m. Hannah Neal.
Military service.

Hayden, William (1600/05-69) Conn.; m. Margaret
Willcoxson. Delegate to court; Military service.

Hayes, John (   -1708) N.H.; m. Mary Horne. Constable.

Hayhurst, Cuthbert (c1633-83) Pa.; m. Mary Rudd.
Proprietor; Minister.

Hayness, John (1594-1653) Mass.-Conn.; m. Mary Har-
lakenden. Governor; Commissioner.

Haynes, John (1621-97) Mass.; m. Dorothy Noyes.
Freeman; Selectman.

Haynes, Rowland (1600-42) Va.; m. ---. Landowner.

Haynes, Thomas (   -1718) Va.; m. ---. Landowner.

Haynes, Walter (1583-1665) Mass.; m. Elizabeth ---.
Selectman; Proprietor.

Haynes    SEE ALSO    Haines

Haynie, John (1625-97) Va.; m. Jane Morris. Justice;
Burgess.

Haynsworth, Richard (c1670-c1712) Va.; m. Margaret
Dyne. Landowner.

Hays, Michael (   -   ) N.Y.; m. ---. Founder.

Hayward, John (   -   ) Va.; m. Margaret ---. Burgess;
Landowner.

Hayworth    SEE    Haworth

Hazard, John (c1693-   ) Va.; m. Frances ---. Landowner.

Hazard, Thomas (1610-80) Conn.; m. Martha ---.
Founder; Magistrate.

Hazen, Edward (1614-83) Mass.; m. Hannah Grant.
Selectman; Judge.

Head, Henry (cl698-1765) Va.; m. Frances Spence.
Landowner.
Head, William ( -1674) Md.; m. Elizabeth ---.
Landowner.
Heale, George (cl650-97/98) Va.; m. Ellen ---.
Justice; Burgess.
Heale, Nicholas ( -1657) Va.; m. Mary ---. Burgess;
Landowner.
Heale, William (cl614-89) N.H.; m. ---. Landowner.
Heard  SEE  Hurd
Hearn, Peter ( -1694) S.C.; m. Joane ---. Member of
Parliament.
Hearne, William (1627-91) Md.; m. Mary ---. Merchant;
Landowner.
Heath, Bartholomew (1610-81) Mass.; m. Hannah Mayes.
Landowner.
Heath, Isaac (1655-84) Mass.; m. --- Fisher. Land-
owner.
Heath, William (cl650-1745) Va.; m. Elizabeth ---.
Landowner.
Heaton, Nathaniel (1610-64) Mass.; m. Elizabeth Wight.
Freeman; Landowner.
Hebard, Robert (1612-84) Mass.; m. Joanna Fairfield.
Landowner.
Hedley, Dennis ( 1650-1741/52) Mass.; m. Joanna
Bullard. Military service.
Helm, Israel (1620-1701) N.J.-Pa.; m. Catherine ---.
Justice.
Helmick, John (1628-  ) Va.; m. ---. Landowner.
Hemingway, Ralph (1613/17-72) Mass.; m. Elizabeth
Hewes; Elizabeth Holbrook. Landowner; Town Clerk.
Hemmenway  SEE  Hemingway
Hempstead, Joshua (1675-1758) Conn.; m. Abigail
Bailey. Justice; Military service.
Henderson, Robert (cl617-cl672) Va.; m. Sarah ---.
Landowner.
Henderson, Samuel (1700-83) Va.; m. Elizabeth
Williams. Sheriff.
Henderson, Thomas (1583-cl619) Va.; m. ---. Judge.
Henderson, Thomas (1634/36-c66) Va.; m. ---.
Landowner.

Henderson, Thomas (    -1799) Va.; m. Sarah Wilkinson.
  Burgess.
Hendricks, Albert (c1640-1714/15) Pa.; m. ---.
  Constable; Supervisor.
Hendricks, Daniel (1610/20-1700) Mass.; m. Dorothy
  (Day) Pike. Freeman; Selectman.
Hendricks, Tobias (    -  ) Pa.; m. ---. Justice.
Hendricksen Sip, Adrian (    -  ) N.J.; m. Geertruje
  Adrain. Landowner.
Hendrixsz,Hendrick (    -1670) N.Y.; m. Anne de Sille.
  Councillor; Magistrate.
Henley,  Robert (c1659-84) Md.; m. ---.   Justice;
  Burgess.
Henley, Thomas (1610/15-58) Va.; m. Elizabeth Reynolds.
  Landowner.
Henry, William (1640-1701) Va.; m. Suzanne ---.
  Landowner.
Henshaw, Joshua (1642-1719) Mass.; m. Mary Elizabeth
  Sumner. Military service.
Herbert, William (1665-c1718) Va.-Md.; m. Mary Lovett.
  Military service.
Hereford, James (c1668-1721) Va.; m. ---. Landowner.
Herndon, Edward (1678-1745) Va.; m. Mary  Waller.
  Landowner.
Herndon, William (1649-1722) Va.; m. Catherine Digges.
  Landowner.
Herrick, Henry (1604-71) Mass.; m. Edith Laskin.
  Military service.
Herrick, Henry (1640-1702) Mass.; m. Lydia Woodbury.
  Constable; Juror.
Herrick, Joseph (1604-  ) Mass.; m. Edith Laskin.
  Representative; Military service.
Herrington  SEE  Harrington
Herman,  Augustine (1605-86) Md.; m. Jannekje Verleth.
  Ambassador.
Herman, Augustine (1630-64) N.Y.; m. ---. Landowner.
Heryford  SEE  Hereford
Hester, Francis (c1662-1720) Va.; m. ---. Founder;
  Freeman.
Het, Rene (    -  ) N.Y.; m. Blanche Dubois. Landowner.

Hew, Peter Lee (1680-   ) Va.; m. ---.  Founder.
Hewes, William (   -1698) Del.-Pa.; m. Deborah ---.
Landowner.
Hewitt, Benjamin (1688-1761) Conn.; m. Ann Palmer.
Landowner.
Hewitt, Thomas (1625-62) Conn.; m. Hannah Palmer.
Landowner.
Hewlett, George (1600-c60) N.Y.; m. ---.  Landowner.
Hewlett, John Lawrence (1595-1658) Va.; m. Ann Marie
Jourdan.  Landowner.
Hewlings   SEE   Hulings
Hewot   SEE   Hewitt
Heyward   SEE   Hayward
Hext, Hugh (   -   ) S.C.; m. ---.  Assemblyman.
Heyden, Jacob Tyssen Von Der (1616-   ) Md.; m. Anna
Hals.  Military service.
Heymon, Henry (c1646-85) Md.; m. Elinor ---.
Landowner.
Heyward, John (   -   ) N.C.-Va.; m. Margaret ---.
Burgess; Landowner.
Heyward, Thomas (1699-1737) S.C.; m. Margaret Wright.
Military service.
Heywood, John (c1612-1707) Mass.; m. Sarah Simonds.
Founder; Constable.
Hibbard, Robert (1613-84) Mass.; m. Jean ---.
Landowner.
Hickman, Elizabeth (1630-98) Pa.; m. Francis Hickman.
Landowner.
Hickman, Francis (   -1685) Pa.; m. Elizabeth ---.
Landowner.
Hickock, Samuel (1687-1745 ) Conn.; m. Sarah Lock-
wood.  Landowner.
Hicks, Robert (1572-1627) Mass.; m. Margaret Winslow.
Founder; Assessor-Treasurer.
Hicks, Robert (1635-1739) Va.; m. Frances ---.
Landowner.
Hicks, William (   -1710) Md.; m. Jane ---.  Land-
owner.
Hiett   SEE   Hyatt
Higbee   SEE   Higby

Higby, Edward  (1615-16-99) Conn.; m. Lydia ---;
Jediah Skidmore. Freeman.

Higdon, Richard (1625-65 ) Va.; m. Jane Brooke.
Attorney; Landowner.

Higgins, Benjamin (1640-90/91) Mass.; m. Lydia Bangs.
Freeman; Military service.

Higgins, Francis (    -   ) Va.; m. Mary ---. Landowner.

Higgins, Richard(1603-1674/75) Mass.; m. Lydia
Chandler. Military service; Council of war.

Higgins, Samuel (1676/77-1761) Mass.; m. Hannah Cole.
Constable; Surveyor.

Higginson, Robert (1610-1649) Va.; m. Joanna Torksy.
Military service.

High, John (1675-1745) Va.; m. Mary ---. Landowner;
Military service.

High, Thomas (1647-88) Va.; m. Hannah ---. Landowner; Military service.

Hightower, John (1695-1764) Va.; m. Mary Bryan.
Landowner.

Higley, John (1647-1714) Conn.; m. Hannah Drake.
Military service; Commissioner.

Hiland, Thomas (    -   ) Mass.; m. Elizabeth ---.
Juror; Proprietor.

Hill, Abraham (1615-1669/70) Mass.; m. ---. Landowner.

Hill, Abraham (c1700-1760) Va.; m. Judith ---.
Military service.

Hill, Henry (1660-1720) Va.; m. Mary ---. Military
service.

Hill, John (1602-64) Mass.; m. Frances ---. Ancient
and Honorable Artillery Company; Selectman.

Hill, Joseph (1602-88) Mass.; m. Rose Clark. Selectman; Deputy to Court.

Hill, Nicholas (c1610-75) Va.; m. Sylvestra Bennett.
Burgess; Military service.

Hill, Robert (1621-77) Va.; m. Mary Webb. Landowner.

Hill, Robert (1642-  ) Va.; m. Mary ---. Landowner.

Hill, Robert (1684-1723) Va.; m. Hannah Briggs;
Mary ---. Landowner.

Hill, Sion (1653/54-   ) Va.; m. --- Green.  Military
service.

Hill, Thomas (1658-1720) Va.; m. Ann Russell.  Military service.

Hill, William (   -1649) Conn.; m. Sarah Jourdain.
Founder; Judge.

Hilleary, Sir  Thomas (1637-97) Va.; m. Elinor Sprigg.
Landowner.

Hilliard, Emanuel (1620-57) N.H.; m. Elizabeth Parkhurst.  Freeman; Landowner.

Hilliard, Timothy (1646-1723) N.H.; m. Orphia Philbrick.  Landowner.

Hills, Joseph (1602-88) Mass.; m. Rose Clarke;
Hannah (Smith) Mellows.  Deputy Speaker.

Hills, William (1608-83) Conn.; m. Phyllis Lyman;
Mary (Warner) Steele; Mary Risley.  Constable;
Landowner.

Hilton, Edward (   -1671) N.H.; m. ---.  Selectman;
Magistrate.

Hilton, William (1628-75) Mass.; m. Rebecca Symmons;
Sarah Greenleaf.  Landowner.

Hinchman, John (c1637-99) N.Y.; m. Elizabeth Emmons.
Proprietor.

Hinckley,  Samuel (1652-97/98) Mass.; m. Sarah Pope.
Landowner.

Hinckley, Samuel (1684-   ) Mass.; m. Mary Freeman.
Landowner.

Hinckley, Thomas (1619-1705/06) Mass.; m. Mercy ---;
Sarah ---; Mary Richards.  Governor.

Hinds, Humphrey (   -   ) Conn.; m. ---.  Landowner.

Hinman, Edward (1609-81) Conn.; m. Hannah(Jennings)
Stiles.  Landowner.

Hinsdale, Robert (   -1675) Mass.; m. Anne Woodward.
Ancient and Honorable Artillery.

Hinton, Sir Thomas (1574-1635) Va.; m. Catherine
Palmer.  Councillor; Member, London  Company.

Hinton,  William (c1620-   ) N.C.; m. ---.  Explorer.

Hitchcock, John (1642-1712) Mass.; m. Hannah Chapin.
Freeman; Deacon.

Hitchcock, John (1650-1716) Conn.; m. Abigail
Morrison.  Proprietor.

Hitchcock, Luke (    -c1659) Conn.; m. Elizabeth
Gibbons.  Selectman.
Hitchcock, Matthias (1610-69) Conn.; m. Elizabeth ---.
Landowner.
Hite, Yost (c1680-1760) N.Y.; m. Anna Marie DuBois.
Judge; Landowner.
Hoagland, Christofiel (1681-1771) N.Y.; m. Adriana
Stoothoff.  Landowner.
Hoar, Hezekiah (1633-93) Mass.; m. Rebekah ---.
Landowner.
Hoar, John (    -1704) Mass.; m. Alice ---.  Military
service.
Hoar, Leonard (1630-75) Mass.; m. Bridget Lisle.
President, Harvard College.
Hobart, Caleb (1633-1711) Mass.; m. Elizabeth Faxon.
Landowner.
Hobart, Edmund (c1570-1646) Mass.; m. Margaret Dewey.
Deputy to Court.
Hobart,  Peter (1604-c1679) Mass.; m. Margaret Dewey;
Elizabeth Ibrook.  Minister.
Hobert   SEE   Hobart
Hobby, John (c1625-1707) Conn.; m. ---.  Landowner;
Deputy to Court.
Hobson, William (    -1659) Mass.; m. Ann Reyner.
Selectman.
Hodgdon, Nicholas (    -  ) Me.; m. Elizabeth (  )
Needham.  Landowner.
Hodges, Charles (1655/65-   ) Conn.; m. Ann ---.
Military service.
Hodges, John (    -1622) Va.; m. Mary ---.  Council
of Safety.
Hodges, John (c1650-1719) Mass.; m. Elizabeth Macey.
Landowner; Military service.
Hodges, Roger (1635-1708) Va.; m. Mary Manning.
Ship owner.
Hodges, W--- (    -c1654) Mass.; m. Mary Andrews.
Landowner.
Hodgkin, John (1648-81) Conn.; m. Mary Bishop.
Landowner; Carpenter.
Hodson   SEE   Hodgden

Hogg, Lewis (1670-1747) Va.; m. Mary Margaret Lindsey.
Landowner.

Hogg, William (1660-1745) Va.-Pa.; m. Barbara Hume.
Founder.

Holbrook, John (1635-   ) Mass.; m. Elizabeth Stream.
Military service; Selectman.

Holbrook, Richard (   -1670) Conn.; m. Agnes ---.
Freeman; Landowner.

Holbrook, Thomas (1601-74/76) Mass.; m. Jane Kingman.
Selectman; Deputy to Court.

Holbrook, Thomas (1624-97) Mass.; m. Joanna Kingman.
Deputy to Court; Military service.

Holcomb, Andrew (   -   ) Va.; m. ---.  Military
service.

Holcomb, Nathaniel (1648-   ) Conn.; m. Mary Bliss.
Representative; Landowner.

Holcomb, Thomas (1597-1657) Conn.; m. Elizabeth
Ferguson.  Deputy to Court; Landowner.

Holcomb, William (   -1680) Va.; m. ---.  Landowner;
Founder.

Holden, Randall (1612-92) R.I.; m. Frances Dundan.
Military service; Councillor.

Holden, Richard (1609-95/96) Mass.; m. Martha Fosdick.
Landowner.

Holden, Simon (1700-86) Mass.; m. Abigail Grover.
Landowner; Military service.

Holden, Stephen (1658/59-1715) Mass.; m. Hannah
Lawrence.  Landowner.

Holden, Stephen (1700-76) Mass.; m. Abigail Graves.
Military service.

Holiday, Thomas (1630-98) Va.; m. ---.  Landowner.

Holiday   SEE ALSO   Holladay

Holladay, Anthony (c1650-1718) Md.; m. Anna ( )
Brewer.  Burgess; Sheriff.

Holladay, John (1675-1742) Va.; m. Elizabeth ---.
Military service; Magistrate.

Holland, Anthony (   -c1702) Md.; m. Isabella Parsons.
Landowner.

Holland, Daniel (   -   ) Va.; m. Joyce ---.  Landowner.

Hollenbeck, Jasper Jacobs (1620-1703) N.Y.; m. ---.
Landowner.
Holliman, Christopher (     -1692) Va.; m. Mary ---.
Landowner.
Hollingsworth, George (     -c1703) Md.; m. ---.
Landowner.
Hollingsworth, Henry (1658-1721) Md.; m. Elizabeth
Atkinson. Surveyor; Sheriff.
Hollingsworth, John (     -1699) N.J.; m. Grace ---.
Constable; Assemblyman.
Hollingsworth, Valentine (c1632-1711) Del.; m. Ann
Rea. Assemblyman.
Hollis, William (1696 -     ) Md.; m. Anna Rhodes.
Landowner.
Hollister, John (c1612-65) Conn.; m. Joanna Trent.
Deputy to Court; Military service.
Holloman, Christopher (c1630-91) Va.; m. Judith or
(Mary)---. Landowner.
Hollowell, Thomas (c1625-87) Va.; m. Alice ---.
Landowner; Quaker.
Holman, James (c1680-1759) Va.; m. Sarah Woodward.
Burgess; Landowner.
Holman, William (1594-1652/53) Mass.; m. Winifred
---. Landowner.
Holmes, David (     -1659) Mass.; m. Joan ---.
Landowner.
Holmes, Edward (1697-1702) N.C.; m. Elizabeth ---.
Landowner.
Holmes, George (1594-1645) Mass.; m. Deborah ---.
Freeman; Landowner.
Holmes, Nathaniel (1639-1711) Mass.; m. Patience
Topliffe. Deputy to Court; Military service.
Holmes, Obediah (1607-82) R.I.; m. Catherine Hyde.
Judge; Councillor.
Holmes, Richard (1667-c95) Mass.; m. Alice ( )
Knight. Landowner.
Holstein, Matthias (Paulsten) (1644-1708) Pa.; m.
---. Landowner.
Holstein, Matthias (1681-c1737) Pa.; m. Britta Rambo.
Landowner.

Holton, William (1611-91) Mass.-Conn.; m. Mary ---.
Founder; Landowner.

Holyoke, Edward (    -1660) Mass.; m. Prudence Stockton.  Freeman; Representative.

Holyoke, Elizur (1633-76) Mass.; m. Mary Pynchon.
Landowner.

Homer, John (1690-1717) Mass.; m. Margery Stevens.
Merchant Marine service.

Hood, Jan (1699-1742) N.Y.; m. Rachel Van Bunschoten.
Constable; Road surveyor.

Hood, Jasper (c1670-  ) N.Y.; m. Catherine Andrees.
Landowner.

Hood, John (    -1721) Pa.; m. Ann ---.  Constable;
Assemblyman.

Hooe, Rice (1598-c1655) Va.; m. Sarah ---; Catherine
Taliaferro.  Burgess; Landowner.

Hooe, Rice (c1661-1726) Va.; m. Frances Townshend.
Justice; Military service.

Hooker, Thomas (c1586-1647) Conn.; m. Susanna Pym;
Susanna Garbrand.  Minister.

Hooper, Henry (    -1676) Md.; m. Sarah ---.  Landowner; Minister.

Hopkins, Arthur (1690-1767) Va.; m. Elizabeth Pettus.
Justice; Sheriff.

Hopkins, Gerard (c1658-1693/94) Md.; m. Thomasine
Eard.  Landowner.

Hopkins, John (1613-54) Mass.; m. Jane Strong.
Freeman; Juror.

Hopkins, Robert (c1625-c1677) Va.; m. Katherine ---.
Landowner.

Hopkins, Stephen (1588-1644) Mass.; m. Elizabeth
Fisher; Ann Dudley.  Councillor; Assistant Governor.

Hopwood, John (1615-  ) Va.; m. Susan Chatterton.
Landowner.

Horry, Daniel (c1660-1696) N.C.-S.C.; m. Elizabeth
Garnier.  Huguenot; Landowner.

Horsmanden, Warham (1627-91) Va.; m. Susannah ---;
or Mary Nevill.  Burgess.

Horton, Barnabus (1600-80) N.Y.-Conn.; m. Mary Lang-
ton.  Magistrate; Constable.

Horton, Hugh ( - ) Va.; m. Mary Snowdall. Land-
owner.
Hosford, William ( -1660) Conn.; m. Jane ( )
Fowkes. Deputy to Court.
Hoskins, John ( -1648) Mass.-Conn.; m. Ann Fiske
or Ann Fyler. Deputy to Court.
Hosmer, James (1605-85) Mass.; m. Ann ---; Mary ---;
Alice ---. Freeman.
Hosmer, James (1637-76) Mass.; m. Sarah White.
Military service.
Hotchkiss, John (1643-89) Mass.; m. Elizabeth Peck.
Landowner.
Hotchkiss, Samuel (c1621-63) Conn.; m. Elizabeth
Clevery. Landowner.
Houchens, Edward (c1661-c1737) Va.; m. Rebecca ---.
Landowner.
Hough, Edward ( - ) N.H.; m. Ann ---. Landowner;
Military service.
Hough, James (1688-1740) Conn.; m. Hannah Clark.
Landowner.
Hough, Richard (1660-1705) Pa.; m. Margery Clawes.
Assemblyman.
Hough, William (1619-83) Mass.; m. Sarah Calkins.
Landowner.
Houghton, Ralph (1623-1706) Mass.; m. Jane Stowe.
Town clerk.
Houghton, William (c1685-1749) N.C.; m. Mary Luten.
Military service.
House, John (1610/14-84) Mass.; m. Annis Peabody.
Freeman; Surveyor.
House, William (1642-1703) Conn.; m. Sarah Bidwell.
Landowner.
Houston, Alfred (1572- ) Va.; m. Ruth Sconse.
Minister.
Houston, John (1688/90-1748/49) Va.; m. Margaret
Cunningham. Landowner.
Houston, Robert ( -c1694) Md.; m. Grace Benson.
Landowner.
Hovey, Daniel (1618-92) Mass.; m. Abigail Andrews.
Selectman.

Howard, Cornelius (1637-1680/90) Md.; m. Elizabeth
Todd. Military service.
Howard, John (    -1696) Md.; m. Susanna (Norwood)
Stevens. Surveyor.
Howard, John (c1615-60) Va.; m. Margaret Clarke.
Burgess; Landowner.
Howard, John (c1621-c1651) Mass.; m. Martha Hayward.
Military service.
Howard, John (1667/68-1704) Md.; m. Katherine Green-
berry) Ridgley. Landowner.
Howard, Joseph (1676-1736) Md.; m. Hannah Dorsey.
Landowner.
Howard, Joshua (1665-86) Md.; m. Joanna O'Carroll.
Landowner.
Howard, Matthew (1609-59) Md.; m. Ann Hall. Land-
owner.
Howard, Matthew (c1640-91) Va.+Md.; m. Sarah Dorsey.
Landowner; Surveyor.
Howe, Abraham (c1603-93) Mass.; m. Hannah Ward.
Freeman; Founder.
Howe, Edward (1575-1639) Mass.; m. Elizabeth ---.
Deputy to Court.
Howe, Isaac (1628-88) Conn.; m. Elizabeth Waterbury.
Landowner.
Howe, Job (    -1705) S.C.; m. Sarah ---.    Commission-
er; Speaker of the House.
Howe, John (1602-80/87) Mass.; m. Mary ---.  Select-
man; Military service.
Howe, John (1630/40-67/75) Mass.; m. Mary ---;
Elizabeth Ward. Landowner; Freeman.
Howe, Samuel (1642-1715) Mass.; m. Martha Bent.
Military service.
Howe, Thomas (1590-1665 ) Mass.; m. Mary Burr.
Landowner.
Howe, Thomas (1656-1733) Mass.; m. Sarah Hosmer.
Selectman; Town Treasurer.
Howell, Andrew (    -  ) Va.; m. Mary Pitt. Landowner.
Howell, Edward (1584-1655) Mass.; m. Frances ---.
Councillor; Deputy to Court.
Howell, Edward (    -1699) N.Y.; m. Mary ---. Land-
owner.

Howell, James (c1646/56-1706) Del.; m. ---. Land-
owner.
Howell, John (1624-96) N.Y.; m. Susannah ---. Land-
owner.
Howell, John (c1660-   ) Pa.; m. Mary Williamson.
Landowner.
Howell, John (c1690-1737) Va.; m. ---. Landowner.
Howell, Joseph (   -1749/50) N.C.-Md.; m. Elizabeth
---; Margaret ---. Assemblyman; Justice.
Howell, Matthew (   -1728) Va.; m. Mary Lane.
Military service.
Howerton, William (c1650-98) Va.; m. ---. Burgess;
Landowner.
Howland, Henry (   -1671) Mass.; m. Mary Newland.
Juror; Landowner.
Howland, John (1592-1672) Mass.; m. Elizabeth Tilley.
Mayflower Compact.
Hoyt, John (1610/15-87/88) Mass.; m. Frances ---.
Proprietor.
Hoyt, Walter (1616-98) Conn.; m. Rhoda ( ) Taylor.
Selectman.
Hubbard, George (1591-1684) Conn.; m. Mary Bishop;
Elizabeth Watts. Deputy to Court.
Hubbard, John (1664-1747) Mass.; m. Elizabeth Stevens;
Mary Brown. Surveyor of Highways.
Hubbard, Richard (c1631-61) Mass.; m. Sarah Bradstreet.
Deputy to Court.
Hubbard, Robert (1613-84) Mass.; m. Jean ---.
Landowner.
Hubbard, Samuel (1610-58) Conn.; m. Tracy Cooper.
Founder of a church.
Hubbard, William (c1595-1670) Mass.; m. Judith Knapp.
Freeman; Minister.
Hubbell, Richard (1627-99) Conn.; m. Elizabeth Meigs.
Deputy to Court.
Hubbell, Samuel (   -   ) Conn.; m. Elizabeth ---.
Landowner.
Hudspeth, Ralph (c1660-1718) Va.; m. Margaret Eyres.
Landowner.
Hughes, William (1670-c1770) Pa.; m. ---. Landowner.

Hulet    SEE    Hewlett

Hulick, Jochem (1650-1723) N.Y.; Jacomynete Van
Pelt.  Landowner; Military service.

Huling, Lars (c1610-c34) Pa.; m. ---.  Landowner.

Huling, William (1657-1713) N.J.; m. Dorothy Eves.
Proprietor.

Hull, Benjamin (c1639-1713) Mass.-N.J.; m. Rachel
Yorke.  Judge; Tax collector.

Hull, Cornelius (1626-95) Conn.; m. Rebecca Jones.
Landowner; Deputy to Court.

Hull, George (1590-1659) Conn.; m. Thomasina Mitchell.
Freeman; Deputy to Court.

Hull, Joseph (1594-1665) Mass.; m. Joanna ---; Agnes
---.  Military service; Minister.

Hull, Richard (c1610-62) Conn.; m. ---.  Assemblyman.

Hull, Tristram (c1624-66) Mass.-Conn.; m. Blanche ---.
Sea Captain; Selectman.

Hulme, George de (c1650-1714) Pa.; m. Ellen ---.
Landowner.

Hume, George (1698-1760) Va.; m. Elizabeth Proctor.
Surveyor; Military service.

Humphrey, Elizabeth (Rees) (  -  ) Pa.; m. Samuel
Humphrey.  Landowner.

Humphrey, Lydia (   -1685) Pa.; m. Ellis Ellis.
Landowner.

Humphrey, Michael (1620-95) Conn.; m. Priscilla
Grant.  Landowner.

Humphrey, Samuel (   -c1682) Pa.; m. Elizabeth Rees.
Landowner.

Humphrey, Samuel (1656-1736) Conn.; m. Mary Mills.
Landowner.

Humphreys, Walter (   -1698 ) N.J.; m. Mary Osborne.
Landowner.

Humphreys, William (1610-87) Va.; m. ---.  Civil
Officer.

Hungerford, Sir Thomas (1602-63) Conn.; m. Hannah
Willey.  Landowner; Constable.

Hungerford, Thomas (1648-1714) Conn.; m. Mary Green.
Landowner.

Hungerford, William Bartholomew (1640-97) Conn.; m.
Mary Johnson. Military service.

Hunnewell, Richard (1645-1703) Me.; m. Elizabeth
(Stover) Sylvester. Military service.

Hunnewell, Roger (c1600-54) Me.; m. Elizabeth Stover.
Military service.

Hunt, Ephraim (1610-87) Mass.; m. Anne Richards.
Military service.

Hunt, Ralph (c1613-77)  Conn.-N.Y.; m. Elizabeth
Jessup. Freeman; Magistrate.

Hunt, William (1599-c1676) Va.; m. Tabitha Edloe.
Physician.

Hunter, Samuel (1675-1724) Md.; m. Lettice ---.
Landowner.

Hunter, William (c1650-c1720) Va.; m. Elizabeth ---.
Justice; Landowner.

Hunting, John (   -1688) Mass.; m. Easter Seabourne.
Freeman; Elder.

Huntington, Christopher (1624-91) Conn.; m. Margaret
Baret; Ruth Rockwell. Military service.

Huntington, Margaret (Baret) (  -  ) Mass.; m.
Christopher Huntington. Landowner.

Huntington, Simon (1629-1707) Conn.; m. Sarah Clark.
Deputy to Court.

Huntington, Thomas (c1629-88) N.J.; m. --- Swayne;
Hannah ---.  Founder; Assemblyman.

Huntley, William (c1670-1708) Pa.; m. Mary ---.
Landowner.

Hurd, John (  -  ) Va.; m. Margaret ---. Landowner.

Hurd, John (1640-  ) Conn.; m. ---. Civil engineer.

Hurd, Luke (c1630-47) Mass.; m. Sarah Wyatt. Landowner.

Hurlbut, Thomas (1684-1771) Conn.; m. Sarah ---.
Landowner.

Hurst, John (   -1724) Va.; m. Mary ---. Landowner.

Huskins, Thomas (1617-79) Mass.; m. Mary Wells; Rose
( ) Hillier. Selectman; Ancient and Honorable
Artillery Company.

Hussey, Christopher (c1597-1686) N.H.; m. Theodora
Batchelder. Selectman; Military service.

Hussey, John (1635-c1711) N.H.-Del.; m. Rebecca
Perkins. Assemblyman; Minister.
Hussey, Mary (Wood) (1575-1650/57) N.H.; m. John
Hussey. Landowner.
Husted, Angel (1620-1706) Conn.; m. Rebecca Sherwood.
Landowner.
Husted, Robert (1595-1653) N.Y.; m. Elizabeth Miller.
Landowner.
Hutchens   SEE   Hutchins
Hutchings, John V. (1691-1768) Va.; m. Amy Godfrey.
Burgess; Mayor.
Hutchings, Richard (c1660-1712) Va.; m. Jane ---.
Landowner.
Hutchins, Francis (   -1698) Md.; m. Elizabeth ---;
Mary ---. Justice; Assemblyman.
Hutchins, John (1604-74) Mass.; m. Frances ---.
Founder.
Hutchins, Nicholas (   -   ) Va.; m. Polly Strangeman.
Landowner.
Hutchinson, Ann (Marham) (1591-1643) Mass.; m.
William Hutchinson. Landowner.
Hutchinson, Richard (1602-c82) Mass.; m. Alice
Bosworth. Surveyor; Landowner.
Hutchinson, Thomas (c1640-89) N.J.-N.Y.; Dorothy
Storr. Founder; Proprietor.
Hutchinson, William (1586-1642) Mass.-R.I.; m.
Anne Marbury. Freeman; Governor.
Hutchinson, William (1698-   ) N.J.; m. Ann Simpson.
Justice.
Huxford, Thomas (1638-   ) Mass.; m. Esther Norton.
Landowner.
Huxley, Thomas (   -1721) Conn.; m. Sarah Spencer.
Freeman; Military service.
Huyck, Jan Hans (1600-54) N.Y.; m. Lizabeth Pieters.
Merchant; Landowner.
Hyatt, John (1674-1726 ) Pa.; m. Mary Smith. Land-
owner; Quaker.
Hyde, Jonathan (1626-1711) Mass.; m. Mary French.
Military service.
Hyde, William (1597-1681/82) Conn; m. Joanna ( )
Abell. Founder; Proprietor.

Hyland, Samuel (1700- ) Mass.; m. Mary Tampton.
  Founder.

## -I-

Ice, Frederick (1700-c1788) Va.; m. Eleanor ( )
  Lewiston. Landowner.
Ijams, William ( -1703) Md.; m. Elizabeth Cheney.
  Original land grant.
Ilsley, William (1608-81) Mass.; m. Barbara Pope.
  Churchman.
Ingalls, Edmund (1598-1648) Mass.; m. ---. Founder.
Ingalls, Henry (1627-1718/19) Mass.; m. Ann ---.
  Freeman; Landowner.
Ingersoll, John (1640-95) N.Y.; m. Jane Skidmore.
  Landowner.
Ingersoll, John (1674- ) N.Y.; m. ---. Landowner;
  Military service.
Ingram, John (c1600-54) Va.; m. Jane ---. Juror;
  Landowner.
Inman, Robert ( -1702) Va.; m. Mary ---. Service
  in Indian wars.
Innis, James ( -1690) Pa.; m. ---. Physician.
Irby, Edmund (c1665-1733) Va.; m. Elizabeth Douglas.
  Landowner.
Irish, Nathaniel (c1650-1730) N.J.; m. Sarah Newhall.
  Justice.
Irish, Nathaniel (1680-1749) N.J.-Pa.; m. Lydia
  Cadwalader. Justice.
Ironmonger, Samuel ( -1630) Va.; m. Bridget Cord-
  ray. Landowner.
Ironmonger, Thomas (c1650-1724) Va.; m. Mary Scales.
  Councillor.
Ironmonger, William (1629-95) Va.; m. Elizabeth Jones.
  Landowner.
Isaac, Richard (1679-1759) Md.; m. Sarah Pottenger.
  Landowner.
Isham, Henry (1628-77) Va.; m. Catherine (Banks)
  Royall. Landowner; Military service.
Isham, John (1654-1713) Mass.; m. Jane Parker.
  Proprietor.
Isler, William (c1690- ) N.C.; m. Hester Williams.
  Military service.

Ives, John (1578-1684) Mass.; m. ---. Vice-Admiral.
Ives, William (1607-48) Conn.-Mass.; m. Hannah ---.
Military service.
Ivey, George (1604-51) Va.; m. Ann Argent. Landowner.
Ivey, George (1638/40-89) Pa.-Va.; m. Hannah Blanch.
Landowner.
Ivory, Nicholas ( - ) Va.; m. ---. Landowner.
Ivy  SEE  Ivey

-J-

Jackman, James (1618-94) N.H.; m. Jemima ---. Free-
man; Landowner.
Jackson, Edward (c1602-81) Mass.; m. Frances ---.
Deputy to Court.
Jackson, Ephraim (1658-1733) Pa.; m. Rachel Newlin.
Landowner.
Jackson, Henry (1606-86) Conn.; m. ---. Freeman;
Landowner.
Jackson, John (1600-66) N.H.; m. Joan ---. Selectman;
Juror.
Jackson, John (1645-1725) N.Y.; m. Elizabeth (Seaman)
Hallet. Councillor; Military service.
Jackson, Samuel (c1619-82) Mass.; m. Esther Sealis.
Freeman; Member Plymouth Company.
Jackson, Samuel (1645-1712) Conn.; m. Jediah ---.
Landowner.
Jackson, Thomas ( -1636/42) Md.; m. ---. Landowner;
Founder.
Jackson, William ( - ) Va.; m. ---. Landowner;
Military service.
Jacob, John (1629/31-1726) Md.; m. Anne Cheney.
Landowner; Justice.
Jacob, Nicholas ( -1657) Mass.; m. Mary Gilman.
Freeman; Selectman.
Jacob, Richard (1645-66) Va.; m. ---. Landowner.
Jaconsen, Aertse ( - ) N.Y.; m. Annetje Gerritts.
Landowner.
Jagger, Jeremiah (1606/10-59) Conn.; m. Elizabeth ---.
Military service.

James, Aaron (   -   ) Pa.; m. Elizabeth Fieldhouse.
Landowner.
James, James (   -1769) Pa.; m. Sarah Mitcher.
Landowner.
James, John (   1696) Va.; m. Sarah Taylor. Surveyor; Landowner.
James, Thomas (1595-1683) Mass.; m. Olive Ingoldsby.
Minister; Freeman.
James, Walter (c1630/32-   ) Va.; m. ---. Landowner.
Jameson, James (c1700-1736/42) Va.; m. Margaret ---.
Constable.
Jamison, James (1650-1720) Pa.; m. ---. Military
service.
Jamison, John (1680-1736) Va.; m. Margarite ---.
Landowner; Military service.
Janes, William (1610-90) Mass.; m. Hannah Bascom.
Recorder; Teacher.
Janes, William (1654-90) Conn.-Mass.; m. Hannah
Broughton. Minister; Teacher.
Janny, Thomas (1634-76) Pa.; m. Margery Heath.
Justice; Councillor.
Jans, Annetje (1605-65) N.Y.; m. Roeloff Janse.
Landowner.
Janse, Roeloff (   -1638) N.Y.; m. Annetje Jans.
Landowner.
Jansen deMandeville, Gillis (   -c1683)N.Y.;m. Altie
Pieterst Hendrich. Landowner.
Jaques, Henry (1617-86) Mass.; m. Anna Knight.
Committeeman; Constable.
Jarman, John (1680-   ) Md.-N.C.; m. ---. Landowner.
Jarman, Robert (c1685-1761) Md.; m. Mary Mead.
Landowner.
Jarnette SEE deJarnette
Jarratt, Devereux (1700-60) Va.; m. Elizabeth ---.
Landowner.
Jarratt, Robert (1625/27-1709) Va.; m. Mary ---.
Military service.
Jarratt, Thomas (c1635-c1700) Va.; m. ---. Military
service.
Jarrett SEE Jarratt

Jarvis, George Wookey (1610-98) Mass.-N.Y.; m. Rebecca Cornell.  Landowner.

Jarvis, Samuel (1698-1779) N.Y.; m. Naomi Brush. Military service.

Jaudon, Sarah (Bertonneau)(Michaud)(   -c1696) S.C.; m. Elie Jaudon.  Huguenot; Landowner.

Jayne, William (1618-1714) N.Y.-Conn.; m. Ann (Jennings) Biggs.  Landowner; Military service.

Jefferson, John (   -   ) Va.; m. ---.  Landowner; Councillor.

Jefferson, Thomas (c1650-1697) Va.; m. Mary Branch. Councillor.

Jefferson, Thomas (1679-1725) Va.; m. Mary Field. Justice; Sheriff.

Jenkins, David (   -   ) Pa.; m. Margaret Rees. Landowner.

Jenkins, Edward (1643-99) Mass.; m. Lettie ( ) Hanford.  Representative.

(Ap) Jenkins, Thomas (1642-1727) Md.; m. Ann Spaulding.  Landowner.

Jenks, Jonathan (1688-  ) R.I.; m. Mary Slack. Landowner.

Jenks, Joseph (1603-83)Mass.; m. Mary Terwyn.  First iron works.

Jenks, Joseph (1632-1717) R.I.; m. Esther Ballard. Founder.

Jenks, Nathaniel (1662-1723) Mass.-R.I.; m. Hannah Bosworth.  Military service.

Jenne, John (c1585-1644) Mass.; m. Sarah Carey. Landowner.

Jennery, Lampert (c1593-1674) Mass.; m. Thomasin Hewes.  Freeman.

Jenness, Francis (1634-1716) N.H.; m. Hannah Swain. Landowner.

Jennings, Charles (c1649-1710) N.C.; m. Mary ---. Clerk of Court.

Jennings, Charles (1680-  ) N.C.; m. Jane Lattimore. Landowner.

Jennings, Edmund (c1659-1720) Va.; m. Frances Corbin. Attorney-General.

Jennings, Henry (1642-1705) Pa.; m. Margaret Bussie.
Landowner.
Jennings, John(c1620-1685/86) Conn.; m. Ann Youngs.
Landowner.
Jennings, Jonathan (1653-1733) Conn.; m. Susannah ---.
Landowner.
Jennings, Joshua (c1620-75) Conn.; m. Mary Williamson.
Landowner.
Jennings, Samuel (1640-1706/09) N.J.; m. Ann Ollive.
Acting Governor; Proprietor.
Jennings, William (1625-90) Va.; m. ---. Landowner.
Jennings, William (1676-1775) Va.; m. Mary Jane
Pulliam. Military service.
Jepson, John (1610-   ) Mass.; m. Emma Coddington.
Landowner; Military service.
Jerauld, Jacques (c1680-1760) Mass.; m. Martha Dupuis.
Physician; Landowner.
Jernigan, Thomas (c1645-c1704) N.C.; m. ---. Land-
owner.
Jessup, John (c1600-   ) Conn.; m. Mary ---. Land-
owner.
Jett, Peter (1630/33-88) Va.; m. Mary Triplett.
Landowner.
Jewett, Joseph (1609-60/61) Mass.; m. Mary Mallison.
Freeman; Founder.
Jewett, Joseph (1654-1735) Mass.; m. Rebecca Law.
Freeman; Military service.
Jewett, Maximillion (1607-84) Mass.; m. Ann ---.
Freeman; Deputy to Court.
Jewett, Nehemiah (1643-1719/20) Mass.; m. Exercise
Pierce. Speaker of House, Justice.
Jobe, Andrew (1650-1722) N.H.-Pa.; m. Elizabeth Ver-
non. Sheriff.
Johns, Richard (1639-1703) Va.; m. Elizabeth Kensey.
Proprietor; Burgess.
Johnson, Anthony (1688-1721) Md.; m. Catherine Smith.
Landowner.
Johnson, Daniel (   -1715) Md.; m. Frances ---.
Landowner.
Johnson, Edward (1598-1672) Mass.; m. Susan Munnter.
Ancient and Honorable Artillery Company.

Johnson, Isaac (1616/17-75) Mass.; m. Elizabeth
  Porter.  Ancient and Honorable Artillery Company.
Johnson, John (c1590-1659) Conn.-Mass.; m. Margery
  Scudder; Grace (Negus) Fawer.  Freeman; Juror.
Johnson, John (1674/80-1711) Va.; m. Lucretia Massie.
  Military service; Landowner.
Johnson, Jonathan (c1696-1769) Va.; m. Priscilla
  Tignor.  Juror.
Johnson, Josiah (1669-1739) Mass.; m. Martha Whitmore;
  Deborah(Fifield) Jackson.  Selectman.
Johnson, Sir Nathaniel (c1645-1713) S.C.; m. ---.
  Governor.
Johnson, Richard (c1612-66) Mass.; m. Alice ---.
  Freeman;  Constable.
Johnson, Richard (1627-99) Va.; m. Susannah Duncombe.
  Councillor.
Johnson, Thomas (c1699-   ) Md.-Va.; m. Ann Jennings.
  Governor.
Johnson, William (1622-1704) Mass.-Va.; m. Esther
  Wiswell.  Military service.
Johnston,  Edward (c1638-1705) Va.; m. Elizabeth
  Walker.  King's Commissioner.
Johnston, Thomas (1670-1751/52) N.C.; m. ---.
  Justice.
Johnston, William (1697-1796) Va.; m. Ann Chew.
  Burgess.
Johnstone, John (c1660-1732) N.J.; m. ---.  Landowner.
Jones, Edward (c1640-90) Va.; m. ---.  Landowner.
Jones, Edward (c1670-1731) N.C.; m. Abigail Shugan.
  Landowner.
Jones,  Ellis (c1637-   ) Pa.; m. Jane ---.  Landowner.
Jones, James (1640/47-1719) Va.; m. Sarah ---.
  Landowner.
Jones, John (1593-1665) Mass.-Conn.; m. Sarah ---.
  Minister.
Jones, John (   -1708) Pa.; m. Ann Prichard;
  Margaret ---.  Landowner.
Jones, Matthew (c1600-82) Va.; m. Elizabeth Albright-
  on.  Burgess.
Jones, Orlando (1680-1719) Va.; m. Martha Macon.
  Burgess.

Jones, Peter (1630/35-c87)Va.; m. Margaret Wood.
  Military Service; Landowner.
Jones, Richard (1607-65) Va.; m. Jane ---. Landowner.
Jones, Richard (1665-1747) Va.; m. Amy Batte. Mili-
  tary service.
Jones, Richard (1670-   ) Conn.; m. ---. Proprietor.
Jones, Robert (c1620-76) Va.; m. Sarah Frances
  Burdette. Military service.
Jones, Robert (c1633-c1706) Mass.; m. Joanna Osgood.
  Military service.
Jones, Roger(1640-1701) N.C.-Va.; m. Dorothy Walker.
  Ship captain.
Jones, Rowland (1644-94) Va.; m. Elizabeth Bicknor;
  Ann Lang. Minister.
Jones, Samuel (1630-66) Conn.; m. Mary Bushnell.
  Military service.
Jones, Thomas (c1635-75) Va.; m. Mary Rapps. Land-
  owner.
Jones, Walter (   -1697) Md.; m. Alice ---. Survey-
  or; Councillor.
Jones, William (1610-90) Conn.; m. Hannah Barlowe.
  Founder; Landowner.
Jones, William (   -1705) Md.; m. Elizabeth ---.
  Justice; Magistrate.
Joor, Joseph (c1670-1720) S.C.; m. ---. Military
  service.
Jordan, Arthur (1629-98) Va.; Elizabeth Bevin, (Bar-
  win or Barwill). Landowner.
Jordan, Arthur (1677-1751) Va.; m. Sarah ---.
  Landowner.
Jordan, George (1654-1715) Va.; m. Mary ---. Land-
  owner.
Jordan, Robert (1611-79) N.H.-Me.; m. Sarah Winter.
  Deputy President; Commissioner.
Jordan, Samuel (c1578-1624/25) Va.; m. Cecilly
  Reynolds. Landowner.
Jordan, Thomas (1600-44) Va.; m. Lucy Corker. Burgess;
  Landowner.
Jordan, Thomas (1634-99) Va.; m. Margaret Brasseur.
  Burgess.

Jorvis   SEE   Jarvis

Joslin, Nathaniel (1627-94) Mass.; m. Sarah King.
Covenant for town; Landowner.

Joslin, Thomas (1591-1661) Mass.; m. Rebecca Marlowe.
Proprietor.

Journesy, Maynard (Meynard) (1630/40-78) N.Y.; m.
Lysbeth Dumon (Dumont). Military service.

Joy, Thomas (c1611-78) Mass.; m. Joan Gallop.
Architect.

Joyner, Nathan (1685/90-1770) N.C.; m. Ann ---.
Selectman.

Judd, Thomas (1608-88) Mass.-Conn.; m. Ann ---;
Clemence Mason. Freeman; Founder.

Judson, Joseph (1619-90) Conn.; m. Sarah Porter.
Military service; Deputy to Court.

-K-

Kasselburgh   SEE   Castlebury

Kay, James (c1635-89) Va.; m. Sarah Ivason. Justice;
Landowner.

Kearney, Barnaby (   -1735/37) Va.; m. Elizabeth
Godwin. Justice; Sheriff.

Keaton, Henry (c1670-1716/18) N.C.; m. ---. Landowner.

Keeler, Joseph (1682-1757) Conn.; m. Elizabeth
Whitney. Landowner.

Keeler, Ralph (1613-72) Conn.; m. Sarah Whelpley.
Landowner.

Keeler, Samuel (1655-1713) Conn.; m. Sarah St. John.
Landowner.

Keeling, Thomas (1608-65) Pa.-Va.; m. Ann ---. Military service.

Keene, John (1657-1723) Md.; m. Mary Hopewell.
Justice; Military service.

Keene, Matthew (c1659-1730/31) Va. m. Bridget ---.
Landowner.

Keene, Richard (1623-75) Md.; m. Mary ( ) Hodkins.
Landowner.

Keene, Thomas (1593-1662/63) Va.; m. Margie Thorley.
Landowner.

Keeney, Joseph (1666-   ) Conn.; m. Hannah Hills.
Landowner.

Keeter, Nicholas Melchertse (1675-   ) N.Y.; m. Jane
Vandermark. Military service.

Keim, Johannes (1675-1753) Pa.; m. ---. Landowner.

Keith, Alexander (c1681-1721) Md.; m. Christian
Farquahar. Juror; Landowner.

Keith, George (1638-1715) Pa.-Va.; m. Elizabeth
Johnston. Minister.

Kellam, Richard (1619-1703) Va.; m. Sarah ---.
Landowner.

Kellogg, Daniel (1630-88) Conn.; m. Bridget Bouton.
Selectman.

Kellogg, Joseph (1626-1707) Conn.; m. Joanna Foote;
Abigail Torry. Selectman; Military service.

Kellogg, Samuel (1630-1711) Mass.; m. Sarah (Day)
Gubb. Landowner; Petitioner.

Kelsey, William (c1601-80) Conn.; m. Bethia Hopkins.
Deputy to Court.

Kemball    SEE    Kimball

Kemp, Robert (1648-1702) Md.; m. Elizabeth Webb.
Landowner.

Kemper, Johann George (1672-1754) Va.; m. Ailsa
Utterback. Landowner.

Kemper, John (1635-70) Va.; m. Anna Law. Military
service.

Kendall, Francis (1620-1708) Mass.; m. Mary Tidd.
Landowner; Military service.

Kendall, William (1600-86) Va.; m. Sarah ( ) Mathews.
Burgess; Military service.

Kendrick, John (1670-1715) Va.; m. ---. Landowner.

Kennard, Nathaniel (1694/96-1742) Md.; m. Jane ---.
Landowner.

Kennard, Richard (c1663-98) Md.; m. Mary(Pullen)
Howell. Landowner.

Kennedy, William (c1660-c1700) Pa.; m. Mary ---.
Landowner.

Kenner, Richard (1650-96) Va.; m. Elizabeth Worsham.
Burgess; Justice.

Kenniston, John (c1615-77) N.H.; m. Agnes ---.
Landowner; Military service.

Kennon, Richard (1619/20-1696) Va.; m. Elizabeth
Worsham. Justice.

Kenrick, John ( -1686) Mass.; m. Ann Smith. Freeman; Constable.

Kent, Richard ( -1654) Mass.; m. Emma ---. Freeman; Attorney.

Kern, William ( - ) Pa.; m. Maria Margaret ---.
Landowner.

Kerr, James (1686-1770) Va.; m. Jane Robinson (or)
Gordon. Founder.

Kester, Elizabeth (Cassell) (1639-c91) Pa.; m. ---.
Landowner.

Kester, Gertrude (Streyper) ( -1707) Pa.; m. Paul
Kester. Landowner.

Ketcham, Edward (1590/98- ) Mass.; m. Sarah ---.
Freeman; Landowner.

Keter, Melchior Claessen (1645-1721) N.Y.; m. Susan
(Verplank) Richards. Military service.

Kettle, Richard (1609-80) Mass.; m. Esther Ward.
Landowner.

Keurlis, Peter ( - ) Pa.; m. Elizabeth ---.
Landowner.

Kewilis    SEE    Keurlis

Key, John (1674-1700) Va.; m. Martha Tandy. Landowner.

Key, Moses (c1675-1758) Pa.; m. Elizabeth Yearsey.
Assemblyman; Landowner.

Keyes, Robert ( -1647) Mass.; m. Sarah ---.
Landowner.

Keyser, Dirck Gerritz (1635-1714) N.Y.-Pa.; m.
Elizabeth Hempel. Minister.

Kezar, John (1651-96/97) Mass.; m. Hanna Davis.
Military service.

Kibbe, Elisha (1643-1735) Conn.; m. Rachel Cooke;
Mary Partridge. Landowner.

Kidder, James (1626-76) Mass.; m. Anne Moore. Military service.

Kierstede, Hans (c1612-66) N.Y.; m. Sara Roeloffe.
Physician.

Kilbourne, Ebenezer (1665-1711) Conn.; m. Grace
Bulkey. Military service.

Kilbourne, John (1624-1703) Conn.; m. Naomi ---;
Sarah Bronson. Tax collector.
Kilbourne, Thomas (1573-1639) Conn.; m. Frances ---.
Proprietor; Landowner.
Killam (Killiam) Samuel (c1598-  ) Mass.; m. Alice
Goodale. Landowner.
Killiam   SEE   Killam
Killingworth, William (   -1709) Va.; m. Avis ---.
Landowner.
Kimball, Benjamin (1637-95) Mass.; m. Mercy Hazel-
tine. Military service; Juror.
Kimball, John (1631-98) Mass.; m. Mary Bradstreet.
Landowner.
Kimball, John (1645-1714) Mass.; m. Hannah Bartlett.
Deputy to Court.
Kimball, Richard (c1595-1676) Mass.; m. Ursula Scott.
Freeman; Proprietor.
Kimball, Samuel (c1651-1716) Mass.; m. Mary Witt.
Military service.
Kimball, Thomas (1633-76) Mass.; Mary ( ) Smith.
Constable; Selectman.
Kimberly, Thomas (1604-72) Conn.; m. Alice Atwood.
Military service.
Kimbrough, John (1654-1716) Va.; m. Margaret Berke-
ley; --- Douglas. Justice; Landowner.
Kincheloe, Cornelius (1650-1724) Va.; m. --- Williams.
Landowner.
Kincheloe, Cornelius (1670-1746) Va.; m. ---.
Landowner.
Kinchen, William (   -   ) N.C.; m. ---. Magistrate;
Sheriff.
Kinchen, William (c1681-1735) Va.; m. Elizabeth
Ruffin. Landowner; Sheriff.
King, Clement (c1693-   )Mass.-R.I.; m. Elizabeth
---. Constable.
King, Henry (c1650-1714) Va.; m. Katherine ---.
Landowner.
King, John (1600-70) Mass.-Conn.; m. Mary Bainbridge.
Treasurer; Military service.
King, John (1640-1703) Mass.; m. Sarah Hatton.
Military service.

King, Michael (   -c1673) Va.; m. Elizabeth ---.
Military service.
King, Robert (1636-80) Va.; m. Hannah Scarborough.
Military service.
King, Thomas (1595/1600-1676) Mass.; m. Anne Collins.
Military service.
King, William (1595-1650) Mass.; m. Dorothy Hayne.
Landowner.
King, William (1650-1716) Va.; m. Judith Payton.
Military service.
Kingman, Henry (1595-1666) Mass.; m. Joane ---.
Proprietor; Landowner.
Kingsbury, Ephraim (1681-1756) Conn.; m. Phebe Main.
Military service; Deputy to Court.
Kingsbury, Henry (1615-87 ) Mass.; m. Susannah ---.
Landowner.
Kingsbury, Joseph (1656-c1676) Mass.-Conn.; m.
Milicent Ames; Love Ayer.  Landowner.
Kingsley, John (c1635-78/79) Mass.; m. Olive Jones.
Signer of covenant; Freeman.
Kinnicutt, Roger (c1640-96) Mass.; m. Joanna Shepard-
son.  Military service.
Kirby, John (1623/24-77) Conn.; m. Elizabeth Hinds.
Landowner.
Kirby, Joseph (1610/14-  ) Conn.; m. Margaret ---.
Founder.
Kirk, John (1660-1705) Pa.; m. Joan Ellet.  Con-
stable.
Kirkham, Thomas (1646-77) Conn.; m. ---.  Tax
collector.
Kirkham, Thomas (   -  ) Conn.; m. Jane ---.
Constable.
Kirtley, Francis (1690-1763) Va.; m. Margaret
Roberts.  Military service; Landowner.
Kissam, John (1644-c1695) N.Y.; m. Susannah Thorne.
Landowner.
Kittredge, John (   -1676) Mass.; m. Mary Little-
field.  Founder.
Klingensmith, Joseph (   -  ) Pa.; m. Elizabeth
Rinehart.  Factory owner.

Klyn, Jans Cornellieson (   -   ) Pa.-N.J.; m. ---.
Landowner.
Knapp, Nicholas (   -1670) Conn.-Mass.; m. Elinor
Lockwood. Proprietor.
Knapp, Samuel (1668-1738) Conn.; m. Hannah Bushnell.
Landowner; Military service.
Knickerbocker, Herman Jansen (1648-1723) N.Y.; m.
Elizabeth van de Bogart. Military service.
Knight, Giles (1653-1726) Mass.- Pa.; m. Abigail
Antill; Mary English. Quaker; Landowner.
Knight, Nathaniel (1645-1713) S.C.; m. ---. Governor;
Landowner.
Knight, Philip (1625-1745) Mass.; m. Margaret Wilkins.
Landowner.
Knight, Thomas (1662-1748) Pa.; m. Elizabeth Browne.
Landowner.
Knight, Walter (1585/87-c1653) Mass.; m. Elizabeth ---.
Landowner.
Knight, William (   -1655) Mass.; m. Elizabeth ---.
Constable; Freeman.
Knott, George (   -1648 ) Mass.; m. Martha Sargeant.
Landowner.
Knott, James (1594-1651) Va.; m. Elinor Butler.
Military service; Landowner.
Knowles, Henry (1609-70) m. ---. Freeman; Landowner.
Knowles, Richard (   -1670/75) Mass.; m. Ruth Bower.
Landowner; Ship captain.
Kobel, Henry (   -   ) Pa.; m. ---. Military service.
Kollock, Jacob (1692-1772) Del.; m. Alice Shepheard.
Landowner.
Kool, Barent Jacobsen (c1610-   ) N.Y.; m. Marretje
Leendertzde Graw. Burgher.
Kornegay, George (1688-1773/74) N.C.; m. Susannah
---. Military service.
Kunders, Thomas (1648-92) Pa.; m. Elin Streypers.
Landowner.
Kuntz, John George (   -1748) Pa.; m. Catherine ---.
Landowner.
Kuster, Johannes (   -1708) Pa.; m. Elizabeth Cassell.
Burgess; Surveyor.

Kuster, Paulus (1630-1707) Pa.; m. Gertrude Strepyers.
Committeeman; Overseer of fences.
Kuykendall, Jacom Luerson (    -1656) N.Y.; m. ---.
Landowner.

-L-

Lackland, John (c1696-1741) Md.; m. ---.  Landowner.
Lacy, Thomas (   -  ) Va.; m. Ann Burnley.  Landowner.
Ladd, Daniel (    -1693) Mass.; m. Ann ---.  Landowner;
Selectman.
Ladd, John (1653-79) Va.; m. Mary ---.  Military
Service.
Ladd, John (1669-1725) Va.; m. Elizabeth Warner.
Councillor.
Ladd, Samuel (1649-97/98) Mass.; m. Martha Corliss.
Military service.
Laicon, Peter Nilsson (    -1693) Pa.; m. ---.
Landowner.
Lake, Daniel (    -1727) N.Y.; m. Sarah (or Alice)
Polyon.  Military service.
Lake, John (1619/96) N.J.; m. Anne Spicer.  Military
service.
Lake, John (    -1729) N.Y.; m. Neeltje Classen.
Elder; Military service.
Lake, Margaret Reade (1598-1672) Mass.; m. John Lake.
Landowner.
Lake, Thomas (1615-76) Me.; m. Mary Goodyear.  Free-
man; Military service.
Laker, Benjamin (   -  ) N.C.; m. Jean Day.  Land-
owner.
Lakin, William (1624-1700) Mass.; m. Lydia Browne.
Military service.
Lamar, Thomas (    -c1714) Va.; m. Ann Pottenger.
Landowner.
Lambdin, Robert (c1638-1683/84) Md.; m. ---.
Landowner.
Lambdin, William (    -1727) Va.; m. Sarah (Elliott)
Auldborn.  Landowner.
Lambdon  SEE  Lambdin

Lambert, Francis (    -1647) Mass.; m. Jane ---.
 Freeman; Landowner.
Lambert, Roger (    -c1716) N.J.; m. Eleanor ---.
 Proprietor; Assemblyman.
Lambert, Thomas (    -    ) N.J.; m. Joanne Terry.
 Landowner.
Lambert, Thomas (1645-85) Mass.; m. Edna Northend.
 Military service.
Lamberton, Cornelius (    -    ) N.Y.; m. Altien Brack-
 house.  Landowner.
Lambeth, John (1690-1746) Va.; m. Mary Meredith.
 Military service; Landowner.
Lamprey, Henry (1616-1700) N.H.; m. Gillyen ---.
 Landowner.
Lanback, Christian (1699-1768) Pa.; m. Susanna
 Catherine ---.  Military service; Ranger.
Lancaster, Henry (1605-1705) Mass.; m. Sarah ---.
 Selectman; Landowner.
Landon, Hannah (Hubbard) (1668-1742) N.Y.; m. Nathan
 Landon. Landowner.
Landon, Nathan (1664-1714) N.Y.; m. Hannah Hubbard.
 Landowner.
Lane, Joseph (1668/69-c1740) N.C.; m. Julian ---.
 Landowner; Vestryman.
Lane, Robert (1631-1718) Conn.; m. Sarah Pickett.
 Assemblyman; Landowner.
Lane, Samuel (1628-82 ) Md.; m. Margaret Burrage.
 Justice; Commissioner.
Lane, Thomas (1634/35-1708/09) Va.; m. Elizabeth Jones.
 Military service.
Langdon, Tobias (1620-64) N.H.; m. Elizabeth Sher-
 burne.  Landowner.
Langford, John (1699-1740) Va.; m. Rebecca ---.
 Landowner.
Langhorne, John (1672/73-  ) Va.; m. Anne Wade.
 Burgess; Landowner.
Langhorne, Thomas (1645/1710) Pa.; m. ---.  Assembly-
 man.
Lanier, Clement (1678-1750) Va.; m. Sarah ---.
 Landowner.

Lanier, John (1631-   ) Va.; m. Lucrece ---.  Military
service; Landowner.

Lanier, John (1655-1717) Va.; m. Elizabeth Bird;
Sarah ( ) Edmunds.  Military service.

Lanier, Nicholas (1700-79) Va.; m. Mary Nance.  Military service.

Lanier, Sampson (cl653-1743) Va.; m. Sarah ---.
Landowner.

Lanier, Sampson (1682-1743) Va.; m. Elizabeth Washington.  Justice; Vestryman.

Lansing, Gerritt Frederick (   -1679) N.Y.; m. ---.
Landowner.

LaPrade, Andrew (1663-1726) Va.; m. Ann ---.  Huguenot;
Landowner.

Larkin, John (1614-72) Md.; m. Katherine ---.  Landowner.

Larkin, John (cl640-cl704) Md.; m. ---.  Landowner.

LaRoche, James (1694-1720) S.C.; m. Frances ---.
Christian ---.  Landowner.

Laroux, Franz (   -cl684) N.Y.; m. Sara ---.  Huguenot; Landowner.

Laroux    SEE ALSO  Larue

Larue, Abraham (cl673-1712) N.Y.; m. Magdalene Gille.
Landowner.

Latham, Cary (1612-85) Mass.; m. Elizabeth (Masters)
Lockwood.  Proprietor.

Latham, Daniel (cl642-1707) Va.; m. Sarah ---.
Shipwright; Landowner.

Latham, William (   -cl648) Mass.; m. ---.  Mayflower
Compact.

Lathrop, John (cl590-1653) Mass.; m. Hannah House.
Minister.

Lathrop, John ( 1645-   ) Mass.; m. Mary Cole.  Landowner.

Latimer, Jonathan (1698-1778) Conn.; m. Borrod
Denison.  Military service.

Latimer, Robert (1664-1728) Conn.; m. Elizabeth
Butolph.  Councillor; Military service.

LaTourette, Jean (cl651-1733) N.Y.; m. Marie Mercereau.
Justice.

Lattin, Richard (1610-72/73) Mass.; m. ---.  Landowner.

Law, John (1605-77)Mass.; m. Susannah Todd.  Landowner; Military service.

Law, John (1635-59/60) Mass.; m. Lydia Draper.  Landowner; Founder.

Lawrence, David (   -1709) N.H.; m. ---.  Constable;
Military service.

Lawrence, Elisha (1666-1724) N.J.; m. Lucy Stout.
Landowner.

Lawrence, Enoch (1648/49-1744) Mass.; m. Ruth (Whitney) Shattuck.  Military service.

Lawrence, George (1637-1708/09) Mass.; m. Elizabeth
Crisp.  Surveyor; Landowner.

Lawrence, John (   -  ) N.C.; m. Mary ---.  Landowner.

Lawrence, John (   -1652) Va.; m. Margaret Murphy.
Landowner.

Lawrence, John (1609-67) Mass.; m. Elizabeth ---;
Susanna Batchelder.  Freeman.

Lawrence, John (   -c1696) Va.; m. Mary ---.  Landowner.

Lawrence, Joseph (1688-1756) Conn.; m. Mary Warren.
Surveyor; Representative.

Lawrence, Nathaniel (1639-1724) Mass.; m. Sarah Morse.
Freeman.

Lawrence, Robert (1639-63) Va.; m. Elizabeth ---.
Justice.

Lawrence; Thomas (1588/89-1624/25) N.Y.- Conn.; m.
Joane Anstrother.    Military service.

Lawrence, William (   -  ) N.J.; m. Elizabeth Scudder.
Deputy to Court; Burgess.

Lawrence, William (1623-80) N.Y.; m. Elizabeth
Gildersleeve.  Landowner.

Lawrence, William (c1635-94) N.C.; m. Rachel Welsh.
Landowner.
Lawrence, William (   -1732) N.Y.; m. Deborah Smith.
Council of Safety.
Laws, John (   -1697) Md.; m. Katherine Bozman.
Landowner.
Lawson, Hugh (1700-1772) Va.; m. ---.  Judge.
Lawson, Richard (1600-59) Va.; m. ---.  Landowner.
Lawson, Roland (1661-  ) Mass.; m. ---.  Justice.
Lawton, Thomas (c1614-81 ) R.I.; m. Grace(Parsons)
Bailey; Elizabeth Salsburie.  Freeman; Commissioner.
Lay, Robert (1617-89) Conn.; m. Sarah Fenner.  Depu-
ty to Court.
Lea, William (1654-1703) Va.; m. Mary Green.  Land-
owner.
Leach, John  (c1640-96) Md.; m. Ireland ---.  Land-
owner; Vestryman.
Leach, Lawrence (1580-1662) Mass.; m. Elizabeth ---.
Freeman; Juror.
Leach, Richard (1617-87) Mass.; m. Sarah ---.  Free-
man; Constable.
Leake, Richard (1691-1784) Va.; m. Elizabeth ---.
Landowner.
Leake, William (1664-1725) Va.; m. Mary Bostick.
Processioner of land.
Lear, John (c1630-95/96) Va.; m. Mary (Oldis) Bastard.
Councillor; Burgess.
Learned, Isaac (1623-57) Mass.; m. Mary Sterner.
Selectman; Deacon.
Learned, William (1590-1645) Mass.; m. Judith Goodith.
Freeman; Founder.
Leatherwood, John (c1650-c1715 ) Md.; m. Martha ---.
Landowner.
Leavens, Benjamin (1652-1724) Conn.; m. Elizabeth
Church.  Landowner.
Leavitt, John (1608-91) Mass.; m. Sarah Gilmore;
Mary Lovett.  Landowner; Representative.
Leavitt, Samuel (c1641-1707) N.H.; m. Mary Robinson.
Landowner; Selectman.
Leavitt, Thomas (1616-96) N.H.; m. Isabelle (Bland)
Astor.  Exeter Covenant.

Lebaron, Francis (1668-1704) Mass.; m. Mary Wilder
Physician.

Lecompte, Anthony (c1636-c1673) Md.; m. Esther
Dotlands. Landowner; Justice.

Lee, Hancock (1653-1709) Va.; m. Mary Kendall.
Landowner.

Lee, Henry (c1620-57) Va.; m. Marah Adkins. Burgess;
Justice.

Lee, John (1620-90) Conn.; m. Mary Hart. Freeman;
Proprietor.

Lee, John (1686-1739) N.C.-Va.; m. ---. Surveyor;
Landowner.

Lee, Richard (1590-1660)Va.; m. Ann Silk; Ann Constable; Ann Hancock; Elizabeth Bandy. Attorney
General; Burgess.

Lee, Richard (c1675-c1756) N.C.; m. ---. Landowner.

Lee, Thomas (1690-1750) Va.; m. Hannah Ludwell;
Elizabeth Keene. Landowner.

Leete, William (1611/13-83) Conn.; m. Anne Payne.
Governor; Council of War.

LeFevre, Andries (   -   ) N.Y.; m. ---. Landowner.

LeFevre, Isaac (1669-1751) Pa.; m. Catherine Ferree.
Military service.

LeFevre, Simon (1640-90) N.Y.; m. Elizabeth Deyo.
Landowner.

Leffingwell, John (1688-1773) Conn.; m. Sarah Abel.
Freeman; Landowner.

Leffindwell, Thomas (1622-1714/15) Conn.; m. Mary
White. Selectman; Commissioner.

Leffingwell, Thomas (1649-1724) Conn.; m. Mary Bushnell. Freeman; Landowner.

Leftwich, Ralph (1628-   ) Va.; m. Ellinor Cousins.
Landowner.

Leftwich, Thomas (1660-1730) Va.; m. Mary North.
Landowner.

Legare, Solomon (1662-1760 )S.C.; m. ---. Landowner;
Churchman.

Legrand, Pierre (c1665-1719) Va.; m. ---. Landowner.

LeHew   SEE   Hew

Leigh, William (1639-1704) Va.; m. Alice ---.
Burgess; Military service.

Leighton, John (1661-1724) Me.; m. Honor Langdon.
Selectman; Military service.

Leland, Henry (1625-80) Mass.; m. Margaret Badcock.
Landowner; Builder.

Lemar, John (1645-94) Md.; m. ---. Landowner.

Lenoir, David Lewis (1686-1777) Va.; m. Ann Terrell.
Landowner.

Leonard, Henry (1620-95) N.J.; m. Mary ---. Landowner.

Leonard, Henry (1656-1739) N.J.; m. Lydia ---.
Sheriff.

Leonard, John (   -1676) Mass.; m. Sarah Healy. Proprietor.

Leonard, Thomas (1641-1713) Mass.; m. Mary Watson.
Town Clerk; Judge.

Leroy, Hugh (c1616-94) Va.; m. ---. Huguenot; Landowner.

Lesesne, Isaac (1674-1736) S.C.; m. Frances Netherton.
Landowner.

Letton, Caleb (c1690-1763) Md.; m. Grace Burton.
Landowner.

Levering, John Wishart (1649-1745) Pa.; m. Magdelena
Baker. Huguenot; Landowner.

Levermore, John (1606-84) Mass.; m. Grace Sherman.
Military service.

Lewis, Charles (1696-1779) Va.; m. Mary Howell.
Military service.

Lewis, David (1670-   ) N.Y.; m. Maria Philips.
Military service.

Lewis, David (1685-1779) Va.; m. Ann Terrell.
Military service.

Lewis, Edmund (1601-50/51) Mass.; m. Mary ---.
Selectman; Landowner.

Lewis, Henry (1640-88) Pa.; m. Margaret (Prothera)
Philbin. Proprietor; Juror.

Lewis, James (   -1663 ) Mass.; m. Sarah Jenkins.
Freeman; Military service.

Lewis, John (1635/40-c1710) Va.; m. Isabella Warner;
Elizabeth O'Brissel. Burgess; Judge.

Lewis, John (1664-1725) Va.; m. Elizabeth Warner;
Isabel Miller. Councillor.

Lewis, Joseph (    -1706) Conn.; m. Elizabeth Case.
Proprietor.
Lewis, Ralph (    -1712) Pa.; m. Mary ---. Landowner.
Lewis, Robert (1607-56) Va.; m. Mary Jones; Elizabeth
--- . Landowner.
Lewis, Thomas (1580/90-1637/40) Me.; m. Elizabeth
Marshall. Landowner.
Lewis, William (1592-1693) Conn.; m. Felix Collins.
Freeman; Founder.
Lewis, William (    -1690) Conn.; m. Mary Hopkins.
Town Recorder.
Lewis, William (    -1708) Pa.; m. Ann ---. Land-
owner.
Lewis, Zachary (1650-c1719) Va.; m. Mary Walker.
Attorney; Landowner.
Libby, Henry (1647-1732) Me.; m. Honor Hinkson.
Military service.
Libby, John (1602-82) Me.-Mass.; m. Mary ---.
Military service.
Libby, John (1636-1720) Me.; m. Agnes ---. Landowner.
Lide    SEE    Lloyd
Light, John Peter (1675-1750) Pa.; m. Sarah Strick-
land. Minister; Surveyor.
Lightfoot, Goodrich (1685/90-1738) Va.; m. Mary Chew.
Military service.
Lightfoot, John (1598-c1647) Va.; m. Elizabeth
Phillips. Councillor; Military service.
Lightfoot, John (c1635-1707) Va.; m. Anne Goodrich.
Military service.
Ligon, Richard (1657-1724) Va.; m. Margaret ---;
Mary Worsham. Landowner.
Ligon (Lygon) Thomas ( 1625/28-76) Va.; m. Mary
Harris. Burgess; Military service.
Lillard, Jean (1668-c1734) Va.; m. Mildred Jones.
Landowner.
Lillington, Alezander (1643-97) N.C.; m. Elizabeth
(Cooke) Cooper. Deputy Governor; President of
Council.
Lincoln, Mordecai (1686-1736) Pa.; m. Mary Robeson;
Hannah Salter. Landowner.

Lincoln, Samuel (1617/19-70) Mass.; m. Martha ---.
Selectman; Military service.

Lincoln, Thomas (1600-83) Mass.; m. Mary ---.
Military service.

Lindley, Francis (    -1704) N.J.; m. Susanna Culpeper.
Civil office.

Lindsay, David (1603-67) Va.; m. Susannah ---; Margaret Colville. Minister.

Lindsey, Alexander (1610-85) N.Y.; m. Cathlyn Dongan.
Landowner.

Linthicum, Thomas (1640-1702) Md.; m. Jane ---.
Founder; Quaker.

Linton, Moses (    -1692) Va.; m. Elizabeth ---.
Landowner.

Linton, Richard (c1630-65) Mass.; m. Elizabeth ---.
Proprietor.

Lippincott, Richard (1613-83) Mass.-N.J.; m. Abigail
---. Assemblyman; Councillor.

Lipscomb, Thomas (1700-70) Va.; m. Sarah MackGehee.
Landowner.

Litchfield, Lawrence (1614-49) Mass.; m. Judith Dennis.
Landowner; Ancient and Honorable Artillery.

Little, Samuel (1665-1727) Pa.; m. Rachel Minshall.
Landowner.

Little, Thomas (    -1671/72) Mass.; m. Anna Warren.
Landowner.

Littlebury, Thomas (    -c1655) Va.; m. Ellynore ---.
Landowner.

Littlefield, Edmund (c1600-61) Me.; m. Annie Austin.
Grand Juror.

Littlehale, Richard (    -1661) Mass.; m. Margaret
Lauthon. Town clerk; Landowner.

Littleton, Nathaniel (1622-84) Va.; m. Anne (Southey)
Horsmanden. Commander in Chief; Magistrate.

Livermore, John (c1638-1718/19) Mass.; m. ---.
Freeman; Selectman.

Livezey, Thomas (1627-91) Pa.; m. Ellen ---. Juror.

Livingston, Robert (1654-1728) N.Y.; m. Alida Schuyler. Landowner.

Lloyd, Edward (1603-66) Va.-Md.; m. Frances ( )
Watkins; Alice Grouch.

Lloyd, Robert (1669-1714) Pa.; m. Lowry Jones. Land-
owner.
Lloyd (Lide), Thomas (1640-94) Pa.;m. Mary Jones.
Councillor; Magistrate.
Lobdell, Joshua (1671-1743) Conn.; m. Mary Burwell.
Landowner.
Lobdell, Simon )    -1717) Conn.; m. Persis Pierce.
Landowner; Military service.
Locke, John (1627-96) N.H.; m. Elizabeth Berry.
Military service.
Lockett, Thomas (    -1686) Va.; m. Margaret Osborne.
Landowner.
Lockhart, James (    -1675) Va.; m. ---. Landowner.
Lockwood, Jonathan (1634-88) Conn.; m. Mary Ferris.
Freeman; Military service.
Lockwood, Robert (1600-58) Conn.-Mass.; m. Susana
Norman. Freeman; Military service.
Loesch, George (1699-  ) N.C.; m. Anna (Christina)
Wallborn. Justice; Military service.
Lofland    SEE    Loughland
Loftin, Leonard (1654-1710/20) N.C.-Pa.; m. Elizabeth
---.    Assemblyman; Vestryman.
Loftin, William (    -1703/04) Md.; m. Elizabeth ---.
Landowner.
Logan, David (c1700-67) Pa.; m. Jane McKinley.
Military service.
Logan, George (    -1721) N.C.; m. Frances ---.
Assemblyman; Commissioner.
Logan, James (1674-1751) Pa.; m. Sarah Read. Safety
Council.
Loker, John (c1608-53) Mass.; m. Mary Draper. Free-
man; Oath of Fidelity.
Lombard, Thomas (c1610-71) Mass.; m. Joyce ---.
Military service.
Long, Philip (1678-1753) Va.; m. ---. Military
service.
Long, Robert (1595-1664) Mass.; m. Sarah Tupor;
Elizabeth ---. Ancient and Honorable Artillery
Company.
Longfellow, William (1650-90) Mass.; m. Anne Sewall.
Landowner.

Loomis, Joseph (1590-1658) Mass.-Conn.; m. Mary White.
Landowner.

Loomis, Nathaniel (1626-88) Conn.; m. Elizabeth Moore.
Freeman; Military service.

Lord, Francis (    -1739) Md.-Va.; m. Sarah ---.
Deputy clerk.

Lord, Richard (1685-1750) Me.; m. Mary Goodwin.
Selectman.

Lord, Robert (1603-83) Mass.; m. Mary Waite.  Deputy
to Court; Military service.

Lord, Thomas (1585-c1668) Conn.; m. Dorothy Bird.
Founder; Proprietor.

Lord, William (1623-78) Conn.; m. ---.  Founder.

Loring, Caleb (1674-1732) Mass.; m. Lydia Gray.
Landowner.

Loring, Thomas (    -1661) Mass.; m. Jane Newton.
Proprietor.

Lothrop    SEE    Lathrop

Lott, Peter (    -1687) N.Y.; m. Gertrude ---.
Magistrate; Landowner.

Loud, Francis (    -c1726) Mass.; m. ---.  Landowner;
Military service.

Loughland, Dorman (c1647-87) Va.; m. Mary ---.
Landowner.

Loughland, John (1675/78-1731/33) Va.-Del.; m.
Priscilla ---; Mary Field.  Landowner.

Love, Alexander (c1680-c1727) Va.; m. ---.  Landowner.

Love, Ephraim (1694-c1772) Pa.-Va.; m. Elizabeth ---.
Military service.

Lovejoy, John (1622-90) Mass.; m. Mary Osgood.
Military service.

Lovelace, Sir William (1583-1627) Va.; m. Anne Barne.
Founder.

Lovell, Robert (1595-1672) Mass.; m. Elizabeth ---.
Military service.

Lovell, Robert (    -c1700) Va.; m. Elinor ---.
Landowner.

Lovett, Daniel (c1622-92) Mass.; m. Joanna Blatt.
Landowner.

Lovett, Lancaster (1638/44-72) Va.; m. Mathsheba ---
(or Anne)---.  Churchwarden.

Low, Thomas (1605-77) Mass.; Margaret Todd. Selectman; Landowner.

Lowden, Richard (1610/12-1700) Mass.; m. Mary Cole.
Freeman.

Lowe, John (    -1701) Md.; m. Rebecca ---. Military
service.

Lowell, John (1595-1647) Mass.; m. Elizabeth Gooch;
Elizabeth Goodale. Commissioner.

Lowell, Percival (1571-1654) Mass.; m. Rebecca ---.
Proprietor.

Lubbertson, Frederick Van Den Kreest (1609-80) N.Y.;
m. Tryntje Hendricks. Magistrate; Landowner.

Lucas, Thomas (c1646-c1675) Mass.; m. ---. Military
service.

Lucas, Thomas (c1675/79-1722) Md.; m. Dorothy ---.
Military service.

Luce, Henry (1640-87/89) Mass.; m. Remember Litchfield.
Landowner; Surveyor.

Luckin   SEE   Lukin

Ludlam, William (1600-65) Mass.-Conn.; m. Clemence
Fordham. Juror; Landowner.

Ludlow, Roger (c1590-1664) Conn.; m. Mary Cogan.
Deputy Governor.

Ludwell, Phillip (c1660-c1739) Va.; m. Lucy Higginson. Governor.

Lukin, Edward (  -  )Va.; m. ---. Member of Virginia
Company.

Lum, John (c1620-73) Conn.; m. --- Strickland.
Deputy to Court.

Lumpkin, Jacob (1644-1708) Va.; m. Ann ---. Landowner; Military service.

Lunsford, Sir Thomas (c1610-c53) Va.; m. Elizabeth
Kemp. Councillor; Military service.

Lunt, Henry (   -1662) Mass.; m. Ann ---. Proprietor; Freeman.

Lunt, Henry (1652/53-1709) Mass.; m. Jane Skipper.
Military service.

Lunt, Skipper (1679-1770) Mass.; m. Elizabeth Brown.
Military service.

Lusby, Robert (c1630-1673/74) Md.; m. Dorothy ---.
Landowner.

Lusby, Robert (1664/66-    ) Md.; m. Mary Baldwin.
Inspector; Landowner.
Luther, John (c1600-    ) Mass.; m. Elizabeth ---.
Landowner.
Luther, Samuel (1636-1716) Mass.; m. Mary Abell.
Minister; Selectman.
Luycaszen, Andries (c1595-    ) N.Y.; m. Jannetje Sebyns.
Fire warden; Burgher.
Luyster, Cornelius (1662-1727) N.J.; m. Jannetje
Pietersen. Military service; Landowner.
Lyddall, George (1620-1705) Va.; m. Barbara Bowker.
Military service.
Lyddell   SEE   Lyddall
Lygon   SEE   Ligon
Lyle, Robert (1698-1765) Pa.; m. Mary Gillaland.
Justice.
Lyman, John (1623-90) Mass.; m. Dorcas Plumb.  Mili-
tary service.
Lyman, Richard (1580-1640) Conn.-Mass.; m. Sarah Osb-
orne.  Freeman; Proprietor.
Lyming, John (    -1717) N.J.; m. Patience Wainwright.
Military service.
Lynde, John (1648-1723) Mass.; m. Mary Pierce.  Mili-
tary service.
Lynde, Jonathan (c1683-c1756) Mass.; m. Hannah Nichols.
Selectman; Deputy to Court.
Lynde, Nathaniel (1659-1729) Conn.; m. Susannah
Willoughby.  Judge; Treasurer of Yale College.
Lynde, Simon (c1624-87) Mass.; m. Hannah Newdigate.
Ancient and Honorable Artillery Company Company;
Governor's Assistant.
Lynde, Thomas (1593-1671) Mass.; m. Mary ---.  Free-
man; Proprietor.
Lynde, Thomas (1616-93) Mass.; m. Elizabeth ---.
Landowner.
Lynn, John (1685-1752/69) Va.; m. Margaret ---.
Justice; Constable.
Lyon, Henry (c1625-1703) Conn.; m. Elizabeth Bateman.
Founder; Judge.
Lyon, John (1655-1736) Conn.; m. Rebecca Hull.
Committeeman; Surveyor of Roads.

Lyon, Margaret ( -1705) Conn.; m. Richard Lyon.
Landowner.
Lyon, Richard (1630-78) Conn.; m. Margaret ---.
Landowner.
Lyon, Thomas (1621-89/90) Conn.; m. Mary Hoyt.
Landowner.
Lyon,Thomas (1673-1739) Conn.; m. Abigail Ogden.
Military service.
Lyon, William (1620-72) Mass.; m. Sarah Ruggles.
Ancient and Honorable Artillery Company.

-M-

McCarty, Dennis ( - ) Va.; m. --- Billington.
Burgess; Justice.
McCarty, Florence ( -1717) Va.; m. Mary Wright.
Landowner.
McClelland, John (1700- ) Pa.; m. Ruete Rupp.
Minister; Builder.
McClendon, Dennis(1641-1706) N.C.; m. Elizabeth ---.
Landowner. Justice.
McClothlan, Robert (c1630-90) Mass.; m. Joanna Warner.
Townsman.
McClure, Samuel(1690-1761)Va.; m. Agnes. Founder.
McCorkle, William ( - ) Pa.; m. ---. Military
service.
MacCubin, John (c1642-c86) Md.; m. Elinor ---.
Landowner.
McDonald, Bryan (1645-1707) Del.; m. Mary Combe.
Surveyor; Landowner.
McDonald, Bryan (1686-1757) Del.; m. Catherine
Robinson. Landowner.
McDonnel SEE McDonald
MacFarland, James (1695-1770) Pa.; m. Jeannette Bu-
chanan. Landowner.
MacFarlane SEE MacFarland
McGehee, Thomas (1645-1727) Va.; m. Ann Bastrop.
Military service.
MacGregor, James (1656-1727) Va.; m. Mary Mumford.
Landowner.

Maciartie;  McCarthy  SEE  McCarty
MackClaflin;  MackClothlan  SEE  McClothlan
McKendree,James (1700-64) Va.; m. Mary ---. Land-
  owner.
Mack Gehee;  Magee  SEE  McGehee
McKenney, John (c1668-97) Mass.; m. ---. Landowner.
McKinne, Barnaby (1673-1740) Va.; m. Mary ---.
  Assemblyman; Justice.
McKinnie;  McKinney  SEE  McKinne
Macklin, William (    -1752) Va.; m. ---, Councillor.
Mackmelion, John (c1663-1704) Va.; m. Ann Frances
  Harrison. Landowner.
McKnight, John (1625-1768) Md.; m. Jane Wallace.
  Founder.
McKnight, John (1660-1714 ) Md.; m. Jane Alexander.
  Oath of Loyalty.
McKnitt  SEE  McKnight
McLaughlin  SEE ALSO  McClothlan
McLendon  SEE  McClendon
McMurtrie Joseph (1685-1762) Pa.; m. Ann Boone.
  Military service.
McMurtie  SEE  McMurtrie
Macock, Samuel (    -1622) Va.; m. ---. Governor's
  Council; Landowner.
Macon, Gideon (c1648-1702) Va.; m. Martha Woodward.
  Burgess; Secretary to Governor.
Macoy, Michael (    -c1682) Va.; m. Anne ---.
  Landowner.
Macy, Thomas (1608-82) Mass.; m. Sarah Hopcott.
  Magistrate; Juror.
Macy, Thomas (1687-1769) Mass.; m. --- Porter; Deborah
  Coffin. Military service; Landowner.
Maddeson  SEE  Madison
Maddox, Alexander (    -1659) Va.; m. Elizabeth White.
  Landowner.
Maddox, Samuel (1638-84) Md.; m. Ann Netley;
  Margaret Townley. Military service.
Madison, Isaac (   -  ) Va.; m. Mary ---. Councillor.
Madison, John (1623-83) Va.; m. Isabel (Minor) Todd;
  Rebecca ---. Ship builder; Landowner.

Madison, John (1666-   ) Va.; m. Isabella (Minor)
Todd. Landowner; Sheriff.
Magruder, Alexander (1610-77) Md.; m. Margaret
Braithwaite; Elizabeth Hawkins. Landowner.
Magruder, Samuel (1654-1711) Md.; m. Sarah Beall.
Justice; Burgess.
Maine, Ezekial (c1650-1714) Conn.; m. Mary ---.
Landowner; Deputy to Court.
Maine, Ezekial (1673-1727) Conn.; m. Mary ---.
Landowner.
Mainwaring, Roger (   -1653) Md.; m. Mary ---.
Minister.
Malin, Randal (c1651-c1700) Pa.; m. Elizabeth ---;
Mary Conway. Landowner.
Mallory, Roger (1635-1705) Va.; m. ---. Magistrate.
Maltby, William (   -1699) Pa.; m. Mary Roades.
Landowner; Builder.
Manchester, Thomas (1615/20-91) R.I.; m. Margaret
Wood. Landowner; Military service.
Mandall, John (   -   ) Mass.; m. ---. Landowner.
Mandeville, Giles Jansen de (c1630-1701) N.Y.; m.
Eloje(Peters)Hendricks. Landowner.
Maner, John (1665-1729) N.C.; m. Elizabeth ---.
Justice.
Mangum, John (1680-1737) Va.; m. Frances Bennett.
Landowner.
Manlove, Mark (c1650-84) Md.; m. Elizabeth Grier.
Justice.
Mann, John (1631-94) S.C.; m. Mary ---. Landowner.
Mann, John (c1700-84) N.C.; m. Ann Vubcebt. Military
service; Congressman.
Mann, Richard (1652-1725) Mass.; m. Elizabeth Sutton.
Landowner.
Mann, Samuel (1647-1719) Mass.; m. Esther Ware.
Minister; Freeman.
Mann, William (1607-62) Mass.; m. Mary Jarred.
Landowner.
Manning, William (1614-90) Mass.; m. Dorothy ---.
Military service.
Mansell, David (c1600-72) Va.; m. ---. Landowner.

Mansfield, Richard (    -1655) Conn.; m. Gillian
Drake. Military service; Landowner.
Manson, Peter (c1675-1721) Va.; m. Elizabeth Chapman.
Military service.
Mapes, Thomas (1628-86) Conn.; m. Sarah Purrier.
Surveyor; Justice.
Maples, Thomas(c1640-65) Va.; m. ---. Landowner.
Mapp, John (c1654-87) Va.; m. Mary ---. Landowner.
Marable, George (    -c1720) Va.; m. Mary Hartwell.
Landowner; Sheriff.
March, Hugh (1622-93) Mass.; m. Judith ---. Land-
owner.
Marchant, John (1679/80-1767) Mass.; m. Elizabeth
Daggett. Constable; Landowner.
Marcy, John (1662-1724) Mass.; m. Sarah Hadlock.
Landowner.
Marion, Benjamin (c1685-  ) S.C.; m. Perinne Bou-
tignon. Landowner.
Maris, George (1632-1705) Pa.; m. Alice Wilsmith.
Councillor.
Maris, John (1669-1747) Pa.; m. ---. Juror; Assembly-
man.
Markham, William (1615-50) Pa.; m. Ann Penn. Deputy
Governor.
Markham, William (1635-1704) Pa.; m. Elizabeth ---.
Deputy Governor.
Markland, Mathew (1609-87) Md.-Va.; m. Margaret Jones.
Constable; Assemblyman.
Marselis, Jan Van Bonnel (    -1722) N.Y.; m. Annatje
Gerritse. Landowner.
Marsh, Jonathan (1649-1730) R.I.-Mass.; m. Dorcas
Dickinson. Landowner; Founder.
Marsh, Onesiphous (1630-1713) Mass.; m. Hannah Cutler.
Landowner.
Marsh, Robert (1635-c88) Pa.; m. Sarah ---. Land-
owner.
Marsh, Samuel (1620-83) Conn.-N.J.; m. Comfort ---.
Freeman; Military service.
Marsh, Thomas (1616-56) Md.; m. Margaret Hartford.
Commissioner; Judge.

Marsh, Thomas (1617-1700) Conn.; m. Jane Clements.
Landowner.
Marshall, Humphrey (1660-1711) Va.; m. Anne ---.
Sheriff; Attorney.
Marshall, John (1586-1660) Conn.; m. ---. Military
service; Landowner.
Marshall, John (Of the Forest) (1591-1657) Va.; m.
Jane Berkeley. Military service; Landowner.
Marshall, John (1610-87) Va.; m. ---. Landowner;
Military service; Landowner.
Marshall, Samuel (    -1675) Conn.; m. Mary Wilton.
Landowner.
Marshall, Thomas (1611-89) Mass.; m. Rebecca ---.
Ancient and Honorable Artillery Company; Military
service.
Marshall, Thomas (1634-1704) Va.; m. Martha ---.
Burgess; Military service.
Marshall, William (    -1673) Va.; m. Katherine
Hebden. Landowner.
Marsham. Richard (c1638-1713) Md.; m. Katherine Brent.
Justice.
Marston, Thomas (1640-c82) Va.; m. Elizabeth Marvell.
Landowner.
Martiau, Nicholas (1591-1657) Va.; m. Jane ( )
Berkeley. Burgess; Military service.
Martien, William (1591- ) Va.; m. Jane Elizabeth
Beach. Military service.
Martin, Abram (1642-c80) Va.; m. Elizabeth Marshall.
Military service; Landowner.
Martin, Edward (1700-45) Mass.; m. Rebekah Peck.
Military service.
Martin, Jean (1674-1739) Va.; m. Marguerite ---.
Assemblyman.
Martin, John (1620-87) N.J.-Pa.-N.C.; m. Hester
Roberts. Founder.
Martin, John (c1640-1711) Va.; m. Martha Brunwell.
Burgess; Landowner.
Martin, John (1683-1756) Va.; m. Letitia ---.
Burgess; Landowner.
Martin, Martin (1678-1760) Va.; m. Sarah Hix.
Surveyor; Minister.

Martin, Moses (1686-c1740) Pa.; m. Margaret Battle.
Landowner.

Martin, Thomas (c1655-  ) Pa.; m. Margery Munderhall.
Landowner.

Martindale, John (1676-1750) Pa.; m. Mary Bridgeman.
Landowner.

Marvel, John (1632-1707) Va.; m. Ann ---.  Landowner.

Marvin, Matthew (1600-80/87) Conn.; m. Elizabeth
Gregory. Deputy to Court; Proprietor.

Marvin, Reinold (    -1622) Conn.; m. Mary ---.
Proprietor.

Marye, James (    -1767) Va.; m. Letitia Maria Ann
Staige. Minister.

Mason, Francis (c1584-1648) Va.; m. Mary ---; Alicia
---.  Justice; Sheriff.

Mason, Francis (1639-96) Va.; m. Elizabeth ( ) Binns.
Sheriff; Justice.

Mason, Frederick (1663-1743) Va.; m. Louise Phelps.
Landowner.

Mason, George (1626-86) Va.; m. Mary French.
Landowner; Sheriff.

Mason, George (1670-1716) Va.; m. Mary Fowke.
Burgess; Military service.

Mason, Hugh (c1605-1678) Mass.; m. Hester Wells.
Deputy to Court; Military service.

Mason, James (1612-70) Va.; m. Ann Huntington.
Burgess.

Mason, Joel (1642-1717) Va.; m. Susan Cross.
Landowner.

Mason, John (1600-72) Conn.; Ann  Peck.  Deputy
Governor; Military service.

Mason, John (c1690-1763) Va.; m.  Elizabeth ---.
Military service.

Mason, Robert (    -1701) Md.; m. Susannah Little.
Sheriff; Treasurer.

Mason, Sampson (1649-76) Mass.; m. Mary Butterworth.
Military service; Landowner.

Massey, Nicholas (1663-  ) Md.; m. Catherine ---.
Landowner.

Massey   SEE ALSO   Massie

Massie, Charles (1686-1736) Va.; m. Ann Macon.
Burgess; Landowner.
Massie, Peter (1639/40-1719) Mass.; m. Penelope
(Ashley) Cooper; Mary ---. Military service;
Surveyor.
Massie, Thomas (     -1733) Va.; m. Mary Walker.
Landowner.
Masters, John (     -1639) Mass.; m. Jane Masters.
Freeman; Landowner.
Masury, Lawrence (1646-1706) Mass.; m. Mary Kibben.
Military service.
Matheny, William Wentworth (1666-1705) Md.; m.
Frances (Norgraves) Mason. Constable.
Mather, Richard (1596-1669) Mass.-Conn.; m. Catherine
Holt. Minister; Military service.
Mathews, John (1639-1707) Va.; m. Ann ---. Surveyor;
Landowner.

Mathews, John (1661-1702) Va.; m. Elizabeth Travendi
(Travenor). Landowner; Military service.
Mathews, Thomas (1622-75) Md.; m. Jane Cockshutt.
Proprietor; Justice.
Mathewson   SEE   Matthewson
Matteson, Henry (1646-c1711) R.I.; m. Hannah Parsons.
Founder.
Matthews, Anthony (     -1692) Va.; m. Ann ---;
Elizabeth Beddoi. Landowner.
Matthews, Roger (  -  ) Md.; m. Hannah ---.
Landowner.
Matthews, Samuel (1592-1660) Va.; m. Frances Hinton.
Governor; Military service.
Matthews, Samuel (1629-1661/2) Va.; m. ---. Landowner.
Matthews, Samuel  (1685-1718) Va.; m. --- Braxton;
Catherine Dunstall; Margaret ---. Landowner.
Matthewson, James (     -1703) R.I.; m. ---. Deputy
to Assembly.
Mattingly, Thomas (     -1664) Md.; m. Elizabeth ---.
Landowner.
Mattoon, Philip (c1645-96) Mass.; m. Sarah Hawks.
Military service.

Maudlin, Ezekial (    -1705/06) N.C.; m. Hannah
  Nicholson. Landowner.
Maultsby, John Roades (1690-1758) Pa.; m. Mary
  Anthony. Quaker; Ferryman.
Maultsby, William (    -1699) Pa.; m. Mary Roades.
  Quaker.
Maund, William (1669-1741) Va.; m. Elizabeth Foreman.
  Landowner.
Maupin, Daniel (1699/1700-1788) Va.; m. Margaret Via.
  Military service.
Maupin, Gabriel (1651-1720) Va.; m. Marie Spencer.
  Military service.
Mauzy, John (1675-1718) Va.; m. --- Conyers. Minister;
  Landowner.
Maverick, John (1578-1635) Mass.; m. Mary Gye.
  Minister; Freeman.
Maverick, Samuel (1602-   ) Mass.; m. Amias Colles.
  Landowner.
Maxey, Edward (    -1740) Md.; m. Susanna ---.
  Landowner.
Maxson, John (1638-1720) R.I.; m. Mary Mosher.
  Minister.
Maxwell, James (1697-1768) N.C.; m. Mary Simons.
  Justice.
Maycock, Samuel (1580-1622) Va.; m. Sarah ---.
  Councillor.
Mayes,William (1574-1635) Va.; m. ---. Minister.
Mayhew, Thomas (1593-1682) Mass.; m. Abigail Parkins;
  Jane Paine. Deputy to Court; Freeman.
Maynard, John (c1606-72) Mass.; m. Mary (Starr) Axtell.
  Carpenter.
Mayo, John (c1590-1676) Mass.; m. Tamison ---.
  Minister.
Mayrant, Nicholas (1692-c1724) S.C.; m. Susannah
  Gaillard. Huguenot; Assemblyman.
Meacham, Isaac (1642-   ) Mass.; m. Deborah (Browning)
  Perkins. Landowner.
Meacham   SEE ALSO   Mechem
Mead, John (c1634-97) Conn.; m. Hannah Potter.
  Assemblyman; Landowner.

Mead, John (1692-  ) Pa.; m. Mary Abrell. Quaker.

Mead, William (1600-63) Mass.; m. ---. Landowner.

Meador, John (1637-94) Va.; m. Elizabeth White.
Landowner.

Meadors, Thomas (c1655-  ) Va.; m. ---. Negotiator
with Indians.

Meadows  SEE  Meadors

Mebie, Jan Pieter (   -1725) N.Y.; m. Anna Peters
(Boomsboom). Founder.

Mechem, Francis (   -1758) Pa.; m. Ellen Pierce.
Military service.

Mechem  SEE ALSO  Meacham

Meek, Walter (c1679-  ) Md.; m. Jane Reede. Landowner.

Meeker, Daniel (1659-94/95) Conn.; m. Elizabeth Ogden.
Landowner.

Meeker, Robert (   -1684/85) Conn.; m. Susanna
Turberfield. Landowner.

Meeker, William (1620/25-70/71) Mass.-Conn.-N.J.; m.
Sarah Preston; Hannah ---. Proprietor.

Meekins, Thomas (   -1687) Mass.; m. Sarah ---.
Freeman; Representative.

Meese, Henry (   -1682) Va.; m. Anne ---. Justice;
Burgess.

Meigs, John (1612-71/72) Conn.; m. Thomasine Fry.
Deacon; Landowner.

Meigs, Vincent (1583-1658) Conn.; m. --- Churchill.
Freeman; Landowner.

Mellichamp, William (   -c1774) S.C.; m. Sara St. Lo.
Justice; Landowner.

Mellows, Abraham (c1570-1639) Mass.; m. Martha Bulkley. Founder.

Melvin, David (1690-1745) Mass.; m. Mary Farrar.
Military service.

Melyn, Cornelis (1600-65) N.Y.; m. Janetje Adriaens.
Petitioner; Military service.

Mendenhall, Benjamin (1666-1740) Pa.; m. Ann Pennell.
Assemblyman.

Mendenhall, John (1683-  ) Pa.-N.C.; m. Elizabeth
Maris. Coroner; Constable.

Mentiall  SEE  Minshull

Mercer, Moses (1667-    ) N.Y.-N.J.; m. ---. Landowner.
Mercier, Francis (    -1717) Md.; m. Margaret Wildon.
  Secretary of First Free School.
Meredith, Thomas (c1620-1718) Va.; m. ---. Landowner.
Meriwether, Nicholas (1631-98) Va.; m. Elizabeth
  Woodhouse. Burgess; Justice.
Meriwether, Nicholas (1667-1744) Va.; m. Elizabeth
  Crafford. Burgess; Military service.
Merrell  SEE  Merrill
Merriam, Joseph (1600-41) Mass.; m. Sarah Goldstone.
  Transporter of freight and passengers.
Merrick, Thomas (1620-1704 ) Mass.; m. Elizabeth
  Tilley. Landowner.
Merrill, Nathaniel (1601-55) Mass.; m. Susanna
  Wilterton. Proprietor.
Merrill, Richard (1642-1727) N.Y.; m. Sarah or
  Susanna Wells. Assessor; Supervisor.
Merriman, John (c1600-80) Va.; m. ---. Deputy to
  Court; Military service.
Merriman, Nathaniel (1613-94) Conn.; m. Joan ---.
  Founder; Military service.
Merriman  SEE  Merryman
Merritt, Henry (1590-1652) Mass.; m. ---. Landowner.
Merritt, John (    -1676) Mass.; m. Elizabeth ---.
  Landowner.
Merryman, Charles (    -1722) Md.; m. Audrey ---;
  Mary Boone. Military service.
Merryman, Charles (    -1775) Md.; m. Mary ---.
  Military service.
Merryman  SEE ALSO  Merriman
Mershon, Henry (1672-1738) N.J.-N.Y.; m. Anne Hough-
  ton. Landowner.
Metcalf, Michael (1586-1664) Mass.; m. Sarah Ellwyn.
  Selectman; Teacher.
Meyer, Daniel (    -1761) Pa.; m. ---. Landowner.
Meyer  SEE ALSO  Demeyer
Micou, Paul (1658-1736) Va.; m. Margaret LeRoy.
  Justice; Physician.
Middlebrook, John (1610-86) Mass.-Conn.; m. Mary
  Turney. Military service.

Middlebrook, Joseph (  -  ) Mass.-Conn.; m. Mary
  Bateman. Military service.
Middleton, Arthur (1681-1737) S.C.; m. Sarah Powell.
  Deputy Proprietor; Governor.
Middleton, Edward (   -1685) Va.-S.C.; m. ---.
  Councillor; Landowner.
Middleton, Robert (1651-1705) Md.; m. Mary Wheeler.
  Military service.
Mighell, Thomas (1606-54) Mass.; m. Ellen ---.
  Civil officer; Landowner.
Milbourne, John (1624-1703) Conn.; m. Naomi ---.
  Landowner.
Miles, John (1602/03-93/94) Mass.; m. Jane Reed.
  Landowner.
Miles, Richard (  -  ) Conn.; m. Katharine Constable.
  Landowner; Deputy to Court.
Miles, Richard (1622-  ) Pa.; m. ---. Landowner.
Miller, Abraham (  -  ) Pa.; m. ---. Landowner.
Miller, Andrew (1628-1718) N.Y.; m. Margaret ---.
  Landowner.
Miller, Simon (1642-84) Va.; m. Margaret (Prosser)
  Widoein. Military service.
Miller, Thomas (1609/10-80) Pa.or Conn.; m. Sarah
  Nettleton. Landowner.
Miller, Thomas (c1624-75) Mass.; m. Sarah Marshfield.
  Surveyor.
Miller, Thomas (1687-1755) Conn.-Pa.; m. Isabella ---.
  Landowner.
Miller, William (  -  ) N.H.; m. Hannah ---.
  Proprietor,
Miller, William (   -1690) Conn.; m. Patience ---.
  Military service; Landowner.
Mills, George (1585-1674) N.Y.; m. Rebecca ---.
  Landowner.
Mills, Simeon (1613-70) Conn.; m. Sarah Bissell.
  Landowner.
Mills, Simeon (1637-83) Conn.; m. Mary Buell.
  Founder; Military service.
Milner, Francis (c1654-c1710) Va.; m. ---. Burgess;
  Military service.

Milward, Thomas (    -1653) Mass.; m. Ann Goodale.
   Landowner.
Mims, Thomas (1623-92) Va.; m. Elizabeth ---.
   Landowner.
Mims, Thomas (1680-1718) Va.; m. Mellyanne Martin.
   Landowner.
Miner, Manasseh (1647-1728) Conn.; m. Lydia Moore.
   Landowner.
Miner, Thomas (1608-90) Conn.; m. Ann (Elizabeth)---;
   Grace Palmer; Isabella Harcoxe deFrolilay.  Magis-
   trate; Commissioner.
Minor, Doodes (1640-94/95) Va.; m. Elizabeth Cocke.
   Landowner.
Minor, John (    -1698) Va.; m. Ellinor ---.
   Landowner.
Minott, James (1653-1735) Mass.; m. Rebecca Wheeler.
   Physician.
Minshull, Jeffery (1621/22-75) Md.; m. Frances Cars-
   ley.  Founder.
Minshull, Thomas (    -   ) Del.; m. Margaret ---.
   Landowner.
Mirick, John (c1614-75) Mass.; m. Elizabeth Waybourne.
   Freeman; Landowner.
Mitchell, Experience (1609-89) Mass.; m. Jane Cooke.
   Proprietor; Landowner.
Mitchell, Henry (    -1705) Va.; m. ---.  Landowner.
Mitchell, Henry (c1694-1754) Va.; m. Tabitha Brown;
   Sarah ---.  Landowner.
Mitchell, John (c1649-1710) Mass.; m. Mary Prior.
   Landowner.
Mitchell, John (c1675-1754-55) Va.; m. Catherine ---.
   Landowner.
Mitchell, Joseph (1685-1754) Mass.; m. Bathsheba
   Lombard.  Landowner.
Mitchell, Thomas (c1660-1741) Mass.; m. Margaret ---.
   Military service; Deputy to Court.
Mixon, John (    -   ) Va.; m. ---.  Landowner.
Moberley, Edward (  1700-87) S.C.; m. Susannah deRiel.
   Military service.
Moffett, Robert (    -1742) Pa.; m. Margaret Stuart.
   Landowner; Burgess.

Molines    SEE    Mullins
Molyneux    SEE    Mullins
Monet, Isaac (1640-1715) Md.; m. Catherine Pillot.
   Landowner.
Monet, Isaac (1670-1748) Md.; m. Elizabeth Williams.
   Landowner.
Monroe, Andrew (1630-68) Va.; m. Elizabeth Alexander.
   Assemblyman; Commissioner.
Monroe  SEE ALSO  Munro
Montagne, Jean de la (1595-1670) N.Y.; m. Rachel
   DeForest. Military service.
Montague, Peter (1603-59) Va.; m. Cicely Mathews.
   Burgess.
Montague, Peter (1634/39-c1703) Va.; m. Mary (Doodes)
   Minor. Burgess; Commissioner.
Montfort, Peter (c1616-61) N.Y.; m. Saera dePlancke.
   Magistrate; Landowner.
Moon, John (    -1655) Va.; m. Susan ---; Prudence ( )
   Wilson. Burgess; Landowner.
Moon, William (c1602-    ) Va.; m. ---. Landowner.
Moore, Andrew (    -1719) Conn.; m. Mary Nash; Sara
   Phelps. New Haven Compact; Deacon.
Moore, Augustine (c1683-1742/43) Va.; m. Mary Todd.
   Military service; Burgess.
Moore, Francis (1586-1671) Mass.; m. Catherine ---.
   Freeman; Landowner.
Moore, Henry (1682-1745) Va.; m. Mary ---. Land-
   owner; Military service.
Moore, Isaac (    -    ) Mass.; m. ---. Deacon.
Moore, James (1640-1706) S.C.; m. Margaret Berringer.
   Governor.
Moore, James (1667-1723) N.C.-S.C.; m. Elizabeth
   (Beauford) Yeomans. Governor.
Moore, John (1580-1659) Va.; m. Elizabeth ---.
   Burgess.
Moore, John (    -1677) Conn.; m. Abigail ---.
   Freeman; Juror.
Moore, John (1659-1732) S.C.; m. Rebecca Axtell.
   Judge; Landowner.
Moore, John (1674-c1736) N.J.; m. Hope Robbins.
   Military service.

Moore, Miles (c1618-   ) Conn.; m. Isabel Joyner.
Freeman; Landowner.
Moore, Richard (c1610-84) Md.; m. ---. Landowner.
Moore, Samuel (1630-88) N.J.; Mary Ilsley. Town
Clerk; Landowner.
Moore, Thomas (c1615-91) N.Y.; m. Martha Youngs.
Deputy to Court; Constable.
Moore, Thomas (1645-80) Mass.-Conn.; m. Ann ---.
Landowner; Military service.
Moore, William (   -1698/99) Md.; m. Rachel ---.
Military service.
Moore, William (1699-1726/27) N.C.; m. Elizabeth ---.
Justice; Landowner.
Moore   SEE ALSO   More
Moorman, Thomas (   -1647) Va.; m. Elizabeth Clark.
Landowner; Vestryman.
Moorman, Zachariah (c1620-c1669) Va.; m. Mary
Elizabeth Candler. Landowner.
More, Richard (1613/14-96) Mass.; m. Christian Hunt;
Jane Hollingsworth. Mayflower Compact.
More   SEE ALSO   Moore
Morehead, John (1682-1768) Va.; m. ---. Landowner.
Morel   SEE   Morrell
Morgan, Anthony (   -   ) Va.; m. Elizabeth ---.
Landowner.
Morgan, Edward (   -   ) Pa.; m. Elizabeth ---.
Yeoman; Landowner.
Morgan, Francis(c1638-   ) Va.; m. ---. Civil office.
Morgan, Henry (1615/16-63) Md.; m. Frances ---.
Justice; Sheriff.
Morgan, James (1607-1685) Conn.; m. Margery Hill.
Selectman; Deputy to Court.
Morgan, Miles (1616-99) Mass.; m. Prudence Gilbert.
Selectman.
Morgan, Morgan (1688-1766) Del.; m. Catherine Garret-
son. Civil officer; Landowner.
Morgan, Robert (1675-1730) Va.; m. Elizabeth Torksey.
Landowner.
Morrell, Thomas (   -1704) N.Y.; m. Hannah ---.
Landowner.

Morrell, Thomas (1660/62-  ) N.Y.; m. Martha ---.
Landowner.
Morrell  SEE ALSO  Morrill
Morrill, Abraham (    -1662) Mass.; m. Sarah Clement.
Ancient and Honorable Artillery Company.
Morrill, Isaac (1588-1661) Mass.; m. Sarah ---.
Ancient and Honorable Artillery Company.
Morrill, John (1640-c1720) Me.; m. ---. Constable;
Landowner.
Morrill  SEE ALSO  Morrell
Morris, Anthony (1654-1721) Pa.; m. Mary Jones.
Councillor; Justice.
Morris, David (1660-1720) Pa.; m. Mary Philipin.
Landowner.
Morris, Edward (1652-  ) Conn.; m. Grace Bett.
Deputy to Court; Selectman.
Morris, Lewis (1671-1746) N.Y.; m. Estella Graham.
Legislator; Governor.
Morris, Nicholas (1605-64) Va.; m. Martha ---.
Military service.
Morris, Richard (1616-72) N.Y.; m. Sarah Poole.
Landowner; Magistrate.
Morris, Thomas (    -1673) Conn.; m. Elizabeth ---.
Founder; Landowner.
Morris, Thomas (    -1710) Va.; m. ---. Landowner.
Morris, William (    -1745) Va.; m. ---. Justice;
Military service.
Morriset, Pierre (    -c1734) Va.; m. Elizabeth Faure.
Huguenot.
Morrison, Richard (    -c1691) N.J.; m. Sarah ---.
Landowner.
Morse, Anthony (1606-86) Mass.; m. Mary ---; Ann ---.
Landowner.
Morse, Anthony (1662-1710) Mass.; m. Sarah Pike.
Freeman; Military service.
Morse, Jeremiah (1651-1715/16) Mass.; m. Elizabeth
Hamant. Military service.
Morse, John (    -c1641) Mass.; m. ---. Landowner.
Morse, Joseph (c1615-58) Mass.; m. Hannah Phillips.
Freeman.

Morse, Samuel (1587-1654) Mass.; m. Elizabeth Jasper.
Proprietor.

Mortenson, Morton (c1655-c1730) Pa.; m. Margaret ---.
Landowner.

Morton, Andrew (     -c1727) Va.; m. ---.  Landowner.

Morton, George (1565-1684) Mass.; m. Juliana Carpenter.  Landowner.

Morton, John (     -1721) Va.; m. Joanna ( ) Hughes.
Landowner.

Morton, Joseph (     -1688) S.C.; m. Elinor ---.
Governor.

Morton, Nathaniel (1613-85) Mass.; m. Lydia (Fenton)
Cooper.  Secretary.

Morton, Thomas (1690-1731) Va.; m. Elizabeth Woodson.
Military service.

Moseley, Arthur (1630-1702) Va.; m. ---.  Burgess.

Moseley, Henry (1614-56) Va.; m. Ann ---.  Landowner.

Moseley, William (c1608-56) Va.; m. Susanna(Barnett)
Blackmore; Susannah Crookcraft.  Justice.

Moses, John (     -1693) Mass.-Conn.; m. Mary Brown.
Military service; Negotiator.

Mosher, Hugh (1610-94) R.I.; m. Lydia Maxon.  Military service; Landowner.

Moss, Edward (1610-95) Va.; m. Ann Belt.  Landowner.

Moss, Edward (1650-1716) Va.; m. ---.  Justice.

Moss, John (1650-1717) Conn.; m. Martha Lathrop.
Deputy to Court; Founder.

Moss, Robert (     -c1689) Va.; m. Rebecca ---.
Landowner.

Mott, Adam (1596-c1661) Mass.; m. ---.  Military
service.

Mott, Adam (1619-90) Mass.-R.I.; m. Jane Hulet (Hewlett).  Military service.

Mott, George (     -c1674) Va.; m. Elizabeth ---.
Landowner.

Mott, Joseph (1661-1735) N.Y.; m. Mariam ---.
Landowner.

Mott, Nathaniel (1630-   ) Mass.; m. Hannah Shooter.
Founder.

Moulton, John (1599-1649/50) Mass.-N.H.; m. Ann ---.
Founder.

Moulton, Robert (1615-55 )  Mass.; m. Abigail ---.
  Shipbuilder; Landowner.
Moulton, Thomas (1614-   )  N.H.; m. Martha ---.
  Freeman; Landowner.
Mounier, Pierre (c1674-c1715) S.C.; m. Louise Robinet.
  Landowner; Huguenot.
Mountjoy, Edward (   -   ) Va.; m. Elizabeth Monroe.
  Landowner.
Mounts, George (c1635-1705) R.I.; m. Katherine Borden.
  Assemblyman.
Mounts, Providence (   -   ) Va.; m. Elizabeth Hannah
  Meter.  Military service.
Mower, Richard (1595-1668) Mass.; m. Alice ---.
  Landowner.
Mowry, Nathaniel (c1644-1717/18) R.I.; m. Johannah
  Inman.  Proprietor; Landowner.
Moyers, Nicholas Jacob (1668-   ) Pa.; m. Elizabeth
  Caroline ---.  Landowner.
Mudd, Thomas (1647-97) Md.; m. Sarah Boarman.  Land-
  owner.
Mudge, Jarvias (1608-53) Mass.; m. Rebecca Elsen.
  Military service.
Mudgett, Thomas (   -   ) Mass.; m. ---.  Civil office.
Mulford, John (1606-86) Conn.; m. ---.  Deputy to
  Court; Judge.
Mulford, William (1620-87) N.Y.; m. Sarah Akers.
  Founder; Constable.
Mullica, Eric Pallson (1636-1704) N.J.; m. Inglebord
  Helm.  Landowner.
Mullins, William (1578-1621) Mass.; m. Alice ---.
  Mayflower Compact.
Mumford, Edward (    -1690) Va.; m. Mary Watkins.
  Landowner.
Mumford, Joseph (1690-1735) Va.- N.C.; m. Ann ---.
  Justice.
Mumford, Thomas (   -   ) Va.; m. ---.  Landowner.
Munger, Nicholas (1630/31-68) Conn.; m. Sarah Hall.
  Landowner.
Munro, William (1625-1717) Mass.; m. Martha George.
  Civil Officer; Landowner.

Munson, Joseph (1677-1725) Conn.; m. Margery Hitchcock. Selectman; Landowner.

Munson, Samuel (1643-93) Conn.; Martha Bradley.
Freeman; Recorder.

Munson, Thomas (c1612-85) Conn.; m. Susan or Joanna
---. Military service; Legislator.

Murdaugh, John (    -1718) Va.; m. ---. Landowner.

Murray, James (c1671-1704) Md.; m. Jemima Morgan.
Military service.

Muse, John (1633-1723) Va.; m. ---. Landowner.

Musgrove, Cuthbert (c1653-87) Md.; m. Dorothy ---.
Landowner.

Musgrove, John (1685-1746) Md.-Va.; m. ---. Landowner.

Musick, George (1664-1754) Va.; m. Ann ---. Landowner.

Mygatt, Joseph (c1595-1680) Conn.; m. Ann ---.
Freeman; Proprietor.

### -N-

Nabbs, Thomas (    -    ) Md.; m. ---. Proprietor.

Nalle, Martin (1670-1728) Va.; m. Mary Alden. Constable; Military service.

Nance, Richard (c1610-c1690) Va.; m. Alice ---.
Landowner.

Napier, Rene (    -1751) Va.; m. Sarah LaForte.
Huguenot.

Nash, Jacob (    -    ) Va.; m. Abigail Dyer. Military
service; Councillor.

Nash, Thomas (1590-1658) Conn.; m. Margery Baker.
Deputy to Court; Landowner.

Nason, Richard (1606-96) Mass.; m. Sarah Baker.
Juror; Selectman.

Naylor, John (1654-1727) Pa.; m. Jane Cutler. Landowner.

Neale, Abner (1696-1772) Va.-N.C.; m. Judith Toulson.
Justice; Guardian of Orphans.

Neale, Daniel (1620-    ) Va.; m. Ellinor ---. Burgess;
Sheriff.

Neale, James (1615-84) Md.; m. Anna Gill. Burgess;
  Councillor.
Neal, Walter (1633-1717) N.H.; m. Mary Ayers. Select-
  man; Military service.
Needham, Anthony (1628-1705) Mass.; m. Ann Potter.
  Military service.
Nelme, Richard (1615-52) Va.; m. Anne ---. Landowner.
Nelson, Ambrose ( -c1717) Md.; m. Martha ---.
  Landowner.
Nelson, Provost ( -c1685) Va.; m. Ann Harlow.
  Landowner.
Nelson, Thomas ( -1648) Va.; m. Joan Dummer.
  Landowner.
Nelson, Thomas (1635-1712) Mass.; m. Mary Hunt.
  Town Clerk.
Nesmith, James (1697- ) N.H.; m. Elizabeth McKeen.
  Landowner; Military service.
Nevill; Nevil  SEE  Neville
Neville, James (1640-c1698) Va.; m. Elizabeth ---.
  Military service.
Neville, James (1650-c1718) N.C.; m. ---. Landowner.
Neville, James (1686-1752) Va.; m. ( ) Keene.
  Military service.
Neville, John (1612-64) Md.; m. Bridget Thomsley
  (Thornbay). Councillor.
Newberry, Thomas (1594-1636) Mass.; m. Joanne Dali-
  nett; Martha ---. Landowner; Representative.
Newbold, Michael (1623-1712) N.J.; m. Anne ---.
  Landowner; Councillor.
Newcomb, Andrew (1618-86) Mass.; m. ---. Sea Captain.
Newcomb, Andrew (1640-1706) Mass.; m. Anne Bayes.
  Constable; Juror.
Newcomb, Francis (1605-92) Mass.; m. Rachel ---.
  Landowner.
Newcomb, Jonathan (1685/86-1742) Mass.; m. Deborah ---.
  Landowner.
Newcomb, Peter (1648-1725) Mass.; m. Susannah Cutting.
  Surveyor.

Newdigate, John (1580-1665) Mass.; m. Ann (Towsen)
  (Hunt) Draper. Selectman; Freeman.

Newell, Abraham (1584-1672) Mass.; m. Frances ---.
Sponsor of Harvard University.

Newhall, Joseph (1658-1706) Mass.; m. Susannah Farrar.
Landowner.

Newhall, Thomas (1630-87) Mass.; m. Elizabeth Potter.
Military service.

Newland, William Henry (c1605-94) Mass.; m. Rose
Holloway.  Committeeman; Military service.

Newlin, Nathaniel (1665-1729) Pa.; m. Mary Mendenhall.
Councillor; Quaker.

Newlin, Nicholas  (c1629/30-99) Pa.; m. Elizabeth
Paggott.  Landowner; Quaker.

Newman, Henry (1690-1774) Md.; m. Nelly ---.  Landowner.

Newman, John (1611-77) Va.; m. --- Woodbridge.
Landowner.

Newman, Thomas (1584-1659) N.Y.; m. Mary Mourton.
Magistrate.

Newton, James (1653/54-1737) Conn.; m. Mary Hubbell.
Deputy to Court; Military service.

Newton, John (1639-97) Va.-Md.; m. Rose Allerton;
Rose (Tucker) Gerrard.  Justice.

Newton, Richard (c1609-1701) Mass.; m. Anne Loker.
Military service.

Newton, Roger (1616-83) Conn.; m. Mary Hooker.
Landowner; Minister.

Nichols, Francis (1590-1650) Conn.; m. Ann Wynes.
Founder; Landowner.

Nichols, Marvin Curtis (1649-1722) Va.; m. Catherine
Digges.  Landowner.

Nichols, Richard (     -1732) Mass.; m. Abigail Damon.
Freeman; Landowner.

Nichols, Thomas (     -1646) Mass.; m. Rebecca Joslin.
Proprietor.

Nicholson, Samuel (     -1685) N.J.; m. Anne ---.
Justice; Landowner.

Nicholson, William (1638-1721) N.C.; m. ---.  Burgess.

Nicholson, William (     -1728) Va.; m. Alice ---.
Landowner.

Niles, Samuel (1674-1762) Mass.; m. Elizabeth Thacher;
Jane Reed.  Minister; Military service.

Nims, Godfrey (c1660-1705) Mass.; m. Mary (Miller)
   Williams. Landowner.
Nixon, Zacharias (    -1691) N.C.; m. Elizabeth Page.
   Landowner.
Noble, Joseph (1689-1740) Md.; m. Mary Wheeler.
   Landowner.
Noble, Thomas (1632-1704) Mass.; m. Hannah Warriner.
   Appraiser; Landowner.
Noe, John (    -1751) N.Y.-N.J.; m. Elizabeth (Damaris)
   Gerard. Landowner.
Noe, Peter (    -1710) N.Y.-N.J.; m. Margaret Clark.
   Landowner.
Norfleet, James (    -1732) Va.-N.C.; m. Sarah Gordon;
   Mary Sumner. Justice.
Norfleet, Thomas (1640-95) Va.; m. ---. Military
   service; Assemblyman.
Norfleet, Thomas (1670-1746) Va.; m. Mary Marmaduke.
   Landowner.
Norman, Henry (c1660-1711) N.C.; m. Anne Hancock.
   Juror; Landowner.
Norman, Isaac (c1670-  ) Va.-Md.; m. Anne Telson;
   Frances Courtney. Landowner.
Norman, Richard (    -1682) Mass.; m. ---. Landowner.
Norris, Edward (1584-  ) Mass.; m. Elvira ---.
   Minister.
Norris, Nicholas (1640-  ) N.H.; m. Sarah Coxe.
   Military service.
Norris, Thomas (c1608-74) Va.; m. Ann Hynson. Land-
   owner; Juror.
Norris, William (c1690-c1724) Va.; m. Susannah
   Gardner. Clerk of Court.
Norsworthy, Tristram (    -1660) Va.; m. Ann ---.
   Burgess; Landowner.
North, John (1615-1691/92) Conn.; m. Hannah Bird.
   Freeman; Proprietor.
Northend, Ezekiel (1622-98) Mass.; m. Edna Bailey.
   Selectman.
Northrup, Joseph (1637-69) Conn.; m. Mary Norton.
   Landowner.
Northrup, Stephen (1600-87) R.I.; m. Elizabeth
   Harrington. Proprietor; Freeman.

Northup; Northrop   SEE   Northrup

Norton, Freegrace (1688-   ) Conn.; m. Sarah Martin. Landowner.

Norton, George (    -1659) Mass.; m. Mary ---. Selectman.

Norton, George (1641-96) Mass.-Conn.; m. Nancy (Barber) Gillett. Selectman.

Norton, Henry (1618-57) Me.; m. Margaret ---. Landowner.

Norton, John (c1622-   ) Conn.; m. Dorothy ---. Landowner.

Norton, John (c1700-   ) Va.; m. ( ) --- Miller. Landowner.

Norton, Nicholas (1610-90) Mass.; m. Elizabeth ---. Military service.

Norton, Thomas (1582-1645) Conn.; m. Grace Wells. Military service.

Norwood, Francis (1635-1709) Mass.; m. Elizabeth Coldham. Landowner.

Norwood, John (   -   ) Va.; m. Lydia Ledbetter. Sheriff.

Norwood, William (1615-1703) Va.; m. Lydia Jordan. Landowner.

Nostrand, Jacob Jansen (   -   ) N.Y.; m. Jannetje Jacobse. Brewer; Landowner.

Noyes, James (1608-56) Mass.; m. Sarah Brown. Landowner.

Noyes, Nicholas (1615/18-1701) Mass.; m. Mary Cutting. Deputy to Court; Deacon.

Noyes, Peter (c1591-1657) Mass.; m. Abigail ---. Selectman; Deputy to Court.

Nucum   SEE   Newcomb.

Nunn, Thomas (c1690-c1740) Va.; m. Elizabeth ---. Landowner.

Nunn, William (   -   ) N.C.; m. Elizabeth Loften. Justice.

Nuthall, John (1620-45) Md.; m. Elizabeth (Bacon) Holloway. Justice.

Nutman, James (1662-1739) N.J.; m. Sarah Prudden. Assessor; Constable.

Nutter, Christopher (1640-1703) Md.; m. Mary Dorman.
Landowner.
Nutter, John (1671-1702) Md.-Del.; m. Elizabeth ---.
Landowner.
Nutting, John (1620/25-71) Mass.; m. Sarah Elizabeth
Eggleston. Military service.
Nye, Benjamin (1620-90) Mass.; m. Katherine Tupper.
Supervisor of highways; Military service.

-O-

Oates, James (1644/45-1703) N.C.; m. Elizabeth Wyatt.
Attorney; Assemblyman.
Odell, Thomas (1670-1711) Md.; m. Sarah(Ridgeley)
Brewer. Landowner.
Offley, John (   -  ) Md.; m. ---.  Commissioner;
Landowner.
Ogden, John (1608-81) Conn.-N.J.; m. Jane Bond.
Landowner.
Ogden, Richard (   -1687) Conn.; m. Mary ---.
Landowner.
Ogle, John (1640-83) Del.; m. Elizabeth Wollaston;
Eleanor Pringle. Landowner.
Olcott, Thomas (1609-54) Conn.; m. Abigail ---.
Proprietor.
Oldage, Richard (   -1660) Conn.; m. ---.  Land-
owner.
Oldham, John (   -1680) Va.; m. Abigail ---.
Landowner.
Oldham, Samuel (c1600-c1655) Va.; Jane Bessell.
Landowner.
Oldham, Samuel (1680-1759) Va.; m. Elizabeth Newton.
Military service.
Oldis, Joseph (   -1692) S.C.; m. ---.  Deputy
Secretary; Deputy Registrar.
Oldis, Thomas (c1604-c1658) Va.; m. Elizabeth ---.
Burgess; Justice.
Oldys  SEE  Oldis
Oliver, John (c1627-c1652) Va.; m. Ellen ---.
Landowner.

Oliver, Thomas (c1568-1659) Mass.; m. Ann ---.
Landowner.
Oliver, Thomas (1601-c1640) Va.; m. Mary ---. Land-
owner.
Olmstead, James (1580-1640) Conn.; m. Joyce Cornish.
Freeman, Constable.
Olmstead, Nicholas (1619-84) Conn.; m. Sarah Loomis.
Freeman; Surveyor.
Olmstead, Richard (1612-86) Conn.; m. ---. Deputy to
Court; Military service.
Olney, Thomas (1600-82) R.I.; m. Mary Ashton; Mary
Small. Founder; Landowner.
Omohundro,Richard ( -1698) Va.; m. Anne Moxley.
Landowner.
O'Neill, Hugh ( - ) Del.; m. Annie Cox. Landowner.
Onge, Frances ( -c1638) Mass.; m. Francis Onge.
Landowner.
Ordway, James (1618-c1702) N.H.; m. Ann Emery.
Proprietor.
Ormsby, Richard (1602-64) Mass.-Me.; m. Sarah Wanton.
Landowner.
Orton, Thomas (1613-41) Conn.; m. Margaret Poll.
Deputy to Court; Landowner.
Osborn, John ( -1689) Conn.; m. Ann Oldage.
Landowner.
Osborn, Joseph (1636-98) N.J.; m. Priscilla Roberts.
Landowner.
Osborn, Richard (1613-c84) N.Y.; m. ---. Landowner.
Osborne, Stephen (1634- ) N.J.; m. Sarah ---.
Founder.
Osborne, Thomas (1580-1633) Va.; m. ---. Burgess;
Military service.
Osborn, Thomas (1595-1686) Conn.-Mass.; m. Mary
Goatly. Founder; Military service.
Osgood, John (1595-1651) Mass.; m. Sarah ---. Select-
man; Military service.
Ostrander, Pieter Pietersen (1648- ) N.Y.; m.
Catrina ---. Landowner.
O'Sullivant, John Thomas (c1634-c93) Va.; m. Mary
Hayes; Sara Gore. Landowner; Explorer.

Otis, John (1581-1667) Mass.; m. Margaret ---.
Landowner; Yeoman.
Otis, John (1621-84) Mass.; m. Mary Jacob. Oath of
Fidelity; Military service.
Otis, John (1657-1727) Mass.; m. Grace Hayman.
Freeman.
Otis, John (1687-1759) Mass.; m. Hannah Churchill.
Landowner.
Otis, Joseph (1665-1754) Mass.; m. Dorothy Thomas.
Judge.
Otney, George (1642-66) Md.; m. Sarah Marsh. Military
service.
Outlaw, Edward (    -1714) Va.; m. ---. Landowner.
Overton, James (1688-1748) Va.; m. Elizabeth Garland.
Justice; Military service.
Overton, William (1638-97) Va.; m. Elizabeth Waters;
Mary (Claiborne) Rose. Landowner.
Oviatt, Thomas (1672-1749/50) Conn.; m. Mary  Baldwin.
Landowner.
Owen, Griffith (    -1718) Pa.; m. Sarah ---.
Physician.
Owens, John (c1698-1757) Va.; m. Phoebe ---. Select-
man; Landowner.
Owen, Owen (1690-1741) Pa.; m. Anne Wood. Landowner;
Sheriff.
Owens, Richard (1624-93) Md.; m. Ann ---. Landowner.
Owen, Sir Richard (1662-1716) Md.; m.  Rachel Roberts.
Landowner; Military service.
Owen, Robert (c1612-85) Del.-Pa.; m. Jane Vaughn.
Landowner.
Owen, Robert (1657-97) Pa.; m. Rebecca Humphrey.
Justice; Councillor.
Owen, Sullivant (c1700-c27) Va.; m. Margaret Hewlett.
Landowner.
Owsley, Thomas (1663-1700) Va.; m. Anne Harris; Anne
Gesty. Minister; Burgess.
Owsley, Thomas (1696-1751) Va.; m. Ann West. Military
service.
Oxenbridge, John (1608-74) Mass.; m. Frances Woodward.
Minister; Landowner.

Pace, George (1620-54) Va.; m. Sarah Maycock.
Landowner.
Pace, Richard (1590-1628) Va.; m. Isabella Smyth.
Military service; Landowner.
Pace, Richard (    -1738) Va.; m. Rebecca ---.
Landowner; Juror.
Packard, Sam (1698-  ) Mass.; m. Elizabeth Lathrop.
Military service.
Packer, James (1681-1765) Conn.; m. Abigale Avery.
Selectman; Landowner.
Page, Lady Alice Lukin (1625-98) Va.; m. Col. John
Page. Landowner.
Page, Isaack (    -1681) N.C.; m. Damaris Shattuck.
Proprietor.
Page, John (1627-92) Va.; m. Fanny Burwell; Lady
Alice Lukin. Justice; Burgess.
Page, Mann (1691-1730) Va.; m. Judith Wormeley.
Councillor; Landowner.
Page, Matthew (1645-1703) Va.; m. Mary Mann. Land-
owner.
Page, Thomas (1615-76) Va.; m. --- Allen. Landowner.
Paine, Anthony (1586-1650) R.I.; m. ---. Landowner.
Paine, Elisha (    -1735) Mass.; m. Rebecca Doane.
Deputy to Court; Selectman.
Paine, Thomas (1586-1631) Mass.; m. Katherine
Marassant. Shipowner; Representative.
Paine, Thomas (c1610/11-1706) Mass.; m. Mary Snow.
Constable; Deputy to Court.
Paine, William (c1598-1660) Mass.; m. Ann ---, or
Hannah ---. Landowner.
Paine    SEE ALSO    Payne
Palfrey, Peter (    -1663) Mass.; m. Edith ---.
Freeman; Landowner.
Palin, Henry (c1630-89) Va.-N.C.; m. ---. Landowner.
Palk, Samuel (c1665-1710) Mass.; m. Sarah Brabrook.
Landowner.
Palmer, Gershom (1644-1718) Conn.; m. Ann Denison.
Landowner.
Palmer, John (1615-1704) Va.; m. ---. Landowner.
Palmer, John (c1660-1745) Pa.; m. Christiana ---;
Martha Sonaby. Landowner.

Palmer, Martin (1625-1702) Va.; m. --- ( ) Crenshaw.
Military service.
Palmer, Samuel (1675-1728) N.Y.; m. Mary Sutton.
Surveyor; Military service.
Palmer, Walter (c1585-1661) Conn.-Mass.; m. Rebecca
Short. Founder; Constable.
Palmer, William ( -c1637) Mass.; m. Frances ---.
Landowner; Magistrate.
Palsgrave, Richard ( -1656) Mass.; m. Ann ---.
Landowner.
Pancoast, John ( -1694) N.Y.-N.J.) m. Elizabeth
---. Constable; Assemblyman.
Pannill, William ( -1677) Va.; m. Katherine ---;
Frances Sterne. Landowner.
Parcell; Parsell SEE Pearsall
Pardee, George (1624-1700) Conn.; m. Katherine Lane.
Minister; Ferryman.
Parish SEE Parrish
Park, Parke and Parkes (Filed in One Alphabet)
Parke, Daniel (1628-79) Va.; m. Rebecca Evelyn.
Burgess; Physician.
Park, Richard (1602-c66) Mass.; m. Margery Crane;
Sarah (Collier) Brewster. Landowner.
Parke, Robert (c1585-1664) Conn.; m. Marthy Chaplin.
Freeman; Selectman.
Parks, Robert (1651-1707) Mass.-Conn.; m. Rachel
Leffingwell. Military service.
Parker, Abraham (1612-85) Mass.; m. Rose Whilock.
Freeman; Founder.
Parker, Edward (1598-1662) Conn.; m. Elizabeth (Wood)
Potter. Moderator.
Parker, George (1617/29-74) Va.; m. Florence Elzey.
Military service; Sheriff.
Parker, Hananiah (1638-1724) Mass.; m. Elizabeth
Browne. Representative; Military service.
Parker, Jacob ( -1669) Mass.; m. Sarah ---.
Military service; Town Clerk.
Parker, James (c1617-1700) Mass.; m. Elizabeth Long.
Representative; Military service.
Parker, James (1653-1731) Mass.; m. Elizabeth Sexton.
Civil Officer.

Parker, John (1648-1711) Conn.; m. Hannah Bassett.
Landowner.

Parker, Richard (1630-1679/81) Va.; m. Elizabeth
Bailey. Physician.

Parker, Thomas (1581-1663) Va.; m. ( ) Peter Montague.
Landowner.

Parker, Thomas (1656-98) Mass.; m. Mary Fletcher.
Selectman; Military service.

Parker, Thomas (c1667-1717) Va.-N.C.; m. Jean ---.
Landowner.

Parker, William (c1615-76) Va.-Md.; m. Ann Powell.
Assemblyman.

Parkhurst, George (c1588-c1655) Mass.; m. Phebe ---.
Freeman; Landowner.

Parmelee, John (1585-  ) Conn.; m. Hannah ---.
Plantation Covenant.

Parnell, John (1690-  ) Va.; m. ---. Landowner.

Parr, John (c1612-c1644) Md.; m. ---. Landowner.

Parrish, Edward (c1640-80) Md.-Va.; m. Clara ---.
Landowner.

Parrish, Humphrey (c1660-1743) Va.; m. Mary ---.
Proprietor; Landowner.

Parrott, Francis (1640-1715) N.C.; m. Frances Johnson.
Justice.

Parrott, Richard (1620-86) Va.; m. Sarah Dale;
Margaret ---. Commissioner; Justice.

Parshall, David (1682-1725/26) Conn.; m. Mary Gardiner.
Landowner; Military service.

Parshall, Israel (1680-1738) N.Y.; m. Joanna Swezey.
Landowner; Military service.

Parshall, James (1640/50-1701) N.Y.; m. Elizabet
Gardiner. Landowner.

Parsons, Benjamin (   -1689) Mass.; m. Sarah Vore.
Deacon.

Parsons, Jeffrey (c1631-89) Mass.; m. Sarah Vinson.
Landowner.

Parsons, John (1617-83) Mass.; m. Mary Bliss.
Freeman.

Parsons, John (1620-  ) Va.; m. Frances ---.
Landowner.

Parsons, Jonathan (1668-   ) Mass.; m. Margaret Marshfield. Minister.

Parsons, Joseph (1618-83) Mass.; m. Mary Bliss.
Military service.

Parsons, Thomas (c1605-1661) Conn.; m. Lydia Brown
Landowner; Military service.

Parsons, Thomas (c1620-84) Md.; m. Isabella ---.
Landowner.

Partridge, George (   -1676) Mass.; m. Sarah Tracy.
Constable; Surveyor.

Partridge, Nathaniel (c1680-1722) S.C.; m. Anne ---.
Provost Marshal.

Partridge, Ralph (c1630-58) Mass.; m. Patience ---.
Minister.

Partridge, Samuel (1645-1740) Mass.; m. Mehitable
Crow. Judge; Military service.

Paschall, William (1693-1774) N.C.; m. Reliance ---.
Landowner.

Paslay, Peasley   SEE   Pasley

Pasley, Robert (c1670-   ) Va.; m. Ellenor ---.
Interpreter.

Pasley, William (c1630-90) Va.; m. ---.   Proprietor;
Landowner.

Patch, Nicholas (1597-1673) Mass.; m. Elizabeth
Owsley. Freeman; Landowner.

Pate, Thomas (c1650-1702) Va.; m. Elizabeth ---.
Physician; Burgess.

Paterson, James (c1700-36) Pa.; m. Susanna Howard.
Landowner; Indian Trader.

Paterson, Lucas (   -1687) N.J.; m. Cristina ---.
Landowner.

Patten   SEE   Patton

Patton, William (   -1669) Mass.; m. Mary ---.
Founder; Surveyor.

Pauling   SEE   Pawling

Paulk, Samuel (1665-1711) Mass.; m. Sarah Brabook.
Landowner.

Paullin, Henry (c1660-1723) Pa.; m. Sarah ---.
Landowner.

Paullin, Thomas (   -   ) Va.; m. Elizabeth ---.
Justice; Civil Officer.

Pawling, Henry (     -1691/92) N.Y.; m. Neelije Roosa.
  Sheriff; Councillor.
Paxson, James (     -1722) Pa.; m. Jane ----.  Burgess;
  Landowner.
Paxson, William (1648-1709) Pa.; m. Mary Partington.
  Landowner.
Paxson, William  (1675-1718) Pa.; m. Abigail Powell.
  Landowner.
Paybody  SEE  Peabody
Payne, Sir John  (1590-1668) Va.; m. Millicent ----.
  Landowner.
Payne, Sir John (1615/20-90)  Va.; m. Lettice Lawson;
  Margaret ----.  Landowner.
Payne, Moses (1581-1643) Mass.; m. Mary Benison;
  Elizabeth.  Freeman; Landowner.
Payne, Stephen (c1613-1679) Mass.; m. Rose ----.
  Military service; Landowner.
Payne, William (1652-98) Va.; m. Elizabeth Pope.
  Justice; Landowner.
Payne, William (1692-1776) Va.; m. Alicia Jones.
  Sheriff; Tobacco inspector.
Payne  SEE ALSO  Paine
Payson, Edward (   -   ) Mass.; m. Mary Elliot.
  Freeman.
Payson, Edward (1657-1732) Mass.; m. Elizabeth Phillips.
  Minister; Freeman.
Peabody, Francis (c1614-97/99) Mass.; m. Mary Foster;
  Lydia ----.  Freeman; Landowner.
Peabody, John (1590-1667) Mass.; m. Isabel Harper.
  Freeman; Town Clerk.
Peabody, William (1620-1707) Mass.; m. Elizabeth Alden.
  Proprietor.
Peake, Christopher (     -1667) Mass.; m. Dorcas French.
  Landowner.
Pearce, George (1662-1752) R.I.; m. Alice Hart.
  Landowner.
Pearce, Giles (1651-98) R.I.; m. Elizabeth Hall.
  Councillor; Assemblyman.
Pearce, Richard (1615-78) R.I.; m. Susannah Wright.
  Landowner.

Pearce    SEE ALSO    Peirce; Pierce

Pearsall, Nicholas (    -   ) Conn.; m. Sarah ---.
  Constable.
Pearsall, Thomas (c1654-c96) N.Y.; m. Mary Seaman.
  Landowner.
Pearson, Edward (    -1689) Pa.; m. Sarah Burgess.
  Landowner.
Pearson, Enoch (1690-1740) Pa.; m. Mary  Smith.
  Landowner.
Pearson, James (1670-1746) Pa.-Va.; m. Susanna Furas.
  Quaker.
Pearson, John (1660-   ) Del.; m. ---.  Landowner.
Pearson, Thomas (c1660-1734) Pa.; m. Margery Smith.
  Councillor; Supervisor of highways.
Pease, John (1630-89) Conn.; m. Ann Cummings.  Land-
  owner.
Pease, John (1654-1734) Mass.-Conn.; m. Margaret
  Adams.  Selectman; Landowner.
Peck, Henry (    -1651) Conn.; m. Joan Walker.  New
  Haven Compact; Landowner.
Peck, Joseph (1587-1663) Mass.; m. Rebecca Clark.
  Commissioner; Deputy to  Court.
Peck, Nicholas (c1630-1710) Mass.; m. Rebecah Bosworth.
  Deputy to Court; Military service.
Peck, Robert (1580-1656) Mass.; m. Anne ---.  Minister.
Peck,  William (1601-94) Conn.; m. Elizabeth Holt.
  Proprietor; Assemblyman.
Peckham, John (1595-1696) R.I.; m. Mary Clark.
  Founder.
Peckman, William (1647-1734) R.I.; m. Elizabeth Clarke;
  Susanna ---.  Minister.
Pedden, James (    -1693/94) Va.; m. Jane ( ) Huggins.
  Landowner.
Peden    SEE    Pedden
Peek, Jan (    -   ) N.Y.; m. Maria DeTruy.  Landowner.
Peeler, Johannes (1698-1748) N.C.; m. Elizabeth March.
  Landowner.
Peeples David (1616-59) Va.; m. Elapet Mackie.
  Justice; Military service.

Peirce, John (      -c1683) N.C.; m. Mary ---. Land-
owner.
Peirce, John (1672-   ) N.C.; m. Sarah ---. Landowner.
Peirce, William (      -1651) Va.; m. ---. Councillor;
Burgess.
Peirce   SEE   Pearce; Pierce
Peirsey, Abraham (      -1627/28) Va.; m. Elizabeth
Draper. Burgess; Commissioner.
Pell, Sir John (1643-1700) N.Y.; m. Rachel Pinkney.
Landowner.
Pelletreau, Elie (      -1730) N.Y.; m. Marie Benoist.
Collector of taxes; Constable.
Pels, Hendrich (c1686-c1742) N.Y.; m. Sophia Palmetier.
Military service.
Pells; Peltz   SEE   Pels
Pember, Agnes (Way)(1660-1732/33) Conn.; m. Thomas
Pember. Nurse; Doctress.
Pemberton, James (1622-96) Mass.; m. Sarah Marshall.
Landowner.
Pence, George (1638-64) Va.; m. Catherine. Military
service.
Pendarvis, Joseph (      -c1694) S.C.; m. ---. Assem-
blyman; Justice.
Pendleton, Brian (1599-1681) Mass.; m. Eleanor Price.
Councillor; Freeman.
Pendleton, Edmund (1665-1750) R.I.; m. Mary ---.
Landowner.
Pendleton, James (1626/27-1709) Mass.; m. Hannah
Goodman. Ancient and Honorable Artillery Company.
Pendleton, Henry (1683-1721) Va.; m. Mary Taylor.
Landowner.
Pendleton, Philip (1654-1721) Va.; m. Isabella Hurt.
Burgess; Deputy Clerk.
Pengree, Moses (1610-96) Mass.; m. Abigail Clement.
Deputy to Court; Selectman.
Penick, Edward (1655-94) Va.; m. Elizabeth ---.
Landowner.
Penn, William (1609-c1652) Va.; m. Elizabeth Markham.
Landowner.
Pennington, Thomas (c1640-c1702) Va.; m. Sarah ( )
Lewis. Military service.

Pennock, Joseph (1677-1711) Pa.; m. Mary Levis.
Landowner.
Penny, Humphrey (     -1683) Conn.; m. Mary Hull.
Landowner; Freeman.
Pennypacker, Hendrick (1674-1754) Pa.; m. Eve Umstat.
Surveyor; Proprietor.
Pepper, Robert (     -1682) Mass.; m. Elizabeth
Johnson. Landowner.
Pepperell, William (1646-1734) Me.; m. Margery Bray.
Justice; Councillor.
Perault, Charles (     -1717) Va.; m. Margaret ---.
Vestryman.
Perdeux   SEE   Perdue
Perdue, Henri (1585-   ) Md.; m. Anne DesJardins.
Merchant; Landowner.
Perham, John (1632-1720) Mass.; m. Lydia Shipley.
Freeman.
Perisho, James (1700/01-c1754) N.C.; m.  Sarah ---.
Overseer of highways.
Perkins, Constantine (1682-1770) Va.; m. Ann Pollard.
Landowner.
Perkins, Isaac (1611-85) N.H.; m. Susanna Wise.
Founder; Constable.
Perkins, Jabez (1677-   ) Conn.; m. Hannah (Lathrop)
Buck. Landowner.
Perkins, Jacob (1624-1700) Conn.; m. Elizabeth Whipple.
Military service.
Perkins, John (1590-1654) Mass.; m. Judith Gater.
Deputy to Court; Military service.
Perkins, Nicholas (1614-56) Va.; m. Elizabeth Hardynge;
Mary Parker. Landowner.
Perkins, Nicholas (1641-1711)Va.; m. Sarah Childress.
Landowner.
Perkins, William (1607-82) Mass.; m. Elizabeth Wooton.
Minister.
Perley, Allen (1608-75) Mass.; m. Susanna Bokeson.
Landowner.
Peronneau, Samuel (c1672-1722) S.C.; m. Joanne Collin.
Elder.
Perrin, Daniel (c1645-1719) N.J.-N.Y.; m. Marie
Thorol; Elizabeth ---. Landowner.

Perrin, John (1614-74) Mass.; m. Ann ---.  Surveyor;
Town Clerk.

Perrott, Francis (     -1717) N.C.; m. Frances Johnson.
Landowner.

Perrott, Richard (1645-  ) Va.; m. Elizabeth Burgess.
Vestryman.

Perry, Ezra (c1625-89) Mass.; m. Deborah Burge.
Freeman; Landowner.

Perry, John (     -1642) Mass.; m. Anna Phipps.
Freeman.

Perryn  SEE  Perrin

Pers, John (c1588-1661) Mass.; m. Elizabeth ---.
Freeman; Deputy to Court.

Person, John (c1658-  ) Va.; m. Frances ---.
Councillor.

Peters, Andrew (c1636-1713) Mass.; m. Mercy (Bearnley)
Wilborne.  Military service.

Peterson, Cornelius (  -  ) N.Y.; m. Letitia Vanderbilt.  Military service.

Pettijohn  SEE  Pettyjohn

Pettingill, Richard (1620-95) Mass.; m. Joanna Ingersoll.  Juror.

Pettit, Nathaniel (c1640-1718) N.J.; m. Mary Dailey.
Tax collector; Quaker.

Pettit, Thomas (c1610-68) N.Y.; m. Christian Mellowes.
Town Marshal.

Pettus, Sir Thomas (1552-1620) Va.; m. Cecily King.
Councillor.

Pettus, Sir Thomas (1598-1669) Pa.; m. ---.
Landowner.

Pettus, Thomas (1610-60) Va.; m. Elizabeth Durrent.
Councillor; Military service.

Petty, Christopher (     -1740) Va.; m. Mary ---.
Landowner.

Petty, William (     -c1747) N.J.; m. Jane ---.
Landowner; Founder.

Pettyjohn, James (c1635-  ) Va.; m. Isabella ---.
Civil Officer.

Pettyjohn, John (1662-1733) Va.; m. ---.  Landowner.

Peurifoy  SEE  Purefoy.

Peverell, Daniel (     -c1692) Md.; m. Hannah ---.
Landowner.
Peyton, Henry (c1631-59) Va.; m. Ellen Partington.
Landowner; Burgess.
Peyton, Sir Henry (1690-1756) Va.; m. Katherine Bate-
man.  Landowner.
Peyton,  Robert (c1640-94) Va.; m. ---.  Attorney;
Military service.
Peyton, Valentine (1686-1755) Va.; m. Frances (Burr)
Harrison.  Justice; Military service.
Peyton, Valentine (     -1786) Va.; m. Margaret
Gwatkin.  Military service.
Phelps, George (c1606-87) Mass.; m. Frances ( ) Dewey.
Military service.
Phelps, Nathaniel (1677-1746) Conn.; m. Hannah Bissell.
Military service.
Phelps, Samuel (c1625-99) Mass.-Conn.; m. Sarah
Griswold.  Landowner.
Phelps, Timothy (1639-1719) Conn.; m. Mary Griswold.
Military service.
Phelps, William (1599-1672) Conn.; m. Elizabeth ---.
Commissioner; Governor's  Assistant.
Phelps, William (1657-  ) Conn.; m. Abigail Stebbons.
Committee of Safety.
Philbrick, James (c1622-74) N.H.; m. Ann Roberts.
Landowner.
Philbrick, Thomas (     -1667) Mass.-N.H.; m. Eliza-
beth ---.  Proprietor.
Philbrick, Thomas (1624-1700) N.H.; m. Hannah (French)
White.  Selectman.
Phillips, Benjamin (1658-c85) Mass.; m. Sarah Thomas.
Military service.
Phillips, George (1562-1644) Mass.; m. Elizabeth
Sargent; Elizabeth Welden. Minister;  Founder.
Phillips, John (1602-77) Mass.; m. Joanna ---;
Faith Doten.  Founder.
Phillips, John (1696-  ) R.I.; m. Sarah ---.  Landowner.
Phillips, Richard Freeman (1622-  ) Mass.; m. ---.
Military service.
Phillips, Samuel (     -1696) Mass.; m. Sarah Appleton.
Minister.

Phillips, Samuel (1662-1720) Mass.; m. Hannah Gillam.
Minister; Bookseller.

Phillips, Theophilus (1653-89) Conn.-N.J.; m. Ann
Hunt. Surveyor; Magistrate.

Phillips, Theophilus (1675-1709) N.J.-Conn.; m.
Frances Elizabeth Betts. Founder Presbyterian Church.

Phillips, William ( - ) Va.; m. ---. Military
service.

Phillips, William ( -1683) Mass.; m. Mary ---.
Landowner.

Phillips, Zerubabel (1632-89) Conn.; m. ---. Commissioner; Constable.

Philpot, Thomas ( - ) Va.; m. ---. Military
service.

Pickard, John ( -1683) Mass.; m. Jane Crosby.
Deputy to Court.

Pickens, Andrew ( - ) Pa.-N.C.; m. Ester Jean
Bonneau. Justice; Coroner.

Pickens, John ( -1767/73) S.C.-Pa.; m. Eleanor
Pakens. Justice; Sheriff.

Pickens, William Andre (1670- ) Md.; m. Margaret ---.
Military service.

Pickering, John (1674-1739) Mass.; m. ---. Constable;
Selectman.

Pickett, Henry (1641-1702) Va.; m. Sarah ---. Landowner; Physician.

Pickett, William (c1585-1640) Va.; m. Sarah Stoner.
Subscriber to Virginia Company.

Pickett, William (1600-84) Va.; m. Ann Sanford
(Sandford). Landowner.

Pierce, Abraham ( -c1673) Mass.; m. Rebecca ---.
Landowner; Military service.

Pierce, Daniel (1600-77) Mass.; m. Sarah ---; Ann ( )
Milward. Proprietor.

Pierce, Daniel (1638-1704) Mass.; m. Elizabeth
Milward. Military service.

Pierce, John (c1588-1661) Mass.; m. Elizabeth ---.
Deputy to Court; Military service.

Pierce, Joshua ( - ) Mass.; m. Martha ---.
Freeman.

Pierce, Michael (1615-76) Conn.-Mass.; m. Persis
Eames. Military services.
Pierce, Thomas (1608-53) Mass.; m. Elizabeth ---.
Deputy to Court.
Pierce, William (1631-1702) Va.; m. Sarah Underwood.
Military service.
Pierce    SEE ALSO    Pearce; Peirce
Pierpont, James (1659-1714) Conn.; m. Mary Hooker.
Minister.
Pierrepont, John (1619-82) Mass.; m. Thankful Stow.
Deputy to Court.
Piersey, Abraham (1577-1628) Va.; m. Elizabeth Draper;
Frances Hinton.  Merchant; Treasurer.
Pierson, Abraham (1613-78) N.J.-Conn.; m. Abigail
Wheeling.  Minister.
Pierson, Henry (1620-66) N.Y.; m. Ann (Valentine)
Williams.  Founder; Military service.
Pierson, Henry (    -1680) Conn.; m. Mary  Cooper.
Landowner.
Pierson, Thomas (1640/42-1701) N.J.; m. Mary Harrison.
Constable; Fence Viewer.
Pietersen, Abraham (c1607-   ) N.Y.; m. Tryntje
Melchiors.  Miller, Landowner.
Pike, John (1573-1654) N.J.-Mass.; m. Dorothy Day.
Freeman; Attorney.
Pike, John (1605-88) N.J.; m. Mary  Tarville.  Land-
owner; Councillor.
Pike, Robert (1616-1706) Mass.; m. Dorothy Day; Sarah
Sanders; Martha Goldmyer.  Selectman; Military
service.
Pike, Samuel (1650-   ) N.J.; m. Jean ---.  Landowner.
Piles, John (    -   ) Md.; m. Sarah Jarboe.  Military
service.
Pinckney, Phillip (    -1688) Conn.; m. Jane---.
Landowner.
Pindall, Thomas (1650-1710) Va.; m. Mary ---.  Land-
owner.
Pingrey    SEE    Pengree
Pinkard, John (1635-90) Va.; m. Elizabeth ---.
Burgess.
Pinkham, Richard (    -c1672) Me.-N.H.; m. Julia ---.
Constable.

Pinney, Humphrey (     -1683) Conn.; m. Mary Hall.
Selectman; Landowner.
Pintard, Anthony (1660-1729) N.J.; m. ---. Judge.
Pitcher, Andrew (     -1660) Mass.; m. Margaret ---.
Landowner.
Pitkins, William (1635-94) Conn.; m. Hannah Goodwin.
Attorney General; Assemblyman.
Pitman, Thomas (1615-84) Va.; m. Frances ---.
Landowner; Miller.
Pitney, James (     -     ) Mass.; m. ---. Landowner.
Pitt, Robert (c1605/10-72/74) Va.; m. Martha Lear.
Burgess; Councillor.
Place, Francis (c1625-c60) Va.; m. ---. Landowner.
Plaice   SEE   Place
Platt, Richard (1603-c84) Conn.; m. Mary Wood.
Founder; Minister.
Pleasant, George (1669-97) Va.; m. Dorothy ---.
Landowner.
Pleasants, John (1644-98) Va.; m. Jane (Larcom)
Tucker. Landowner.
Pledge, John (     -1720) Va.; m. Dorothy ---.
Landowner.
Plumb, John (1594-1648) Conn.; m. Dorothy ---.
Landowner.
Plumer   SEE   Plummer
Plumley, Charles (     -1683) Pa.; m. Margery Page.
Landowner.
Plummer, Francis (c1594-1672/73) Mass.; m. Ruth ---.
Freeman; Juror.
Plummer, Sampson (1699-   ) Me.; m. Elizabeth Libby.
Military service.
Plummer, Thomas (c1645-94) Md.; m. Elizabeth Stockett.
Landowner.
Plympton, John (c1620-77) Mass.; m. Jane Daumin.
Freeman; Ancient and Honorable Artillery Company.
Pocahontas  (1595-1617) Va.; m. John Rolfe.  Aided
early settlers.
Poindexter, George (1627-92) Va.; m. Susannah Nichols.
Landowner; Shipowner.
Poindexter, Thomas (1675-1719) Va.; m. Sarah Crawford.
Landowner.

Polhemus, Johannes Theodorus(     -1676) N.Y.; m.
Katherine Van Werven. Minister.

Polk   SEE ALSO   Pollock

Polk, Robert Bruce (1640-1703/04) Md.; m. Magdeline
(Tasker) Porter. Landowner; Military service.

Pollard, Robert (c1650-c1700) Va.; m. ---. Landowner.

Pomeroy, Caleb (1641-91) Conn.-Mass.; m. Hepzibah
Baker. Landowner.

Pomeroy, Eltweed (1585-1673) Mass.; m. Margery
Rockett. Freeman; Selectman.

Pond, Daniel (1661-97) Mass.; m. Abigail Shepard;
Mary Kilbourne. Selectman; Military service.

Pond, Ephraim (1656-1704) Mass.; m. Deborah Hawes.
Military service.

Pond, Robert (1667-1750) Mass.; m. Joanna Lawrence.
Proprietor.

Pond, Samuel (     -1650/54) Conn.; m. Sarah Ware.
Landowner.

Pontus, William (     -1653) Mass.; m. Wyber Hausen.
Freeman; Juror.

Poole, Edward (1609-64) Mass.; m. Sarah Pumey.
Military service.

Poole, Richard (     -1674) Va.; m. Florence ---.
Landowner.

Poole, William (1700-69) Va.; m. Sarah ---.
Military service.

Poore, John (     -1667) Mass.; m. Judith ---;
Margaret Champney. Founder.

Poore, John (1615-84) Mass.; m. Sarah ---. Juror.

Pope, Humphrey (1645-95) Va.; m. Elizabeth Hawkins.
Landowner.

Pope, John (1675-1725) Mass.; m. Elizabeth Bourne.
Landowner.

Pope, John (c1699-1735) N.C.; m. Elizabeth Pope;
Mourning McKinnie. Commissioner; Assemblyman.

Pope, Nathaniel (1610-60) Va.; m. Lucy ---. Commissioner; Military service.

Pope, Seth (1648-1727) Mass.; m. Deborah ---. Selectman; Magistrate.

Pope, Thomas (1608-83) Mass.; m. Sarah Jenney.
Landowner.

Pope, William (c1634-c1700) Va.; m. Marie ---.
Landowner.

Porter, Benjamin (1678-1725) Va.; m. Ann ---.
Landowner.

Porter, Benjamin (1697-1761) Va.; m. Hannah Ingram.
Landowner.

Porter, Daniel (    -1690) Conn.; m. Dorothy ---.
Surgeon.

Porter, John (1596-1676) Mass.; m. Mary ---.  Deputy
to Court; Military service.

Porter, John (c1664-1712) Va.-N.C.; m. ---.  Attorney
General.

Porter, John (1590-1648) Conn.; m. Rose ---; Anne
White.  Constable; Grand Juror.

Porter, Richard Preserve ( 1658-   ) Conn.; m. Ruth---.
Surgeon; Landowner.

Porter, Samuel (    -1717/18) Va.; m. ---.  Freeman;
Landowner.

Porter, Samuel (1681-1770) Mass.; m. Sarah Bradstreet.
Landowner.

Porter, Thomas (    -1697) Conn.; m. Sarah Hart.
Landowner; Deacon.

Porter, William (    -1705) Va.; m. Jane ---.
Landowner.

Porter, William (1693-1749) Pa.; m. Mary Price.
Military service.

Posey, Francis (1605/15-57/58) Md.; m. Elizabeth ---.
Burgess; Assemblyman.

Post, Stephen (1600-59) Conn.; m. Ellinor(Chandler)
Panton.  Proprietor; Constable.

Post, Thomas (c1620-91) Mass.; m. Susannah ---.
Landowner; Freeman.

Pottenger, John (1643-1735) Md.; m. Mary Beall.
Landowner.

Potter, Nathaniel (c1644-   ) Mass.; m. Dorothy ---.
Rhode Island Compact.

Potter, Robert (1610-55) R.I.; m. ---.  Freeman;
Founder.

Potter, Robert (c1639-1702) Mass.; m. Ruth Driver.
  Landowner.
Potter, Samuel (1664-1729) N.Y.; m. Ada Bradford.
  Landowner.
Potter, Stokes (    -1718) Mass.; m. Elizabeth Sherman.
  Landowner.
Potter, Thomas (1630-1703) R.I.-N.J.; m. Ann ---.
  Landowner.
Potter, William (1608-60) Conn.; m. Frances ---.
  New Haven Compact.
Potts, David (1670-1730) Pa.; m. Alice Croasdale.
  Assemblyman.
Potts, Jonas (1660/70-c1754) Pa.; m. Mercy ---.
  Landowner.
Pound, John (c1632-90) Pa.-N.J.; m. Winifred ---.
  Proprietor.
Pound, Winifred (c1639-c1700) Pa.; m. John Pound.
  Landowner.
Povall, Robert (1650-1728) Va.; m. Elizabeth Hooker.
  Surveyor; Juror.
Powel   SEE   Powell
Powell, Benjamin (    -   ) Va.; m. ---.   Landowner.
Powell, John (1669-1747) Va.; m. Esther Bowles.
  Landowner.
Powell, Mary (Place) (1645-c1701) Va.; m. Thomas Powell.
  Landowner.
Powell, Rowland (    -   ) Pa.; m. Maud Richards.
  Landowner.
Powell, Thomas (1640-1701) Va.; m. Mary Place.
  Landowner.
Powell, Walter (1620/25-95) Va.; m. Margaret Berry.
  Landowner.
Powell, William (1580-1621) Va.; m. Elizabeth Welles
  or Magdalin Stitt.  Burgess; Military service.
Powers, Isaac (1665-1735) Mass.; m. Mary (Pontter)
  Winship.  Landowner; Military service.
Powers, Jerahmeel (1639-1708) Pa.; m. Frial Sheppard.
  Military service.
Power, Walter (1639-1709) Mass.; m. Trial Shepard.
  Founder.

Powhatan (     -1613) Va.; m. ---.  Indian chief.

Poythress, Francis (     -c1649) Va.; m. ---.  Burgess;
Landowner.

Prather, Jonathan (1530-80) Va.-Md.; m. ---.  Landowner.

Prather, Thomas (1604-80) Va.; m. Mary ---.  Landowner.

Prather, Thomas (1673-1712) Md.; m. Martha Sprigg.
Landowner.

Pratt, John (1620-55) Conn.; m. Elizabeth ---.
Proprietor.

Pratt, Joshua (     -1656) Mass.; m. Bathsheba Fay.
Landowner; Constable.

Pratt, Matthew (     -1672) Mass.; m. Elizabeth Bates.
Landowner.

Pratt, Thomas (c1620-92) Mass.; m. Frances ---.
Landowner.

Pratt, William (1622-78) Conn.; m. Elizabeth Clark.
Military service; Deputy to Court.

Preble, Abraham (c1604-63) Me.; m. Judith Tilden.
Magistrate; Councillor.

Prence,Thomas (c1600-73) Mass.; m. Patience Brewster;
Mary Collier; Mary ( ) Freeman.  Governor; Councillor of War.

Prentice, John Valentine (     -   ) Conn.; m. Hester
Nichols.  Landowner.

Prentice, Thomas (1621-1710) Mass.; m. Grace ---.
Military service.

Prentice, Valentine (     -   ) Mass.; m. ---.  Landowner.

Prentice    SEE ALSO    Prentiss

Prentiss, Samuel (1680-1723) Mass.; m. Esther Hammond.
Landowner, Freeman.

Prescott, James (1640-81) N.H.; m. ---.  Landowner;
Oath of Fidelity.

Prescott, John (1604-81) Mass.; m. Mary(Rozer) Platt.
Town Covenant; Military service.

Prescott, Jonas (1640-1723) Mass.; m. Mary Loker.
Deputy to Court; Military service.

Pressnall, Jacob (1684-1716) Va.; m. Mary Maupin.
Landowner.

Preston, Richard (1621-69) Va.-Md.; m. Margaret ---.
Landowner.
Preston, William (1590/95-1647) Conn.; m. Mary Sea-
brook. Deacon.
Preston, William (1624-  ) Pa.; m. Jane Lawson.
Builder; Landowner.
Prevost, David (   -   ) N.Y.; m. Margaret Ten Waert.
Military service.
Prewitt, Roger (1700-  ) Va.; m. Judith (Vaul) Allen.
Military service.
Prewitt   SEE ALSO   deProuitt
Price, Edward (1650-c99) Pa.; m. Jean Mabley.
Minister.
Price, John (1580/84-1636) Va.; m. Ann Matthews;
Mary ---. Assemblyman; Councillor.
Price, Thomas (     -1701) Md.; m. Elizabeth Phillips.
Councillor.
Prickett, John (c1698-c1760) N.J.; m. ---. Landowner.
Priest, Degory (c1579/c1590-  ) Mass.; m. Sarah
(Allerton) Vincent. Mayflower Compact.
Priest, James (c1637-c76) Mass.; m. Elizabeth ---.
Freeman; Landowner.
Prime, Mark (   -1683) Mass.; m. Ann ---. Landowner.
Prince, Edward( -1675/83)Va.; m.---. Landowner; Burgess.
Prince, Thomas (1658-96) Mass.; m. Ruth Turner.
Landowner.
Prince   SEE ALSO   Prence
Prindle, William (c1630-96) Conn.; m. Mary Desboron-
ger. Proprietor; Oath of Fidelity.
Pritchard, Obadiah (   -   ) Md.; m. Margaret ---.
Landowner.
Pritchard, Robert (     -1679) Va.; m. Frances ---.
Landowner.
Pritloe, John (   -   ) N.C.; m. Elizabeth ---.
Landowner.
Proctor, George (     c1738) Va.; m. Mary ---. Free-
man; Military service.
Proctor, John (     -c1696) Va.; m. Mary Bennett.
Landowner.
Prothro, Evan (1650-1709) Del.; m. Elizabeth Morgan.
Landowner; Quaker.

Prout   SEE   Prewitt

Prouty, Richard (1652-1708) Mass.; m. Demaris Torry.
Military service; Landowner.

Provost, Johannes (1630-  ) N.Y.; m. Sarah Staats.
Sheriff; Clerk of Court.

Prudden, Peter (1591-1656) Conn.; Joanna Boyer.
Minister.

Pruyn, John (1667-  ) N.Y.; m. Emilia Sanders.
Alderman.

Pryor, Robert (c1663-  ) Va.; m. Betty Virginia Green.
Landowner.

Pugh, Ellis (1656-1718) Pa.; m. Sinah ---.   Quaker;
Minister.

Pugsley, Matthew (c1663-1730) N.Y.; m. Mary Hunt.
Landowner.

Pullen, Richard (c1643-88) Md.; m. Ann ---.   Councillor.

Pulliam, James (    -   ) Va.; m. Mary ---.   Landowner.

Pulliam, John (1670-1734) Va.; m. Agnes ---.   Landowner.

Purcell, Thomas (    -   ) N.J.; m. Christian Van
Woggelum.  Landowner.

Purcell   SEE ALSO   Pearsall

Purden, John (1692-1767) Del.; m. Mary (Holland)
Lockwood.  Landowner; Freeman.

Purdy, Francis (1595-1658) Conn.; m. Elizabeth
Brundage.  Landowner.

Purefoy, Nicholas (c1679-c1770) Va.; m. Mary Cuthrell.
Minister.

Purefoy, Thomas (1578-1656/60) Va.; m. Lucy Ranson.
Justice; Councillor.

Purington, Hezekiah (1675-1717) Mass.; m. Mary Scammon.  Elder; Military service.

Purnell, Thomas (1619-94) Md.-Va.; m. Elizabeth
Dorman.  Burgess; Judge.

Purrier, William (1599-1676) Mass.-N.Y.; m. Alice ---.
Proprietor; Deputy to Court.

Pursell, Thomas (1667-  ) N.Y.; m. Christiana Van
Woggelum.  Landowner.

Pusey, Ann (Stone) Worley (c1650-1717) Pa.; m. Henry
Worley.  Juror.

Putnam, Edward (1654-1747) Mass.; m. Mary Holton.
Deacon.
Putnam, Elisha (1685-1745) Mass.; m. Susanna (Trask)
Fuller. Town Clerk; Treasurer.
Putnam, John (1579-1662) Mass.; m. Priscilla Deacon.
Deputy to Court; Military service.
Putnam, Thomas (1614-86) Mass.; m. Ann Holyoke.
Selectman; Highway builder.
Pyle, Robert (1660-1730) Pa.; m. Ann Stovey. Assembly-
man; Justice.
Pyncheon, William (1590-1662) Vt.-Mass.-Conn.; m.
Anna Andrews. Treasurer; Governor.

-Q-

Queen, Samuel (1630-1713) Md.; m. Katherine Marsham.
Landowner.
Quick, Jacob Theunissen (c1636-89) N.Y.; m. Neeltje
Cornelis. Landowner.
Quick, Theunis Thomassen (1600/05-c66) N.Y.; m.
Vroutje (Janse) Horing; Belijtjen Jacobus. Builder.
Quisenberry, John (1627-1714) Va.; m. Anne Pope.
Landowner.

-R-

Radcliff, James (    -    ) Pa.; m. Mary Elizabeth West.
Minister.
Radclift, Charles (1640-    ) Va.; m. Elizabeth Taylor.
Landowner.
Ragdell    SEE    Ragsdale
Ragland, Evan (c1650-1717) Va.; m. ---. Landowner.
Ragsdale, Godfrey (1620-44) Va.; m. Mary Cookney;
Sarah Woodson. Landowner.
Ragsdale, Godfrey (1644-1703) Va.; m. Rachel ---.
Landowner; Military service.
Raidford, Philip (1656-1724) Va.; m. Sarah ---.
Landowner.
Raiford, Matthew (1687-1758 ) N.C.; Mourning ---.
Landowner; Justice.
Raines, Rowland (c1600-42) Va.; m. ---. Landowner.

Rambo, Peter Gynnarson (1605-98) Pa.; m. Bretta ---.
Justice; Warden.

Ramey, Jacob (1630-1721) Va.; m. Mary (Spencer) Miles.
Landowner.

Ramsay    SEE    Ramsey

Ramsey, William (1648-1712) Md.; m. Sabina Bladen-
burgh. Surveyor; Collector of customs.

Ramsey, Zerland (    -    ) N.C.; m. Letitia ---.
Landowner.

Rand, Francis (    -1691) N.H.; m. Cristine ---.
Landowner.

Rand, Robert (    -1639/40) Mass.; m. Alice ---.
Landowner.

Rand, Thomas (    -1731) N. Y.; m. ---.   Landowner;
Military service.

Randall, Christopher (    -1684/85) Md.; m. Johanna
Norman. Landowner.

Randall, John (c1675- ) Va.; m. Mary Johns. Landowner.

Randolph, Henry (1623-73) Va.; m. Judith Soan.
Assemblyman.

Randolph, Henry (1689-1726) Va.; m. Elizabeth Eppes.
Military service.

Randolph, Isham (c1684-1742) Va.; m. Jane Rogers.
Burgess; Military service.

Randolph, Sir John (    -    ) Va.; m. ---.
Attorney; Speaker of House.

Randolph, William (1651-1711) Va.; m. Mary Isham.
Burgess; Councillor.

Randolph, William (1681-1742) Va.; m. Elizabeth
Beverly. Councillor; Burgess.

Randolph    SEE ALSO    Fitzrandolph

Ranney, Thomas (c1616-1713) Conn.; m. Mary Hubbard.
Landowner.

Ransom, James (1640- ) Va.; m. ---.   Burgess.

Ransom, Peter (1615-58) Va.; m. ---.   Burgess;
Landowner.

Rapelje, Joris Hansen (1600-65) N.Y.; m. Catalynje J.
Trice (Tricot). Magistrate; Landowner.

Rapelje, Sarah (1625- ) N.Y.; m. Hans Hausen Bergen.
First white female born in New Amsterdam.

Ratcliffe, Richard (c1648-1718) Md.-Va.; m. Elizabeth
---; Mary Caterne. Landowner.
Rathbone, John (1634-   ) R.I.; m. Margaret Didge.
Assemblyman;  Grand Juror.
Raven, John (    -1717) S.C.; m. Elizabeth ---.
Landowner.
Raven, Luke (    -1737) Va.; m. Sarah ---.  Ranger;
Landowner.
Ravenscroft, Samuel (    -1695) Va.; m. Dyonsia
Savage. Military service.
Rawlins    SEE    Rollins
Rawls, George (c1632- )Va.; m. ---.  Landowner.
Rawson, Edward (1615-93) Mass.; m. Rachel Perne.
Selectman; Minister.
Ray, William (1685-1760) Md.; m. ---.  Landowner.
Raymond, Richard (    -   ) Conn.; m. Judith ---.
Freeman.
Raymond,  William (1637-1709) Mass.; m. Hannah Bishop.
Deputy to Court; Military service.
Rea, Alexander (c1683-1769) N.C.; m. ---.  Landowner.
Read, Andrew (1637-97) Va.; m. Elizabeth Coleman.
Landowner.
Reade, George (1608-74) Va.; m. Elizabeth Martiau.
Burgess; Military service.
Reade, John (1660-1733) Mass.; m. Elizabeth Holden.
Landowner.
Read, Margaret (1672-   ) Mass.; m. John Lake. Land-
owner.
Reade, Thomas (    -   ) Va.; m. Lucy Gwyn. Landowner.
Reade, William (c1612-   ) Mass.; m. Avis Deacon.
Freeman.
Reading, John (c1656-1717) N.J.; m. Elizabeth ---.
Proprietor; Recorder.
Reagan, Daniel (c1656-c1696) Va.; m. Jane Gross.
Landowner.
Reams, John (c1677-c1728) Va.; m.  Alice ---.
Landowner.
Reams, Thomas (1698-1773) Va.; m. Elizabeth ---.
Landowner; Surveyor.
Reaves; Reeves    SEE ALSO    Rives; Ryves

Rediat, John (1607-87) Mass.; m. Ann Volt.  Proprietor; Military service.

Redman, Solomon (1677-1749) Va.; m. Mary Stewart.
Landowner.

Reed, Thomas (c1639-c1719) N.H.; m. Elizabeth ---.
Landowner.

Reems SEE Reams

Reese, Sir David (c1699- ) Pa.; m. ---.  Minister.

Rees, Edward Ap ( -1728) Pa.; m. Mabby Evan;
Rebecca Humphrey.  Quaker minister.

Reeves, James ( -1697) Conn.; m. Mary Purrier.
Freeman.

Reeves, Mark ( -1694) N.J.; m. Ruth Hunt; Ann Hunt.
Proprietor; Landowner.

Regan SEE Reagan

Relfe, Thomas ( -1717) N.C.; m. Mary Jennings.
Vestryman; Justice.

Relfe, William (c1676-1741) N.C.; m. Keziah ---.
Landowner; Church warden.

Relille SEE Relyea

Relyea, Dennis ( - ) N.Y.; m. Jeanne Elizabeth
LeRoy.  Landowner.

Remay; Reme SEE Remey

Rembert, Andre ( -1736) S.C.; m. Anne Bressau.
Landowner.

Remey, Abraham (1677- ) Va.; m. ---.  Vestryman.

Remey, Jacob (c1635-1721) Va.; m. Mary Spencer.
Landowner.

Remington, John ( -1667) Mass.; m. Elizabeth Rowley.
Freeman.

Ressequie, Alexander (1689-1752) Conn.; m. Sara
Bontecue.  Assemblyman.

Revell, Randall (1613-87) Md.; m. Katherine Scarburgh.  Burgess; Sheriff.

Reyner, Humphrey ( -1660) Mass.; m. ---.  Freeman;
Delegate to Court.

Reynolds, Christopher (1611-54) Va.; m. Elizabeth ---.
Landowner.

Reynolds, John (c1612-57) Conn.; m. Sarah ---.  Freeman; Landowner.

Reynolds, John (c1637-1701) Mass.; m. Judith Palmer.
 Civil officer.
Reynolds, Nathaniel (c1627-1708) R.I.; m. Priscilla
 Brackett. Landowner; Military service.
Reynolds, Robert (1639-59) Mass.; m. Mary ---.
 Freeman.
Rhodes, Henry (1608-75) Mass.; m. Elizabeth White.
 Military service.
Rhodes, Hezekiah (1660-1744) Va.; m. Elizabeth
 Nichols. Landowner.
Rhodes, John (    -   ) Va.; m. ---. Landowner.
Rhodes, John (    -1701) Pa.; m. Elizabeth ---.
 William Penn's Council; Landowner.
Rhys, Hannah (1656-1741) Pa.; m. Jones Rhys. Land-
 owner.
Rhys   SEE ALSO   Rice
Rice, Edmund (c1594-1665) Mass.; m. Thomasina Frost.
 Landowner; Selectman.
Rice, Edward (1618/19-1718) Mass.; m. Anne ---.
 Deacon; Landowner.
Rice,Nathaniel (    -   ) Va.; m. Mary  Bullock.
 Provincial Secretary.
Rice, Robert (    -c1668) Mass.; m. Elizabeth ---.
 Freeman.
Rice, Thomas (    -1711) Va.; m. Marce ---. Overseer;
 Processioner.
Rich, Richard (    -1692) Mass.; m.  Sarah Roberts.
 Landowner.
Richard, John (1606-   ) Conn.; m. Lydia Stocking.
 Founder.
Richards, Joseph (1640-1710) Pa.; m. Jane ---.
 Landowner.
Richard, Mawd (    -   ) Pa.; m. Rowland Powel.
 Minister; Landowner.
Richards, Thomas (1590-1651) Mass.-Conn.; m. Walthean
 Loring.   Ancient and Honorable Artillery; Selectman.
Richardson, Amos (c1623-83) Mass.-Conn.; m. Mary ---.
 Governor's Assistant.

Richardson, Ezekial (1602-47) Mass.; m. Susanna ---.
Landowner.
Richardson, Isaac (1697-1726) N.C.; m. Katherine
Gandy. Landowner.
Richardson, John (1674-   ) Va.; m. Mary  Dubois.
Landowner.
Richardson, John (    -1710) Del.; m. Elizabeth ---.
Assemblyman; Justice.
Richardson, Joseph (    -1681) Mass.; m. Anna (Riggs)
Wilson.  Pledged Association Test.
Richardson, Lawrence (1606-66) Md.; m. Sarah ---.
Landowner.
Richardson, Richard (1677-1742) Va.; m. --- Burchell.
Sheriff; Burgess.
Richardson, Robert (    -1682) Md.; m. Susanna ---.
Landowner.
Richardson, Samuel (1635/36-1719) Pa.; m. Eleanor ---.
Councillor; Justice.
Richardson, Stephen (c1652-c1694) Conn.; m. Lydia
Gilbert.  Freeman; Military service.
Richardson, Thomas (1608-51) Mass.; m. Mary ---.
Freeman; Founder.
Richardson, William (    -1699) Va.-Md.; m. Elizabeth
Talbot.  Landowner.
Richbourg    SEE   De Richbourg
Richi, Jacob (c1645-   ) N.C.; m. ---.  Landowner.
Richmond, Edward (1632-96) R.I.; m. Abigail Davis.
Attorney General.
Richmond, John Webb (1594-1664) Mass.; m. Katherine
St.John.  Landowner; Commissioner.
Rickard, Giles (1597-   ) Mass.; Joan Gilson.  Survey-
or; Constable.
Ricketts, William (1622-1700) Md.; m. Mary Goodwin.
Landowner.
Ricks, Isaac (1638-1723) Va.; m. Katheren ---.
Landowner.
Riddick, James (1650-   ) Va.; m. Ann ---.  Burgess.
Ridgeway, Richard (1654-1722/23) Pa.-N.J.; m. Abigail
Stockton; Elizabeth Chamberlain.  Landowner.
Ridgley, Henry (1625-1710) Va.-Md.; m. Elizabeth Howard;
Sarah Hamer.  Burgess; Councillor.

Ridgley, Henry (1669-1700) Md.; m. Katherine (Green)
Garry. Assemblyman; Justice.
Ridgley, William (1678-1719) Md.; m. Jane Westall.
Landowner.
Ridley, Nathaniel (1675-1719) Va.; m. Elizabeth Day.
Sheriff; Military service.
Riggs, Edward (     -  ) Mass.; m. Elizabeth Roosa.
Military service; Landowner.
Riggs, Edward (1590-1672) Mass.; m. Elizabeth ---.
Military service.
Riggs, James (1664-1744) Md.-Mass.; m. ---. Ranger.
Riggs, John (1622-  ) Va.; m. ---. Landowner.
Ring, Andrew (c1618-1692/93) Mass.; m. Deobrah Hopkins.
Landowner.
Ring, Eleazar (1658-1749) Mass.; m. Mary Shaw.
Landowner.
Ringgold, Thomas (1610-72/73) Md.; m. ---. Assembly-
man; Justice.
Ringo, Philip Jan (1620-62) N.J.-N.Y.; m. Gertrude
Cornelis Trommols. Sheriff; Judge.
Ripley, Joshua (     -1739) Conn.; m. Hannah Bradford.
Landowner.
Risden, Philip (     -  ) Va.; m. ---. Landowner.
Risley, Richard (1615-48) Conn.; m. Mary ---. Mili-
tary service.
Rith, Leonhard (1691-1747) N.Y.; m. Elizabeth Cath-
rina ---. Military service.
Rittenhouse, William (1644-1708) Pa.; m. ---. Paper
maker; Landowner.
Rivers, William (c1636-85) Va.; m. ---. Landowner.
Rives, George (     -  ) Va.; m. ---. Landowner.
Rives, Timothy (c1670-1716) Va.; m. Mary ---; Judith
---. Military service.
Rives, William (1616-60) Va.; m. ---. Landowner.
Rives, William (c1683-1746) Va.; m. Elizabeth Foster.
Landowner; Military service.
Robbins, Daniel (1640-1714) N.J.; m. Hope ---. Con-
stable; Overseer of highways.
Robbins, Jeremiah (c1675-1747) N.Y.; m. ---. Mili-
tary service.

Robbins, John (1610/20-60) Conn.; m. Mary Welles.
Representative.
Robbins, John (1645/49-1689/90) Conn.-N.Y.; m. Mary
Boardman. Deputy to Court.
Robbins, Richard (      -1680) Mass.; m. Rebecca ---.
Landowner.
Robbins, Richard (1687-   ) Mass.; m. Martha Curtis.
Fence viewer.
Roberson, Israel (1698/1700-c1760) Va.; m. Sarah ---.
Military service.
Roberson, Nicholas (1665/67-c1716) Va.; m. --- Marks.
Landowner.
Roberson; Robeson     SEE ALSO     Robertson
Robert, Pierre (1656-1715) S.C.; m. Jeanne Braye.
Huguenot Minister.
Robert, Pierre (1680-1731) S.C.; m. Judith de
Broudeaux. Minister.
Roberts, Hugh (      -c1683) Pa.; m. Elizabeth Williams.
Councillor; Minister.
Roberts, John (1658-1724) Va.; m. Elizabeth Trammell.
Military service.
Robins, Edward (1602-41) Va.; m. ---. Burgess;
Virginia Company.
Robins, John (1636-1709) Va.; m. Esther Littleton.
Military service.
Robins, Obedience (1600-62) Va.; m. Grace(O'Neill)
Waters. Burgess: Councillor.
Robins     SEE ALSO     Robbins
Roberts, Thomas (1600-73/74) N.H.; m. Rebecca Hilton.
Governor
Roberts, Thomas (1647-1719) Va.; m. Rose ---.  Justice;
Landowner.
Robertson, George (1662-1739) Va.; m. Mary Worsham.
Minister.
Robertson, John (     -   ) N.J.; m. ---.  Landowner.
Robertson, William (1675-1740) Va.; m. Christina
Ferguson. Secretary to Council.
Robertson     SEE ALSO     Roberson; Robinson
Robeson, Andrew (1654-1720) Pa.-N.J.; m. Mary Spencer.
Proprietor; Assemblyman.

Robinett, Allen (c1633-94) Pa.; m. Margaret ---.
Landowner.
Robinson, Charles (c1695-1754) Va.-N.C.; m. Sarah ---.
Assemblyman; Judge.
Robinson, Christopher ( 1645-95) Va.; m. Elizabeth
Potter; Agatha Obert. Burgess; Secretary of State.
Robinson, Cornelius (1630/35-c75) Va.; m. ---.
Surveyor; Landowner.
Robinson, John (c1616-75) Mass.; m. Elizabeth
Trickley. Landowner; Selectman.
Robinson, John (1654-97/98) N.Y.; m. Jeanne ---.
Assemblyman.
Robinson, John (c1700-    ) Va.; m. Mary Evans.
Military service.
Robson, Humphrey (1655-84) Mass.; m. Elizabeth North-
end. Freeman.
Roby, Henry (1618-88) N.H.; m. Ruth Moore. Select-
man.
Rochester, Nicholas (1640-1719) Va.; m. ---. Land-
owner.
Rocketts    SEE    Ricketts
Rockhould, Robert (1615-59) Md.; m. Sarah ---.
Landowner.
Rockwell, John (    -1676) Conn.; m. Elizabeth Weed.
Freeman; Landowner.
Rockwell, William (1591-1640) Mass.; m. Susannah
Capen. Freeman; Selectman.
Rockwood, Nicholas (1628-80) Mass.; m. Margaret
Holbrook. Military service.
Rodes; Roads; Roades    SEE    Rhodes
Rodman, John (1682-1759) N.Y.-N.J.; m. Mary Scammon.
Physician.
Roe, David (    -c1707) N.Y.; m. Mary ---. Landowner.
Roe, John (    -1707) Mass.; m. Hannah (Purrier)
Punerborn. Landowner.
Roe, William (1616-1707) N.Y.; m. --- Hedger.
Military service.
Roeloff, Sarah (1626-93) N.Y.; m. Hans Kierstede.
Interpreter.
Rogers, Giles (1643-1730) Va.; m. Rachel Eastham.
Landowner.

Rogers, James (1615-85) Conn.; m. Elizabeth Rowland.
Deputy to Court; Proprietor.
Rogers, John (1611-92) Mass.; m. ---. Freeman;
Commissioner.
Rogers, John (1617-83) Va.; m. Mary Booth. Burgess.
Rogers, John (1662-99/1700) N.J.; m. Mary Groom.
Landowner.
Rogers, Joseph (1607/08-78) Mass.; m. Hannah ---.
Councillor; Military service.
Rogers, Nathaniel (1598-1655) Mass.; m. Margaret Crane.
Minister.
Rogers, Thomas (1551-1621) Mass.; m. Grace Makin.
Mayflower Compact.
Rogers, William (1600-64) N.Y.; m. Anne Sherman.
Landowner.
Rohrer, Johann (    -    ) Pa.; m. Dorothea ---.
Military service.
Roignon   SEE   Runyon
Rolfe, John (1585-1622) Va.; m. Pocahontas.
Councillor; First Recorder General.
Rolfe, Thomas (1615-   ) Va.-N.C.; m. Jane Poythress.
Landowner.
Rollins, James (1690/91-   ) N.H.; m. Hannah ---.
Landowner.
Rollins, Thomas (  c1641-1706) Mass.-N.H.; m. Rachel
Cox.  Justice; Assemblyman.
Rongnion, Vincent (1648-1713) N.J.; m. Ann Boutcher.
Landowner.
Roosa, Albert Heymans (1621-79) N. Y.; Wyntie Ariens.
Magistrate; Military service.
Root, Jacob (c1660-1731) Conn.; m. Mary Frary.  Free-
man; Landowner.
Root, John  (1608-84) Mass.-Conn.; m. Mary Kilbourne.
Landowner.
Root, Thomas (1605-94) Conn.; m. ---.  Founder.
Roper, John (c1640-c1690) Va.; m. ---.  Vestryman;
Processioner.
Roscoe, William (1664-1700) Va.; m. Mary Wilson.
Burgess; Sheriff.
Rose, Robert (1594-1664) Conn.; m. Margery ---.
Constable; Deputy to Court.

Rosenkrans, Alexander (1661-1745) N.Y.; m. Marrergens
dePue. Committeeman.
Rosenkrans, Dirck (1674-1708/17) N.Y.; m. Winje
Kursteche. Trustee.
Rosenkrans, Harmon Hendricks (    -1697) N.Y.; m.
Magdalene Dircks. Proprietor.
Ross, Andrew (    -1703/04) Mass.; m. Milcah Snow.
Deacon; Deputy to Court.
Ross, Francis (1665-    ) S.C.; m. ---. Landowner.
Ross, George (    -1705) N.J.; m. Constance Little.
Freeman.
Ross, James (1635-90) Mass.; m. Mary Goodenow.
Landowner.
Ross, Joseph (1683-1778) Conn.; m. Sarah Utley.
Proprietor.
Ross, Reuben (    -1722) Va.; m. Elizabeth ---.
Landowner.
Ross, Thomas (1630-94/95) Mass.; m. Seeth Holman.
Military service; Landowner.
Ross, William (c1680-1758) Va.; m. Armula Whiteside.
Landowner.
Rossiter, Bryan (1610-72) Conn.; m. Elizabeth Alsop.
Magistrate; Physician.
Rossiter, Sir Edward (    -    ) Mass.; m. Jane Samwell.
London Company.
Roulston, John (1658-1717) Mass.; m. Mercy ---.
Military service.
Rountree, Francis (1649-1743) Va.; m. Sarah Coleman.
Landowner.
Rouse, John (1610/14-84) Mass.; m. Annie Peabody.
Freeman.
Row, Thomas (    -1703) Md.; m. Ann ---. Landowner.
Rowlette, Peter (1637-    ) Va.; m. Frances ---.
Founder.
Rowley, Henry (    -1673) Mass.; m. Sarah Palmer;
Ann ( ) Blossom. Freeman; Deputy to Court.
Rowley, Moses (c1630-1705) Conn.; m. Elizabeth
Fuller. Freeman; Constable.
Rowley, Shubael (1660-1714) Conn.; m. Catherine
Crippen. Landowner.

Rowlings, Richard (1651-96) Md.; m. Jane ---.
  Tobacco inspector; Landowner.
Royall,Joseph (1600-58) Va.; m. Katherine Banks.
  Founder, Landowner.
Royce, Robert (      -1676) Conn.; m. Elizabeth ---.
  Constable; Councillor.
**Rozer   SEE   Rozier**
Rozier, Benjamin (      -1681) Va.; m. Ann Sewall.
  Judge, Sheriff.
Rozier, John (1603-60) Va.; m. Elizabeth Hillier.
  Minister.
Rucker, John (1678-1742) Va.; m. Susannah Phillips.
  Landowner; Vestryman.
Rucker, Peter (c1670/73-c1743) Va.; m. Elizabeth
  Fielding; Patey ---.  Landowner.
Rudd, Jonathan (      -1658) Conn.; m. Elizabeth Leaven-
  worth.  Oath of allegiance; Military service.
Rudd, Joseph (1678-1744) Va.; m. Avis ---.  Landowner.
Ruffin, Robert (1646-93) Va.; m. Elizabeth Prime.
  Census taker; Sheriff.
Ruffin, William ( c1617-c77) Va.; m. ---.  Landowner.
Ruggles, John (1581-1663/64) Mass.; m. Barbara ---.
  Freeman; Founder.
Ruggles, John (1633-1713) Mass.; m. Mary Gibson.
  Freeman; Military service.
Ruggles, Samuel (1658-1715) Mass.; m. Martha Wood-
  bridge; Mary Custis.  Landowner.
Ruggles, Thomas (1584-1644) Mass.; m. Mary Carter or
  Curtis.  Landowner.
Rulon, David (c1660-c1740 ) N.J.; m. Mary ---.  Land-
  owner.
Rumph, Jacob (      -    ) S.C.; m. Ann Clawyler.  Mili-
  tary  service.
Rundel, William (1647-1714 ) Mass.-Conn.; m. Abigail
  Tyler.  Landowner.
Runyon, Vincent (1645-1713) N.J.; m. Ann Martha
  Boucher.  Landowner.
Rusco, William (1594-    ) Conn.; m.  Rebecca ---.
  Landowner.
Rush, John (1620-99) Pa.; m. Susanna Lucas.  Landowner.

Russell, John (1577-1660) Mass.; m. ---. Freeman;
Town Clerk.
Russell, John (    -1676) Mass.; m. Elizabeth ---.
Landowner.
Russell, Mary (Sterling) Heatly (1699-1754) S.C.; m.
Richard Heatly; Captain Charles Russell. Landowner.
Russell, Nicholas (c1620-c60) Va.; m. ---. Landowner.
Russell, Peter (c1655-1746) Va.; m. Sarah ---. Land-
owner.
Russell, Richard (c1570-1667) Va.; m. Elizabeth ---.
Landowner.
Russell, William (    -1661) Mass.; m. Martha Davys.
Selectman; Carpenter.
Rust, Samuel (1666-1734) Va.; m. Martha ---. Judge;
Surveyor.
Rutherford, Robert (1640-1728) Va.; m. Margaret Vawter.
Constable; Landowner.
Rutter, Thomas (c1669-1729/30) Pa.; m. Rebecca Staples.
Minister.
Ryerson, Martin (1640-87) N.J.; m. Annetje Rapelje.
Magistrate; Landowner.

-S-

Sabin, William (    -1687) Mass.; m. ---. Landowner.
Sablet; Soblet    SEE    Sublett
Sackett, Richard (1683-1746) N.Y.; m. Margery Sleade.
Military service; Tax collector.
Sage, David (1639-1703) Conn.; m. Mary Wilcox. Land-
owner.
St. John, Matthias (1603-69) Conn.; m. Elizabeth ---.
Military service.
Saint Leger, Sir Warham (1579-1631) Va.; m. Dame Mary
Hayward. Burgess.
Sale, Anthony (1699-  ) Va.; m. Elizabeth Willis.
Landowner.
Salisbury, Sylvester (1629-79) Conn.; m. Elizabeth
Beck. Military service.
Sallee    SEE    Saller
Saller, Abraham (    -1720) Va.; m. --- Penault.
Huguenot; Military service.

Salter, Richard (c1724-  ) Conn.-N.J.; m. Sarah Bowne.
Deputy to  Court; Judge.

Saltonstall, Gurdon (1639-1707) Conn.; m. Elizabeth
Ward.  Governor; Minister.

Sammons, James (1695-1765) Va.; m. Phillis Ivey.
Landowner.

Sample, William (c1665-c93) Md.; m. Judith Boyer.
Landowner.

Sampson, Abraham (     -1686) Mass.; m. --- Nash.
Freeman; Military service.

Sampson  SEE ALSO  Samson

Sams, Bonum ( c1663-c1717) S.C.; m. Elizabeth Brewton.
Landowner; Proprietor.

Samson, Henry (1614-85) Mass.; m. Ann Plummer.  Landowner.

Sanborn, John (    -  ) N.C.; m. Anne Bachilor.
Military service.

Sanborn, John (1620-92) N.H.; m. Mary Tuck; Margery
Page; Elizabeth Sherburn.  Councillor; Assemblyman.

Sanborne, Richard (1655-  ) N.H.; m. Ruth Moulton.
Military service.

Sanborn, Samuel (1611-85) N.H.; m. Rebecca Gibbins.
Military service.

Sanborn, William (1622-96) N.H.; m. Mary Moulton.
Landowner.

Sanders, James (1650-1717) Va.; m. Sarah Scrimshire.
Landowner.

Sanders, John (1613-43) Mass.; m. Priscilla Grafton.
Landowner.

Sanders, Lawrence (c1645-1704) S.C.; m. Sarah Earp.
Landowner.

Sanders  SEE ALSO  Saunders

Sandford,  Robert (1615/17-75/76) Conn.; m. Ann Adams.
Landowner.

Sandford  SEE ALSO  Sanford

Sandidge  SEE  Sandridge

Sandridge, John (    -1707/08) Va.; m. Mary Vaughn.
Landowner.

Sands, James (1622-95) Mass.R.I.; m. Sarah Walker.
Deputy to Court; Commissioner.

Sands, Sarah (Walker) (1643-1731) Mass.; m. James
Sands. Landowner.
Sanford, Ezekial (1637-83) Conn.; m. Rebecca Whelpley.
Freeman; Landowner.
Sanford, John (     -   ) Mass.; m. ----. Founder.
Sanford, John (     -1653) R.I.; m. Bridget Hutchinson.
Governor.
Sanford, John (1649-93) Va.; m. Sarah Wodehouse.
Justice; Landowner.
Sanford, Peleg (1634-1701) R.I.; m. Mary Coddington.
Governor.
Sanford, Richard (1599-c1678) Mass.; m. Margery ---.
Freeman; Landowner.
Sanford, Robert (     -1738) Va.; m. Mary Muse. Land-
owner.
Sanford, Samuel (1643-91) Conn.; m. Hannah Brownson.
Landowner.
Sanford, Thomas (1600/10-81) Conn.; m. Dorothy
Meadors; Sarah ---.    Freeman; Landowner.
Sanford   SEE ALSO   Sandford
Sappington, Thomas (     -1721) Md.; m. Mary Rutland.
Founder.
Sargent, William (1602-82) Mass.; m. Sarah ---;
Elizabeth ----.   Lay Minister; Selectman.
Sartor, John William (1700-77) Va.-S.C.; m. Mary Grey.
Lawyer; Landowner.
Satcher, John (1686-1729) Pa.; m. Mary Elizabeth
Loftus. Assemblyman.
Saunders, Edward (1625-72) Va.; m. Mary E. ( ) Hudnall.
Justice; Physician.
Saunders, Tobias (     -1688) R.I.; m. Mary Clarke.
Founder; Assemblyman.
Saunders, Woodward (1632-c84) Va.; m. Barbara King.
Landowner.
Saunders   SEE ALSO   Sanders
Savage, Anthony (c1607-95) Va.; m. Alice Stafford.
Justice; Sheriff.
Savage, Arthur (1680-1735) Mass.; m. Faith Phillips.
Constable; Military service.
Savage, John (     -1684/85) Mass.-Conn.; m. Elizabeth
Dubbin. Freeman; Military service.

Savage, Thomas (1594-1627) Va.; m. Hannah Tyng.
Military service.

Savage, Thomas (1607/08-81) Mass.; m. Faith Hutchinson. Freeman; Military service.

Savage, Thomas (1640-1703) Mass.; m. Elizabeth
Scotten. Deputy to Court; Military service.

Savage Thomas (1669-1728) Va.; m. Alicia Harmenson.
Justice; Military service.

Savage   SEE ALSO   Savidge

Savidge, Robert (1635-98) Va.; m. Mary ---. Landowner.

Savidge   SEE ALSO   Savage

Sawin, John (1680-1760) Mass.; m. Joanna Lyon. Military service.

Sawtell, Richard (    -1694) Conn.-Mass.; m. Elizabeth
Post. Proprietor; Town Clerk.

Sawyer, Thomas (1600-c53/54) Va.; m. Frances ---.
Sheriff; Justice.

Saxton, George (    -1689) Mass.; m. Katherine ---.
Landowner.

Saye   SEE   Desaye

Sayles, John (1633-81) R.I.; m. Mary Williams. Landowner.

Sayles, John (1692-1777) R.I.; m. Elizabeth Comstock.
Landowner.

Sayre, Thomas (    -   ) Va.; m. Hannah Foster.
Indian Scout.

Sayre, Thomas (1597-1670) Mass.-N.Y.; m. ---. Founder;
Landowner.

Sayward, James (1667-1736/37) Mass.; m. Deobrah ---.
Selectman; Landowner.

Scaife, Jonathan (    -1709) Pa.; m. Anne ---.
Juror; Assessor.

Scales, William (c1610-82) Mass.; m. Ann ---. Founder.

Scarborough, Edmund (1584-1635) Md.; m. Hannah Butler.
Burgess; Commissioner.

Scarborough, Edmund (1617-71) Md.; m. Mary Littleton.
Burgess.

Scarborough, John (1646-1706) Mass.; m. Sarah Oakley.
Landowner; Minister.

Scarborough, John (1667-1727) Va.-Pa.; m. Mary Pierson.
Minister; Landowner.
Scarborough, William (     -1776) Va.; m. Sarah ---.
Military service.
Scarburgh  SEE  Scarborough
Schenck, Johannes (1656-1748) R.I.; m. Maria Magdalena
Hass; Margaretha deBoeckhorst. Town Clerk.
Schenck, Martin (1584-   ) N.Y.; m. Margarette deBoer-
hurst. Military service.
Schenck, Roelof Martense (1630-1704) N.Y.; m. Noeltje
Van Couwenhoven; Annetje Wyckoff. Landowner.
Schermerhorn, Jacob Jan (1622-88) N.Y.; m. Janetje
(Seger) Van Egmonborn. Magistrate; Landowner.
Schermerhorn, Lucas (1675-1743) N.Y.; m. ---. Mili-
tary service.
Schlegel  SEE  Slagle
Schofield, Daniel (c1595-1669/70) Conn.-Mass.; m.
Mary Young; Sarah ---. Landowner; Marshal.
Schomp, Pieter (1648-   ) N.J.; m. Stanchy ---.
Founder; Military service.
Schoonmaker, Hendrick (1632-81) N.Y.; Elsie Janse;
Janse Van Braestede. Military service.
Schouten, Jan Lempo (1600-   ) N.J.; m. ---. Sheriff.
Schumaker, Peter (1622-1707) Pa.; m. ---. Landowner;
Quaker.
Schuyler, David Pieterse (1669-1715) N.Y.; m. ---.
Councillor; Mayor.
Schuyler, Philip Pieter (1625/28-83) N. Y.; m. Margaret
Van Slicktenhorst. Military service; Deputy to Court.
Schwab, Jost (1656-1739) Pa.; m. Katherine Wolfharbin.
Huguenot.
Scofield  SEE  Schofield
Scothorn, Robert (1659-1708) Pa.; m. Mary Gibbons.
Grand Juror; Attorney.
Scott, Catherine (Marbury) (     -1687) R.I.; m. Richard
Scott. Landowner.
Scott, Daniel (1655-1723/24) Md.; m. Jane Johnson.
Landowner.
Scott, Edmund (1591-1690) Conn.; m. Elizabeth (Fuller)
Upson. Landowner; Proprietor.

Scott, Edward (c1649-91) Conn.; m. Hannah Bird. Proprietor.

Scott, Hugh (1630-1718) Pa.; m. Violet ---. Founder.

Scott, John ( - ) Va.; m. Jane Todd. Military service.

Scott, John (c1630/35-90) Mass.; m. Sarah Bliss. Landowner.

Scott, Richard (1607-80/81) R.I.; m. Catherine Marbury. Proprietor; Assemblyman.

Scott, Thomas ( - ) Va.; m. Ann Baytop. Committee of Safety.

Scott, Thomas (1594-1654) Mass.; m. Elizabeth Struth. Church Warden; Treasurer.

Scott, William ( - ) Pa.; m. ---. Landowner.

Scottow, Joshua (1614/15-98) Mass.; m. Lydia ---. Military service.

Scranton, John (c1610-71) Conn.; m. Joanna ---. Burgess; Assemblyman.

Screven, William (c1629-1713) S.C.; m. Brigett Cutt. Founder; Organized church.

Scribner, John ( -1675)N.H.;m.Mary ---. Landowner.

Scribner, Thomas (1651-1713) N. H.; m. Hannah Welsh. Landowner.

Scripture, Samuel (1675- ) Mass.; m. Elizabeth Spalding. Military service.

Scruggs, Richard (1597- ) Va.; m. Martha Drury. Vestryman; Landowner.

Scudder, Henry (c1617-61) N.Y.; m. Catherine Estey. Landowner.

Scudder, Jonathan (1646-90) N.Y.; m. Sarah Brown. Military service.

Scudder, Thomas (c1590-1657 ) Mass.; m. Elizabeth Lowers. Landowner.

Scudder, Thomas (1615-90) Mass.; m. Mary Ludlam. Landowner.

Seabrook, Robert (1652-1710) S.C.; m. ---. Commissioner; Speaker of House.

Sealis, Richard ( -1653) Mass.; m. ---. Deacon.

Sealy, Richard (1620/21-c70) N.H.; m. ---. Commissioner; Oath of Allegiance.

Seaman, Benjamin (1649-1733) N.Y.; m. Martha Titus. Landowner.

Seaman, Benjamin (1685-1720) N.Y.; m. Jane Nott.
Landowner.

Seaman, John (1603/04-95 ) Mass.-N.Y.; m. Martha Moore;
Elizabeth Strickland. Landowner.

Searle, Robert (1640-1717) Mass.; m. Deborah Salter.
Town Clerk.

Searle, Samuel (1662-91) Mass.; m. Deborah Bragg.
Oath of Allegiance.

Searle, William ( -1667) Mass.; m. Grace ---.
Landowner.

Sears, Richard (1590-1676) Mass.; m. Dorothy Thacher.
Juror; Constable.

Seaton, James (1690-1744) Va.; m. Grace Clements.
Landowner.

Seaver, Ebenezer (1687-1773) Mass.; m. Margaret Heath.
Landowner.

Seaver, Robert (1608-83) Mass.; m. Elizabeth Ballard.
Selectman.

Seavey, William (1601-1686/88) N.H.; m. Mary ---.
Selectman.

Seay, John (c1675- ) Va.; m. ---. Landowner.

Sebrina, Cornelis (1653-1723) N.Y.; m. Altie
(Fredericks) Lubberts. Assemblyman.

Sedgwick, Robert (1613-56) Mass.; m. Johanna ---.
Military service; Deputy to Court.

Seely, John ( - ) Mass.; m. Mary Walker. Freeman; Military service.

Seeley, Robert (1601-67) Conn.-Mass.; m. Mary ---.
Military service; Deputy to Court.

Selden, John ( -1754) Va.; m. Grace Boswell.
Justice; Sheriff.

Selden, Samuel (c1660-1720) Va.; m. Rebecca Yeo.
Attorney.

Selden, Thomas (1616-55) Conn.; m. Hester Wakeman.
Landowner.

Selleck, David (c1614-54) Mass.; m. Susan Kilkey.
Subscriber to free school.

Seller, Samuel (1620-84) Pa.; m. Anna Gibbons.
Landowner.

Sellman, John ( -1707) Md.; m. Elizabeth ---.
Landowner.

Semmes, Marmaduke ( -1693) Md.; m. Fortune Metford.
Landowner.

Settle, Francis (1635-1707) Va.; m. Elizabeth ---.
Mary ( ) Williams.  Juror; Landowner.

Severance, Joseph (1682-1766) Conn.; m. Anne Kellogg.
Military service.

Sewall   SEE   Sewell

Seward, Obadiah (1644-  ) N.Y.; m. Ann Biggs.  Landowner.

Seward, William (1627-  ) Conn.; m. Grace Norton.
Deputy to Court; Assemblyman.

Sewell, Henry (    -1644) Va.-Md.; m.  Alice Willoughby.  Burgess.

Sewell, Henry (c1625-64) Md.; m. Jane Lowe.  Secretary
of Province.

Sewell, Henry (1631-91) Md.-Mass.; m. Johanna Warner.
Landowner.

Seymour, Richard (1604/05-55) Conn.; m. Mercu Ruscoe.
Landowner.

Shackleford, Roger  (1629-90) Va.; m. Mary Palmer.
Parish Warden.

Sharpe, John (1643-76) Mass.; m. Martha Vase.  Military service.

Sharples, John (1624-85) Pa.; m. Jane Moor.  Landowner.

Shattuck, Damaris (    -1674) R.I.; m. ----.  Landowner.

Shattuck, John (1647-75) Mass.; m. Ruth Whitney.
Military service.

Shattuck, William ( 1620-75) N.J.; m. ---.  Landowner.

Shattuck, William (1622-72) Mass.; m. Susanna ---.
Proprietor; Landowner.

Shaw, Anthony (    -1705) Mass.-R.I.; m. Alice Stonard.
Landowner.

Shaw, Benjamin (1641-1717) N.H.; m.  Esther Richardson.  Councillor.

Shaw, Robert (1594-1661) N.H.; m. Ann ---.  Juror;
Selectman.

Shawhan, Darby (1672/73-1736) Md.; m. Sarah Meeks.
Landowner.

Shearman, John (1612-70) Mass.; m. Martha Palmer.
Military service.

Shedd, Daniel (1620-1708) Mass.; m. ---.  Military
service.

Sheffield, Edmund (1612-1705) Mass.; m. Mary Woody.
Selectman.

Shelbourne, Augustine (1690-1748) Va.; m. ---. Landowner.

Shelbourne, Thomas ( - ) Va.; m. Elizabeth ---.
Landowner.

Shelburne SEE Shelbourne

Sheldon, Isaac (1629-1708) Mass.; m. Mary Woodford;
Mehitable ( ) Ensign. Founder.

Sheldon, John (1629-1706) R.I.; m. Sarah Palmer.
Landowner.

Sheldon, John (1658-1743) Mass.-Conn.; m. Hannah
Stebbins; Mary Woodford. Selectman; Deacon.

Sheldon SEE ALSO Shelton

Shelton, Daniel (1666-1728) Conn.; m. Elizabeth
Welles. Shipowner.

Shelton, James (c1580-1668) Va.; m. Ann ---. London
Company.

Shelton, James ( -1684) Md.; m. Hannah ---.
Landowner.

Shelton, James (c1630-1716) Va.; m. Mary Bathurst;
Susan Rich; Mary Aston. County Clerk.

Shelton, John (c1620- ) Va.; m. Susan Roth. Landowner.

Shelton, John (1649-1706) Va.; m. Jane Chilton.
Vestryman.

Shelton, John ( -1750) Va.; m. ---. Landowner.

Shelton, Ralph (1685-1733) Va.; m. Mary ---. Survey-
or; Appraiser.

Shelton, Richard ( - ) Va.; m. Susanna ---.
Landowner.

Shelton, Thomas (c1610-84) Va.; m. Hannah Wood.
Landowner.

Shelton, William (c1663-c1725) Va.; m. Hannah Armistead.
Justice; Sheriff.

Shelton SEE ALSO Sheldon

Shepard, Edward (1600-49) Mass.; m. Violet (Stanley)
Wolterton. Selectman; Freeman.

Shepard, John (c1678-1756 ) Mass.; m. Elizabeth Woodruff. Landowner.

Shepard, Ralph (1603/06-93) Mass.; m. Thankful Lord.
Dedham Covenant.
Shepard, Robert (1648-  ) Mass.; m. Mary ---.
Landowner.
Shepard  SEE ALSO  Sheppard; Shepherd
Shepardson, Daniel (   -1644) Mass.; m. Joanna ---.
Blacksmith.
Shepherd, Thomas (1615-90) Va.; m. ---.  Landowner.
Sheppard, John (   -   ) Va.; m. Jean ---.  Burgess.
Sheppard, Robert (1604-53/55) Va.; m. Elizabeth
Spencer.  Burgess; Military service.
Sheppard  SEE ALSO  Shepard; Shepherd
Sheppey, Thomas (1603-  ) Va.; m. Elizabeth ---.
Landowner.
Sherborn; Sherburn  SEE  Sherbourne
Sherbourne, Henry (c1611-80) N.H.; m. Rebecca Gibbons.
Landowner.
Sherbourne, John (1615-93) N.H.; m. Elizabeth Tucke.
Selectman; Military service.
Sherbourne, Samuel (   -   ) Mass.; m. Love Hutchings.
Selectman; Military service.
Sheriff  SEE  Shreve; Shreves
Sherman, Edmund (c1572-1641) Conn.; m. Judith Angier.
Freeman; Proprietor.
Sherman, John (1616-85/91) Mass.; m. Mary Launce.
Minister; Freeman.
Sherman, Joseph (1650-1730) Mass.; m. Elizabeth
Winship.  Military service.
Sherman, Peleg (1638-1719) R.I.; m. Elizabeth Lawton.
Landowner.
Sherman, Philip (1610/11-87) R.I.-Mass.; m. Sarah
Odding.  Portsmouth Compact; Freeman.
Sherman, Samuel (1620-1700) Conn.; m. Sarah Mitchell.
Deputy to Court.
Sherwood, Thomas (1586-1655) Conn.; m. Alice ---.
Committeeman; Landowner.
Shine, Daniel (   1757) N.C.; m. Elizabeth Green.
Landowner.
Shinn, James (   -   ) N.J.; m. Abigail Lippincott.
Minister; Landowner.

Shinn, John (1632-1712) N.J.; m. Jane ---. Land agent; Freeholder.

Shipley, Adam (c1640-96/98) Md.; m. Lois ---. Juror; Military service.

Shipley, John ( -1678) Mass.; m. Ann ---. Landowner.

Shipley, John (1660-1736) Mass.; m. Lydia Lakin. Landowner.

Shipman, Edward ( 1697) Conn.; m. Elizabeth Comstock. Landowner.

Shipp, Josiah (c1660-1720) Va.; m. Jane ---. Burgess; Juror.

Shipp, William ( - ) Va.; m. Sarah ( ) Julian. Burgess; Landowner.

Shippey, Richard (c1675-1708) Va.; m. Eleanor Mott. Landowner.

Shippey, Thomas (1608- ) Va.; m. Elizabeth ---. Landowner.

Shippy; Shappey SEE Shippey

Shoemaker, Heinrich Jochenese ( -1681) N.Y.; m. Elsie(Janse)Van Breestede. Military service.

Shoemaker, Jacob (1665-1722) Pa.; m. Margaret Gove. Sheriff; Landowner.

Short, John (c1650-1721/30) Va.; m. ---. Physician.

Short, William (c1613-59) Va.; m. Elizabeth ---. Committee of Safety.

Shotwell, Abraham (1646-1719) N.J.; m. Elizabeth Burton. Oath of Allegiance; Landowner.

Shreve, Thomas (c1620-75) R.I.; m. Martha ---. Landowner.

Shropshire, St. John (1666-1718) Va.; m. Elizabeth Winkfield. Minister.

Shugan; Shugar SEE Shugart

Shugart, John (c1670-1726) Va.-Pa.; m. Elizabeth ---. Landowner; Military service.

Shurtleff, William (1624-66) Mass.; m. Elizabeth Lettice. Military service; Constable.

Sibley, John (1607-61) Mass.; m. Rachel Pickworth. Selectman; Landowner.

Silliman, Daniel ( -1690) Conn.; m. Peaceable Eggleston. Landowner; Naval service.

Simcock, Jacob (1660-1716) Pa.; m. Alice Maris.
Landowner; Military service.

Simcock, John (1630-1703) Pa.; m. Elizabeth Budd.
Councillor; Proprietor.

Simmons, Moses (    -    ) Mass.; m. ---. Landowner.

Simmons, William (1648-93) Va.; m. Elizabeth ---.
Landowner.

Simonds, William (1611/12-72) Mass.; m. Judith (Phippen) Harward. Military service.

Simonds  SEE ALSO  Simons

Simons, Benjamin (    -1717) S.C.; m. Mary Esther
Dupre. Huguenot; Landowner.

Simons, Samuel (1696-1759) S.C.; m. Elizabeth Bonneau.
Landowner.

Simons  SEE ALSO  Simonds

Simpson, John (    1764) N.C.; m. Mary ---. Military
service.

Sims, George (1643-    ) Va.; m. Dorothy Everard.
Landowner.

Sinckler  SEE  Sinkler

Sinclair, John (c1630-c1700) N.H.; m. Deborah ---.
Landowner.

Singletary, Richard (c1599-1687) Mass.; m. Susanna
Cook. Selectman; Landowner.

Sinkler, John (c1630-c1700) N.H.; m. Mary ---.
Landowner; Selectman.

Sip, Adrian Hendricksen (    -    )N.J.; m. Geerttruje
Ariens. Landowner.

Sisson, James (    -1734) Mass.; m. Lydia Hathaway.
Landowner.

Sisson, Jonathan (1689-1775) Mass.; m. Mary Wood.
Landowner.

Sisson, Richard (1608-84) Mass.; m. Mary ---.
Secretary of Colony.

Skelton, Samuel (1584-1634) Mass.; m. Susannah Travis.
Freeman; Minister.

Skidmore, Thomas (1600-84) Conn.-Mass.; m. Ellen ---.
Landowner.

Skiff, James (c1610-c88) Mass.; m. Margaret Reeves.
Selectman; Proprietor.

Skillman, Thomas (1635-90) N.Y.; m. Sarah Pettit.
Freeholder; Landowner.
Skinner, Richard (1626-77) Va.; m. Elizabeth Hill.
Landowner.
Skinner, Thomas (      -1675) Md.; m. ---. Justice;
Commissioner.
Skinner, William (    -  ) Mass.; m. ---. Landowner.
Skipper, William (1597-c1640) Mass.; m. Sarah Fisher.
Minister.
Skipwith, Sir Grey (1600-66) Va.; m. Ann Kemp.  Sheriff.
Vestryman.
Skipwith, Sir Grey (      -1680) Va.; m. Elizabeth or
Bridget. Landowner.
Skipwith, Sir William (1670-1730) Va.; m. Sarah
Peyton. Vestryman; Justice.
Slack, William (      -1727) Mass.; m. Mary ---. Land-
owner.
Slagle, Christopher Frederick (1675-1772) Pa.; m.
Anna Maria Aistrin.  Constable; Landowner.
Slason, George (      -1695) Mass.; m. Mary Jennings.
Legislator; Landowner.
Slaughter, Francis (1630-56) Va.; m. Elizabeth Under-
wood.  Justice; Military service.
Slaughter, Francis (1652-1718) Va.; m. Margaret
Hudson.  Landowner.
Slaughter, Francis (1700-66) Va.; m.  Ann Lightfoot.
Landowner; Military service.
Slaughter, John (1617-  ) Va.; m. ---. Landowner.
Slaughter, Robert (1680-1726) Va.; m. Frances Ann
Jones.  Landowner.
Slawson, George (      -1695 ) Mass.; m. ---. Legis-
lator.
Slecht, Cornelius Barentse (c1620-71) N.Y.; m.
Tryntje Tysse Bos.  Assemblyman; Military service.
Slecht, Hendrick Cornelius (      -1697/99) N.Y.; m.
Elaje B. Lieveling.  Member, Reformed Dutch Church.
Slocum, Anthony (c1590-1689/90) Mass.-R.I.; m. Mary
Harvey; Jane Harvey.  Freeman; Surveyor.
Slocum, Giles (1610-82) R.I.; m. Joan ---.  Quaker.
Slocumb   SEE   Slocum

Small, Edward (   -   ) Mass.; m. Elizabeth ---.
Landowner.
Smallwood, James (1638-1718) Md.; m. Hester Evans.
Sheriff; Military service.
Smith, Alexander (c1631-96) Va.; m. Mary Anne Cocke.
Vestryman; Constable.
Smith, Alexander (1684-1777) Va.-N.C.; m. Elizabeth
Whitfield. Assemblyman.
Smith, Andrew (1670-96) Conn.; m. Sarah Tomlinson.
Landowner.
Smith, Arthur (1638-97) Va.; m. Sarah Jackson. Bur-
gess; Military service.
Smith, Benjamin (c1686-   ) Mass.; m. ---. Landowner.
Smith, Charles (1680-1710) Va.; m. Dorothy Peyton.
Surveyor; Military service.
Smith, Christopher (   -1676) R.I.; m. Alice ---.
Military service; Deputy to Court.
Smith, Giles (c1603-70) Conn.; m. ---. Landowner.
Smith, Henry (1588-1648) Conn.; m. Dorothy ---.
Minister.
Smith, Henry (c1607-87) Mass.; m. Elizabeth ---.
Proprietor; Freeman.
Smith, James (1645-90) Mass.; m. Sarah Coker.
Snowshoe maker.
Smith, Jeremiah (1656-1726) N.Y.; m. Anne Cornell.
Military service.
Smith, John (1595-c1648) R.I.; m. Alice ---. Founder.
Smith, John(1613-84) Va.; m. Anna Jones. Landowner.
Smith, John (   -1696) Va.; m. Jane Cocke. Military
service.
Smith, John (1614-1710) Mass.; m. Susanna Hinckley.
Minister.
Smith, John (1687/90-1777/83) N.C.; m. Elizabeth
Whitfield. Assemblyman.
Smith, John (1698-1776) Va.; m. Margaret Harrington.
Military service.
Smith, John Rex (c1630-c94) Mass.; m. Elizabeth Wood.
Landowner.
Smith, John Rock (c1665-   ) N.Y.; m. ---. Landowner.
Smith, Joseph (1651-1718) Va.; m. ---. Landowner.
Smith, Lawrence (c1650-1700) Va.; m. Mary ---.
Burgess, Councillor.

Smith, Nehemiah (1605-84) Conn.; m. Sarah Ann Bourne.
  Military service; Landowner.
Smith, Nicholas (    -    ) Va.; m. ---. Burgess.
Smith, Philip (1611-84) Conn.; m. Rebecca Foote.
  Deacon; Representative.
Smith, Richard (1630-91/92) N.Y.; m. Sarah Folger;
  Joanne Quarles. Landowner.
Smith, Samuel (1602-80) Conn.; m. Elizabeth Goodwin.
  Deputy to Court; Selectman.
Smith, Samuel (c1661-1748) Mass.; m. Elizabeth Wells.
  Deputy to Court; Commissioner.
Smith, Simon (1625-87) Conn.; m. Elizabeth ---.
  Freeman; Proprietor.
Smith, Thomas (1587-   ) Va.; m. Adria Gurganey.
  Subscriber to Virginia Company.
Smith, Sir Thomas (1612-69) Va.; m. ---. Landowner.
Smith, Thomas (1648-94) S.C.; m. Barbara Atkin.
  Landgrave;Governor.
Smith, Thomas (1663-1738) S.C.; m. Mary Hyrne.
  Councillor.
Smith, Thomas (1691-   ) Va.; m. Saban Smith. Land-
  owner.
Smith, William (1590-1645) Va.; m. Anne ---. Land-
  owner.
Smith, William (1660-1743) Pa.-Va.; m. Mary Croasdale.
  Landowner.
Smith, William (1687-1724) Va.; m. Elizabeth Ballard.
  Landowner.
Smithwick, Edward (1647-1716) N.C.; m. Africa ---;
  Sarah Woolard. Landowner; Assemblyman.
Smithwick, Hugh (1661-   ) N.C.; m. ---. Landowner.
Smock, Hendrick Matthyse (c1638-1708) N.Y.; m. Guerte
  Harmens. Magistrate.
Smoot, Richard (    -1678) Va.-Md.; m. ---. Land-
  owner.
Smoot, William (1596/97-1668/70) Md.-Va.; m. Grace (   )
  Wood. Military service.
Smute   SEE   Smoot
Snedeger, Jan (    -1679) N.Y.; m. Annetje Rys.
  Magistrate.

Snodgrass, John (1690-1773) Va.; m. ---. Landowner.
Snow, Anthony (        -1692) Mass.; m. Abigail Warren.
  Deputy Governor; Councillor.
Snow, Nicholas (        -1676) Mass.; m. Constance Hopkins.
  Deputy to Court; Military service.
Snow, Thomas (      -    ) Mass.; m. Milach ---. Freeman;
  Town Officer.
Snowden, Richard (        -1711) Md.; m. ---. Landowner.
Soane, Henry (1620-62) Va.; m. Judith ---. Burgess;
  Speaker of House.
Soane, William (1651-1714) Va.; m. ---. Speaker of
  House; Burgess.
Sollers, John (        -1699/1700) Md.; m. Ann ---.
  Commissioner; Justice.
Somerby, Andrew (1610-86) Mass.; m. Abigail Freeman.
  Freeman; Landowner.
Somerby, Anthony (1667-1744) Mass.; m. Elizabeth
  Crawford. Landowner.
Soper, John (1654-c1725) Md.; m. ---. Landowner.
Sorrell, Robert (        -1682) Va.; m. Rebecca Woodward.
  Military service.
Soule, George (1590-1680) Mass.; m. Mary Becket.
  Legal adviser; Military service.
Soule, George (c1624-1704) Mass.; m. Debora ---.
  Landowner.
South, George (      -    ) Md.-Va.; m. ---. Landowner.
South, John (1625-    ) Va.; m. Sarah ---. Landowner.
Southery, Robert (        -1685) Pa.; m. ---. Landowner.
Southworth, Constant (1615-79) Mass.; m. Elizabeth
  Collier; Elizabeth Alden. Freeman; Deputy to Court.
Spalding    SEE    Spaulding
Sparhawk, Nathaniel (1597-1647) Mass.; m. Mary Angier.
  Deputy to Court.
Sparkman, John (      -    ) Va.; m. Dorothy ---. Land-
  owner.
Sparrow, Richard (c1580-1660) Mass.; m. Theodora ---.
  Landowner.
Spaulding, Edward (1594-1670) Mass.-Conn.; m. Margaret
  ---; Rachel---. Founder; Military service.
Spaulding, Nathaniel (1687-    ) Mass.; m. Johanna ---.
  Military service.

Spaulding, Thomas (c1635-1700) Md.; m. Catherine ---.
Landowner.
Spearman, Job (c1677-1767/71) Va.; m. Elizabeth ---.
Landowner.
Spearman, John (c1644-c97) Va.; m. Susannah ---.
Landowner.
Speed, James (1679-1719) Va.; m. Mary Pulley. Land-
owner.
Speight, Francis (1614-  ) Va.; m. ---. Landowner.
Speir, James (1675/80-1731) N.C.; m. Anne ---.
Surgeon.
Spence, Alexander (    -1698) Va.; m. Elizabeth
Browne. Burgess; Landowner.
Spence, William (    -1623) Va.; m. ---. Burgess;
Assemblyman.
Spencer, Gerard (1576-c1645) Conn.; m. Alice ( ) Whit-
bread. Military service.
Spencer, Gerard (1614-85) Conn.; m. Hannah Lobdell;
Rebecca (Porter) Clark. Deputy to Court; Military
service.
Spencer, Gerard (1674-1752) Conn.; m. Sarah Douglas.
Military service.
Spencer, John (c1646-84) R.I.; m. Susannah ---.
Juror; Town Clerk.
Spencer, Thomas (c1607-87) Mass.; m. Sarah Harding.
Proprietor; Military service.
Spencer, William (1587-c1637) Va.; m. Alice ---.
Landowner.
Spencer, William (1611-40) Mass.; m. Agnes Tucker.
Boston Charter; Military service.
Spicer, Peter (c1656-  ) Conn.; m. Mary Buscot.
Military service.
Spicer, Thomas (1600-59) R.I.; m. ---. Treasurer;
Delegate to Court.
Spillman, Thomas (c1698-1740) Va.; m. Anne ---.
Landowner.
Spinks, John (c1691-  ) Va.; m. ---. Landowner.
Spinning, Humphrey (c1630-89) N.J.; m. Abigail
Hubbard. Founder; Landowner.
Spivey, Matthew (    -1717) Va.; m. ---. Military
service.

Spofford, John (1612-74) Mass.; m. Elizabeth Scott.
Landowner; Military service.
Spofford, John (1648-97) Mass.; m. Sarah Wheeler.
Landowner.
Spofford, John (1678-1735) Mass.; m. Dorcas Hopkinson.
Landowner.
Spooner, Samuel (1653-1739) Mass.; m. Experience
Wing. Constable; Juror.
Spooner, William (1622-83/84) Mass.; m. Hannah Pratt.
Founder; Surveyor.
Spotswood, Alexander (1676-1740) Va.; m. Jane (Butler)
Brayne. Governor.
Sprague, Ephraim (1685-1754) Mass.; m. Deborah Wood-
ward. Landowner.
Sprague, Francis (      -c1669) Mass.; m. Lydia ---.
Plymouth Tavernkeeper.
Sprague, John (c1623-76) Mass.; m. Ruth Basset.
Councillor; Military service.
Sprague, Ralph (1599-1650) Mass.; m. ---.  Deputy to
Court; Ancient and Honorable Artillery Company.
Sprague, Ralph (1632-1703) Mass.; m. Joan Corbin.
Freeman; Constable.
Sprague, William (1609-75) Mass.; m. Millicent Eames.
Founder; Collector of taxes.
Sprigg, Edward (1677-1753) Md.; m. Mary Belt.  Justice;
Military service.
Sprigg, Thomas (1630-1704) Md.-Va.; m. Eleanor Nut-
hall.  Justice; Sheriff.
Sprigg, Thomas (c1670-c1730) Md.; m. Margaret ---.
Assemblyman; Military service.
Springer, Charles (1658-1735) Del.; m. Marie(Hend-
rickson) Dather.  Landowner.
Sproul, Samuel (c1690-c1773) Va.; m. Margaret ---.
Overseer of roads.
Spruill, Godfrey (      -    ) Va.; m. Mary ---.  Land-
owner.
Spruill, Godfrey (      -1718) N.C.; m. Johanna ---;
Susanna ---.  Landowner.
Sprye, Oliver (c1649-    ) Md.; m. Joanna ---.  Land-
owner.

Spry, Phineas (     -1741/42) S.C.; m. --- Huggins.
Landowner.
Spur, Robert (1610-1703) Mass.; m. Ann ---. Freeman.
Stackhouse, James (    -    ) Va.; m. ---. Landowner.
Stackhouse, Thomas (c1664-1744) Pa.; m. Grace Heaton.
Assemblyman; Quaker.
Stacy, Mahlan (1638-1703) N.J.; m. Rebecca Ely.
Founder; Councillor.
Stacy, Simon (     -c1649) Mass.; m. Elizabeth Clarke.
Proprietor.
Stafford, William (1606-44) Md.; m.  Frances Mason.
Anne ---. Landowner.
Stalcop (alias)  SEE   Andriessen
Stainwood, Philip (1628-72) Mass.; m. Jane ---.
Landowner; Selectman.
Stamps, Timothy (1603-98) Va.; m. Margaret Frizzell.
Landowner.
Stanclift, James (c1666-1712) Conn.; m. ---. Land-
owner.
Standiford  SEE   Stanford
Standish, Miles (1584-1659) Mass.; m. Barbara ---;
Rose ---.  Mayflower Compact; Treasurer.
Stanfield, Francis (    -    ) Pa.; m. Grace ---.
Assemblyman.
Stanford, William (     -1718) Md.; m. Rachel Salsbury.
Landowner.
Stanley, Christopher (c1603-46) Mass.; m. Susanna ---.
Freeman; Proprietor.
Stanley, Edward (     -1726) Va.; m. Martha ---. Land-
owner.
Stanley, James (c1688-1756/60) Va.; m. Catherine
Hutchins. Landowner.
Stanley, John (1624-45) Conn.; m. Sarah Scott.
Proprietor.
Stanley, John (1691-1783) Va.; m. Martha Hutchins.
Landowner; Founder.
Stanley, Thomas (1598-1663) Mass.; m. Hannah ---;
Bennett ---.  Deputy to  Court; Ancient and Honor-
able Artillery Company.

Stanley, Timothy (1603-48) Conn.; m. Elizabeth
Morrice. Landowner.

Stansborough, Josiah (c1600-61) Mass.-N.Y.; m. Francy
Cransden. Elder; Landowner.

Stansbury, Tobias (1652-1709) Md.; m. Jane Dixon;
Sarah Raven. Military service.

Stanton, John (1641-1713) Conn.; m. Hanna Thompson.
Military service.

Stanton, Thomas (1616/17-76/77) Conn.; m. Anne Lord.
Interpreter; Judge.

Stanwood  SEE  Stainwood

Stanyon, Anthony (1611-35) Mass.-N.H.;m. Mary ---;
Ann ( ) Portage. Town Clerk; Magistrate.

Stapp, Abraham (1650-1714) Va.; m. Dorothy Moss.
Attorney; Juror.

Stapp, Joshua (1688-1783) Va.; m. Martha Coffey.
Landowner.

Starbuck, Edward (1604-90) Mass.; m. Katherine
Reynolds. Surveyor; Proprietor.

Stark, Aaron (c1602-85) Mass.; m. ---. Military
service.

Starkweather, John (1646-1703) Mass.-Conn.; m. Ann
---. Pound keeper; Landowner.

Starkweather, Robert (    -1674) Mass.; m. Janet
Roberts. Landowner.

Starr, Comfort (1589-1659) Mass.; m. Elizabeth ---.
Deputy to Court; Surveyor.

Starr, John (1626-1704) Mass.; m. Martha Bunker.
Surveyor; Juror.

Starr, Joseph (1676-1758) Conn.; m. Abigail Baldwin.
Tax collector; Constable.

Starr, Josiah (1657-1715/16) Mass.; m. Rebecca ---.
Justice; Town Clerk.

Starr, Thomas (1615-58) Conn.-Mass.; m. Rachel ---.
Surgeon.

Stathum, Thomas (    -    ) Mass.; m. Ruth Udol.
Landowner.

Steadman, Isaac (1605-78) Mass.; m. Elizabeth ---.
Landowner; Proprietor.

Steadman, John (    -1675) Conn.; m. Vuilet ---.
Military service.

Stearns, Charles ( - ) Mass.; m. Rebecca Gibson.
Landowner; Military service.

Stearns, Isaac (1630-71) Mass.; m. Mary Barker.
Military service.

Stearns, Nathaniel (1620/22- ) Mass.; m. Mary Stone.
Military service; Deputy to Court.

Stearns, Shubal (1655-1734) Mass.; m. ---. Military
service.

Stebbins, Edward ( -1668) Conn.;m. Frances Tough.
Constable; Proprietor.

Stebbins, Rowland (1594-1671) Mass.; m. Sarah Whiting.
Selectman; Landowner.

Stebbins, Thomas (1620-83) Mass.; m. Hannah Wright.
Surveyor; Selectman.

Steele, John (1591-1624/25) Conn.; m. Rachel Talcott.
Proprietor; Town Clerk.

Steele, John (c1626-c53) Conn.; m. Mercy Warner.
Landowner; Military service.

Steele, John (1647-1737) Conn.; m. Ruth Judd. Freeman; Landowner.

Stegg, Thomas ( -1651) Va.; m. ---. Landowner;
Burgess.

Stephens, John (c1606-62) Conn.-Mass.; m. Elizabeth
Parker; Mary ---. Military service.

Stephens, Peter ( - ) Va.; m. Mary Christina ---.
Founder; Military service.

Steptoe, Anthony (1653-1709) Va.; m. Lucy Stephens.
Landowner.

Sterling, Daniel (1673-1747) Conn.; m. Mary ( ) Ely.
Military service.

Sterling, George (1660- )S.C.; m. Rachel ---.
Landowner; Merchant.

Sterling, John ( -1741) Md.; m. Mary Martin.
Landowner.

Sterling, William (1632-1719) Mass.; m. Elizabeth ---.
Proprietor.

Sterrett, Benjamin (c1695-1739) Pa.; m. ---. Landowner.

Stetson, Robert (1615-1703) Mass.; m. Honor Tucker.
Deputy to Court; Selectman.

Stevens, Benjamin (c1676-1743) Conn.; m. ---. Military service.

Stevens, Cyprian (1647-   ) Mass.; m. Mary Willard. Constable, Military service.

Stevens, John (1611-88/89) Mass.; m. Katherine ---. Landowner.

Stevens, John (1639-90) Mass.; m. Joanna Thorne. Landowner.

Stevens, John (1670-   ) Mass.; m. Dorothy Hubbard. Landowner.

Stevens, Joseph (1680-1767) Mass.; m. Prudence Rice. Town Clerk; Selectman.

Stevens, Richard (    -1715) Mass.; m. Mary Lincoln. Landowner.

Stevens, William (1630-87) Md.; m. Magdalen ---. Judge; Councillor.

Stevenson, Edward (    -1716) Md.; m. Mary ---. Landowner; Assemblyman.

Stevenson, Thomas (1615-65) N.Y.; m. Mary (Bullock) Redmond; Mary Bernard. Military Service.

Stevenson, Thomas (    -   ) Conn.; m. Elizabeth Lawrence. Commissioner; Justice.

Stevenson, Thomas (1674-1719) Pa.; m. Sarah (Jennings) Pennington. Assemblyman; Justice.

Steward, Alexander (    -1731) Mass.; m. Deborah (Redaat) Forbes. Military service.

Stewart, John (    -   ) Va.; Elizabeth Sturman. Landowner; Military service.

Stewart, William (c1685-1717) Va.; m. ---. Landowner.

Stickney, William (1592-1665) Mass.; m. Elizabeth ---. Selectman; Clerk of Market.

Stiles, Francis (1602-c1663) Conn.; m. Sarah ---. Landowner.

Stiles, John (1593-1662) Conn.; m. Rachel ---; Dorcas Burt. Landowner; Founder.

Stillman, George (1654-1728) Conn.; m. Rebecca Smith. Juror; Selectman.

Stillman, John (1693-1775) Conn.; m. Mary Wolcott. Assessor.

Stillwell, Nicholas (c1610-71) Va.; m. ---. Military service.

Stinchcomb, Nathaniel (c1671-1710) Md.; m. Hannah
Randall. Military service.
Stinson, Robert (1700-80) Me.-Mass.; m. Catherine
Carr. Military service.
Stith, Drury (c1660-c1740) Va.; m. Susanna Bathurst.
Justice; Surveyor.
Stith, Drury (c1695-1740) Va.; m. Elizabeth Buckner.
Justice; Military service.
Stith, John (1638-93) Va.; m. Jane ( ) Parsons.
Lawyer; Burgess.
Stith, John (c1700-58) Va.; m. Elizabeth Anderson.
Burgess; Military service.
Stockbridge, John (1608-57) Mass.; m. Elizabeth Sloan.
Landowner.
Stockett, Henry ( -1682) Md.; m. Katherine ---.
Landowner.
Stockett, Thomas ( -1670/71) Md.; m. Mary Welles.
Judge; Sheriff.
Stocking, George (1582-1683) Conn.-Mass.; m. Ann ---.
Chimney viewer.
Stocking, Samuel ( -1683) Conn.; m. Bethia Hopkins.
Founder; Military service.
Stockley, John ( -1673) Va.; m. Elizabeth ---.
Physician; Landowner.
Stockstill, Edward (c1700-83) Md.; m. Catherine ---.
Landowner.
Stockton, Richard (1630-c1707) N.J.; m. Abigail ---.
Military service.
Stockwell, Quinton ( -1715) Conn.; m. Abigail
Bullard. Constable; Military service.
Stoddard, Anthony ( -1686/87) Mass.; m. Mary
Downing. Landowner.
Stoddard, John (1619-c64) Conn.; m. Mary Foote.
Coroner's Jury.
Stokeley, Francis ( -1656) Va.; m. ---. Landowner.
Stokeley, John ( -1673) Va.; m. Elizabeth ---.
Physician; Landowner.
Stokes, Christopher (c1600-c46) Va.; m. ---. Land-
owner; Burgess.
Stokes, John (1600-c61) Va.; m. Ann ---. Landowner.

Stokes, Sylvanus (1636-c1704) Va.; m. Mary Bishop.
Juror; Landowner.

Stone, Anna (Howe) Treadwaye (    -    ) Mass.; m.
John Stone. Landowner.

Stone, George (1597-1670) Va.; m. Mary Wernow.
Proprietor; Subscriber to Virginia Company.

Stone, Gregory (1590-1672) Mass.; m. Margaret Garrad;
Lydia ( ) Cooper. Landowner; Deputy to Court.

Stone, Hugh (1638-1732) R.I.; m Abigail Busecot.
Landowner.

Stone, John (1595-1667) Mass.; m. Mary ---.  Founder;
Ferryman.

Stone, John (1618-83) Mass.; m. Anna Howe.  Landowner;
Elder.

Stone, John (1658-c1735) Mass.; m. Sarah (Nutting)
Farnsworth.  Military service.

Stone, Samuel (1602-63) Mass.-Conn.; m. ---.  Minister; Teacher.

Stone, William (1603-60) Va.-Md.; m. Verlinda (Cotton)
Graves.  Governor; Justice.

Stonestreet, Thomas (    -1706) Md.; m. Elizabeth ---.
Landowner; Military service.

Stoothoop, Elbertson (1620-88) N.Y.; m. Aeltje
Cornelese Cool.  Burgomaster.

Stope, Christopher (1612-72) Va.; m. ---.  Landowner.

Storm, Dirck (1630-1715) N.Y.; m. Maria Monfoort.
Town Clerk.

Storrs, Samuel (c1640-1719) Conn.; m. ---.  Churchman;
Landowner.

Stoughton, Thomas (1624-84) Conn.; m. Mary Wadsworth.
Founder.

Stout, Penelope (von Prinkis) (1615-1705) N.J.;
m. Richard Stout.  Negotiator with Indians.

Stout, Richard (    -1703) N.J.; m. Penelope von
Prinkis.  Landowner; Indian Commissioner.

Stoutenburgh, Peter (1613-98) N.Y.; m. Eve Afegy Van
Tienhoven.  Treasurer; Landowner.

Stovall, Batholomew (1665-1721) Va.; m. Ann Burton.
Landowner.

Stovall, John (c1698-1781) Va.; m. Dorcas ---.
Military service.

Stover, Sylvester (1628-c1650) Me.; m.  Elizabeth
Norton.  Landowner.

Stowe, John (1581-1653) Mass.; m. Elizabeth Biggs.
Proprietor; Freeman.

Stowell, Samuel (1620-84) Mass.; m. Mary Farrow.
Landowner.

Stower, Nicholas (    -1646) Mass.; m.  Amy ---.
Freeman; Founder.

Strachey, William (c1570-  ) Va.; m. Frances Forster.
Secretary of the Colony.

Stranyan, Anthony (1611-  ) Mass.; m. Mary ---; Ann
( ) Portage.  Landowner.

Stratton, Edward (c1630-88) Va.; m. Elizabeth Thurston;
Martha Shippey.  Landowner; Juror.

Stratton, Mark (c1679-1759) N.Y.; m. Ann Hancock.
Landowner.

Strayhorn, Gilbert (1680-  ) Va.; m. Nancy ---.
Landowner.

Street, Nicholas (1603-74) Mass.; m. Mary ( ) Newman.
Minister.

Streing, Daniel (c1661-1706) N.Y.; m. Charlotte Le-
Mestre.  Justice; Military service.

Strickland, John (c1600-72) Conn.; m. Martha ---.
Juror; Sergeant.

Strickland, Matthew (    -1698/99) Va.; m. Elizabeth
---.  Landowner.

Strickland, Matthew (    -1730) Va.; m. Ann Braswell.
Landowner.

Strickler, Abraham (1667-1744) Pa.; m. Elizabeth
Crawford; Mary Ruffner.  Landowner.

Stricjker, Jan (c1617-1697/98) N.Y.; m. Lammetje Seu-
bring.  Military service.

Strode, Edward (1697-  ) Va.; m. Eleanor ---.  Military service.

Strong, Christopher (    -  ) S.C.; m. Jeannette
Symington.  Landowner.

Strong, Jedediah (1637-1733) Mass.; m. Freedom Wood.
Constable.

Strong, John (1605-99) Mass.-Conn.; m. Abigail Ford.
Elder; Deputy to Court.

Strother, Francis (1700-56) Va.; m. Susannah Dabney.
Military service.

Strother, William (1630-c1702) Va.; m. Dorothy
Savage; Elinor ---. Landowner; Sheriff.

Strother, William (1653-1726) Va.; m. Margaret Thornton. Sheriff; Justice.

Stroud, Barnard (1694-1783) N.J.; m. Keziah Harker.
Landowner.

Stroud, John (      -1737) N.J.; m. Hannah ---. Landowner.

Strycker, Jan (1615-87) N.Y.; m. Lamhertje Seubering.
Chief Magistrate; Landowner.

Strycker, Jan (1684-1770) N.Y.; m. Margarita Schenk.
Military service.

Strycker, Pieter (1653-1714) N.Y.; m. Annetje Berenes.
Judge; Sheriff.

Stuart, Alexander (1680-1714) Pa.; m. Mary Baily.
Landowner.

Stuart, Archibald (1689/90-1759) Pa.-Va.; m. Janet
Brown. Road overseer; Ranger.

Stuart, Robert (1700-83) Pa.; m. Martha Richardson.
Landowner.

Stubblefield, George (c1635-   ) Va.; m. ---. Landowner.

Stubblefield, John (c1659-1748) Va.; m. Ann ---.
Landowner.

Stubblefield, Robert (c1659-1748) Va.; m.  Ann ---.
Landowner.

Stubblefield, Thomas (c1685/90-1758) Va.; m. Ellen
(Hackley) Doniphan. Military service.

Stubbs, John (c1630-c71) Va.; m. ---. Landowner;
Surveyor of highways.

Stump, John (      -1747) Md.; m. Mary Catherine Baker-
in. Landowner.

Sturges, Edward (1613-95) Mass.; m. Temperance
Gorham; Elizabeth Hinckley. Deputy to Court;
Selectman.

Sturges, John (1623-97/98) Conn.; m. Deborah Barlow.
Selectman; Freeman.

Sturges, John (      -1743/44) Conn.; m. Abigail ---.
Landowner.

Sturman, Thomas (c1584-c1654) Va.; m. Ann ---. Burgess; Military service.

Sublett, Abraham (1655-1715) Va.; m. Susannah Dupuy. Landowner.

Sublett, Pierre Louis (1686-1754) Va.; m. Marte Martain. Landowner.

Suddarth, James (1680-1753) Va.; m. Mary Pepper. Freeman; Landowner.

Sumlin; Sumrall   SEE   Summerell

Summerell, Thomas (1680-1755) Va.; m. Ann ( ) Cobb. Landowner.

Sumner, William (1605-89) Mass.; m. Mary (West) Swift. Freeman; Selectman.

Sumner, William (1668-  ) Va.; m. ---. Landowner.

Supplee, Andros (1634-1726) Pa.; m. Gertrude Stressinger. Landowner.

Sutliff, Nathaniel (1672-1732) Mass.; m. Sarah Savage. Selectman; Constable.

Sutton, George (1610-99) N.C.; m. Sarah Tilden. Overseer of Highways.

Sutton, William (1641-1718) N.J.; m. Demaris Bishop. Constable; Town Clerk.

Swaine, William (1589-1664) Mass.-Conn.; m. ---. Judge; Governor.

Swann, Samuel (1610-82) N.C.; N.J.; m. Joanne Ward. Deputy to Court; Military service.

Swann, Thomas (1616-80) Va.; m. Margaret Delton; Sarah Cod; Sarah Chandler; Ann ( ) Browner; Mary Mansfield. Burgess; Councillor.

Swann, William (c1585-1638) Va.-N.C.; m. Judith ---. Attorney; Land registrar.

Swayn   SEE   Swaine

Swayze, John (c1619-  ) N.Y.-Conn.; m. ---. Landowner.

Swayze, Samuel (1658-  ) N.Y.; m. Mary Betts. Town Officer.

Swayze, Samuel (1680-1759) N.J.; m. Penelope Horton. Judge.

Sweetser, Seth (1606-62) Mass.; m. Bethia Cook. Landowner.

Swett, Benjamin (1626-77) N.H.; m. Hester Weare. Military service.

Swett, John (c1595-1651/52) Mass.; m. Sarah ---.
Freeman; Founder.
Swift, William (    -1644) Mass.; m. Joan ---.  Land-
owner.
Swift, William (1627-1705/06) Mass.; m. Ruth ---.
Military service; Deputy to Court.
Sylvester, Joseph (1638-90) Mass.; m. ---.  Landowner.
Sylvester, Richard (    -1663) Mass.; m. Naomi ---.
Freeman; Landowner.
Symes  SEE  Sims
Symonds, Samuel (c1595-1678) Mass.; m. Martha Read.
Lieutenant Governor; Deputy to  Court.
Symons, Jeremiah (1655-1715) N.Y.-N.C.; m. Ann ---.
Justice; Burgess.
Symons, Thomas (c1641/49-1706) N.C.; Rebecca White.
Landowner.
Syng, Philip (1676-1739) Md.; m. Abigail Murdock.
Goldsmith.

- T -

Taber, Ebenezer (1693-1772 ) R.I.; m. Abigail ---.
Landowner.
Taber,Philip (1605-69) Mass.-R.I.; m. Lydia Masters.
Freeman;  Assemblyman.
Taber, Thomas (1636-1720) Mass.; m. Mary Thompson.
Selectman; Military service.
Taft, Robert (1640-  ) Mass.; m. Sarah ---.  Select-
man; Founder.
Talbot, Matthew (1699-1759) Va.; m. Mary Williston.
Landowner.
Talbot, Richard (    -1666) Md.; m. Elizabeth Ewen.
Proprietor.
Talcott, John (    -  ) Mass.; m. Prudence ---.
Military service.
Talcott,  John (1562-1659) Mass.; m. Ann Skinner.
Freeman; Landowner.
Talcott, John (c1590-1688) Mass.; m. Ellen Wakeman.
Military service.
Talcott, John (1620-59) Conn.; m. Dorothy Mott.
Governor's Assistant; Commissioner.

Talcott, Samuel (1635-   ) Mass.; m. Hannah Holyoke.
Landowner.
Taliaferro, Francis (1656-1720) Va.; m. Elizabeth
Catlett. Sheriff.
Taliaferro, John (1656-1720) Va.; m. Sarah Smith.
Sheriff; Military Service.
Taliaferro, Richard (1665-1715) Va.; m. Sarah Smith.
Landowner.
Taliaferro, Robert (1625-72) Va.; m. Katherine Dedman;
Alice Grymes. Landowner; Sheriff.
Taliaferro, Robert (1635/36-1700) Va.; Katherine
Grymes; Sara Grymes. Landowner; Sheriff.
Taliafro; Talifro; Talifer   SEE   Taliaferro
Tallmadge; Talmadge   SEE   Talmage
Tallman, Peter (c1623-1708) R.I.; m. Joan Briggs; Ann
Hill; Esther ---. Attorney; Commissioner.
Talmage, James (1654-90) Conn.; m. Abigail Bishop.
Military service.
Talmage, Thomas (1617-91) N.Y.; m. Elizabeth ---.
Founder; Recorder.
Tandy, Henry (1660-1702) Va.; m. Rebecca ---. Land-
owner; Military service.
Taney, James (1612/13-   ) Mass.; m. Ann Hatch. Mili-
tary service.
Taney, Michael (   -   ) Md.; m. Mary ---. Landowner.
Taney, Roger Montfort (1600-35) Md.; m. Elizabeth ---.
Deputy to Court.
Tanner, Joseph (   -1688) Va.; m. Mary ---. Clerk
of Court; Landowner.
Tanner, William (1660-1740) R.I.; m. Elizabeth Cot-
trell; Mary (Tosh) Babcock; Elizabeth Shelton.
Landowner.
Tapp, Edmund (   -1653) Conn.; m. ---. Landowner.
Tappan, Abraham (c1606-72) Mass.; m. Susanna Taylor.
Freeman; Selectman.
Tappan, Isaac (1653-   ) Mass.-N.J.; m. Hannah Kent.
Landowner.
Tappan, Isaac (1673-   ) N.J.; m. Nancy Wilkinson.
Landowner.
Tapscott, Edward (   c1659-1730) Va.; m. Elizabeth Hill.
Landowner.

Tarbell, Thomas (1618-81) Mass.; m. Mary ---;
Susanna ( ) Lawrence. Founder; Proprietor.
Tarbox, John (      -1674) Mass.; m. Rebekah ---.
Landowner.
Tarkington, John (1640-96) N.C.; m. Prudence ---.
Landowner.
Tarkington, John (c1679/80-1715) Md.; m. Martha ---.
Landowner.
Tarlton, Stephen (      -1688) Va.; m. Susanna ---.
Vestryman.
Tarpley, James (1692-1765) Va.; m. Mary Camp.  Land-
owner.
Tarpley, John (c1647-1739) Va.; m. Ann Glasscock.
Justice; Sheriff.
Tarrant, Leonard (      -1718) Va.; m. Mary Brooks.
Sheriff; Landowner.
Tasker, Thomas (      -1699/1700) Md.; m. Eleanor Dent.
Landowner; Treasurer.
Tate, James (1617-64) Va.; m. Mary Anne ---.
Minister.
Tate, Robert (c1685-1751/53) Va.; m. ---.  Landowner;
Processioner.
Tatum, Edward (1665-1739) Va.; m. Rebecca Rives.
Landowner.
Tatum, Nathaniel (1599-1638) Va.; m. Ann ---.  Mili-
tary service.
Tatum, Nathaniel (      -1685/86) Va.; m. Mary ---.
Military service.
Tatum, Nathaniel (1688/90-1737/39) Va.; m. Elizabeth
Godfrey.  Military service.
Taylor, Anthony (1607/11-87) N.H.; m. --- Phillips.
Founder; Landowner.
Taylor, Edward (1642-1729) N.J.; m. Ruth Wyllys.
Minister.
Taylor, George (      -1706) Va.; m. Martha Tomlin.
Minister; Burgess.
Taylor, James (1575-1658) Va.; m. ---.  Ship builder.
Taylor, James (1635-98) Va.; m. Frances Walker; Mary
(Bishop) Gregory.  Landowner; Justice.
Taylor, James (1674-1729) Va.; m. Martha Thompson.
Burgess; Surveyor.

Taylor, John (    -1646) Conn.; m. Rhoda ---. Land-
owner.
Taylor, John (    -1676) Md.-Va.; m. Margaret ---.
Landowner.
Taylor, John (1625-1702) Va.; m. Alice Gascoigne.
Landowner; Justice.
Taylor, John (1641-1709) Mass.; m. Thankful Woodward.
Landowner.
Taylor, John (    -1712) Va.; m. ---. Landowner.
Taylor, John (1696-1780) Va.; m. Catherine Pendleton.
Justice; Landowner.
Taylor, Joseph (c1672-1774) Pa.; m. Elizabeth Haines.
Landowner.
Taylor, Philip (1680-1732) Pa.; m. Ann Conway.
Assemblyman.
Taylor, Richard (    -1678/79) Va.; m. Sarah ---.
Landowner.
Taylor, Robert (1633-95) Pa.; m. Mary Hayes. Land-
owner.
Taylor, Robert (c1680-  ) N.Y.; m. ---. Landowner.
Taylor, Samuel (1688-1733) Mass.; m. Mary Hitchcock.
Landowner.
Taylor, Thomas (c1626-57) Va.-N.C.; m. Anne ---.
Burgess; Landowner.
Taylor, William (1619-c76) Va.; m. Elizabeth Kings-
mill. Burgess; Councillor.
Teackle, Thomas (1624-95) Va.; m. ---. Landowner.
Teague, Edward (c1660-97) Md.; m. Susan ---. Land-
owner.
Teal, Edward (c1682-1720/21) Md.; m. Hannah (Randall)
Stinchcomb. Ranger; Bondsman.
Tefft, John (    -1676) R.I.; m. Mary Barber. Free-
man; Military service.
Teller, William (1616-1701) N.Y.; m. Marie Verleth;
Margaret Dedehasen. Landowner.
Temple, Abraham (1652-1738) Mass.; m. Deborah Hadlock.
Military service.
Temple, Joseph (1666-1760) Va.; m. Anne Arnold.
Justice; Sheriff.
Tenney, Samuel (1667-1747) Mass.; m. Sarah Boynton.
Elder; Moderator.

Tenney, Thomas (1614-99) Mass.; m. Ann Magill.
Military service.

Terhune, Albert (1619-85) N.Y.; m. Geertse ---.
Landowner.

Terrell, Blackabee (c1670-1732) Va.; m. ---.
Landowner.

Terrell, David (1695/1700-1759) Va.; m. Agatha Chiles.
Military service.

Terrell, Joel (1700-  ) Va.; m. Sarah Oxford.
Founder; Landowner.

Terrell, John (1675-c1764) Va.; m. Elizabeth ---.
Landowner.

Terrell, Richmond (c1656-  ) Va.; m. Catherine Crump.
Landowner.

Terrell, Timothy (1658/68-1727) Va.; m. Elizabeth
Foster. Landowner; Vestryman.

Terrell, William (1635-1727) Va.; m. Susanna Waters.
Council of Safety.

Terry, Samuel (c1661-1730) Conn.; m. Martha Crane.
Landowner.

Terry, Thomas (1607-71) N.Y.; m. Mary ---.  Founder;
Landowner.

Teurneur SEE Turner

Thacher, Anthony (1588/89-1667) Mass.; m. Elizabeth
Jones. Landowner.

Thacher, John (1638/39-1773) Mass.; m. Rebecca
Winslow. Selectman; Deputy to Court.

Thacher, Peter (1651-1727) Mass.; m. Theodora Oxenbridge. Landowner.

Thacher, Peter (1665-1736) Mass.; m. Thankful Sturgis.
Judge; Selectman.

Thacher, Thomas (1620-78) Mass.; m. Elizabeth Partridge.
Minister.

Thacker, Henry (1663-1710) Va.; m. Elizabeth Payne.
Sheriff; Justice.

Thayer, Ferdinando (1628-1712) Mass.; m. ---.  Military service.

Thayer, Richard (1601-95) Mass.; m. Dorothy Morimore.
Military service.

Thelaball, James (1625-93) Va.; m. Elizabeth Mason.
Huguenot; Landowner.

Theweatt, James ( - ) Va.; m. ---. Landowner.

Thigpen, James (1627-79) N.C.; m. Elizabeth ---; Elyn
---. Landowner.

Thomas, Christopher (1609-70) Md.-Va.; m. Elizabeth
Wiggins. Burgess.

Thomas, Evan ( -c1700) Pa.; m. Mary ---. Landowner.

Thomas, John (1585-c1653) Va.; m. Dorothy ---. Landowner.

Thomas, John (1621-76) Mass.; m. Sarah Pitney. Landowner.

Thomas, John (1690-1782) Va.; m. Sarah ---. Landowner.

Thomas, Joseph (c1680-1735) N.C.; m. Alice ---. Ship
Master.

Thomas, Philip (c1614-1702/03) Va.; m. ---. Landowner.

Thomas, Philip (1620-75) Md.; m. Sarah Harrison.
Justice; Commissioner.

Thomas, Richard (c1673-1744) Pa.; m. Grace Atherton.
Landowner.

Thomas, Tristram (1626-86) Md.; m. Ann Coursey.
Commissioner.

Thomas, William (1613-65) Va.; m. Rebecca ---. Landowner.

Thomas, William ( -1687) N.C.-Va.; m. Elizabeth ---.
Landowner.

Thomason, William (1695-1750) S.C.-Va.; m. Mary Arnold.
Landowner.

Thompson, John (1616-96) Mass.; m. Mary Cook. Military service.

Thompson, John (1638-97) Va.; m. Sarah ---. Military
service.

Thompson, John (1658-1727) Va.; m. Alice ---. Landowner.

Thompson, John (c1676-1752) Mass.-Va.; m. Elizabeth ( )
Salway; --- Rootes. Minister.

Thompson, Jonathan (1663-1748) Mass.; m. Frances
Whitmore. Landowner.

Thompson, William (1597-1649/50) Md.; m. Anne ---.
Landowner.

Thompson, William (c1599-1666) Mass.-R.I.; m. Abigail
---. Minister.

Thompson, William (1623-60) Md.; m. Mary Breton.
Landowner.

Thompson, William (    -1699) Va.; m. Katherine ---.
Minister.

Thorndyke, John ( -1668) Mass.; m. Elizabeth Stratton.
Founder.

Thorne, William (c1603-65) N.Y.; m. Sarah ---. Landowner.

Thornton, Francis (1651-1726) Va.; m. Alice Savage.
Justice; Burgess.

Thornton, Francis (1682-1729) Va.; m. Mary Taliaferro.
Military service; Burgess.

Thornton, Luke (1642-1725) Va.; m. Anne ---. Landowner.

Thornton, Rowland (1685-1748) Va.; m. Elizabeth Cut-
lett. Justice.

Thornton, William (1620-  ) Va.; m. Avice Russell;
Elizabeth Howland. Landowner.

Thornton, William (1642-1708) Va.; m. Elisie Belling-
ton. Landowner.

Thornton, William (1699-1745) Va.; m. Elizabeth ( or
Ann) Meaux. Landowner.

Thoroughgood, Adam (1602-c40) Va.; m. Sarah Offley.
Landowner; Burgess.

Thorpe, John (1595-1669/89) Mass.; m. Susanna ---.
Freeman; Deputy to Court.

Thorpe, Thomas (c1636-73) N.J.; m. Rebecca ---.
Landowner.

Thorpe, Thomas (    -1704) Va.; m. Martha ---;
Florinda Bigwell. Surveyor; Landowner.

Threlkeld, Christopher (c1665-1711) Va.; m. Mary ---.
Landowner.

Throckmorton, Gabriel (1665-1737) Va.; m. Frances
Cooke. Justice; Sheriff.

Throckmorton, John (1600-84) R.I.; m. Rebecca Colvill.
Landowner.

Throckmorton, John (1633-79) N.J.; m. Frances Mason;
Rebecca ---. Landowner; Vestryman.

Throop, William (1657-1704 ) R.I.; m. Mary Chapman.
Selectman; Surveyor.

Thruston, Edward (1636-1717) Va.; m. Susanna Perry.
Physician.
Thruston, Edward (1678-1761) Va.; m. Elizabeth Hous-
den. Physician.
Thruston   SEE ALSO   Thurston
Thurman   SEE   Thurmond
Thurmond, Philip (1576-1650) Va.; m. ---. Councillor;
Military service.
Thurmond, Philip (1640-1720) Va.; m. ---. Councillor;
Military service.
Thurmond, Richard (c1683-1710) Va.; m. Mary ---.
Military service.
Thurston, Daniel (    -1693) Mass.; m. Ann Pell.
Landowner; Military service.
Thurston, Damiel (1661-1738) Mass.; m. ---. Military
service.
Thurston, Edward (1617-1707) R.I.; m. Elizabeth Mott.
Commissioner; Governor's Assistant.
Thurston, John (1651-   ) Mass.; m. Margaret ---.
Freeman; Landowner.
Thurston, Thomas (1633-1704) Mass.; m. Sarah Thaxton.
Town Clerk; Justice.
Thurston   SEE ALSO   Thruston
Thwing, Benjamin (1619-73) Mass.; m. Deborah ---.
Proprietor.
Tibbetts, Henry (1590-c1676) N.H.-R.I.; m. Elizabeth
---. Juror; Landowner.
Tibbetts, Henry (    -1713) R.I.; m. Sarah Stanton.
Constable; Juror.
Tichenor, Martin (1626-   ) N.J.; m. Mary Charles.
Landowner.
Tidwell, Richard (c1630-92) Va.; m. ---. Freeman;
Tobacco viewer.
Tiffany, Humphrey (1624-88) Mass.; m. Elizabeth ---.
Justice; Proprietor.
Tilden, Nathaniel (1583-1641) Mass.; m. Lydia Huck-
stepp. Town Officer; Elder.
Tilden, Thomas (c1618/19-1703) Mass.;. m. Mary Holmes.
Military service.

Tilden, Thomas (c1668-1728) Mass.; m. Hannah Mandall.
Landowner.

Tileston, Timothy (1636-97) Mass.; m. Sarah Bridgman.
Deputy to Court.

Tilghman    SEE    Tillman

Tilley, Elizabeth (1592-1672/78) Mass.; m. John Tilley.
Mayflower Compact.

Tilley, John (    -1621) Mass.; m. Elizabeth ---.
Mayflower Passenger.

Tillman, Christopher (    -c1619) Va.; m. Anna Sanders.
Landowner.

Tillman, Christopher    (    -1652) Va.; m. Ruth Devon-
shire. Landowner.

Tillman, George (1685-1756) Va.; m. Mary House.
Landowner; Military service.

Tillman, Gideon (1650-1720) Md.; m. Margaret Maneux.
Founder; Churchman.

Tillman, Richard (1626-75/76) Md.; m. Mary Foxley.
Surgeon; High Sheriff.

Tillman, Roger (c1650-1717) Va.; m. Winnefred Austin;
Susannah ( ) Parham. Landowner.

Tilney, John (1618-1701) Va.; m. Ann Smith. Commissioner; Military service.

Tilson, Edmund (    -1660) Mass.; m. Joanna ---.
Freeman; Landowner.

Tilton, Daniel (1646-1715) Mass.-N.H.; m. Mehitable
Sandborn. Assemblyman; Speaker of House.

Tilton, Daniel (1677-1744) N.H.; m. Elizabeth (Hilliard)
Shaw. Landowner.

Tilton, John (1620-88) N.Y.; m. Mary Graves; Mary
Goodie. Founder; Town Clerk.

Tilton, Peter (    -1696) Mass.; m. Elizabeth ---.
Founder; Freeman.

Tilton, William (c1618-53) Mass.; m. Susanna ---.
Freeman; Selectman.

Tingley, Palmer (1614-   ) Mass.; m. Anna Fosdick.
Military service; Landowner.

Tipping, William (1630-1714) Md.; m. Elizabeth ---.
Landowner.

Tipton, Edward (1618-72) Md.; m. Elizabeth ---;
Margaret Downing. Shipowner.

Tipton, Jonathan (1618-   ) Md.; m. Sarah Steptoe.
Landowner.

Tipton, Jonathan (1689-1757) Md.; m. Sarah Pearce;
Elizabeth Adams. Landowner.

Titus, Edmund (c1630-1701) N.Y.; m. Martha Washburn.
Landowner.

Titus, Robert (1600-54) Mass.-N.Y.; m. Hannah ---.
Deputy to Court.

Todd, Christopher (1617-86) Conn.; m. Grace Middlebrook. Landowner.

Todd, Joseph (1645-99) Pa.; m. Joane ---.  Merchant.

Todd, Thomas (1619-77) Md.-Va.; m. Anne Gorsuch;
Elizabeth Bernard. Burgess; Assemblyman.

Tomes  SEE  Toms

Tomkies, Charles (   -1739) Va.; m. Mary Alexander.
Physician; Justice.

Tompkins, Humphrey (   -   ) Va.; m. Hannah Bennett.
Landowner; Virginia Company.

Tompkins, Ralph (1585-1666) Mass.; m. Katherine Foster.
Landowner.

Tompkins, Samuel (   -1655) Va.; m. Sarah Trivilyan.
Landowner.

Tompkins, Samuel (1696-c1763) Va.; m. Martha ---.
Landowner.

Toms, Francis (1636-1712) N.C.-Md.; m. Priscilla
Nicholson. Landowner; Tax Collector.

Tooke, James (1575-1659/62) Va.; m. ---.  Landowner;
Clerk of Court.

Toomer, John (c1667-   ) S.C.; m. Mary ---. Landowner.

Toppan  SEE  Tappen

Topping, Thomas (c1636-c86) Conn.; m. Emma ---.
Magistrate; Military service.

Torrey, James (1615-85) Mass.; m. Ann Hatch. Military service.

Torrey, William (1608-90) Mass.; m. Elizabeth Fry.
Clerk of House; Ancient and Honorable Artillery
Company.

Tottenham, Henry (   -1726) Mass.; m. Anna ---.
Landowner.

Tourneur  SEE  Turner

Tousey, Thomas (1688-1761) Conn.; m. Hannah Clark. Minister.

Tower, Ibrook (1643/44-1732) Mass.; m. Margaret Harding. Landowner.

Tower, John (1609-1701) Mass.; m. Margaret Ibrook. Freeman; Military service.

Tower, John (1637-    ) Mass.; m. ---. Landowner.

Towles, Henry (1652-1721) Va.; m. Ann Stokeley. Landowner; Constable.

Towles, John Stokeley (1690-1757) Va.; m. Ann Vallet; --- ( ) Wharton. Landowner.

Towne, William (c1606-72) Mass.; m. Joanne Blessing. Landowner.

Towner, Richard (c1650-1722) Conn.; m. Mary ---. Landowner.

Townley, Richard (c1628-1711) N.J.; m. Elizabeth (Smith) Carteret. Military service; Deputy to Court.

Townsend, Henry (    -1695) N.Y.; m. Anne Cole. Landowner.

Townsend, Richard (1616-70) Conn.-N.Y.; m. Elizabeth Weeks. Town Clerk.

Townshend, Richard (1606-52) Va.; m. Frances Baldwin. Burgess; Landowner.

Townshend, Robert (1640-75) Va.; m. Mary Langhorne. Landowner.

Tracy, Stephen (1596-1655) Mass.; m. Typhosa Lee. Constable; Surveyor.

Tracy, Thomas (1610-85) Conn.; m. Mary ( ) Mason. Military service; Assemblyman.

Tracy, Winston (1681-    ) Conn.; m. Rachel Ripley. Landowner.

Travis, Edward (1594-c1663) Va.; m. Ann Johnson. Burgess.

Travis, Henry (1654-    ) Mass.; m. Bridget ---. Landowner.

Traylor, Edward (1596-1673) Va.; m. Louise Pascal. Landowner.

Traylor, Edward (1639-78) Va.; m. Martha Randolph. Landowner.

Traylor, Edward (c1670-1740) Va.; m. Elizabeth Perkinson. Landowner.

Treadwell, Edward (1608-60) Mass.; m. Sara Massengale. Proprietor.

Treat, James (1634-1708/09) Conn.; m. Rebecca Lattimer. Military service; Council of Safety.

Treat, Richard (1589-1669) Conn.; m. Alice Gaylord. Proprietor; Commissioner.

Treat, Robert (1624-1710) Conn.; m. Jane Tapp. President of United Colonies; Governor.

Treherne, George (1630-c84) Md.; m. Ann Commody. Landowner; Assemblyman.

Trezavant, Daniel (c1660-1726) S.C.; m. Susanne Maulard. Landowner.

Trigg, Daniel (1651-1716) Va.; m. Susanna Docia Johns. Landowner.

Triplett, Francis (c1645-1701) Va.; m. Abigail ---. Landowner.

Tripp, John (1610-78) R.I.; m. Mary Paine. Founder; Councillor.

Troope, Robert ( -c1666) Md.; m. ---. Landowner.

Trowbridge, James (1637-1715 ) Mass.; m. Margaret Jackson. Military service; Selectman.

Trowbridge, John (1661-1686/89) Conn.; m. Ann Leete. Landowner.

Trowbridge, Thomas (1590-1672) Conn.-Mass.; m. Elizabeth Marshall. Ancient and Honorable Artillery Company.

Trowbridge, William (1633-88) Mass.-Conn.; m. Elizabeth (Lambert) Sellivant. Landowner.

Truax, Philip (c1586-1649/53) N.Y.; m. Susanna DuChesne. Landowner.

True, Henry (1644-1735) Mass.; m. Jane Bradbury. Freeman; Selectman.

Truman, James (1603-72) Md.; m. Anne Storer. Physician.

Trumble, John (1607-57) Mass.; m. Ellinor Chandler. Freeman; Town Clerk.

Tuck, Robert ( -1664) N.H.; m. Joanna ---. Physician; Selectman.

Tucker, John (    -1671) Va.; m. Rose ---. Landowner.
Tucker, Robert (1604-82) Mass.; m. Elizabeth Allen.
Town Clerk; Selectman.
Tucker, William (1574-1644) Va.; m. Mary Thompson.
Burgess.
Tudor, Owen (c1620-90) Conn.; m. Mary Loomis. Land-
owner.
Tufts, Peter (1617-1700) Mass.; m. Mary Pierce.
Founder; Landowner.
Tuggle, Henry (1670-1743) Va.; m. Elizabeth (Baldwin)
Browne. Constable; Surveyor.
Tuggle, Thomas (    -    ) Va.; m. Mary Tarrant.
Landowner.
Tugwell; Tuggell    SEE    Tuggle
Tullos, Claud (1641-1700) Va.; m. Sarah Rodham.
Constable; Landowner.
Tunstall, Richard (c1697-c1782) Va.; m. Ann Hill.
Burgess; Town Clerk.
Tupper, Thomas (1578-1676) Mass.; m. Anna ---.
Founder; Council of War.
Turk, Robert (c1657-    ) Va.; m. ---. Landowner.
Turner, Daniel (1626-73) N.Y.; m. Jacqueline deParisia.
Magistrate; President, Mayor's Court.
Turner, Edward (c1631-1709) Md.; m. Mary ---. Land-
owner.
Turner, Humphrey (c1593-1673) Mass.; m. Lydia Gamer.
Representative; Councillor.
Turner, Nathaniel (    -1646) Mass.-Conn.; m. Margaret
Leachland. Military service.
Turner, Thomas (    -    ) Mass.; m. Sarah Hiland.
Landowner.
Turner, Thomas (    -    ) Mass.; m. Hannah Jenkins.
Landowner.
Turner, William (1645-76) Md.; m. Mary McLemore;
Frances ---. Minister; Military service.
Turnley, Francis (1662-    ) Va.; m. ---. Landowner.
Turnley, John (1690-    ) Va.; m. ---. Landowner.
Turpin, William (c1634-85) Md.; m. Margaret Ivory.
Landowner.
Tuthill, Henry (1580-1618)Mass.-N.Y.; m. Alice ---.
Freeman; Constable.

Tuthill, Henry (1612-1648/50) Mass.; m. Bridget --;
Margaret ---. Freeman; Proprietor.
Tuttle, Edward (c1628-90) Conn.; m. Alling Ball.
Proprietor.
Tuttle, John (1618-63) N.H.; m. ---. Landowner.
Tuttle, John (c1646-1720) N.H.; m. Dorothy ---;
Mary ---. Selectman; Judge.
Tuttle, Simon (1647-1719) Conn.; m. Abigail Beach.
Proprietor.
Tuttle, William (1609-73) Conn.; m. Elizabeth ---.
Proprietor; "Night Watch."
Twining, Nathaniel (1689-1753) Pa.; m. Sarah Kirk.
Landowner.
Twining, Stephen (1659-1720) Mass.-Pa.; m. Abigail
Young. Landowner.
Twining, William ( -1659) Mass.; m. ---. Military
service.
Twining, William (1625-70) Mass.; m. Anna Doane;
Elizabeth Deane. Military service.
Twitchell, Benjamin (1599-1675/76) Mass.; m. Mary
Riggs. Landowner.
Tyler, Charles (1657-1739) Conn.; m. Rebecca Potter.
Landowner.
Tyler, Henry (1604-72) Va.; m. Ann ---. Justice;
Landowner.
Tyler, Job (1619-1700) Mass.; m. Mary ---. Landowner.
Tyler, Moses (1641/42-1727) Mass.; m. Prudence Blake.
Landowner.
Tyler, Richard ( -1734) Va.; m. Susannah ---.
Landowner.
Tyler, Robert (1625-74) Md.; m. Joan (Ravins) Reade.
Landowner.
Tyler, Robert (1671/72-1738) Md.; m. Susannah Duval.
Landowner; Magistrate.
Tyler, William (c1620-1701) N.J.; m. Joanna Parson.
Proprietor.
Tyler, William (c1688-1758) Mass.; m. Sarah Royal.
Merchant.
Tyner, Nicholas ( -1752) N.C.-Va.; m. Elizabeth
---. Landowner.

Tyrrell    SEE    Terrell

Tyson, John (1692-1775) N.C.-Va.; m. Priscilla Maybro;
  Sarah ( ) Lewis.  Military service.

Tyson, John (    -c1691) Va.; m. Susanika ---.
  Landowner.

Tyson, Matthias (1686-1727) N.C.; m. Mary Potts.
  Landowner.

Tyson, Reynier (1689-1745) Pa.; m. Margaret Steypers.
  Incorporator.

-U-

Ufford, Thomas (    -1660) Conn.; m. Isabell ---.
  Freeman; Juror.

Underhill, John (1597-1672) N.Y.; m. Helena de Hooch.
  Military service.

Underwood, Joseph (1615-77) Mass.; m. Mary Wilder.
  Freeman; Proprietor.

Underwood, Thomas (c1700-  ) Va.; m. ---.  Landowner.

Underwood, William (c1640-97) Mass.; m. Sarah ( )
  Pellet.  Founder; Selectman.

Underwood, William (1649-1717) Va.; m. Mary Elizabeth Butler; Margaret Moor.  Justice; Military
  service.

Upchurch, Michael (1620-81) Va.; m. Frances Delke.
  Landowner.

Updike, Louris Jansen (1620-59) N.Y.; m. Christian
  ---.  Landowner.

Upham, John (1600-81) Mass.; m. Elizabeth Slade.
  Deputy to Court; Landowner.

Upson, Stephen (1650-1735) Conn.; m. Mary Lee Gwin.
  Deputy to Court.

Upson, Thomas (    -1655) Conn.; m. Elizabeth Fuller.
  Proprietor.

Upton, John (c1620-77) Mass.; m. Eleanor Stewart.
  Military service.

Utie, George (    -1671/74) Md.; m. Susanna Goldsmith.  Assemblyman; Landowner.

Utie, John (c1600-39) Va.; m. Ann ---.  Governor's
  Council.

Utter, Nicholas (c1630/32-  )Conn.; m.  Elizabeth ---.
Landowner.
Uty  SEE  Utie

-V-

Vaden, Henry (c1663-c1729) Va.; m. Elizabeth ---.
Landowner.
Vail, Jeremiah (1618-87) N.Y.; m. Mary (Folger) Paine.
Freeman; Proprietor.
Vail, Samuel (1654-95) N.Y.; m. Elizabeth Hunt.  Land-
owner. Military service.
Valentine, John (c1600-52) Va.; m. Elizabeth ---.
Landowner.
Valentine, John (1654-1724) Mass.; m. Mary Lynde.
Attorney.
Valentine, Richard (1620-84) N.Y.-R.I.; m. ---.
Constable; Landowner.
Valentine, Richard (1666-1725) N.Y.; m. Sarah Halstead.
Assessor.
Valentine, Richard (c1688-1768) N.Y.; m. Mary Pearsall.
Military service.
Vallot, Claude Champagne (1649-92/93) Va.; m. Ann
Jenkinson. Landowner.
Van Alstine, Jan Martense (   -  ) N.Y.; m. Dirckien
Hermans. Landowner.
Van Antwerp, Arent Danielse (   -  ) N.Y.; m. Sara Van
Eps. Landowner.
Van Antwerp, Jan Danielse (1634/35-1717) N.Y.; m.
Maretje Groot. Military service.
Van Ardalen, Symon Janse (1629-1710) N.Y.; m. Pieterje
Claessen. Representative.
Van Barkelo, Willem Janse ( -1683) N.Y.; m. Lysebet
Janse. Landowner.
Van Bebber, Jacob Isaac ( -1705) Pa.; m. Christina
---. Founder.
Van Benschoten, Teunis Eliason (c1671-1719) N.Y.; m.
Gerritaje Gerritts. Landowner; Bridge builder.
Van Benthuysen, Paulus Martense (1625-1717) N.Y.; m.
Catherine Van Kleek. Oath of Allegiance; Inspector.

Van Borckelloo, Wyllem Jansen (1657- ) N.Y.; m.
Lysbet Jane ---. Landowner.
Van Boskirk    SEE    Van Buskirk
Van Brunt, Rutger Joesten (    -c1718) N.Y.; m. ---.
Civil Officer; Landowner.
Van Buren, Cornelis Maessen (c1605-48) N.Y.; m.
Catetyntse Martinse. Military service.
Van Burgh, Johannes Pieterse (1624-97) N.Y.; m.
Catherine Roeleff. Landowner.
Van Buskirk, Laurens Andriessen (    -1694) N.J.; m.
Jannetje Jans Barenton. Assemblyman; Governor's
Council.
Van Cortlandt, Olaf Stevense (1600-84) N.Y.; m.
Annetje Locheineau. Landowner.
Van Couwenhoven, Wolfert Gerretse (1588-1661) N.J.;
m. Noellje Jans. Commissioner; Burgher.
Vanderbilt, Jan Aertzen (    -1705) N.Y.; m. Anneke
Hendrick; Dearber Cornelis. Landowner.
Van Der Burgh, Gysbert Cornelisse (    - ) N.Y.; m.
Lysbet Claasen Van Voorhout. Landowner.
Van Der Burgh, Lucas Dirckse (1654/70- ) N.Y.; m.---.
Military service.
Vanderdonk, Andreaen (1620-55) Del.; m. Jannetkin
Varleth. Councillor; Patroon.
Van Der Heydon, Jacob Tyssen (1616- ) N.Y.; m. Ann
Hals. Military service.
Van Der Hoff, John Garretson (    - ) Del.; m. Ann
---. Landowner.
Van Der Mark, Thomas (1643-93 ) N.J.; m. Jacomyntje
Jacobs. Landowner.
Van Der Veer, Cornelis Janse (c1643-1703) Mass.; m.
Tryntje Gillie. Landowner.
Van Der Veer, Jacob (c1630-96) N.Y.-Del.; m. Katherine
---. Military service; Landowner.
Van Der Vliet, Dirck Janszen (c1687- ) N.Y.; m.
Greetje Gerritse. Military service.
Van Der Voort, Michael Paul (1610/19-92) N.Y.; m.
Marritije Joris Rapalje. Surgeon; Landowner.
Van Deusen, Abraham Pieter (1605- ) N.Y.; m. Tryntje
Melshiers. Registrar; Assemblyman.

Van Deventer, Jacobus (1663-   ) N.Y.; m. Femmetje
  Barents Ridder. Landowner; Commissioner.
Van Deventer, Jan Pieteros (1627-92) N.Y.; m. Maria
  Hoogeboom. Magistrate; Constable.
Van Dolson, Jan Gerrittse (   -   ) N.Y.; m. Gerritje
  Kray. Landowner.
Van Doorn, Pieter (1609-58) N.Y.; m. Catharyn Stilting.
  Landowner.
Van Dorn, Diedlof (   -1688) N.Y.; m. Eleje Jenriaens.
  Landowner.
Van Driest, Jan Barent (   -   ) N.Y.; m. Jannetje
  Van Borkeloo. Landowner.
Van Dyck  SEE  Van Dyke
Van Dyke, Jan Thomasse (1605-73) N.Y.; m. Tryntje
  Haegen. Military service.
Van Eps, Johannes (   -1690) N.Y.; m. Elizabeth
  Janse. Landowner.
Van Etten, Jacob Jansen (   -   ) N.Y.; m. Annetje
  Arianse. Petitioner.
Van Fossen, Arnold (1665-   ) Pa.; m. Mary ---.
  Landowner; Surveyor.
Van Gezel, Gerret (   -   ) Del.-N.Y.; m. ---.
  Secretary to Governor.
Van Gesel, Jacob (c1618-   ) N.Y.; m. Gertrude Reynier.
  Landowner.
Van Hess, Cornelis Hendricks (   -1694) N.Y.; m.
  Mejeke Van der Burghgraff. Military service;
  Landowner.
Van Hoorn  SEE  Van Horn
Van Hoosen, Jan Franse (   -1667) N.Y.; m. Volkie
  Jurrianse. Commissioner.
Van Horn, Christian Barentsen (   -1658) Pa.-Del.;
  m. Jannetje Jans. Landowner; Fire Warden.
Van Horn, Jan Cornellissen (   -c1660) N.Y.; m.
  Hildegard Joris. Military service.
Van Houten, Roelof Cornelis (1628-72) N.Y.; m.
  Gerretje Van Nes. Military service.
Van Kuykendahl, Jacob Laurzen (   -1653) N.Y.; m.
  ---. Military service; Blacksmith.
Van Lear, John George (1667-1748) Pa.; m. Mary
  Branson. Merchant; Apothecary.

Van Leer    SEE    Van Lear

Van Maesterlandt, Anneke Webber Jane (1592-1663) N.Y.;
m. Roelof Janse Van Maesterlandt. Landowner.

Van Meter, Jan Joostan (1624-1706) N.Y.; m. Macyken
Hendricksen. Military service.

Van Meteren    SEE    Van Meter

Van Nieukirk, Garret Cornelis (1635-86/95) N.Y.; m.
Chieltje Cornelissen Slecht. Landowner; Huguenot.

Van Noorden, Pieter Casperson (1600-54) N.Y.; m.
Aichtje Jane ---. Landowner.

Van Nuys, Aucke Janse (    -1694) N.Y.; m. Magdalina
Pieters. Magistrate; Delegate.

Van Patten, Nicholas (1641-   ) N.Y.; m. Affie Dews
Brandt. Justice; Trustee.

Van Pelt, Anthony Dennis (1647-1720/21) N.Y.; m.
Magdalene Helme Joostan. Landowner.

Van Pelt, Leunis Janse Lanen (c1685-1765) N.Y.; m.
Maria Dregeau. Landowner.

Van Pelt, Matthys Janse Lanen (c1626-83) N.Y.; m.
Tryntje ---. Landowner.

Van Pelt, Teunis Janse Lanen (    -1696) N.Y.; m.
Greetje Jans ---. Landowner.

Van Rensaelaer, Jeremias (1632-74) N.Y.; m. Maria
Van Cordtland. Landowner.

Van Schaick, Cornelis Aertzen (1610-67) N.Y.; m.
Belitje Hendrickse. Landowner.

Van Schichtenhorst, Brant (1610-68) N.Y.; m. Aeltie
Weneken; Gerutse Van Schaick. Military service;
Director of a New York Colony.

Van Steltyn, Everet Pels (    -   ) N.Y.; m. Jannaetje
Symens. Landowner.

Van Strycker    SEE    Strycker

Van Swearingen, Garrett (Gerret)(1636-98) Md.; m.
Barbara deBarette; Mary Smith. Councillor; Sheriff.

Van Swearingen, Thomas (1665-1710) Md.; m. Jane Riley.
Landowner.

Van Swearingen, Thomas (c1688-1726) Md.; m. Lydia
Riley. Landowner.

Van Tienhaven, Cornelis (c1600-c64) N.Y.; m. Rachel
Vinge. Provincial Secretary.

Van Tuyl, Abraham (1661-1735) N.Y.; m. Femmetje Dennis.
Landowner.
Van Tuyl, Isaac (c1681-c1728) N.Y.; m. Sarah Lakerman.
Landowner.
Van Vlack, Marinus Roelofse (1675-1747) N.Y.; m.  Dina
Idasse.  Constable.
Van Vliet, Adrain Gerretson (    -   ) N.Y.; m. Agatha
Jan Spruyt.  Landowner.
Van Vliet, Dirck Janszen (    -   ) N.Y.; m. Greetje
Gerritse.  Military service.
Van Voorhees, Stephen Coerten (1600-84) N.Y.; m. ---.
Magistrate; Assemblyman.
Van Vorst, Cornelis (1580-1638) N.Y.; m. Vromietje
Ides.  Landowner.
Van Vorst, Jacobus Garrit (1641-81) N.Y.; m. ---.
Landowner.
Van Vranken, Ryckert Classe (1629-  ) N.Y.; m.
Hillagonda ---.  Mariner.
Van Westervelt, Gurrien (1662-1738) N.Y. ; m.
Cornelia Van Voorhees.  Landowner.
Van Westervelt,  Lubbert Lubberston ( 1620-96) N.J.;
m. Geesie Roelofse.  Landowner.
Van Wick  SEE  Van Wyck
Van Winkle, Jacob Waling (    -1657) N.Y.-N.J.; m.
Tryntje Jacobs.  Landowner.
Van Wyck, Cornelis Barentse (    -   ) N.Y.; m. Anna
Polhemus.  Patroon; Proprietor.
Van Zandt, Gerritt Stoffelse (c1630-  ) N.Y.; m.
Lysbeth Gerritze.  Landowner; Supervisor.
Vassall, William (1592-1655) Va.; m. Anne King.
Council of War; Governor's Assistant.
Vaughan, George (1650-1704) N.Y.; m. Margaret Spink.
Landowner.
Vaughan, Robert (c1597-1669) Md.; m. Mary ---.
Assemblyman; Military service.
Vaughan, Robert (1691-  ) R.I.; m. Joanna Sweet.
Landowner.
Vaughan, William (1630-84) Va.; m. Sarah ---.
Proprietor.
Vaughn  SEE  Vaughan

Vause, John (c1622-c1700) Va.; m. Elizabeth ---.
Landowner.
Vawter, Bartholomew (1685-c1717) Va.; m. Winifred
Hodgson. Landowner.
Vawter, John (1691-1752) Va.; m. Margaret Noel.
Landowner.
Veach, James (1628- ) Md.; m. Mary Gakerlin.  Sheriff;
Military service.
Veatch, John (1700-67) Md.; m. Grace Masters. Land-
owner.
Vedder, Herman Albertus (c1610-1714) N.Y.; m. Maritse
Glen. Magistrate; Landowner.
Veeder, Synom Volkert (1624-96) N.Y.; m. Emgeltie ---.
Founder.
Veitch; Veatch   SEE   Veach
Venable, Abraham (c1685- ) Va.; m. Elizabeth Hicks.
Landowner; Burgess.
Venable, Abraham (1700-68) Va.; m. Martha Davis.
Burgess.
Verberk, Jan Janse (1600-88) N.Y.; m. Mayke Gisberta.
Magistrate.
Verleth, Casper (c1600- ) Md.; m. Judith ---.
Landowner.
Vermilye, Johannes (1601-56) N.Y.; m. Jacomina Jacobs.
Military service.
Vernon, Thomas (    -1698) Pa.; m. Elizabeth ---.
Juror; Landowner.
Ver Planck, Abraham (1575- ) N.Y.; m. Marie ( ) D.
Ross. Landowner.
Vesey, George (    -    ) Va.; m. Joanna ---.  Justice;
Assemblyman.
Vestal, William (1660-1702) Pa.; m. Alice (Glover)
Brunsden. Quaker; Landowner.
Via, Amer (c1664-1708/11) Va.; m. ---. Processioner.
Via, Amer (1688- ) Va.; m. Margaret ---. Military
service.
Viall, John (1618-86) R.I.; m. Elizabeth Smith.
Landowner.
Viall, Jonathan (1674-1724) R.I.; m. Mercy ---.
Landowner.

Viele, Peter Cornelisse (c1680- )N.Y.; m. Johanna
  Mydertie Van den Bogaard. Military service. Landowner.
Vigne, Guillaume (    -1632) N.Y.; m. Adrienne
  Cuvellier. Landowner.
Vinal, Ann (    -1664) Mass.; m. ---. Military
  service.
Vincent, John (1600-c34) Mass.; m. Mary ---. Town
  Officer.
Vinson, John (1649-1712) Mass.; m. Sarah Gurney.
  Landowner.
Vivian, John (    -1705) Va.; m. Margaret Smith.
  Proprietor; Constable.
Voorhees  SEE  Van Voorhees
Vore, Richard (    -1683) Conn.; m. ---. Freeman.
Vreeland, Enoch Michielsen (1647-1717) N.J.; m.
  Aftee Van Hoorn. Judge; Assemblyman.
Vrooman, Adam (1640-1730) N.Y.; m. Engelse Bloom.
  Military service.
Vrooman, Hendrick Meuse (1618-90) N.Y.; m. Geertrey
  Johannis. Landowner.

-W-

Waddy, Samuel (c1649- ) Va.; m. Ann ---. Landowner.
Waddy, Sarah (c1675-1735) Va.; m. John Anderson.
  Landowner; Minister.
Wade, Pearce (1700-70) Va.; m. Elizabeth ---. Land-
  owner.
Wadhams, John (    -1676) Conn.; m. Susannah ---.
  Constable; Landowner.
Wadsworth, Christopher (    -1677) Mass.; m. Grace
  Cole. Selectman; Surveyor.
Wadsworth, William (1595-1675) Mass.; m. Elizabeth
  Stone. Founder; Deputy to Court.
Waight, Abraham (    -    ) S.C.; m. Tabitha Nichols.
  Landowner.
Wailes, Nehemiah (1637- ) Md.; m. ---. Landowner.
Waite, John (1618-93) Mass.; m. Mary Hills. Landowner.
Wakefield, John (    -1674) Me.; m. Elizabeth Little-
  field. Landowner; Commissioner.

Wakeman, John (1594/99-1661) Conn.; m. Elizabeth Hopkins. New Haven Compact; Judge.

Waldo, Cornelius (1624-1700) Mass.; m. Hannah Cogswell. Committee of Safety; Selectman.

Waldo, John (1658-1700) Mass.; m. Rebecca Adams. Assemblyman; Military service.

Waldron, Baron Resolve (1610-90) N.Y.; m. Rebecca Hendricks; Janeke Van Nagle. Deputy Sheriff; Landowner.

Walker, Alexander (c1701-   ) Va.; m. Mary Holdcraft. Landowner; Justice.

Walker, George (c1635-1704) Va.; m. Elizabeth ---. Landowner.

Walker, James (1619/20-91) Mass.; m. Elizabeth Philips. Deputy to Court.

Walker, John (   -1668) Va.; m. Rachel Croshaw; Sarah ---. Burgess; Councillor.

Walker, John (c1655-1707) Del. m. Mary Payner. Justice; Assemblyman.

Walker, John (   -c1712) N.C.; m. Elizabeth ---. Landowner.

Walker, Lewis (   -1728) Pa.; m. Mary Morris. Landowner.

Walker, Philip (c1620-99) Mass.; m. Jane Metcalf. Oath of Fidelity; Military service.

Walker, Richard (1611-87) Mass.; m. Jane Talmadge. Landowner.

Walker, Robert (1607-87) Mass.; m. Sarah Leager. Freeman; Landowner.

Walker, Thomas (c1626-c97) Mass.; m. Mary Stone. Town Treasurer; Freeman.

Walker, Thomas (   -1720) Va.; m. Susanna Peasley. Military service; Landowner,

Wall, Joshua (c1687-c1728) Va.; m. Martha ---. Military service.

Wallace, James (1667-1712) Va.; m. Anne (Shepherd) Wythe. Minister.

Wallace, John (1700-74) Mass.; m. Annis Barnett. Landowner.

Wallbridge, Gustavus (   -1729) Conn.; m. Anna Amos. Military service.

Wallbridge, Henry (    1727) Mass.-Conn.; m. Anna
Amos. Tax Collector.

Waller, John (1617-85) Va.-Md.; m. Mary (Key) Bron-
frett; Alice Major. Landowner.

Waller, John (1673-1754) Va.; m. Dorothy King.
Burgess; High Sheriff.

Waller, William (    -    ) Va.; m. ---. Landowner.

Walling, Thomas (1630-74) R.I.; m. Mary Abbott.
Commissioner.

Wallingford, Benjamin (1678-1740) Mass.-Md.; m.
Elizabeth Browne. Landowner.

Wallingford, Nicholas (1619-81) Mass.; m. Sarah
Travis. Landowner; Master Mariner.

Wallis, Henry (    -c1699) Md.; m. ---. Delegate to
Court.

Waln, Nicholas (1650-1721) Pa.; m. Mary Jane Turner.
Assemblyman; Justice.

Walsworth, William (1646-1703) Conn.; m. Mary Abigail
Seaton. Landowner.

Walters, Walter (c1665-1732) Va.; m. Alice ---.
Juror; Landowner.

Walthall, William (1608-72) Va.; m. ---. Justice;
Landowner.

Walthall, William (c1635-90) Va.; m. Anne Archer.
Landowner.

Walton, George (1690/1700-67) Va.; m. Elizabeth Rowe.
Military service; Justice.

Walton, William (    -1668) Mass.; m. Elizabeth ---.
Minister.

Walton, William (c1700-47) Va.; m. Susannah ---.
Proprietor.

Wanshaer, Jan Janszen (1621-74) N.Y.; m. Baertze
(Hendrick) Kip. Landowner; Military service.

Wanzer   SEE   Wanshaer

Ward, Andrew (1597-1659) Conn.; m. Hester Sherman.
Commissioner; Magistrate.

Ward, Enoch (c1685-1750) Va.; m. Elizabeth Shackel-
ford. Landowner; Justice.

Ward, John (1598-   ) Va.; m. ---.  Burgess.

Ward, John (1625-94) Conn.; m. Sarah ---.  Representative; Justice.

Ward, John (1626-1708) Mass.; m. ---.  Selectman;
Military service.

Ward, Richard (   -1682) Va.; m. Elizabeth ---.
Justice; Commissioner.

Ward, Seth (   -   ) Va.; m. ---.  Assemblyman; Landowner.

Ward, William (1603-87) Mass.; m. ---; Elizabeth ---.
Landowner.

Wardlaw, Robert (1670-c1700) Va.; m. ---.  Landowner.

Ware, Edward (1673-   ) Va.; m.  Elizabeth Garrett.
Landowner; Military service.

Ware, Jacob (c1690-1709) Va.; m. Susanna Adams.
Minister.

Ware, Peter (   -   ) Va.; m. --- Valentine.  Landowner.

Ware, Robert (1602-   ) Va.; m. Jane ---.  Landowner.

Ware, Robert (   -1699) Mass.; m. Margaret Huntung.
Freeman; Landowner.

Warfield, Richard (c1630-1703/04) Md.; m. Elinor
Brown.  Vestryman; Landowner.

Warham, John (1630-70) Conn.; m.  Jane (Dabinot)
Newberry.  Minister.

Warne, Thomas (1652-1722) N.J.; m. Mary (Lord) Gerhart.
Justice; Councillor.

Warner, Andrew (1600-84) Mass.; m. Esther ( ) Selden;
Mary (Humphrey) ---.  Freeman; Proprietor.

Warner, Augustine (1611-74) Va.; m. Mary Markes.
Burgess; Justice.

Warner, Augustine (1642-81) Va.; m. Mildred Reade.
Governor's Council.

Warner, Ichabod (1684-1768) Mass.; m. Mary Metcalf.
Military service.

Warner, John (1615-   ) Mass.-R.I.; m. Priscilla
Hollinder.  Town Clerk.

Warner, John (1645-1712) R.I.; m. Ann Gorton.  Landowner.

Warner, William (c1590-c1648) Mass.; m. Abigail Baker.
Landowner.

Warner, William (1627-1706) Pa.; m. Ann Dide.
Justice; Councillor.
Warren, Arthur (1602-58) Mass.; m. Mary ---. Pro-
prietor.
Warren, Humphrey (1632-73) Md.; m. Susannah Davenport;
Eleanor ---. Maryland Remonstrance; Military
service.
Warren, Humphrey (     -1694) Md.; m. Margery ---.
Justice; Sheriff.
Warren, Jacob (1642-1722) Mass.-Conn.; m. Mary
Hildreth. Freeman; Fence viewer.
Warren, Jacob (1668-1727) Mass.; m. Sarah ---.
Selectman; Landowner.
Warren, James (1698-   ) Me.; m. Mary Goodwin. Land-
owner.
Warren, John (1585-1667) Mass.; m. Margaret ---.
Military service.
Warren, John (1640-1705) Va.; Rachel Sargent. Land-
owner.
Warren, Joseph (c1645-1718) Mass.; m. Experience
Wheelock. Landowner.
Warren, Nathaniel (1624-67) Mass.; m. ---. Military
service.
Warren, Richard (1580-1628) Va.; Elizabeth March.
Mayflower Compact.
Warren, Richard (1646-96) Mass.; m. Sarah Taney.
Landowner.
Warren, Thomas (1624-c70) Va.; m. Elizabeth (Spencer)
Sheppard; Jane King. Burgess.
Warwick, William (     -1720) Md.; m. Mary ---.
Landowner.
Washburn, John (1597-1670) Mass.; m. Margery(Margaret)
Moore. Freeman; Proprietor.
Washburn, John (1629-86) Mass.; m. Elizabeth Mitchell.
Landowner; Military service.
Washburn, William (1601-53) N.Y.; m. Jane ---. Land-
owner.
Washer, Thomas (c1570-c1619) Va.; m. Mary Bruce.
Assemblyman.
Washington, Edward (c1700-92) Va.; m. Mary (Stone)
Barry. Founder; Landowner.

Washington, Henry (1694-1748) Va.; m. Mary Bailey.
Landowner.

Washington, John (1623-61) Va.; m. Mary (Flood) Ford.
Military service.

Washington, John (1627-78) Va.; m. Anne (Pope) Broad-
hurst; Margaret Butler. Burgess; Military service.

Washington, Lawrence (1625-77) Va.; m. Jane Fleming.
Landowner.

Washington, Lawrence (1659-97/98) Va.; m. Mildred
Warner. Justice; Burgess.

Washington, Richard (1659-1724) Va.; m. Elizabeth
Jordan. Landowner; Military service.

Washington, Richard (1691-1763) N.C.; m. Hannah
Murfree. Constable; Military service.

Waterbury, John (1620-58) Conn.; m. Rose Lockwood.
Landowner; Representative.

Waterman, Robert (1612-52) Mass.; m. Elizabeth Bourne.
Freeman; Juror.

Waterman, Thomas (    -1708) Conn.; m. Miriam Elizabeth ---. Landowner.

Waters, Edward (1568-1637) Va.; m. Grace O'Neil.
Burgess; Commissioner.

Waters, John (1606-74) Md.; m. Susannah ( ) White;
Elizabeth Giles. Landowner.

Waters, Lawrence (c1602-87) Mass.; m. Ann Linton.
Proprietor.

Waters, William ( 1623-87) Va.; m. Margaret (Robins)
Clark. Sheriff; Burgess.

Waters, William (1660-1720) Va.; m. Isabel Harmonson.
Burgess; Sheriff.

Watkins, Henry (1638-1716) Va.; m. Rachel ---.
Burgess; Assemblyman.

Watkins, Henry (1685-90) Va.; m. Katherine Pride.
Burgess.

Watkins, Richard (1616-59) Va.; m. ---. Landowner.

Watson, John (    -1706) Va.; m. Alice ---. Landowner.

Watts, John (    -1678/85) Va.; m. Margaret ---.
Landowner.

Watts, Richard (    -1655) Conn.; m. Elizabeth ---.
Proprietor.

Watts, Richard (     -1712) Va.; m. Mary Blagg. Land-
owner.
Waugh, John (1687-1781) Conn.; m. ---. Military
service.
Way,  Robert (1650/60-1725) Pa.; m. Hannah Hickman.
Landowner.
Wear, Robert (1678-1754) Va.; m. Martha ---. Land-
owner.
Weatherbee   SEE   Weatherby
Weatherby, Bartholomew (1586-c1638) Va.; m. Albina
Godby. Landowner.
Weatherby, John (1650-1711) Mass.; m. Lydia Moore.
Military service.
Weatherby, Whitehead (     - ) Pa.; m. ---. Land-
owner.
Weaver, Clement (1591/92-1683) Mass.; m. Rebecca
Holbrook. Landowner.
Weaver, Clement (1619/21-83) R.I.; m. Mary Freeborn.
Military service.
Weaver, Clement (1647-91) R.I.; m. ---. Military
service.
Weaver, Clement (1669-1737) R.I.; m. Hannah Long.
Military service.
Weaver, William (1671-1718) R.I.; m. Elizabeth Harris.
Landowner.
Weaver, Samuel (1604-c1700) Va.; m. Elizabeth ---.
Landowner.
Weaver, William (1695-1759) R.I.; m. Alice ---.
Surveyor.
Webb, Benjamin (1667-1732) Conn.; m. Susanna Ballen-
tine. Landowner.
Webb, Christopher (1630-94) Mass.; m. Hannah Scott.
Town Clerk.
Webb, Edmond (c1648-85) Md.; m. ---. Landowner.
Webb, Giles (c1615-92) Va.; m. Margaret ---; Judith
(Bland) Randolph. Burgess.
Webb, James (c1701-77) Va.; m. Mary Edmonson.
Justice; Landowner.
Webb, John (     -1711) Pa.; m. ---. Landowner;
Quaker.

Webb, Richard (1580-1658) Mass.; m. Grace Wilson.
Surveyor.

Webber   SEE   Weber

Weber, Henry (   -   ) Va.; m. ---.   Justice.

Weber, Samuel (1656-1716) Me.; m. ---.   Military
service.

Webster, Ebenezer (1667-   ) N.H.; m. Hannah Judkins.
Military service.

Webster, John (1590-1661) Conn.; m. Agnes Smith.
Magistrate; Deputy Governor.

Webster, Robert (1627-76) Conn.; m. Susannah Treat.
Landowner.

Wedge, Thomas(c1640-1703) Mass.; m. Joanna Humobrew.
Representative.

Weed, Jonas (1605-76) Conn.; m. Mary ---.   Proprietor.

Weeks, Abraham (1631-91/92) Va.; m. Mildred ---.
Constable.

Weeks, Benjamin (1674-1744/45) N.C.; m. Mary ---.
Landowner.

Weeks, Samuel (1670-1746) N.H.; m. Elinor Hames.
Military service.

Welch, John (1622-83) Md.; m. Mary Damaris Wyatt;
Ann ( ) Grosse. Sheriff; Military service.

Welch, Philip (1640/42-   ) Mass.; m. Harriet Haggett.
Military service.

Welch, Thomas (   -1681) Conn.; m. Hannah Buckingham. Freeman; Deputy to Court.

Welch, William (   -   ) N.C.; m. ---.   Landowner.

Weld, Joseph (1595-1646) Mass.; m. Elizabet Weld;
Barbara Clapp. Freeman; Ancient and Honorable
Artillery Company.

Weldon, Samuel (1650-92) Va.; m. Sarah Efford. Military service; Justice.

Wellborn, John (c1610-   ) Va.; m. ---.   Founder; Landowner.

Wellborn, Thomas (1640-   ) Va.; m. Arcadia Toft.
Sheriff; Judge.

Wellbourn; Willborn   SEE   Wellborn

Welles   SEE   Wells

Wellman, Thomas (1620-72) Mass.; m. Elizabeth ---.
Landowner; Military service.

Wells, James (c1630-97) Conn.; m. Elizabeth Clarke.
Freeman.
Wells, Nathaniel (1600-   ) R.I.; m. ---. Freeman;
Landowner.
Wells, Richard (c1608-67/70) Md.; m. Frances White.
Burgess; Physician.
Wells, Robert (   -   ) Mass.; m. Alice ---. Land-
owner.
Wells, Stephen (   -1723) Va.; m. Elizabeth (Williams)
Settle. Landowner.
Wells, Thomas (1598-1659) Conn.; m. Elizabeth (Deming
or Hunt) Foote; Alice Tomes. Deputy Governor;
Commissioner.
Wells, Thomas (1603-66) Mass.; m. Abigail Warner.
Physician; Ancient and Honorable Artillery Company.
Wells, William (1566-1620) Conn.; m. Elizabeth ---.
Founder.
Wells, William (1608-71) Mass.; m. Mary ---. Attorney.
Welsh   SEE   Welch
Welton, John (   -1726) Conn.; m. Mary ---. Propri-
etor.
Wemple, Jan Barentsen (c1620-63) N.Y.; m. Marirje
Wynderts. Landowner.
Wensley   SEE   Winsley
Wentworth, Charles (1684-1780) Mass.; m. Bethia Fenno.
Selectman; Military service.
Wentworth, William (1615-97) Mass.-N.H.; m. Elizabeth
Kenny; Susanna (Carter) Fleming. Selectman;
Moderator.
Werden, Peter (1608-87) Mass.; m. Mary ---. Land-
owner.
West, Anthony (   -1652) Va.; m. Ann ---. Landowner.
West, Francis (1590-   ) Va.; m. Unity Croshaw.
Governor.
West, John (1590-1651/52) Va.; m. Ann ---. Governor;
Military service.
West, John (1632-89) Va.; m. Ursula Unity Croshaw.
Burgess; Military service.
West, Joseph (1670-   ) Md.; m. Rebecca ---. Landowner.
West, Nathaniel (c1655-1724) Md.; m. Martha Woodward.
Burgess.

West, Robert (    -1637) N.C.; m. Mary Harvey.
Landowner.

West, Samuel (1640/45-1701) S.C.; m. ---.  Landowner;
Committeeman.

West, Thomas (c1670-c1714) Va.; m. Frances ---.
Burgess.

West, William (1695-  ) Md.; m. Esther Duval.  Church
Warden.

Westcott, Stuckeley (1592-1677) R.I.-Mass.; m. Juliana Marchant; Rosanna Hill.  Proprietor; Commissioner.

Westerfeld  SEE  Van Westerfeld

Westmore  SEE  Wetmore

Weston, John (1643-1723) Mass.; m. Sarah Fitch.
Landowner.

Westwood, Worlich (    -1702) Va.; m. Elizabeth
Naylor.  Innkeeper; Landowner.

Wetherbee  SEE  Weatherby

Wetmore, Thomas (1615-81) Conn.; m. Sarah Hall.
Commissioner; Military service.

Whalley, Edward (1615-1718) Mass.; m. Elizabeth Rat-
cliff.  Landowner.

Wharton, Thomas (1664-1718 ) Pa.; m. Rachel ---.
Councillor; Governor.

Wheat, Moses (c1625-1700) Mass.; m. Tamplen ---.
Proprietor; Landowner.

Wheeler, Anne (Halsey) (    -1659) Mass.; m. Thomas
Wheeler.  Landowner.

Wheeler, Ephriam (    -1669/70) Conn.; m. Ann Turney.
Military service.

Wheeler, George (1668-1737) N.H.; m. Abigail Hosmer.
Landowner.

Wheeler, Joan (Bryan) (    -1673) Conn.; m. Thomas
Wheeler.  Landowner.

Wheeler, John (1630-85/94) Md.; m. Mary ---.  Military service.

Wheeler, Moses (1598-1698) Conn.; m. Miriam Hawley.
Landowner.

Wheeler, Richard (    -1675/76) Mass.; m. Sarah
Prescott.  Landowner.

Wheeler, Thomas (    -1653/54) Mass.; m. Anna Halsey.
Landowner.

Wheeler, Thomas (1602-86) Conn.; m. Mary ---. Representative; Military service.
Wheeler, Thomas ( -1669) Mass.; m. Ruth Wood. Military service; Landowner.
Wheeler, Thomas (1620-72) Mass.; m. Sarah Meriam. Freeman; Landowner.
Wheeler, Thomas ( -1704) Mass.; m. Joan Bryan. Landowner.
Wheeler, William (1670-1738) Md.; m. Susanna (Drummond). Landowner.
Wheelock, Ralph (c1600-84) Mass.; m. Rebecca ---. Representative; Freeman.
Wheelwright, John (1594-1679) Mass.; m. Mary Hutchinson. Minister.
Whidden; Whitten SEE Witten
Whipple, John (1617-83) R.I.-Mass.; m. Sarah ---. Military service.
Whipple, Mathew (1605-47) Mass.; m. Anne Hawkins. Landowner.
Whitacre SEE Whitaker
Whitaker, Jabez (1596-1626) Va.; m. Mary Bourchier. Burgess; Councillor.
Whitaker, John (c1671- ) Pa.; m. Jane (Scot) Parker. Landowner.
Whitaker, John ( -1713) Md.; m. Catherine ---. Landowner.
Whitaker, Jonathan (1688-1763) N.J.; m. Elizabeth Jarvis. Landowner.
Whitaker, William (1618-62) Va.; m. ---. Burgess; Councillor.
Whitcomb, John (1588-1662) Mass.; m. Frances Coggan. Freeman; Founder.
White, Edward (1693-1769) Mass.; m. Hannah Wiswall. Military service.
White, Guy ( -1676) Md.; m. Sarah ---. Landowner.
White, Henry (1648-1706) N.C.; m. Rebekah Arnold. Landowner.
White, Jeremiah (1695-1776) Va.; m. Mary Martin. Landowner.
White, John (c1600/10-72/73) Mass.; m. Joan West. Founder; Landowner.

White, John (c1620-70) Va.; m. ---. Burgess.
White, John (    -1685) Md.; m. Sarah Keyser. Military service; Burgess.
White, Joseph (1651-1702) N.J.; m. Elizabeth Church. Quaker; Landowner.
White, Moses (1680-   ) S.C.; m. Mary Campbell. Minister.
White, Patrick (    -1691) Va.; m. Elizabeth ---. Landowner.
White, Peregrine (1660-1727) Mass.; m. Susanna Eames. Selectman; Councillor.
White, Richard (c1623-88) Va.; m. Mary ---. Landowner.
White, Thomas (c1610-29) Mass.; m. ---. Freeman.
White, William (1648-73) Mass.; m. Susanna Fuller; Elizabeth ---. Landowner.
Whitehead, Daniel (1603-68) N.Y.; m. Jeanne Skidmore. Landowner.
Whitehead, Daniel (1646-1704) N.Y.; m. Abigail Stevenson. Landowner.
Whitehead, Isaac (c1630-91) Conn.-N.J.; m. Susannah ---. Town Clerk; Judge.
Whitfield, Matthew (c1607-84) Va.; m. Ann ---. Landowner.
Whitfield, Matthew (    -1708) N.C.-Va.; m. Priscilla Lawrence. Proprietor; Surveyor.
Whiting, James (1609-   ) Va.; m. Ann ---. Landowner.
Whiting, Samuel (1597-1679) Mass.; m. Elizabeth St. John. Minister.
Whiting, William (    -1647) Conn.; m. Susanna ---. Treasurer; Deputy to Court.
Whitman, John (1602-92) Mass.; m. ---. Military service; Magistrate.
Whitmarsh, Ebenezer (1658-1718) Mass.; m. Christian Bayley. Military service.
Whitmer, George (1700-   ) Pa.; m. ---. Landowner.
Whitmore, John (    -1648) Conn.; m. ---. Assemblyman; Landowner.
Whitmore, Thomas (1593-1661) Mass.; m. Hannah Chawkley. Proprietor.

Whitmore, Thomas (1615-81) Conn.; m. Sarah Hall.
Delegate to Court.
Williamson, Richard ( -c1659) Va.; m. Margaret
Sherwood. Landowner.
Williamson, Robert ( -1669) Va.; m. Jane Allen.
Burgess.
Williamson, Robert ( -1726) Va.; m. Katherine
Lewis. Freeman; Landowner.
Whitney, Henry (1620-73) Conn.; m. Sarah ( ) Ketchum.
Freeman; Proprietor.
Whitney, John (1599-1673) Mass.; m. Elinor ---; Judith
Clement. Founder; Military service.
Whitney, John (1620/24-92) Mass.; m. Ruth Reynpids.
Selectman; Military service.
Whitney, Joshua (1635-1719) Mass.; m. Lydia ---;
Mary ---; Abigail Tarball. Military service.
Whitney, Richard (c1624- ) Mass.; m. Martha Coldam.
Freeman; Proprietor.
Whiton, James (c1645- ) Mass.; m. Mary Beal. Land-
owner.
Whittemore SEE Whitmore
Whittier, Thomas (1620-96) Mass.; m. Ruth Green.
Road builder; Deputy to Court.
Whittington, John (1650-1722) Md.; m. Johanna ---.
Assemblyman.
Whittington, William (1616-58/59) Va.; m. Elizabeth
Weston. Military service.
Whittington, William (1649/50-1720) Md.; m. Esther
Littleton; Tabitha (Scarborough) Smart. Burgess;
Justice.
Whittelsey, Jabez (1675-1756) Conn.; m. Lydia Way.
Landowner.
Whittelsey, John (1623-1704) Conn.; m. Ruth Dudley.
Freeman; Attorney.
Whittlesey SEE Whittelsey
Wick, John (1660-1719) N.Y.; m. Temperance Barnes.
Landowner.
Wickenden, William (1614-69) R.I.; m. Alice ---.
Minister; Assemblyman.
Wicker, Joseph (c1685-c1741) N.C.; m. Ruth Musson.
Burgess.

Wicker, Richard (    -1699) Va.-N.C.; m. Margaret ---.
Clerk of Court.

Wickes, Philip (1678-1742) N.Y.; m. Martha Corey.
Landowner.

Wickes, Thomas (1612-71) N.Y.; m. Isabelle Harcourt.
Proprietor; Freeman.

Wickes, Thomas (1650-   ) N.Y.; m. Deborah Platt.
Military service.

Wickliffe, David (1611-42) Md.; m. Jane Rokeby.
Landowner.

Wicks, John (    -1675) Mass.; m. Mary ---. Landowner.

Wiggin, Thomas (1692-1667) N.H.; m. Catherine Whiting.
Governor's Assistant; Governor.

Wight, Henry (    -1673/74) Mass.; m. Alice ---; Jane
Goodenow. Selectman; Constable.

Wightman, Valentine (c1642-1722) N.C.; m. Suzanne
Holmes. Landowner.

Wilbore, Samuel (1585-1656) Mass.; m. Ann Bradford.
Freeman; Constable.

Wilbore, Shadrach (1631-97/98) Mass.; m. Mary Dean.
Town Clerk.

Wicoff   SEE   Wyckoff

Wilcock; Willcox   SEE   Wilcox

Wilcox, Barnabas (    -1690) R.I.; m. Sarah ---.
Justice.

Wilcox, John (1596-1651) Conn.; m. Mary ---. Selectman; Surveyor.

Wilcox, Thomas (1681-1779) Pa.; m. Elizabeth Cole.
Landowner.

Wilcoxon, William (1601-52) Conn.; m. Margaret Birds-
eye. Freeman; Proprietor.

Wilcoxson   SEE   Wilcoxon

Wilder, Edward (1623-90) Mass.; m. Elizabeth Eames.
Freeman; Selectman.

Wilder, Francis (c1650-1723) Va.; m. ---. Churchman;
Landowner.

Wilder, Nathaniel (1652-1704) Mass.; m. Mary Sawyer.
Founder; Military service.

Wilder, Thomas (1618-67) Mass.; m. Ann Eames. Selectman; Landowner.

Wilkins, Bray (     -1696/97) Mass.; m. Anne (Hannah)
Gingell. Landowner.
Wilkins, John (1596-1650) Va.; m. Anna ---. Land-
owner; Burgess.
Wilkins, William (1666-1747) Va.; m. Mary Langley.
Founder; Military service.
Wilkinson, Laurence (1646-92) R.I.; m. Susannah Smith.
Deputy to Assembly.
Wilkinson, Samuel (1641-1727) R.I.; Plain Wickenden.
Justice; Assemblyman.
Wilkinson, William (1612-63) Va.; m. Naomi Hewes;
Margaret Nicholson. Minister.
Wilkinson, William (1643-1705/06) N.C.; m. Esther
Sweatman. Attorney; Speaker, House of Burgesses.
Willard, Simon (1605-76) Mass.; m. Mary (Garrett)
Dunster; Elizabeth Dunston; Mary Sharpe. Judge;
Military service.
Willeston, James (c1676-1736) Va.; m. Ann Hargrove.
Landowner; Military service.
Willet  SEE  Willett
Willett, Edward (     -1704) Md.; m. Tabitha ---.
Landowner.
Willett, Thomas (1610-74) N.Y.-Mass.; m. Mary Hooker.
Council of War; Councillor.
Willett, Thomas (1620-46) N.Y.; m. Roemell ---.
Landowner.
Willett, Thomas (1645-1722) N.Y.; m. Helena Stoothoof.
Governor's Council.
Willey, Isaac (c1640-85) Conn.; m. Johanna ---.
Selectman; Freeman.
Willey, Isaac (1699-1767) Conn.; m. Deliverance
Tolman. Freeman; Landowner.
Willey, John (1648-88) Conn.; m. Miriam Moore.
Landowner; Military service.
Williams, David (1696-1752) Conn.; m. Dorothy Sturgis;
Ruth Bradley. Military service.
Williams, George (c1650-   ) Va.; m. Sarah ---. Land-
owner.
Williams, John (c1600-74) Mass.; m. ---. Freeman;
Proprietor.

Williams, John (1640-80) Va.; m. Anne ---; Eve Smyth.
Landowner.

Williams, Joseph (1644-1724) R.I.; m. Lydia Olney.
Landowner.

Williams, Joseph (1661-1739) N.C.; m. Elizabeth Sawyer.
Surveyor; Assemblyman.

Williams, Joseph (1686-1782) N.C.; m. N.C.; m. Martha
Newborne. Minister.

Williams, Matthew (1606-c28) Conn.; m. Susan ---.
Founder.

Williams, Michael (1617-44) Va.; m. Anne Valentine.
Landowner.

Williams, Rice ( -1701) Va.; m. Mary ---. Landowner.

Williams, Richard (1611-1706) Mass.; m. Frances
Deighton. Founder.

Williams, Robert (1608-93) Mass.; m. Elizabeth Stahl-
man or Stalham; Martha (Strong) Stratton. Freeman;
Trustee, Roxbury School.

Williams, Robert (1642-1734) Pa.; m. Owen Cadwalader.
Landowner.

Williams, Roger (1599-1683) R.I.; m. Mary Barnard.
Governor.

Williams, Roger (1645-77) Va.; m. Joane Frith.
Landowner.

Williams, Thomas (alias Harris) (c1634- ) Mass.;
m. Elizabeth ---. Landowner.

Williams, Thomas (c1693-c1749) Md.; m. Eleanor ---.
Justice; Vestryman.

Williams, Walter ( -1672) Va.; m. ---. Landowner.

Williams, William (c1625-89/90) Conn.; m. Jane West-
over. Freeman; Proprietor.

Williams, William (c1630-64) Va.; m. ---. Minister;
Landowner.

Williams, William ( -1712) N.C.; m. Mary ---.
Minister.

Williamson, Henry ( - ) Va.; m. Katherine Weeks.
Landowner.

Williamson, James ( -1656) Va.; m. Ann Underwood.
Justice.

Willis, George (1589-1645) Conn.; m. Bridget Young;
Mary (Smith) Bysbie. Governor's Assistant. Governor.
Willis, Henry (1691-1740) Va.; m. Mildred (Howell)
Brown. Founder; Burgess.
Willis, John (     -1699) Va.; m. ---. Military
Service.
Willis, Thomas (1583-1660) Mass.; m. Mary Tomlins.
Proprietor; Representative.
Willis, William (c1616-63) Va.; m. ---. Landowner.
Williston, James (1697-1736) Va.-Md.; m. Ann Hargrave.
Landowner.
Willmott; Wilmote  SEE  Wilmot
Willoughby, Francis (     -1671) Mass.; m. Margaret
(Lock) Taylor. Freeman; Selectman.
Willoughby, Thomas (1587-1656) Va.; m. Alice ---.
Burgess; Commissioner.
Wills, Daniel (1633-98) N.J.; m. Elizabeth ---;
Mary Wagstaff. Physician.
Wilmer, Simon (1630-99) Md.; m. Rebecca Tilghman.
Legislator.
Wilmot, Benjamin (1589-1659) Conn.-Mass.; m. Ann ---.
Oath of Fidelity.
Wilmot, John (     -c1719) Md.; m. Jane ---. Landowner;
Merchant.
Wilson, James (     -1712) Va.; m. Elizabeth ---.
Military service.
Wilson, John (1588-1667) Mass.-Conn.; m. Elizabeth
Mansfield. Minister.
Wilson, William (c1646-1713) Va.; m. Jane Willis.
Burgess; Military service.
Wiltbank, Helmanue Frederick (1625/31-83/84) Pa.; m.
Jonekin (Joan) Hull. Military service.
Wiltsee, Hendrick Martensen (1623-1712) N.Y.; m.
Margaritha Meyringhs Jensen. Interpreter; Military
service.
Wiltsee, Phillippe Maton (1590-1632) N.Y.; m. Sophia
Ter Bosch. Builder of Fort.
Wimberly, John (1635-73) Va.; m. ---. Landowner.
Wimberly, John (1650-1715) Va.; m. Frances Welby.
Proprietor; Landowner.

Winans, John (c1640-94) N.J.; m. Susanna Melyn.
Juror; Proprietor.

Winchell, Nathaniel (1633-1700) Conn.; m.  Sarah
Porter.  Landowner.

Winchell, Nathaniel (1665-1741) Conn.; m. Mary Grover.
Military service.

Winchell, Nathaniel (1694-    ) Conn.; m. Abigail
Ruggles.  Landowner; Churchman.

Winchell, Robert (c1600-69) Conn.; m. ---.  Juror;
Recorder.

Winchester, John (1611-94) Mass.; m. Hannah Sealis.
Teacher; Surveyor.

Winchester, William (1670-1757) Md.; m. Joanna ---.
Teacher; Surveyor.

Wing, Deborah (Bachiler) (    -1691) N.H.; m. John
Wing.  Landowner.

Wing, Ebenezer (1594-1786) Mass.; m. Elizabeth Blackmore.  Military service.

Wing, John (1613-89) Mass.; m. Elizabeth Tucker.
Landowner.

Wing, Stephen (1621-1710) Mass.; m. Osheah Dillingham.
Freeman; Constable.

Wingate, John (1636-87) N.H.; m. Sarah (Taylor)
Conway.  Juror; Selectman.

Wingate, Joshua (1670-1769) N.H.-Mass.; m. Mary Lunt.
Selectman; Military service.

Wingfield, John (1623-78) Va.; m. Mary Owens.
Landowner.

Wingfield, Thomas (1670-1720) Va.; m. Mary Stegall.
Landowner.

Winn   SEE   Wynne

Winship, Edward (1612/13-88) Mass.; m. Elizabeth (Parks)
Freeman.  Selectman; Ancient and Honorable Artillery
Company.

Winsley, Samuel (    -1663) Mass.; m. Elizabeth ---;
Anna ( ) Boyd.  Deputy to Court; Commissioner.

Winslow, John (1596-1674) Mass.; m. Mary Chilton.
Oath of Fidelity; Landowner.

Winslow, Josiah (1606-74) Mass.-Conn.; m. Margaret
Bourne.  Deputy to Court.

Winslow, Kenelm (1599-1672) Mass.; m. Eleanor Adams.
Deputy to Court.
Winsor, Joshua (     -1679) R.I.; m. ---. Landowner.
Winstead, Samuel (c1658-1726) Va.; m. Elizabeth ---.
Constable; Landowner.
Winston, John (1680-c1767) Va.; m. Barbara Overton.
Landowner.
Winston, William (    -   ) Va.; m. Sarah Dabney.
Landowner.
Winter, William (c1680-1733) N.J.; m. ---. Grand
Juror.
Winthrop, John (1587-1649) Mass.; m. Mary Forth;
Thomasine Clopton; Margaret Tyndall; Martha Rains-
borough. Landowner.
Winthrop, John (1606-76) Mass.; m. Elizabeth Reade.
Governor.
Wise, John (1618-95) Va.; m. Hannah Scarborough.
Landowner.
Wise, William (1681-1752) Va.; m. Lydia Ladethen.
Landowner.
Wishart, James (c1637-79) Va.; m. Elizabeth Peters.
Landowner.
Withers, James (1680/81-1746) Va.; m. Elizabeth Keene.
Landowner.
Withers, John (     -1693) Va.; m. ---. Landowner.
Withers, William (1636-98) Va.; m. ---. Landowner.
Witherspoon, John (1670-1739) Va.; m. Janette ---.
Landowner.
Withington, Henry (1586-1666) Mass.; m. Elizabeth ---.
Landowner.
Witt, William (1675-1754) Va.; m. Mary ---; Elizabeth
Daux. Landowner; Quaker.
Witten, Thomas (1632-   ) Md.; m. --- Buckley. Land-
owner.
Witter, Josiah (1638-85/90) R.I.; m. Sarah Crandall.
Landowner.
Witter, William (1584-1659) Mass.; m. Annie Churchman.
Landowner.
Wixam, Robert (     -1686) Mass.; m. Alice ---. Mili-
tary service.

Woburn, Joseph Johnson (1628/29-1704) Mass.; m. Hester Wiswell. Selectman.

Woertman, Dirck Jans (c1630-    ) N.Y.; m. Marrietje (Teunis) Denyse. Ferryman; Landowner.

Woodhull, Richard (1620-90) Conn.; m. Deborah Crowe. Magistrate; Justice.

Wofford, William (c1620-c55) Md.; m. Mary ---. Surveyor; Landowner.

Wolcott, Henry (1576-1655) Mass.-Conn.; m. Elizabeth Sanders. Landowner.

Wolcott, Henry (1610-    ) Conn.; m. Sarah Newberry. Assemblyman.

Wolcott, Jonathan (    -    ) Mass.; m. Alice Ingersoll. Freeman; Constable.

Wolcott, Samuel (1656-1708) Mass.; m. Judith Appleton. Landowner; Selectman.

Womack, Abraham (1642-1733) Va.; m. ---. Grand Juror.

Womack, Richard (1655-84) Va.; m. Mary Puckett. Landowner.

Womack, Thomas (1680-1732) Va.; m. Mary Farley. Landowner.

Womack, William (1620-79) Va.; m. ---. Landowner.

Wood, Henry (    -1691) N.J.; m. Hannah ---. Landowner.

Wood, John (1610-35) R.I.; m. Elizabeth ---. Landowner; Councillor.

Wood, John (    -1704) R.I.; m. Mary Peabody. Landowner.

Wood, Jonas Halifax (1613-80) N.Y.; m. Joanna Strickland. Landowner.

Wood, Joseph (1660-1721) Del.; m. Francina Herrman. Landowner.

Wood, Samuel (c1636-1718) Mass.; m. Alice ---. Proprietor.

Wood, Thomas (1635-87) Mass.; m. Ann Todd. Military service.

Wood, William (1582-1671) Mass.; m. Margaret Sawyer. Town Officer.

Wood   SEE ALSO   Woods

Woodbridge, John (1613-95) Mass.; m. Mercy Dudley. Minister.

Woodbury, Isaac (1644-1726) Mass.; m. Mary Wilks.
Mariner.
Woodbury, John (1579-1641) Mass.; m. Joanna Humphrey;
---. Selectman; Deputy to Court.
Woodhouse, Henry (1607-55) Va.; m. Maria ---; Mary
---. Burgess; Commissioner.
Woodhouse, Henry (1635-88) Va.; m. Sarah Keeling.
Landowner.
Woodie, Henry ( -1700) Mass.; m. Elinor Hopkinson.
Freeman; Representative.
Woodley, Andrew ( -1720) Va.; m. ---. Sheriff.
Woodliffe, John (c1585-c1637) Va.; m. Mary Wynne.
Landowner.
Woodman, Edward (1606-94) Mass.; m. Joanna(Schway)
Bartlett. Deputy to Court; Military service.
Woodruff, John (1604-70) N.Y.; m. ---. Founder.
Woodruff, Matthew ( -1682) Conn.; m. Hannah ---.
Freeman.
Woodruff, Thomas (1630- ) N.J.; m. Edith Wyatt.
Sheriff.
Woods, Abner (c1753- ) Va.; m. Mary ---. Landowner.
Woods, John (1654- ) Va.; m. Elizabeth Warsop.
Landowner.
Woods, Michael (1684-1782) Pa.-Va.; m. Lady Mary
Campbell. Landowner.
Woods, Samuel (c1636-1718) Mass.; m. Alice Rushton.
Proprietor.
Woods   SEE ALSO   Wood
Woodson, Benjamin (1666-1723) Va.; m. Sarah Porter.
Landowner.
Woodson, John (1586-1644) Va.; m. Sara Winston.
Surgeon.
Woodson, Joseph (1677-1755) Mass.; m. Hannah ---.
Built garrison.
Woodson, Robert (1634-1707) Va.; m. Elizabeth Ferris.
Burgess; Military service.
Woodson, Sara (Winston) (1599- ) Va.; m. John Wood-
son. Physician's wife.
Woodward, Chrystopher (c1585-c1650) Va.; m. Margaret
---. Landowner.
Woodward, George (1660-96) Massachusetts; m. Lydia
Brown. Military service.

Woodward, Henry (     -1685) Mass.; m. Elizabeth ---.
Physician.

Woodward, Henry (1646-90) S.C.; m. Mary Godfrey.
Indian agent; Landowner.

Woodward, Nathaniel (     -1667) Mass.; m. Margaret
---. Surveyor; Founder.

Woodward, Richard (     -1669) Mass.; m. Rose ---.
Freeman.

Woodward, Richard (c1636-1700) Pa.; m. Jane ---.
Constable; Juror.

Woodward, Richard (     -c1752) Pa.; m. Deborah Stanfield. Constable; Grand Juror.

Woodward, William (1642-80) Md.-Va.; m. --- West.
Landowner.

Woodworth, Joseph (1648-   ) Mass.; m. Sarah Stockbridge. Landowner.

Woodworth, Walter (c1610-85) Mass.; m. ---.  Juror;
Freeman.

Wooldridge, John (    -   ) Va.; m. ---.  Landowner.

Woolford, Roger (     -1701) Va.-Md.; m. Mary Denwood.
Landoffice Clerk.

Woolsey, George (1610-98) Mass.-N.Y.; m. Rebecca
Cornell. Burgher; Town Clerk.

Woolsey, John Jacob (    -   ) Va.; m. --- Moore.
Military service.

Woolson, Joseph (1677-1755) Mass.; m. Hannah ---.
Landowner.

Woolston, John (    -   )N.J.; m. --- Olive. Landowner.

Wolverton, Charles (1660-1746) N.J.; m. Mary Chadwick.
Landowner.

Wootton, Thomas (1585-1669) Va.; m. Sarah ( ) Wood.
Physician.

Worcester, William (     -1663) Mass.; m. Sarah ---.
Minister.

Word, John (    -   ) Va.; m. ---.  Landowner.

Worley, Francis (     -1726) Pa.; m. Mary Brassey.
Surveyor.

Wormeley, Ralph (1650-1701) Va.; m. Elizabeth Armistead. Councillor.

Worrell, Richard (1617-88) Pa.; m. Frances Taylor.
Landowner.

Worsham, John (     -1729) Va.; m. Mary Wynne.  Justice;
Sheriff.
Worsham, William (cl600-60) Va.; m. Elizabeth Little-
berry.  Legislator.
Wirthington, John (1650-1701) Md.; m. Sarah Howard.
Justice; Assemblyman.
Worthington, Nicholas (     -1683) Mass.; m. Sarah
(Bunce) White.  Proprietor.
Worthington,  Samuel (1687-1739) Pa.; m. Sarah Simcock.
Landowner.
Wright, Dionysius (cl640-cl702) Va.; m. Mary ---.
Landowner; Justice.
Wright,  Edward (1625-91) Mass.; m. Elizabeth
(Mellows) Barrett.  Landowner.
Wright, Francis (cl659-cl713) Va.; m. Anne Washington.
Justice.
Wright, James (1671-1764) Pa.; m. Mary ---.  Military
service.
Wright, Joseph (1637-1714) Conn.; m. Mary Stoddard.
Landowner; Deacon.
Wright, Nathaniel (1688-  ) Conn.; m.  Ann ---.
Appraiser.
Wright, Peter (1590-  ) N.Y.; m.  Alice ---.
Founder; Landowner.
Wright, Robert (1632-  ) S.C.; m. Sarah Wren. Justice.
Wright, Samuel (     -1655) Mass.; m. Margaret ---.
Landowner.
Wright, Thomas (1610-c68/69) Mass.-Conn.; m. ---.
Freeman; Selectman.
Wyatt, Conquest (1655-1748) Va.; m. Sallie Pate.
Sheriff; Landowner.
Wyatt, Edward (1619-90) Va.; m. Johe Conquest.
Landowner.
Wyatt, George (1622-c71/72) Va.; m. Susanna ---;
Martha ---.  Landowner.
Wyatt, Haute (1596-1638) Va.; m. Barbara (or Elizabeth)
Mitford; Ann Cox; Lady Jane Furth.  Minister.
Wyatt, John (1684-1768) Va.; m. Jane Pamplin; Eliza-
beth Buckner.  Landowner.
Wyatt, Nicholas (cl620-78) Va.-Md.; m. Dameris Stock-
ett.  Landowner.

Wyborne, Thomas (1580-1656) Mass.; m. Elizabeth ---.
Proprietor; Commissioner.
Wyche, Henry (1648-1712) Va.; m. ---. Minister;
Military service.
Wyckoff, Claes Corneliszen (1597-1674) N.Y.; m.
Margaret Van der Goos. Landowner.
Wyckoff, Pieter Claeson (1625-94) N.Y.; m. Margaret
(Grietje) Van Ness. Magistrate; Landowner.
Wyeth, Nicholas (1595-1680) Mass.; m. Rebecca (Parks)
Andrews. Landowner.
Wygant, Michael (    -  ) N.Y.; m. Anna Catherine ---.
Landowner.
Wyllis    SEE    Willis
Wyman, Francis (c1620-  ) Mass.; m. Abigail Reed.
Landowner.
Wyman, John (1621-84) Mass.; m. Sarah Neitt. Land-
owner.
Wynkóop, Cornelius Evab (1616-74) N.Y.; m. Maria
Janse Langedyck. Landowner.
Wynne, Edward (    -1682) Mass.; m. Joanna ---.
Freeman; Selectman.
Wynne, Joshua (1660-1715) Va.; m. Mary Jones. Burgess;
Justice.
Wynne, Pieter (    -c1677) N.Y.; m. Jannetje Adams.
Landowner.
Wynne, Robert (1622-78) Va.; m. Mary ( ) Poythress.
Burgess; Justice.
Wynne, Thomas (1620-92) Md.; m. Elizabeth ---.
Anne ---. Sheriff; Assemblyman.
Wynne, Thomas (1627-92) Pa.; m. Martha Buttall.
Judge; Surgeon.
Wythe, Thomas (    -1693) Va.; m. Ann ---. Landowner.

-Y-

Yale, Thomas (1616-83) Conn.; m. Mary Turner. New
Haven Covenant.
Yarborough, William (1685-1748) Va.; m. Eleanor ---.
Landowner; Surveyor.
Yardley, William (1638-93 ) Pa.; m. Jane ---. Land-
owner.

Yarnall, Francis (1660/63-1721) Pa.; m. Hannah Baker.
Councillor.

Yates, George (     -1691) Md.; m. Mary (Wells)
Stockett. Deputy Provincial Surveyor.

Yates, Robert (1658-1713) Md.; m. Rebecca (Young)
Tyre. Justice; Commissioner.

Yeamans, John (1610/11-75/76) N.C.; m. --- Limp.
Governor; Landgrave.

Yeardley, Sir George (1579-1621) Va.; m. Temperance
Flowerdean. Deputy Governor; Governor.

Yorke, Richard (     -1673) N.H.; m. Elizabeth ---.
Landowner.

Young, Christopher (c1642-95) N.Y.; m. Mary Budd.
Mariner; Landowner.

Young, Christopher (1677-1727) N.Y.; m. Elizabeth
Moore. Landowner; Military service.

Young, Christopher (1700-86) N.Y.; m. Joanna Parshall.
Landowner.

Young, George (     -     ) Md.; m. Elizabeth ---.
Assemblyman.

Young, John (1598-1671/72) Mass.; m. Mary (Warren)
Gardiner. Minister.

Young, John (1623-98) Mass.-Conn.-N.Y.; m. Mary ---.
Magistrate; Ship Master.

Young, Nicholas (1610-69) Md.; m. Elizabeth Parker.
Burgess; Sheriff.

Yowell, Thomas (1618-c86) Md.-Va.; m. Anne Sturman.
Burgess; Founder.

## ADDENDUM

(The information on the following names was received in the latter part of 1975 too late to include in the main file.)

Alston, John (    -1704) N.C.; m. Ann Wallis. Landowner.

Archer, James (    -1695) Va.; m. Elizabeth Hubbard. Military service; Justice.

Armistead, Anthony (c1585-    ) Va.; m. Frances Thompson. Marshal; Burgess.

-B-

Ball, William (c1670-c1700) Va.-S.C.; m. Margaret Sampson. Military service.

Banister, John (c1600-c61) Va.; m. Joan ---. Juror.

Barber, Thomas (1653-c1718) Va.; m. Elizabeth Peters. Burgess; Tax Collector.

Barber, William (1602-69) Va.; m. Mary ( ) Denbott. Burgess; Military service.

Benson, James (1653-1709) Md.; m. Margaret Withers. Military service.

Bibb, Thomas (1669-1701) N.J.-Pa.-Va.; m. Ruth Kettle. Burgess; Justice.

Bibb, Thomas (1695-1720) N.J.-Pa.; m. Rebecca ---. Landowner.

Blaisdell, Ralfe (    -1650) Me.; m. Elizabeth ---. Landowner; Freeman.

Brazeal, Henry (c1623-c97) Va.; m. ---. Constable; Landowner.

-C-

Chaffee, Nathaniel (1638/42-1721) Mass.; m. Experience Bliss. Grand Juror; Military service.

Chappell, James (1650-1704) Va.; m. Elizabeth Jones. Justice; Sheriff.

Chattwin, Thomas (    -c1678) Va.; m. Elizabeth (Wilkinson) Welsh. Freeman; Landowner.

Chowning, Robert (    -1666) Va.; m. Joane ---.
Freeman; Landowner.
Colgate, Richard (1674-1722) Md.; m. Rebecca Herbert.
Assemblyman; Landowner.
Comstock, Christopher (1635-1702) Conn.; m. Hannah
Platt. Freeman; Military service.
Covington, Henry (c1670-c1741) Md.; m. Mary Blacki-
stone. Landowner.

-D-

Day, Christopher (1665-1748) Pa.; m. Martha ---.
Landowner.
Dowling, Ann (Powell) Coffey (c1680-1774) Va.; m.
Robert Dowling. Plantation overseer in war time.

-E-

Elmore, Thomas (c1675-    ) Va.; m. Mary ---. Landowner.

-F-

Ferris, Zachariah (c1645-1710) Mass.-Conn.; m. Sarah
Blouds. Military service.
Ferris, Zachariah (1676-1757) Mass.-Conn.; m. Sarah
Reed. Landowner.
Field, Abraham (c1638-c74) Va.; m. Mary Ironmonger.
Landowner.

-G-

Gorsuch, Richard (c1637-77) Va.; m. Elizabeth Roe.
Landowner.

-H-
Hammond, Samuel (1652-1728) Mass.; m. Mary Hathaway.
Proprietor; Founder of church.
Harris, Edward (c1636-c1704) Va.; m. Rebecca ---.
Landowner.

Hoochlandt, Cornelis Dirckson (1599-1695) N.Y.; m.
Aeltie Ariaens. Ferryman; Landowner.
Howson, Robert (    -    ) Va.; m. ---. Landowner.
Hubard, John (    -1668) Va.; m. Katherine ---.
Justice; Landowner.

-J-

Jeffries, Robert (1638/39-c78) Va.; m. Alice ---.
Landowner.

-K-

Keys, Solomon (1633-1702) Mass.; m. Frances Grant.
Landowner.
Kip, Hendrick Hendricksen (1600-66) N.Y.; m. Tryndie
Lubberts. Burgher; Councillor.

-L-

Libby, Benjamin (1682-1768) Mass.; m. Sarah Stone.
Selectman; Proprietor.
Lindley, John (    -1704) Pa.-N.J.; m. Susanna
Culpepper. Landowner.

-M-

Mellet, John Peterson (    -1703) N.J.; m. Mary ---.
Blacksmith; Landowner.
Moore, Margaret (Berringer) (1660-    ) S.C.; m. James
Moore. Governor; Landowner.
Moore, Maurice (c1670-1743) S.C.; Elizabeth Porter.
Founder; Military service.
Morris, John (1680-1739) N.C.; m. Mary Simons. Land-
owner.

-N-

Noel, Cornelius (1623-99) Va.; m. Elizabeth Page.
Landowner.

-P-

Parker, Francis (1685-1717) Va.; m. Elizabeth ---.
Landowner.
Parker, Thomas (1629-85) Va.; m. --- King. Landowner;
Vestryman.
Peters, Edmund (     -1676) Va.; m. Elizabeth ---.
Justice; Delegate to Court.
Pickens, John (1654-  ) Va.; m. Esther Jeanne Benoit.
Justice; Sheriff.
Poole, Thomas (1662-  ) Va.; m. ---. Landowner.
Powell, John (1590-c1632) Va.; m. Katherine ---.
Landowner.
Prall, Arent (     -1721) N.Y.; m. ---. Landowner.
Pratt, Phinehas (1590-1685) Mass.; m. Mary Priest.
Landowner.

-R-

Royall, William (c1600-76) Mass.; m. Phoebe Green.
Assistant to Governor; Landowner.

-S-

Schenck, Jan Martensen (     -1688/89) N.Y.; m.
Jannetje Van Voorhees. Landowner.
Shepardson, Damiel (1641-1723) Mass.; m. Elizabeth
(Call) Tingley. Proprietor.
Smead, William (1635-c1703) Mass.; m. Elizabeth
Lawrence. Landowner; Military service.
Spence, Patrick (    -   ) Va.; m. Dorcas ---. Land-
owner.
Stelle, Poncet (1635/40-c1700) N.Y.; m. Eugenie
Lagereau. Huguenot; Innkeeper.
Sutherland, Robert (c1668-  ) Va.; m. ---. Landowner.

-T-

Tapp, John (c1663-c1704) Va.; m. Elizabeth ---.
Landowner.

Tarlton, Richard (1640-1704) N.H.; m. Ruth Stileman.
  Assemblyman.
Terry, Samuel (1633/34-  ) Mass.; m. Anne Lobdell.
  Selectman; Delegate to Court.

-U-

Upchurch, James (    -1765) Va.; m. Elizabeth ---.
  Landowner.
Upchurch, Richard (    -c1700) Va.; m. ---.  Landowner.

-V-

Van Alen, Laurens (1632-1714) N.Y.; m. Elbertje
  (Evertse) Backer.  Assessor; Magistrate.
Vreeland, Hartman Michielson (1610-63) N.J.; m.
  Fitje Hartmans.  Tax Collector; Assemblyman.

-W-

Waugh, John (1630-1706) Va.; m. Elizabeth ---.
  Minister; Burgess.
Wheeler, Thomas (1660-1735) Md.; m. Mary ---.  Land-
  owner.
Williamson, Richard (    -c1659) Va.; m. Margaret
  Sherwood.  Landowner.
Williamson, Robert (    -1669) Va.; m. Jane Allen.
  Burgess.
Williamson, Robert (    -1726) Va.; m. Katherine
  Lewis.    Freeman; Landowner.

## Appendix

In this list will be found the names of ancestors
of members', descent from whom, because of change
in the ruling of the Society (or even as a result
of later information regarding their lineage) are no
longer acceptable in Applications and Supplements.
According to the By-laws of the Society adopted at
the time of organization, proof of lineage from ancestors in the colonies at any date during the colonial period was approved as a credential for membership. In 1942, however, this ruling was changed and
since that time only descent from those who were in
the first twelve British colonies before January 1,
1701, is acceptable. Those admitted under the former ruling before this date continued in full membership, but no more applications in this category were
accepted.

In this list, therefore, will be found names of
those ancestors whose vital dates are later than
1700; applications and supplements of those who had
proven descent from them remain in official files at
Headquarters.

Also included here are the names of several colonists, lineage from whom was formerly accepted, but
has been proven to be incorrect.

-A-

Agee, James (1720/47-1821) Va.;m. Mary Elizabeth Ford.
    Founder.
Agee, Noah (1750-86) Va. ;m.Martha Mask. Landowner.
Agnew, James (1711-70) Pa. ;m. (2) Rebecca Scott.
    Military service.

Alexander, Archibald (1708-80 ) Va.; m. Margaret
Marks. Sheriff; Military service.
Alexander, Philip (1704-53) Va.; m. Sarah Hool.
Peace commissioner.
Allen, James (cl730-93) Va.; m. Ann Bigges.    Military
service.
Anderson, George (cl700-78) Va.; m. --- (---) Cofer.
Military service.
Anderson, Jacob (1731-1822) Va.; m. Mary Callaway.
Landowner.
Anderson, William (1706-76) S.C.; m. Rebecca Denny.
Military service.
Armstrong, Robert (1731-98) Pa.; m. Margaret Cunning-
ham. Military service.
Arnold, William (cl700-74) Va.; m. Elizabeth ---.
Landowner.
Ashe, Samuel (1726-1813) N.C.; m. Mary Porter.
Military service.
Austin, John (1755-1838) Mass.; m. Martha Messer.
Military service.

-B-

Bailey, Samuel (1720-81) Va.; m. Augusta Parks.
Military service.
Baker, John (cl722-92) S.C.; m. Sarah ---.    Council-
lor; Delegate.
Ball, William (1718-85) Pa.; m. Martha Brumfield.
Military service.
Barry, Andrew (1746-1811) S.C.; m. Margaret Moss.
Magistrate.
Bartholomew, Seth (1729-96) Conn.; m. Hepzibah
Robberts. Military service.
Batchelder, David (1710-  ) Mass.; m. Thankful Par-
ham. Landowner.
Batcheller, William (1743-1821) Mass.; m. Lydia
Warren. Minister.
Bedford, Thomas (1725-95) Va.; m. Virginia Mary Cole-
man. Justice; Committee of Safety.
Belknap, Abel (1754-1838) N.Y.-Mass.; m. Bethiah New-
hall. Military service.

Bell, Peter (1733-78) Md.; m. Elizabeth Leiter. Land-
owner; Committee of Safety.
Bibb, Thomas (1722-80) Va.; m. Sarah ---. Military
service.
Biles, William (1702-75) Pa.; m. Ann Stevenson.
Committee of Safety.
Binn, George (1723-55) Pa.; m. Susan Harvey. Assem-
blyman.
Bird, Abraham (1735-1820) Va.; m. Rachel Zeigler.
Military service; Committee of Safety.
Bitting, Ludwig (1702-76) Pa.; m. Lavinia ---. Assem-
blyman.
Black, Samuel (1727-82) Va.; m. Jane Porter. Military
service.
Blackburn, Robert (1746-1808) Va.; m. Sarah Richie.
Landowner.
Blewett, William (1718-1819) N.C.; m. Sarah Gorton.
Justice.
Bloomfield, Timothy (1729-1803) N.J.; m. Sarah Ford.
Committeeman.
Boddie, Nathan (1732-97) Va.; m. Chloe Crudup.
Landowner.
Boddie, William (c1710-72) Va.; m. Mary Bennett.
Landowner.
Bonnell, William (c1810-   ) Conn.; m. Ann Wilmot.
Founder.
Booth, Gideon (1721-   ) Conn.; m. Mary Hubbell.
Selectman.
Bordner, Jacob (1722-92) Pa.; m. Sarah Bolt. Propri-
etor.
Bostick, John (c1710-59) Va.; m. Nancy Wilson or
Henrietta Chesley. Commissioner; Military service.
Bostwick, Chesley (1740-91) S.C.; m. Jane Gervais.
Military service.
Breazeale, Kennon (1753-1858) N.C.; m. Hiskey Griffin.
Landowner.
Brent, Hugh (1739-1813) Va.; m. Elizabeth Barton.
Military service.
Brooke, James (1705-   ) Md.; m. Deborah Snowden.
Landowner.

Brown, Daniel (1737-89) N.C.; m. Mary Miller. Military service.
Brown, Hugh (c1716-94) N.C.; m. Mary Buick. Landowner.
Brown, Jesse (c1716-77) Va.; m. Mary Flanagan. Justice; Military service.
Brown, Joshua (1754-1820) Md.; m. Margaret Mauser. Landowner.
Bryan, Hardy (1712/16-50) N.C.; m. Sarah (Bonner) Worsley. Justice; Military service.
Bryan, William (1724-85) N.C.; m. Elizabeth Smith. Military service.
Buchanan, James (1739-1827) Va.; m. Mary Elizabeth Spear. Military service.
Buchanan, Walter (    -1788) Pa.; m. ---. Justice. Commissioner.
Burckhartt, Christopher (1756-1827) Md.; m. Elizabet Hobbs. Landowner.
Burrus, William (1745-  ) Va.; m. Susanna Terrell. Founder.
Butcher, Samuel (1731-1847) Va.; m. Susanna Marple. Military service.
Byrd, George (1730-1817) Va.; m. Sarah Commander. Overseer of Poor.

-C-

Cabell, Joseph (1732-98) Va.; m. Mary Hopkins. Military service.
Caldwell, Thomas (1724-1802) Va.; m. Mary ---. Justice.
Callaway, William (1714-78) Va.; m. Elizabeth ---; Elizabeth Tilley. Oath of Fidelity; Burgess.
Campbell, Arthur (c1743-1811) Va.; m. Margaret ---. Committee of Safety.
Campbell, George (1735/38-81) Pa.; m. Helen Donaldson. Assistant to Council of Safety; Military service.
Campbell, Patrick (c1743-1804) Pa.; m. Jean ---. Military service.
Cannon, John (1709-84) S.C.; m. --- Allison. Landowner.

Capp, John Michael (1716-50) Pa.; m. Margaret ---.
Oath of Allegiance.
Carleton, Thomas (1721-86) Va.; m. Sarah Sampson.
Landowner.
Carruth, Walter (1703-69) N.C.; m. Sarah ---.
Justice.
Cartwright, John (c1720-80) Md.-Va.; m. Sarah Mills.
Sheriff; Councillor.
Caswell, Richard (1729-89) N.C.; m. Mary Mackilwean.
Assemblyman.
Chambers, Benjamin (1749-1816) Md.; m. Elizabeth
Forman. Military service.
Cherry, Samuel (c1706-54) N.C.; m. Gatsey Llewwlyn.
Military service.
Chesnut, John (1743-1818) S.C.; m. Sarah Cantey.
Military service.
Church, Jonathan (c1740-1827) Mass.; m. Perone Whipple.
Military service.
Churchill, Stephen (1717-51) Mass.; m. Hannah Barnes.
Landowner.
Clapp, George Valentine (1702/03-   ) Pa.; m. Mary
Albright. Military service.
Clifton, William (1716-70) N.C.; m. Susan Sharp.
Attorney General.
Cochran, John (1704-88) N.H.; m. Jennie McKeen.
Landowner.
Cole, John (1718-95) Va.-Md.; m. Mary ---. Landowner.
Coleman, Benjamin (1753-1813) N.C.; m. Elizabeth
Goodman. Military service.
Conger, John (1727-84) N.C.; m. Phoebe Ross. Com-
mittee of Safety.
Conger, John (c1745/50-1801) N.C.; m. Mary Ross.
Town Clerk.
Connor, John (1715-87) Va.; m. Elizabeth Kavanaugh.
Landowner.
Cook, William (1737-1804) Pa.; m. Sarah Simpson.
Military service; Constable.
Cooper, George (1740-1826) Va.; m. Rebecca ---.
Military service.
Cooper, Spencer (    -1809) Va.; m. Anna Crain.
Military service.

Crawford, William (1732-82) Del.; m. Hannah Vance.
Land agent.

-D-

Delaney, Henry (c1720-85) Va.; m. Rebecca (Brodnex)
Walker. Burgess.

Delesdernier, Lewis Frederick (1752-1836) Me.; m.
Sarah Brown. Military service.

Denny, Thomas (1725-74) Mass.; m. Mary (Chaplin)
Starr. Assemblyman.

Devine, William (c1725-1802) Va.; m. Sarah Smith.
Juror; Landowner.

Dickinson, John (1731-90) Va.; m. Martha Patsy Usher.
Military service.

Dickson, Robert (    -1765) Pa.; m. Priscilla Kennedy.
Landowner.

Dillard, Thomas (1721-91) Va.; m. Mary ---. Military
service.

Dockery, Thomas (1745-65) N.C.; m. Rebecca (Ash)
Crosnor. Committeeman.

Dodd, Thomas (1723-1815) N.J.; m. Sarah Newcomb.
Military service.

Dudley, Francis (c1750-1802) Mass.; m. Sarah Wheeler.
Military service.

Durden, John (1716-83) Va.; m. Mary Coleman. Military service.

Durkee, Jeremiah (1727-75) Mass.-Conn.; m. Abigail
Adams. Landowner.

Dutcher, David (1715-75) N.Y.; m. Agatha Freer.
Military service.

-E-

Early, Jeremiah (1705-87) Va.; m. Elizabeth Buford.
Military service.

Early, Jeremiah (1730-79) Va.; m. Sarah Anderson.
Justice; Trustee.

Edwards, Thomas (1719-c1810) Pa.; m. ---. Judge.

Egnar, David (1739-1829) S.C.; m. Mary (Johnson)
Harrison. Landowner.

Elder, John (1706-92) Va.; m. Mary Simpson. Land-
owner.
Ellis, James (1727-85) Md.; m. Mary Veatch. Military
service.
Ervin, Hugh (c1730-85) S.C.; m. Mary Ellison.
Landowner.
Eskridge, William (     -1830) Va.; m. Elizabeth Scott.
Military service.
Estes, Benjamin (c1748-1816) Va.; m. Cecilia Thorpe.
Landowner.
Estill, James (     -1785) Va.; m. ---. Landowner.
Ewing, Robert (1715/23-87) Va.; m. Mary Baker.
Justice; Military service.

-F-

Faison, James (1706-50) N.C.; m. Frances ---. Con-
stable; Military service.
Felder, John Henry (1725-1778/80) S.C.; m. Mary
Elizabeth Shainloffel. First Provincial Congress;
Justice.
Field, Henry (c1718-90) Va.; m. ---. Burgess; Judge.
Fiefield, David (1749-1806) N.H.; m. Abigail Larey.
Military service.
Filbert, John Samuel (1710-86) Pa.; m. Susannah ---.
Proprietor.
Finley, John (1702- ) Va.; m. Thankful Doak.
Military service.
Fleming, William (1717-84) Va.; m. Jane Frame. Land-
owner.
Flemister, Lewis (1746-1807) Va.; m. Ellender Chison.
Military service.
Fox, Peter (1740-82) N.C.; m. Hannah Moore. Founder.
Frederick, Peter (1722-63) N.C.; m. Nancy ---. Mili-
tary service.
Froman, Paul (c1706-83) Pa.-Va.; m. Elizabeth Hite.
Landowner.
Fudge, Jacob (     -1790) S.C.; m. Margaret Gregory.
Landowner.

-G-

Gale, Isaac (1708-93) Mass.; m. Judith Sawyer. Military service.

Garat, William (1715-86) Pa.-Va.; m. Mary Lewis. Assemblyman.

Gilbert, Barnhardt (1724-1802) Pa.; m. Catherine Bender. Military service.

Gillespie, Thomas (1719-97) Pa.; m. Naomi ---. Military service.

Gillham, Ezekial (1732-85) Va.; m. Sarah Clemore. Elder; Landowner.

Gilman, David (1702-80) Mass.; m. Mary Lord. Landowner.

Gilman, John (1744-92) N.H.-Mass.; m. Dorothy Kimble. Landowner.

Glover, John (1732-97) Mass.; m. Hannah Gale. Military service.

Goodman, William ( -1781) N.C.; m. ---. Landowner.

Gorsuch, Charles (1720-1806) Md.; m. Susannah ---. Landowner.

Greenberry, Griffith (1727-1809) Md.; m. Ruth Riggs. Committee of Safety.

Greenweld, Philip Lorentz (1728-1802) Pa.; m. Marie Margaret Foessel. Military service.

Griffith, Thomas Roper (c1740-98) Va.; m. Catherine Greebhill. Landowner.

Grigsby, John (1720-94) Va.; m. Elizabeth Porter. Military service.

-H-

Hale, Samuel (1718-1807) N.H.; m. Mary Wright. Military service.

Hall, Edward (c1710/13-90) Va.; m. Elinor Stuart. Military service.

Hamilton, Archibald (c1720-94) Va.; m. Frances Calhoun. Constable; Military service.

Hammond, Elisha (c1712- ) Mass.; m. Elizabeth Haskell. Landowner.

Handy, Charles (1729-93) R.I.; m. Ann Brown. Deputy
Governor; Military service.
Hardin, Mark (1708-89) Va.; m. Catherine Marr.
Landowner.
Harper, Nicholas (1706-1803) Va.; m. Elizabeth Behre.
Military service.
Harris, Nathan (1712-82) Va.; m. Lucy Stewart.
Landowner.
Harris, Samuel (1708/10-1823) N.C.; m. Martha Laird.
Landowner.
Hart, Anthony (1755-1845) Va.; m. Elizabeth ---.
Founder.
Hatch, Benjamin (1721-96) Mass.; m. Jerusha Phillips.
Military service.
Hawkins, Phileman (1743-78) Va.; m. Sarah Smith.
Military service.
Haynes, John (1701-84) Va.; m. Mary ---. Military
service.
Helphenstein, Peter (1724-89) Va.; m. Katheryne
Berger. Landowner.
Henry, John (c1705- ) Va.; m. Sarah (Winston) Syne.
Burgess; Councillor.
Henry, Patrick (1735-94) Va.; m. Sarah Shelton.
Attorney.
Heyl, Peter (1710-61) N.C.; m. Catherine ---. Land-
owner.
Hicks, Thomas (1725-93) Va.; m. Elizabeth Williams.
Landowner.
Hill, Abraham (c1732-92) N.C.; m. Christian Walton.
Landowner.
Hill, Henry (c1730 -1804) N.C.; m. Sarah Cotton.
Military service.
Hill, William (1710/15-87) N.C.; m. Susannah Smith-
ers. Delegate to Court; Landowner.
Hogg, Peter (1703-82) Va.; m. Elizabeth Taylor.
Attorney; Military service.
Howard, Samuel (1739-1815) N.H.-Mass.; m. Elizabeth
Barrett. Military service.
Howell, Samuel (1723-1807) Pa.; m. Sarah Stretch.
Landowner.

Howell, Samuel (1748-1802) Pa.; m. Margaret Emley. Landowner.

Hubert, Benjamin ( -1825) Va.; m. Mary ( ) Williams. Huguenot.

Hughes, Orlando (1740-68) Va.; m. Elizabeth ---. Landowner.

Hunt, Jonathan (1706-83) N.C.; m. Isabel Hampton. Committee of Safety.

Hunter, James (1735-1809) Mass.-Me.; m. Abigail Williams. Military service.

Huskins, Thomas (1736-1836) N.H.; m. Mary French. Military service.

Hyde, Thomas (1735-1819) Conn.; m. Elizabeth Huntington. Military service.

-I-

Irwin, Robert (1738-1800) N.C.-Pa.; m. Mary Alexander. Military service.

-J-

Jefferson, Peter (1708-57) Va.; m. Jane Randolph. Sheriff; Burgess.

Jennings, Augustine ( -1778) Va.; m. Hannah Williams. Military service.

Jennings, John (1734- ) N.C.; m. Lydia Batte. Military service.

Johnson, Aquilla (1729-84) Va.; m. Elizabeth ---. Military service.

Johnson, Benjamin (1705-50) Va.; m. Agnes Clark. Landowner.

Johnson, Benjamin (1734-69) Va.; m. Mary Moorman. Landowner.

Johnston, William (1715/18-69) Va.; m. ---. Military service.

Jones, Cadwallader (1752-99) Va.; m. Katherine ---. Burgess.

Jones, Robert ( -1766/67) Va.; m. Sarah Cobb. Military service.

Jordan, Thomas (1714-87) N.C.; m. Rachel Speight.
Justice.

-K-

Keinadt, Michael (1720-96) Pa.; m. Margaret Diller.
Shipowner.
Kennedy, Samuel (1730-78) Pa.; m. Sarah Ruston.
Surgeon.
Kent, Charles (     -1800) Mass.; m. Elizabeth Torrence.
Boston Tea Party.
King, Richard (1715-76) Mass.; m. Mary Stowell.
Military service.
Knoll, John (1704-   ) Pa.; m. Ann Mary ---. Land-
owner.
Kobel, Jacob (     -1808) Pa.; m. Margaret Barbara
Emrich. Landowner.

-L-

Lane, Edward (1721-1818) Pa.; m. Sarah Richardson.
Military service.
Lane, Jesse (1733-1806) N.C.; m. Winifred Aycock.
Commissioner; Military service.
Lane, Joseph (c1710-74) N.C.; m. Patience McKinnie.
Commissioner; Justice.
Leach, Elijah (1744-1815) Conn.; m. Elizabeth Tracy.
Landowner.
Lee, Thomas (1729-1816) Va.; m. Mary Bryan. Land-
owner.
Lerue, Peter (1702-   ) Va.; m. Frances Allen.
Landowner.
Lesueur, David (     -1771/72) Va.; m. Elizabeth ---.
Founder.
Lewis, Charles (1729-72) Va.; m. Lucy Jefferson.
Military service.
Lewis, David (1763-1839) S.C.-N.C.; m. Judith ---.
Civil Officer.
Lewis, John (1733-1813) Va.; m. ---. Landowner.
Lewis, Nathaniel (1732/33-1820) R.I.; m. Elizabeth
Hull. Assemblyman; Civil Officer.

Lewis, Robert (1704-66) Va.; m. Jane Meriwether. Landowner.

Lewis, Thomas (1733-1813) Va.; m. ---. Landowner.

Lipscomb, William (1731-1810) Va.; m. Elizabeth Smith. Committee of Safety; Military service.

Lobdell, Joshua (1703-67) Conn.; m. Mary Reynolds. Landowner.

Lobdell, Joshua (1732-67) Conn.; m. Ruth Boughton. Landowner.

Locke, Matthew (1730-1801) Pa.; m. Mary Brandon. Assemblyman.

Logan, Benjamin (1743-1802) Va.; m. Anne Montgomery. Military service.

Love, David (1740-98) N.C.; m. Jean Bleuett. Military service.

Love, Joseph (1725-58) Va.; m. Martha Bryan. Military service.

Lowry, Robert (1743-1823) S.C.; m. Elizabeth ---. Landowner.

Lyle, Matthew (1711-74) Va.; m. Esther Blair. Military service; Founder of Presbyterianism.

-M-

McAllister, Alexander (1715-1800) N.C.; m. Jean Colvin. Military service; Landowner.

McBride, Thomas (1742-69) Mass.; m. Sarah Snow. Landowner.

McCall, Francis (1710-94) N.C.; m. ---. Founder.

McClung, John (1731-1817) Va.; m. Elizabeth Alexander. Landowner.

McClure, Robert (1763-1830) S.C.; m. Marjorie (Pearson) Buffington. Founder.

McCready, Robert (1752-1846) Pa.; m. Anne Levine. Landowner.

McDonald, Flora (1720-90) N.C.; m. Allan McDonald. Military service.

McDowell, John (1743-90) N.C.; m. Jane Park. Military service.

McElroy, Samuel (1745-1806) Va.; m. Mary Irvine.
Military service.
McFarland, John (1708-84) Va.; m. Mary Montgomery.
Military service.
McGriff, Patrick (1750-1810) S.C.; m. Mary Hall.
Military service; Committee of Safety.
McKinley, David (1760- ) Pa.; m. Esther ---. Weaver.
MacLaughlin, George (1735-1815) Mass.; m. Lois Sands.
Military service.
McLellan, Hugh (1710-89) Mass.; m. Elizabeth ---.
Military service.
Mallet, Gideon ( -1771) S.C.; m. Mary Lombard.
Landowner.
Mansfield, John ( -c1780) Conn.; m. Ann (Waldo)
Grady. Military service.
Mask, William (1748-1811) N.C.; m. Anne Smith.
Councillor; Assemblyman.
Mason, David (1730- ) Va.; m. Mary ---. Landowner.
Massie, David (1721-55) Va.; m. Ann ---. Landowner.
Vestryman.
Mather, Increase (1725-94) Mass.; m. Anne Brown.
Minister.
Mathewson, Abraham (1737-1801) R.I.; m. Alice ---.
Landowner.
Maupin, John (1725-1806) Va.; m. Frances Dabney.
Military service.
Maury, Matthew ( -1752) Va.; m. Mary Anne Fontaine.
Huguenot.
Mealman, Adam (1729-1827) Pa.; m. Catherine King.
Founder.
Mercer, James (1713-90) N.C.; m. Sarah Simmons.
Military service.
Merrill, Nathaniel (1702-72) Mass.; m. Esther Warner.
Landowner.
Messer, Samuel (1736-1811) Mass.; m. Sarah Howe.
Military service.
Metcalf, John (1724-79) Va.; m. Rhoda (Dent) Chinn.
Military service.
Meyer, Valentine ( -1797) Pa.; m. Margaret Barbara
Werle. Landowner.

Michaux, Joseph (1737-1807) Va.; m. Judith Woodson.
Landowner.
Mims, David (1701-81) Va.; m. Agnes Wildy.  Landowner.
Montgomery, James (1729-96) Pa.; m. Jane Patterson.
Landowner.
Moore, William (1758-1844) Va.; m. Mary Ingert.
Justice; Landowner.
Morris, William (1722-92) Pa.; m. Elizabeth Stipps.
Landowner; Military service.
Moses, Othniel (1735-56) Conn.; m. Sarah Pinney.
Military service.
Moulton, Abraham (1732-56) N.H.; m. Sarah Morris.
Military service.
Mourning, John (1728-1800) N.C.; m. Sarah Harris.
Committee on Safety; Military service.
Mullins, Matthew (1719-80) Va.; m. Mary Maupin.
Military service.

-N-

Nash, Basil (1758-1848) Md.; m. Ellen Briscoe.  Military service.
Neville, George (1734-1811) Va.; m. Rachel Earle.
Military service.
Newkirk, Henry (1706-85) Pa.; m. Gertrude Hartman.
Landowner.
Nitschman, John (1703-72) Pa.; m. Julianna Haberland.
Minister; Teacher.

-O-

Ogle, Samuel (1710-52) Md.; m. Ann Tasker.  Governor.
Otis, John (1713-92) Mass.; m. Temperance Hinkley.
Landowner.

-P-

Parke, Zebulon (c1727-　　) N.J.; m. Ann ---.  Military service; Landowner.
Parks, Elisha (1725-78) Mass.; m. Mary Ingersoll.
Military service.

Paterson, John (1732-1812) N.C.; m. Isabelle McDuffie.
Military service.
Paterson, William (1745-   ) N.J.; m. Cornelia Bell.
Landowner.
Patton, James (1736-   ) Va.; m. ----. Surveyor.
Pearl, Timothy (1723-89) Conn.; m. Dinah Holt.
Assemblyman.
Pegues, Claudius (1719-90) S.C.; m. Henrietta Butler.
Founder; Justice.
Penn, John (1740-88) Va.; m. Susan Lyme. Attorney;
Landowner.
Perry, Freeman (1733-1813) R.I.; m. Mary Hazard.
Landowner.
Petrie, John Jost (   -1770) N.Y.; m. Gertrude von
Kiuk. Military service; Landowner.
Pettigrew, James (1755-73) Pa.; m. Judith (Hart) De
Shira. Military service; Landowner.
Phelps, Joshua (1729-1809) Conn.; m. Hannah Tarbox.
Military service.
Phelps, Nathaniel (1703-81) Conn.; m. Mary Curtis.
Military service.
Pike, John (1704-76) Va.; m. ----. Landowner.
Pike, William (1751-1806) Conn.; m. Molly (Thorp)
Darrow. Military service.
Pittman, Thomas (c1726-85) Va.; m. Mary Rowe. Magis-
trate.
Poage, John (1726-89) Va.; m. Mary Blair. Magistrate;
Military service.
Pope, Henry (1742-90) N.C.; m. Tabitha Appleton.
Landowner.
Porter, John (1717-1802) Mass.; m. Mary Kimbell.
Military service.
Porter, John (1742-1834) Mass.; m. Lydia Baker.
Landowner.
Powers, Jonathan (1704-75) Pa.; m. Hannah Sawyer.
Military service.
Putnam, Elisha (1715-58) Mass.; m. Lydia Chase.
Military service.

-R-

Rankin, Robert (1732-1820) Va.; m. Masena Marshall.
Military service.
Ray, Nicholas (1747-1819) Md.; m. Prudence (Peters)
Taylor. Military service.
* Reeves, William (1660-cl719) Va.; m. ---. Military
service.
Reynolds, John (1714-84) Md.; m. Elizabeth McKee.
Military service.
Rhodes, Jeriah ( -1812) N.Y.; m. Sophronia Ayres.
Council of Safety.
Rice, Hezekiah (1732-96) N.C.; m. Mary Bullock.
Military service.
Richardson, Richard (1704-80/81) S.C.; m. Mary Eliza-
beth Cantey. Military service.
Richardson, Richard (1741-1818) S.C.; m. Dorcas
Nelson. Military service.
Richardson, William (1743-86) S.C.; m. Ann Magdelen
Guignard. First Provincial Congress.
Riddick, William (1725-1800) Va.; m. Mary Polke.
Burgess.
Robertson, John (1742-1808) Va.; m. Ann Walthall.
Military service.
Robeson, Peter Lord (1785-1851) N.J.; m. Mary Spencer.
Military service.
Robinson, John (1736-1815) Va.; m. Janet Edgar.
Military service.
Ross, David (1753-1825) Va.; m. Susan Sutherland.
Military service.
Rowan, William (1735-1800) Pa.; m. Elizabeth Cooper.
Sheriff.
Rutherford, Griffith (1731-1800) N.C.; m. Elizabeth
Graham. Landowner; Surveyor.
Rutherford, Robert (1734-1814) Va.-N.C.; m. Dorothy
Ann Brooks. Landowner.

* Later information proves descent from above incorrect.

-S-

Sanders, William (1705-    ) S.C.; m. Margaret Moore.
Justice; Military service.
Schneider, J. George (1720-87) Pa.; m. Hannah ---.
Military service.
Scripture, James (1749-1810) Mass.; m. Sibbel Shipley.
Military service.
Scripture, Samuel (1727-    ) Mass.; m. Mary Greene.
Military service.
Seaborn, George (1732-1818) S.C.; m. Grace Greenwood.
Landowner.
Seem, John George (1722-    ) Pa.; m. ---. Military
service.
Seixas, Isaac Mendez (1704-80) N.Y. m. ---. Land-
owner.
Sevier, Valentine (1703-1802) Va.; m. Joanna Goode.
Military service.
Shelby, Evan (1720-94) Md.; m. Letitia Coxe. Mili-
tary service.
Sheppard, Benjamin (1710-91) N.C.; m. Sara Ruffin.
Justice; Military service.
Shertel, Barnhardt (1709-75) Pa.; m. Ursual Hifler.
Landowner.
Shinn, Joseph (1712-59) N.J.; m. Mary Budd. Land-
owner.
Shuey, Daniel (    -1777) Pa.; m. Mary Margaret ---.
Committeeman; Military service.
Shugart, Zachariah (1732-96) Pa.; m. Mary Mulholland.
Sheriff.
Sinclair, Richard (1730-1813) N.H.; m. Mary Cilley.
Military service.
Smith, Drury (1718-70) Va.; m. Martha ---. Justice;
Burgess.
Smith, Jasper (    -1769) N.J.; m. ---. Justice.
Smith, Samuel (1760-    ) N.C.; m. Sallie Williams.
Military service.
Sorrell, Samuel (1753-1811) S.C.; m. --- Newberry.
Assemblyman.
Sparks, Daniel (1740-1810) S.C.; m. --- Stevens.
Military service.

Spaulding, Benjamin (1739-1811) Mass.; m. Patty
Barrett. Military service.

Spofförd, Abel (1718-45) Mass.; m. Eleanor Poor.
Military service.

Stearns, Phinehas (1738-92) Mass.; m. Mary Welling-
ton. Selectman; Military service.

Stewart, Alexander (1753-   ) Pa.; m. Elizabeth Barron.
Committee of Safety.

Strother, John (1721-96) Va.; m. Jane Fussell; Mary
(Willis) Wade. Stamp Act.

Stroud, John (1732-1837) N.J.; m. Sarah Cantey. Military service.

Stuart, David (1733-89) N.C.; m. Elizabeth McQueen.
Landowner.

Sutherland, Robert (1722-87) Va.; m. Joyce Woodstock.
Landowner.

Sutton, John (1736-1818) N.Y.; m. ---. Military
service.

-T-

Talbot, Charles (1723-79) Va.; m. Drusilla Gwin.
Landowner.

Taney, Michael (1702-   ) Md.; m. Dorothy Brooke.
Landowner.

Taney, Michael (1755-99) Md.; m. Monica Brooke.
Landowner.

Tate, James (1701-1801) Va.; m. Mary Doak. Military
service.

Taylor, Henry (c1720-77) Va.; m. Sarah ---. Military service.

Taylor, Matthew (   -1770) N.H.; m. Jeannette ---.
Founder.

Ten Broeck, John (1780-1820) N.J.-Penn.; m. Katie
Lowe. Military service.

Terry, Nathaniel (   -1780/82) Va.; m. Sarah Royall.
Justice; Burgess.

Thomas, Anthony (1759-1824) Md.; m. Lucy Cecil.
Landowner.

Thomas, James (1710-80) N.C.; m. Sarah Barnes.
Landowner.

Thomas, John (1705-88) Va.; m. Christina Graham.
Justice.
Thomas, John (c1720-  ) Va.; m. Jane Black.  Land-
owner.
Thompson, Richard (1735-78) Va.; m. Mary Abataub.
Military service.
Tracy, Percy (1716-1801) Conn.; m. Elizabeth Hyde.
Landowner.
Trotman, Thomas (c1740-  ) N.C.; m. Harrell
Christian.  Founder.
Trow, Israel (1737-69) Mass.; m. Margaret ---.
Military service.
Tucker, Thomas (      -1757) Mass.; m. Elizabeth ---.
Representative; Military service.
Turk, Thomas (1720-1809) Va.; m. Margaret ---.
Military service.
Turner, Harry (1714-51) Va.; m. Elizabeth Smith.
Military service.
Turner, James H. (1707-87) Va.; m. Kerenhappuch
Norman.  Military service.
Tyson, John (1723-1775) N.C.; m. Bethany Hines.
Military service.

-V-

Vandervort, John (1755-1836) N.Y.; m. Mary Elizabeth
---.  Military service.
Van Patten, John (1753-1835) N.Y.; m. Wintie Clute.
Military service.
Van Slyck, Cornelis Antonissen (1734-76) N.Y.; m.
Ota-Tosh.  Landowner.
Varian, Isaac (      -1800) N.Y.; m. Elizabeth De Voun.
Military service.
Vaughan, Cornelius (1729-85) Va.; m. Elizabeth ---.
King's Councillor.
Venable, Abraham (1700-68) Va.; m. Martha Davis.
Justice; Military service.

-W-

Waddell, John (1724-79) Va.; m. Elizabeth Green.
Founder.

Waite, Benjamin (1736-1822) Mass.; m. Lois Gilbert.
Founder.

Waldo, Daniel (1716-87) Mass.-Conn.; m. Susanna
Adams. Founder; Representative.

Waldo, Jonathan (1728-88) Mass.; m. Joanna Mighell.
Landowner.

Waldo, Zechariah (1701-61) Mass.; m. Abigail Griffen.
Landowner.

Walker, George (1745-1833) Va.; m. Eleanor Hicks.
Landowner.

Walker, John (1736-1800) N.C.-S.C.; m. Nancy Ashford.
Military service.

Ward, Benjamin (1703-88) N.C.; m. Mary Ward. Congressman; Justice.

Ward, Edward (1709-91) Md.; m. Casandra Talbot.
Committee of Safety.

Ward, James (1738-1818) N.C.; m. Mary Kent. Landowner.

Waterbury, Daniel (1791-  ) N.Y.; m. Ann Bouton.
Military service.

Watkins, Evan (     -1817) Va.; m. Prudence ---.
Founder.

Weber, Henry (1716-  ) Pa.; m. ---.  Landowner.

Weber, Henry (1729-95) N.Y.; m. Elizabeth Brandon.
Landowner.

Weber, J. Henry (1735-1815) Pa.; m. Elizabeth Filbert.
Landowner.

Williams, John (1745-99) Va.; m. Elizabeth ---.
Deputy to Court.

Williams, Joseph (1748-  ) N.C.; m. Rebecca Landon.
Delegate; Military service.

Williams, Robert (1707-68) N.C.; m. Ann Boykin.
Landowner.

Wilson, Benjamin (1744-1827) Va.; m. Phoebe Davisson.
Burgess; Military service.

Windemuth, John George (1716-82) N.J.; m. Elizabeth
Bernhardt. Miller.

Wingfield, John (1735-98) Va.; m. Sarah Garland.
Military service.
Withington, Peter (1733-77) Pa.; m. Eve Schepler.
Military service.
Wofford, Joseph (1743-1831) S.C.; m. Martha Llewel-
lyn. Military service.
Wolfe, George Wendell (1720-1816) Pa.; m. Ann Eliza-
beth Reid. Military service.
*Wood, Abraham (c1615-1680/83) Va.; m. ---. Mili-
tary service.
Wood, Jonathan (1730-1804) Mass.; m. Rachel ---.
Selectman.
Wood, Samuel (1737-1800) Va.; m. Sarah Reeve.
Military service.
Woods, John (1712-91) Pa.; m. Susannah Anderson.
Military service.
Woods, William (1707-82) Va.; m. Susannah ---.
Military service.
Woodworth, Abner (1724-1809) R.I.; m. Hannah Dyer.
Landowner.
Wooten, Shadrach (1734-1812) N.C.; m. Elizabeth
Allen. Military service.
Wylly, William (1735-1810) Va.; m. Mary ---.
Landowner.


-Y-


Yost, John (1750-    ) Md.; m. ---.    Founder; Gunsmith.


* Later information proves descent from above incorrect.